when
only
God
knew

MICHAEL J. PUGH

When Only God Knew

Trilogy Christian Publishers
A Wholly Owned Subsidiary of Trinity Broadcasting Network
2442 Michelle Drive, Tustin, CA 92780

Manufactured in the United States of America
10 9 8 7 6 5 4 3 2 1
Library of Congress Cataloging-in-Publication Data is available.

ISBN: 978-1-68556-080-5
E-ISBN: 978-1-68556-081-2

TABLE OF CONTENTS

FOREWORD

You and I don't know each other, and, so, I thought that it might be a good idea to tell you who I am. What I am about to tell you is not meant to boast about accomplishments but to tell you why I wrote this book for you.

I guess that you might say that I have done okay by most standards, but I only relatively recently realized that almost all my life meeting those standards was inconsequential to the long view—and was not as satisfying as I expected it would be.

Here is my story in a nutshell.

My life has been filled with what most would probably call successes and accomplishments, even though I now know that I was mostly only chasing my tail.

In high school, I was voted most likely to succeed in my senior year by my classmates and earned college scholarships, having been an Eagle Scout, in honor societies, president of three off-campus organizations, class vice-president, and a lifeguard, among other things.

In college, which I attended on various scholarships and graduated with honors, I was selected to Who's Who Among Students and Omicron Delta Kappa Leadership Honorary, having been, among other things, editor of a campus magazine, co-editor of another campus magazine, assistant editor of my college annual, my fraternity's domain conference chairman and secretary and on the Interfraternity Executive Cabinet, the Student Body Executive Cabinet and the Dean's List.

Then I went to law school, also on scholarship, where I graduated with honors, was on Law Review (for which you can be selected after doing well enough in your studies), was selected for a campus leadership organization, having been Student Body Secretary for Legal Affairs (organizing a tenant's union and legal referral service for students) and elected law school Senator, among other things. During law school, I tested for and became a member of MENSA—you know, the high IQ guys.

After graduating from law school, I was awarded the Jervey Fellowship in Foreign and Comparative Law at Columbia University law school and received an LLM in foreign and comparative law after studying at Columbia University and the University of Munich in then West Germany.

In my summers while at law school and at Columbia before going to the University of Munich, I was a waterfront director at two boy's camps, having earned my American Red Cross water safety instructor certificate.

And you think that would have been enough for me. But it wasn't. I continued to reach.

As I was passing the bar exam and during my legal career, I have clerked for a federal judge, worked as an appellate attorney at the United States Department of Justice in Washington, D.C., taught at two law schools, and been in private practice. I am AV preeminent rated, the highest rating by my peers, and have been selected by one registry in the top one percent (1 percent) of attorneys.

I was also busy when not practicing law. I was a two-term president of a world trade council, president of an organization that provided volunteers to community-wide non-profit organizations, founder and two-term president of a Rotary Club that won Rotary's presidential award in its first year and on numerous other community-wide committees, boards, and councils. I was selected to be a Paul Harris Fellow, a high Rotary honor, by other Rotarians, even before I founded that Rotary Club. I have lectured on various topics.

I was also involved with my kids in coaching tee-ball and Scouting, and I became a Taekwondo Sixth Degree Master Black Belt in the middle of all the above.

Sounds like something, huh? Maybe so, but I was not successful in the most meaningful way as I have come to understand. I came to understand that I was running around in mostly meaningless circles

When Only God Knew

because I had no relationship with Jesus and did not understand who He, God, and the Holy Spirit were. It took some challenging circumstances for me to see that I was not in control, and I thank God for those difficult circumstances and lessons.

Now, God has provided me with all the blessings that I need—Sharon, a smart, beautiful, trustworthy, faithful, godly wife; a peaceful walk on a straighter and narrower path than before with a view from that path that is more beautiful and serene than the view from the wider more destructive path on which I had been aimlessly wandering; and the ability and desire to use whatever gifts I may have from almost fifty years learning and practicing the law to, hopefully, make a difference in your lives.

So, I write this book for you because the Bible informs us that not to speak up when there is "a public charge to testify regarding something (one has) seen or learned about" is a sin. See Leviticus 5:1 (NIV). As a Christian, my public charge comes from the Bible, which tells me to:

1. "Always be prepared to give an answer to everyone who asks you to give the reason for the hope that you have, but to "do this with gentleness and respect"—(1 Peter 3:15, NIV);

2. "demolish arguments and every pretension that sets itself up against the knowledge of God"—(2 Corinthians 10:5, NIV);

3. "[p]reach the word; be prepared in season and out of season; correct, rebuke and encourage—with great patience and careful instruction"—(2 Timothy 4:2, NIV) and,

4. "contend for the faith that was once for all entrusted to God's holy people"—(Jude 1:3, NIV).

I agree with Pastor John Parnell when he said that we, as Christians, "should stand up in public and tell God's truth as [we] see it without worrying that secular listeners may not even agree with our most basic assumptions."[1] I believe that it is my responsibility—duty to you—to state what I know to be the truth—the only reliable truth—in this complicated and challenging world.

I hope that this book will be a blessing to you.

INTRODUCTION

This book asks the reader to consider how biblical authors were able to state facts and principles as to which they had no knowledge or experience. The reader is also asked to consider why many of those facts and principles were only later proven to be accurate and reliable—sometimes thousands of years later—by the secular world. The reader is asked to weigh the evidence and determine, as if on a jury, if the evidence supports the reliability of the Bible and its message.

For thousands of years the Bible was considered a reliable and accurate history of people, places, and events.

Then came the "Age of Reason" in the 18th century. The "Age of Reason" "refers to a period in history where countries such as France and England showed a critical thinking approach to life."[2] That Age "came with humankind questioning almost every belief and way of life," including Christianity.[3] It is the contention of this book that many "thinkers" from—and since—the Age of Reason have, however, been anything but rational, logical, or even "reasonable" when it came to the Bible. Age of Reason philosophers and scientists and many philosophers and scientists since the Age of Reason thought they could reason and knew better than what the Bible said

They were wrong.

One author, Phillip Power, in Mensa Bulletin, the magazine for high IQ members, successfully challenged the ideas that "religion is irrational," and that "people of higher intelligence are capable of higher levels of reason" and that "therefore, their intelligence allows them to see the irrationality of religion."[4] As he points out in the conclusion to the article he wrote in that magazine, "Intelligence doesn't confer prudence, wisdom, or infallibility, as hard a truth as that is to accept for those of us who have been blessed with it."[5] We can all agree to that.

Some of the greatest minds in history—Aristotle, Rene Descartes, St. Thomas Aquinas, St. Augustine, St. Albert the Great, Francis Bacon, Isaac Newton—believed in God.[6] And that belief did not change for most scientists as science has advanced in the modern era.[7] In his book, *100 Years of Nobel Prizes*, which discusses Nobel Prize winners from 1901-2000, Baruch Aba Shalev, a geneticist and author, said,

> Only 11 percent of Nobel laureates claimed to be atheists or agnostics. Interestingly, that was more weighted toward awards for literature (35 percent) than it was toward chemistry (7 percent), physics (5 percent), or medicine (9 percent).[8]

As astrophysicist Joseph Hooten Taylor, Jr., the co-winner of the 1993 Nobel Prize in physics, said, "A scientific discovery is also a religious discovery." He is quoted in the book *50 Nobel Laureates Who Believe in God* by Tihomir Dimitrov as saying, "There is no conflict between science and religion."[9]

This book asks the reader to weigh evidence to determine whether to believe the Bible is reliable as from God and that, therefore, it is also reliable that Jesus Christ was His Son, as it also states. It describes standards used in a courtroom which may be helpful in weighing the evidence. While it is written from a Christian's perspective, I hope that it is useful to those who do not believe, to those who are searching, to those who do not know if they can believe, and to Christian believers in the Bible.

If there is—and there is—substantial evidence that the Bible is accurate and reliable as to historical and scientific facts stated in it, which would only later be proven by the secular world, then it is not a step too far to believe that the Bible is correct as to who Jesus was and why He should be believed.

In fact, if the Bible is reliable as this book contends, then "the fear of the Lord is the beginning of wisdom" and "the beginning of knowledge, [not a person's intelligence,] but fools despise wisdom and instruction." See Psalm 111:10 (NIV) and Proverbs 1:7 and 9:10 (NIV).

It is my firm belief that the evidence, if weighed properly, proves that Jesus is everyone's Savior, that He loves them all, and that He went to a gruesome death on a cross so, through belief in Him, everyone can be saved and have eternal life.

It is also my firm belief that those who do not believe in God either:

1. are uninformed or misinformed,
2. do not understand what they have heard or
3. are willful in that, hearing the truth, they, nonetheless, refuse to believe what they hear.

It is my hope that you will read—consider—what I say here, no matter what preconceived notions you may have. It is more so my hope that this book will help all who read it to believe in the Bible's reliability.

Some readers of this book may have been treated badly by a church and/or its members. They may have turned their backs on the evidence and the truth that results from it because of that. It is my hope that those readers can forgive any unkind treatment which they may have received at the hands of professing Christians. It is my hope that those treated badly by a church and/or its members will remember that we all—Christians and non-Christians alike—have sinned and have fallen and continue to fall short of the glory that God would have for us, but that is not what is intended for us in the Bible. I hope that they will remember that we all make mistakes—mistakes which Jesus, who loves them perfectly, did not make.

As a Christian, one of the essential doctrines of Christianity is that the Bible is the inspired Word of God or "God-breathed" Word. The Bible itself claims to be written by divine inspiration. Chapter 3, verse 16 of 2 Timothy (NKJV) says, "All Scripture is given by inspiration of God, and is profitable for doctrine, for reproof, for correction, for instruction in righteousness."

The English Standard Version (ESV) of the Bible says it this way: "All Scripture is breathed out by God" (2 Timothy 3:16, ESV). In 1 Thessalonians 2:13 (ESV), we find another verse to support this fact:

> And we also thank God constantly for this, that when you received the word of God, which you heard from us, you accepted it not as the word of men but as what it really is, the word of God, which is at work in you believers.

According to Proverbs 30:5 (ESV), "Every word of God proves true." The New International Version of the Bible says it this way, "Every word of God is flawless." See also Psalm 12:6 (NIV).

If the Bible is divinely inspired or God-breathed, one would, at the very least, expect there to be evidence that it contains reliable and accurate facts. This book discusses some of that evidence. If the Bible contains reliable and accurate facts, one could then, without trepidation, take the next step to believe that only through Jesus as one's Savior can one be blessed with eternal life, as the Bible says. As Jesus said in John 14:6 (ESV), "I am the way, the truth, and the life. No one comes to the Father except through Me."

The Bible speaks of many events and facts that were later proven to be accurate, very often despite skepticism as to the accuracy of the facts stated. Some "assumptions widely held in our culture that can be challenged by both information and argument are:"[10]

- Jesus never lived.
- You can't prove God exists.
- There are no such things as miracles.
- There is no evidence that Jesus rose from the dead.

When Only God Knew

- The Bible wasn't written until hundreds of years after the life of Jesus.

The Bible also predicts many events and facts that only later happened and were thereby proven to be accurate (prophecies). This book addresses only some of the many many facts that support the accuracy and reliability of the Bible and were only later proven to be accurate. The Bible was written by over forty authors ... over 1,500 years from different ethnic backgrounds, living on three continents and from various walks of life. The Old Testament contains thirty-nine books and the New Testament twenty-seven books, totaling sixty-six books.[11]

Places and people disappeared geographically and historically, only later to be substantiated by archaeology,[12] history, and other contemporary disciplines. Likewise, scientific statements beyond the ability of the authors to know stated in the Bible would also only later be proven to be true by the secular world.

While I personally know that belief in Jesus Christ as Savior comes from God, Jesus, His Son, and the Holy Spirit, I also know that not everyone agrees. It is my hope that this book will inform convincingly both believers and nonbelievers. It is my hope that, despite what anyone's experiences may have been, they come to rely on the truth of the Bible. Who knows, it may even convince readers who are willful in their unbelief to open their hearts to whom Jesus was.

One purpose of this book is to describe support for some of the various historical, geographical, biographical, and scientific facts that were part of the narrative in the Bible. Another purpose of this book is for the reader to think about how often God reported something in the Bible before mankind found proof of it. The reader can then reach his or her own conclusion, based on weighing the evidence, whether God's knowledge of so many things before mankind's proof of them should cause the reader to believe the remainder of the biblical narrative. At the very least, how often God knew something was true before mankind found proof should cause the reader to want to delve more deeply into matters about which there is controversy.

This book supports the proposition that explaining biblical authors' foreknowledge of events or facts must require one of only two conclusions. The first is that each of the forty authors—from different ethnic backgrounds, living on three continents, differently educated or, by today's standards, uneducated and from various walks of life—each had the foreknowledge to accurately predict events and write about facts which would only later be proven to be accurate. It is not likely that forty authors all independently had the ability to see into the future.

The more reasonable conclusion is that those later proven or reconfirmed events and facts were communicated to those forty writers by an all-knowing, all-present single being who knew the facts well before they would be proven or reconfirmed and also knew that the facts would be proven at some time in the future. That person is contended in this book to be the all-knowing and all-present God of the Bible.

The title of this book, *When Only God Knew*, was chosen because it accurately reflects its theme. It discusses scientific, medical, mechanical, geographical, and historical facts and prophecies talked about in the Bible at a time when only someone besides the writer could know that they would later be proven and/or be used to overcome modern skepticism, thereby confirming the Bible's reliability.

There is too much evidence supporting the conclusion that the Bible is reliable to discuss in this single reference.[13] While one may even be able to challenge the impact of one, two, or a few pieces of evidence that claim to prove the accuracy of the Bible, there is so much evidence of the Bible's accuracy not open to honest challenge that one should, at the very least, begin to consider whether what the Bible says, particularly about salvation through belief in who Jesus was, is worth exploring, if not completely accurate.

When Only God Knew

This book is not and not meant to be exhaustive respecting the evidence that God and His Son, Jesus, exist. Citations to a fact stated in the Bible may be from only one or two of the sources that support the fact. For most of the facts referenced in this book, there are many more sources that support the fact than are cited. The reader may be interested in doing other research or in researching the resources cited and citations contained in the resources cited below.

This book is only designed for the reader to consider three questions. They are:

1. How did biblical authors come by information not then known where they lived?
2. Who knew or could have known that biblical information not then known where biblical authors lived or that subsequently lost information would be rediscovered?
3. Why was there information included in the Bible which was not then known where biblical authors lived and/or information lost to history for which there would later be skeptics?

It is my hope that readers and teachers will add to the proofs that the answer to those questions is that God had such knowledge and informed biblical authors of it or included the information in the Bible so that it could—then and later—support the Bible's accuracy and reliability.

Hopefully, this book will be a quick reference, for some, but only *some*, of the factual proofs[14] that the Bible is accurate—historically, geographically, scientifically, and prophetically—and was written through the God-breathed knowledge of its writers.

Chapter 1 discusses the various standards of proof used in American courtrooms. Those standards may be helpful to the reader in determining if the Bible should be considered reliable. Chapter 2 explains the methodology used. The general reliability of the Old and New Testaments sections of the Bible as a historical document is discussed in Chapter 3. Specific facts are then discussed in Chapters 4 through 11 to support the conclusion that the Bible is a reliable narration of facts and must have come from a knowledgeable source, from someone other than the biblical author.

The conclusion of scholars is, however, that the New Testament contains the most reliable ancient histories ever written. For instance, as discussed in more detail in Chapter 3 of this book, most of the original books of the New Testament were written within thirty-five years of Jesus' reported death. All the original books of the New Testament were written by 96 AD ±, i.e., before the end of the first century AD, only fifty-sixty years ± after the events which they describe. The books of the New Testament were written closer in time to the occurrence of described events than other ancient writings that are considered historically reliable.

The author appreciates all the hard work of the sources cited in this book, has attempted to quote sources of fact where practical, and to cite at least one source for each statement of fact this book contains, even if the statements which deserve to be quoted are paraphrased. My apologies if citations have been omitted. Such was unintentional.

I also appreciate those who have reviewed this book to make it more readable for accuracy and to catch grammatical and syntactic errors.

Finally, this book is written to give readers assurance as to the reliability of the Bible, either as a basis for its defense or as a wake-up call to non-believers. I am convinced above and beyond any reasonable doubt[15] that all the evidence, particularly when taken as a whole, proves that Christ was the Son of God and died so that anyone who believes in Him and repents of his or her sin can have joy-filled eternal life. You may not be convinced as I am, but, particularly if the evidence for the accuracy and reliability of the Bible meets one of the other standards of proof discussed in Chapter 1, it is my hope that you will continue inquiring into what the Bible says and what it can mean to you.

When Only God Knew

Even so, the belief that one being was responsible for the facts, principles, and prophecies discussed in this book is not meant to explain a sufficient basis for salvation and eternal life. It is not. Even though knowing the facts and principles discussed in this book should lead reasoning and reasonable men and women to the inescapable conclusion that the God of the Bible and Jesus are real and to being awestruck by-fearful of God-the fear of God is only the start of wisdom.[16] Even Satan, a fallen angel whom the Bible says will one day be thrown into a lake of fire forever,[17] knew God and Jesus. He did not, does not, and will not accept Jesus as his Savior.

Knowledge about God alone does not bring about salvation or eternal life, as Paul taught in Romans (written 56–57 AD).[18] To repeat what was said above, only Jesus is "the way and the truth and the life," and "no one comes to the Father except through" belief in Him.[19] One must have a personal relationship with Him and accept Him as one's Savior.

PART I

Background

To understand the full impact of the scientific, medicinal, or historical facts found in the Bible, which were later supported by science, archaeology, or another proven historical fact, and to understand why the narrative in the Bible is historically and scientifically reliable, it may be helpful to the reader to understand how evidence and proof are weighed in a courtroom and what the various levels of proof could be. It may also be helpful for the reader to understand why the Bible is generally considered to be more reliable than many other ancient writings considered to provide accurate information.

The three chapters in this part discuss various standards of proof, the methodology used to arrive at the book's narrative, and why the facts contained in the Bible are generally reliable, separate from facts specific to a particular person, place, event or scientific, mathematical, medical, or engineering fact reported in the Bible. Those specific facts will be discussed primarily beginning with chapter 4 in Part II.

CHAPTER 1

Measuring Evidence and Standards of Proof

Judges and juries "weigh" evidence to see if, on balance, the evidence should be believed. The probability as to what facts ultimately show comes from that weighing.[20]

"Absolute proof" is never required in a courtroom; "such a burden would be prohibitive, as few things are capable of absolute proof that removes all possibility of doubt."[21]

While fact finders in a courtroom do not always reach the same conclusion as to what facts ultimately show, it is important for the fact finder to begin by rationally and logically considering facts when weighing evidence for or against a proposition. As one author has said,[22]

> As human beings capable of rational thought, we are obliged to conform our beliefs to reality, not the other way around.
>
> …
>
> To do this, to form beliefs, we must investigate the world and its issues to discover facts and truths about them. This process, which we all employ, is useful for one simple reason: truth is true whether you believe it or not. Truth does not require belief in order to be true, but it does deserve to be believed.
>
> …
>
> First, we assess the evidence and reasons for its truth. Next, we weigh the evidence to determine how

well supported these claims are. Finally, we trust; we exercise faith based on the weight of the evidence. Faith is not Christian-branded hoping or wishing.

While it is appropriate to draw reasonable inferences from the evidence or facts weighed,[23] speculation is not evidence and is not proper when reaching conclusions as to what has been proven.[24] Likewise, feelings, perceptions, conjectures, hunches, gut feelings, guesses, beliefs, arguments, conclusions, suppositions, and unproven and unsupported theories or theoretical possibilities, legal or otherwise, are not evidence.[25]

In a courtroom, the fact-finder ideally makes decisions solely on the evidence presented. I recognize that is difficult to do, including for me, but the attempt to make decisions solely on the evidence is more likely to result in an accurate decision than is relying on biases and assumptions. I have attempted to set aside my biases and assumptions in presenting the evidence that God knew the truth of various things at a time when mankind did not, and I hope that you will, too.

A. Weighing Facts and Defining Proof

There are two ways that one can conclude that the Bible is accurate and reliable. For those who are not believers in Jesus as their Savior or in the existence of God and perhaps for the more skeptical believers, the facts supporting those facts can be "weighed." A conclusion can then be reached as to the likelihood that Jesus died to save those that believe in Him as their Savior or that God exists. As the trier of fact, as in any courtroom, you, the juror here, should be impartial,[26] keep an open mind and wait "until the entire case is presented before reaching a fixed opinion or conclusion"[27] as to the ultimate conclusion you reach.

When Only God Knew

The other way that one can conclude that the Bible is accurate and reliable is through faith without the need to weigh facts. While faith in the accuracy and reliability of the Bible does not necessarily require objective evidence and may be subjective, for the reasons indicated throughout this book, objective evidence can, nonetheless, also be used as proof of its accuracy and reliability.

Proof is defined as "a fact or piece of information that shows that something exists or is true."[28] In determining if the Bible is to be believed or how to defend the reliability of the Bible, the reader may want to apply secular standards of proof, such as those used in a courtroom. There are three generally accepted standards of proof—particularly in American law—which could be used to judge both a skeptic's proposition that the Bible cannot be accurate or from God and the Christian counter-position that the Bible is the reliable Word of God.

B. Preponderance of Evidence

[29]

The first standard by which one may want to judge facts and reach conclusions is called the preponderance of the evidence. The preponderance of the evidence is evidence that by the greater weight supports or that is more likely than not to support a fact or factual conclusion. "'Greater weight of the evidence' means the more persuasive and convincing force and effect of the entire evidence."[30]

The preponderance of the evidence is the standard that is usually applied in civil non-criminal cases in American courtrooms and in some other courtrooms around the world. In cases where this standard is applied, juries and/or judges weigh the evidence as if on a scale. They then decide if the weight of the evidence for a proposition, for example, liability for negligence, is at least slightly more probable or something more than 50 percent than the weight of the evidence for an alternative or opposing proposition, for example, not being liable for negligence. The fact-finders reach a conclusion based on the more probable proposition. In such a case, if anything over 50 percent of the evidence supports a proposition or an opposing proposition, that evidence would be accepted as reliable and, therefore, accurate by the fact finder.

C. Clear and Convincing Evidence

Then there is a more difficult standard of proof to meet, in some cases, again, usually civil cases. That standard is whether the evidence is clear and convincing. The clear and convincing standard applies to some—but far fewer—propositions.

Clear and convincing evidence is more than a preponderance of the evidence and less than evidence beyond a reasonable doubt[31] discussed below. Some American courts have defined clear and convincing evidence as "highly probable" proof of a fact.[32] It is different from the "greater weight of the evidence," i.e., a preponderance, in that it is more compelling and persuasive. Clear and convincing evidence is evidence that is precise, explicit, lacking in confusion, and of such weight that it produces a firm belief or conviction, without hesitation, about the matter in issue.[33]

D. Evidence Beyond Reasonable Doubt

Finally, in American jurisprudence, primarily in criminal cases, decisions are made as to whether the evidence is above and beyond any reasonable doubt. Proof beyond a reasonable doubt has been defined as "proof of such a convincing character that you would be willing to rely and act upon it unhesitatingly in the most important of your own affairs."[34] Reasonable doubt is, however, not merely possible doubt or speculative, imaginary, or forced doubt.[35] Reasonable doubt does not require absolute proof of a proposition.

E. Applying Standards of Proof

In determining what standard of proof the reader may want to apply in judging the reliability and accuracy of the Bible, he or she will be challenged by how to

1. consider evidence,
2. set aside preconceived notions which we all have,
3. focus on the facts as they are presented,
4. reach conclusions based on evidence without considering what the reader thinks is a dominant opinion and
5. avoid groupthink.

The ideal in a courtroom is for the fact finder to consider evidence only based on the proof that is presented. As one author pointed out,

> In these times of fast media and ever-growing Internet, we are under so many external influences that it can be difficult to know when we are thinking for ourselves. Unless you are a discerning, very aware person, you most likely don't even know when your thinking is not your own.
>
> ...
>
> Another trap we fall into when we don't think for ourselves is groupthink. Groupthink, a term coined by Irving Janis in 1972, is a psychological phenomenon that takes place within a group of people who try to avoid conflict and reach agreement without critically evaluating options or alternative ideas.[36]

It is often difficult to set aside preconceived ideas. The allure of thinking like the crowd is seductive and significant. A letter signed by professors from relatively liberal Princeton, Harvard, and Yale and published by Princeton University's James Madison Program, titled "Think for yourself,"[37] warned university students to avoid groupthink. Such warning is equally applicable here. As those professors said, "the current climate on campuses too easily allows for students to be influenced by dominant opinion and groupthink."[38] Likewise, the current climate around discussions of faith may also be affected—infected—by culturally and pseudo-scientific and pseudo-historic "opinion and groupthink." That should be avoided.

> Thinking for yourself means questioning dominant ideas even when others insist on their being treated as unquestionable[, the professors wrote.] It means deciding what one believes not by conforming to fashionable opinions, but by taking the trouble to learn and honestly consider the strongest arguments to be advanced on both or all sides of questions—including arguments for positions that others revile and want to stigmatize and against positions others seek to immunize from critical scrutiny.[39]

What the letter says about students is just as applicable to non-students in non-campus settings. The key element of the letter applicable to the consideration of the facts in this book[40] is that,

> in today's climate, it's all-too-easy to allow your views and outlook to be shaped by dominant opinion... The danger [anyone] faces today is falling into the vice of conformism, yielding to groupthink. At many colleges and universities what John Stuart Mill[41] called "the tyranny of public opinion" does more than

When Only God Knew

merely discourage students from dissenting from prevailing views on moral, political, and other types of questions. It leads them to suppose that dominant views are so obviously correct that only a bigot or a crank could question them.

Another author has described the care to be taken in today's world.[42] He points out that even modern journalism that reports on biblical matters falsely caricatures the Bible and states that the Bible is not reliable or accurate and is full of myth when he said,

> Nor is the press alone in this deception. Radical revisionist biblical scholars and pseudoscholars, like members of the notorious Jesus Seminar, are well aware of this sad sensationalizing formula for success and exploit it regularly. This may, admittedly, be impugning the motives of some in that category who are driven instead by a desire merely to be "politically correct" when it comes to biblical scholarship; that is, to be ultracritical of anything biblical. In this connection, sadly, secular historians of the ancient world often have a much higher opinion of the reliability of biblical sources than some biblical scholars themselves![43]

Whatever standard of proof one uses, this book contends that fair and open-minded readers should be convinced that the Bible is God-inspired and reliable and that, therefore, Jesus Christ died to save everyone who believes in Him.

CHAPTER 2

Method Used

Evidence Supported by Reason and Logic Prove the Existence of God

Chapter 1 described three secular standards of proof which can be applied to determine if the Bible is reliable. Chapter 3 lays out the evidence for the general reliability of the Bible. Chapters 4 through 11 provide examples of dates when a particular fact was stated, or a particular event was predicted in the Bible. It then states the dates when the biblically stated fact was later—sometimes millennia later—proven, confirmed, or reconfirmed to be accurate.

This book is written as an apologetic for the Bible. Apologetics is "a branch of theology devoted to the defense of the divine origin and authority of Christianity,"[44] i.e., "the branch of theology concerned with the defense or proof of Christianity."[45] There are five general approaches to apologetics. They are:

1. Classical Apologetics which emphasizes reason and is very often philosophical in nature;[46]

2. Evidentialism which "focuses on the factual verification of the Christian claims" and usually presents a proposition or fact "like legal cases," appealing "to legal standards of evidence" with an evidential conclusion that "hinges on probability;"[47]

3. Presuppositionalism, which employs "transcendental arguments to make a case." The case is made through deductive reasoning, which "seeks to explain the necessary conditions for some fact or phenomenon" and is

"more concerned with what makes evidence evidential and what makes reason reasonable," usually concluding that "there can be no reason or logic, for example, apart from God;"[48]

4. Fideism, which rejects all three of the above approaches. It argues that they are insufficient "ways to justify the Christian faith" and holds that "faith and faith alone is the only proper way to understand the truth of Christianity"[49] and

5. A combination of two or more of these approaches.

I understand and agree that faith is a proper way to understand the truth of Christianity. Nonetheless, because this book is designed to reach the non-faithful as well as the Christian believer, it takes an evidentialist approach with a pinch of both classical apologetics and presuppositionalism. The premise of this book is that evidence supported by reason and logic prove the existence of God and the reliability of the Bible, including that Jesus died for our sins.

As support for the conclusion that knowledge of the Bible's writers was from God and is reliable, this book discusses scientific, medical, and mechanical principles described in the Bible at a time when the principles were authored

a. by writers with no apparent scientific, medical or mechanical background or with experience contrary to the principle they state,

b. centuries before disciplines were developed on which the accuracy of the principle could or would be measured and/or

c. apparently, centuries before science, medicine, or mechanics caught up with the principle stated in the Bible.

It also discusses historical facts in the Bible, which were long denied until they were recently substantiated, and prophecies in the

When Only God Knew

Bible which only later—in some cases hundreds of years later—came to be and were thereby determined to be accurate.

There are various translations of the Bible originally written in Hebrew, Greek, and Aramaic. Quoted biblical passages and passages which refer to a particular translation will be referred to in this book by their acronym. For example, the American Standard Version of the Bible will be referred to by "ASV," the English Standard Version by "ESV," the King James Version by "KJV," the New American Standard Bible by "NASB," the New International Version by "NIV" and the New King James Version by "NKJV," and the like.

Reference to a particular acronym does not, however, mean that the facts reported in other translations of the Bible contradict the version to which the citation is made. Because one translation may be slightly different from another does not mean that the Bible is not reliable. It only means that the translators of each version may have given a slightly different meaning to a word or phrase. Thus, for example, citing to Mark 6:45-52 (ESV) (written 50-65 AD), for the story of Jesus walking on water does not mean that the same story was not accurately related in the American Standard Version, the King James Version, the New American Standard Bible or the New International Version. They all tell the same story.

By comparing the date(s) when the scientific, medical, or mechanical principle or fact or prophecy was stated in the Bible and the date(s) when it was only later discovered to be correct, i.e., confirmed, this book is designed to show that the principle or fact described in the Bible was stated at a time when the biblical author of the principle, fact or prophecy had no discernible way—aside from being informed by God or, far far less likely, by luck—to know that the principle or fact was accurate or reliable or that the prophesied event would occur. There are so many facts related in the Bible that were later proven to be correct that the chance of luck playing a role has to be discounted. Likewise, many writers of the Bible have generally not been considered to be seers with the ability to predict the future. *If scientific, medical, and mechanical principles are found in the Bible in books written at a time*

a. when the writers had no apparent scientific, medical, and mechanical background or had contrary experience,
b. centuries before disciplines were developed on which the accuracy of the principle could be measured or would be measured, or
c. centuries before science, medicine, or mechanics caught up with the principle stated in the Bible,

one then has to ask how did the writers come to know the scientific, medical and mechanical principle or prophecy to be able to state them accurately?

Such is support for the reliability of the Bible and for the source of its authorship, i.e., God. "Given that Bible writers were not scientists, except possibly the Apostle Luke, and given that the scientific information at their disposal was generally also often misleading, as described below, the accuracy of the Bible can only be attributed to the inspiration of God."[50]

Likewise, by comparing when the historical fact or prophecy was stated in the Bible and when it was later re-discovered after having been denied by skeptics or when the prophecy later came to be, this book also tries to show that the biblical author of the fact or prophecy had no way—aside from being informed by God—to know that the fact or prophecy was accurate or reliable.

One of the reasons why biblically stated facts were only later verified scientifically or through such disciplines as archaeology may have been intentional. Perhaps later proof of accuracy was intended *for the express purpose of later showing* that the Bible fact is reliable and accurate and because skepticism of Bible facts was expected. Perhaps later proof of accuracy was intended as additional proof of the existence of God. This is particularly true where there was no basis for the Bible author of the fact to know that a fact would later be shown to be correct. Modern historians, archaeologists, and anthropologists have only relatively recently found proof of many biblical facts and prophecies.

Both support the proposition that the reliability and accuracy of the Bible should be attributed to the inspiration of God. Both also support the fact that modern historians, archaeologists, and anthropologists will likely find further proof of biblical facts.

It is, consequently, important to note three things. First, it is important to be aware, as you read through this book, of the dates that the books of the Bible were written, i.e., when a scientific, medical, mechanical, or historical fact or prophecy was first related or revealed in the Bible. The fact that the Bible is generally more reliable than any other ancient document and dates when the books of the Bible were written will be discussed in Chapter 3. Particularly in Chapters 4 through 11, when a particular fact or prophecy was first related or revealed in the Bible, i.e., the date that the book of the Bible relating or revealing a particular fact or prophecy was written, will be noted as they are discussed.

Second, it is important to note when the scientific, medical, and mechanical principle, historical fact, or prophecy was later proven to be accurate. The dates when a principle, fact, or prophecy was proven to be accurate will also be noted as they are discussed.

This comparison is particularly significant since skeptics, particularly starting in the Age of Reason in the eighteenth century,[51] began to question facts reported in the Bible, often presuming incorrectly that *all* facts reported in the Bible are a myth. Only in the last two centuries or so have historical, archaeological, anthropological, and scientific tools and evidence been used, or for that matter available, to support the biblical narrative. Those tools have contradicted much of the reported, long-held, and erroneous man-made skepticism as to the Bible's reliability. It seems as if it was decided by someone to state in the Bible

a. accurate scientific, medical, or mechanical principles or facts not subject to scientific proof at the time they were included,

b. historical facts whose accuracy would be later challenged, or

c. prophecies that would only later come true,

in order to overcome the humanistic skepticism as to biblical accuracy and reliability.

When the biblically stated fact, principle, or prophecy was only later substantiated, discovered, or proven, the next question must be, how did the biblical author come by the information? The information was written in the Bible often millennia before it was substantiated, discovered, or proven. If someone knew that there would be skepticism as to the accuracy or reliability of the Bible, comparing the dates when the books of the Bible revealing particular principles, facts, or prophecies were written with the dates when the principles, facts, or prophecies were later proven to be accurate and reliable is proof of someone having knowledge of things or events before they exist or happen. After comparing and considering the many dates no later than the end of the first century AD that the books of the Bible reveal particular facts, principles, or prophecies with the dates, often thousands of years later, when the particular facts, principles, or prophecies were confirmed, logic requires the conclusion that the information must come from someone with foreknowledge, not the biblical writer who first recorded it. That, too, is proof of the existence of God.

Third and finally, it is important to realize that not all information that supports biblical fact, principle, or prophecy has yet been discovered or revealed. Historians, scientists, archaeologists, and others continue to make new discoveries that continue to confirm the reliability of biblical facts and the Bible. It is expected that, if history is any indicator, new facts will continue to be discovered, confirming facts stated in the Bible, which had been completed by the end of the first century AD.

CHAPTER 3

Biblical Reliability Generally

Old and New Testaments

Chapters 4 through 11 below identify particular facts reported in a book of the Bible written on or about a particular date and leaves the reader to consider the consequence of only later determining that the fact is accurate and of reaching, or not, a logical conclusion as to who knew the information at the time it was included in the Bible. Separate from the specific proofs of reliability found in chapters 4 through 11, however, there is a good basis for knowing that the Bible is also a generally reliable narrative of the facts which it contains.

The issue for consideration in this Chapter is whether the Bible is considered to be generally trustworthy,[52] a separate issue from whether a particular fact is later proved to be reliable. This chapter discusses, generally, why the Bible as a whole is considered trustworthy and reliable by most scholars who study ancient history.

The reader may be aware, however, that there are those who argue that the Bible is a mere unreliable, inaccurate myth. In considering whether the Bible is factually accurate and reliable, the reader may need to know that "secular historians of the ancient world often have a much higher opinion of the reliability of biblical sources than some biblical scholars themselves."[53] The view that the Bible is a myth and unreliable does not represent even the majority view in biblical scholarship today. University of Arizona archaeologist William Dever, for example, is well known for his objection to the term "biblical archaeology," since it seems to convey a probiblical bias; yet he assails some of the unwarranted conclusions of biblical minimalists in a strongly worded article in BAR [*Biblical Archaeology Review*]: "Save Us from

Postmodern Malarkey." He does not have kind words for the mini-malists in his book, What Did the Biblical Writers Know and When Did They Know It? either. "I suggest," he writes, "that the revisionists are nihilist not only in the historical sense but also in the philosophical and moral sense."[54]

Moreover, "for some who have heard statements from pseudo-archaeologists that deny various biblical accounts and personalities, it may be helpful for them to realize that as time goes on, more and more archaeological evidence surfaces that supports the Bible."[55]

In determining the reliability of the Bible and, consequently, its accuracy, it is important to consider the source of information in it, such as (a) eye witness accounts which confirm the reported events as in the Gospels of Matthew and John and in the book of Acts, (b) whether the information was the result of an inquirer's interview of a first-hand witness as in the Gospels of Mark and Luke, (c) what historians and archaeologists report as an accepted fact and (d) whether a stated fact was later proven to be accurate. The more current the reported information in the Bible is to the related event, and the more copies that exist of the written information, the more it is reliable and accurate.

To compare the dates when the Bible revealed or related particular facts or prophecies with the dates when the scientific, medical, and mechanical principles, historical facts, and prophecy was later proven to be accurate, it is important to understand when the various books of the Bible were written. Section A below contains a chart to which you may want to refer as you read this book for the date on which a particular proposition or fact was described in the Bible. This chapter, after presenting that chart, then discusses why the Bible is considered an accurate transcription in a general sense.

Following the chart below with the dates the books of the Bible were written is a section on Old Testament reliability followed by a section on New Testament reliability. In particular, as to the section on New Testament reliability, the reader should note that there

When Only God Knew

are more and more current copies of the New Testament than of any other ancient writings relied on by historians, which makes the New Testament far more reliable for historical fact than other ancient writings.

A. Dates Books of the Bible Were Written [56]

The dates in the following chart, while approximations, are taken from various articles written on the subject and are generally reliable. In every event, however, the dates the books of the Bible are generally agreed to have been written were sometimes years, sometimes decades, sometimes centuries, and sometimes millennia before the stated fact in that book was later proven to be accurate. As for the book of Job, it is unknown when it was written or by whom. It is, however, believed to be the oldest book in the Bible, and the approximations of the date it was authored range from as early as 2000 BC.[57]

In Biblical Order			
Old Testament		New Testament	
Genesis	1450–1405 BC	Matthew	50–65 AD
Exodus	1450–1405 BC	Mark	50–65 AD
Leviticus	1450–1405 BC	Luke	60–61 AD
Numbers	1450–1405 BC	John	80–90 AD
Deuteronomy	1450–1405 BC	Acts	62–70 AD
Joshua	c. 1405–1385 BC	Romans	56–57 AD
Judges	c. 1043 BC	1 Corinthians	55 AD
Ruth	c. 1375–1010 BC	2 Corinthians	55–57 AD
1 Samuel	c. 931–722 BC	Galatians	49–50 AD
2 Samuel	930–722 BC	Ephesians	60–62 AD
1 Kings	c. 561–538 BC	Philippians	60–62 AD
2 Kings	c. 561–538 BC	Colossians	60–62 AD
1 Chronicles	450–430 BC	1 Thessalonians	51 AD
2 Chronicles	450–430 BC	2 Thessalonians	51–52 AD
Ezra	457–444 BC	1 Timothy	62–64 AD
Nehemiah	445–400 BC	2 Timothy	66–67 AD

In Biblical Order			
Old Testament		*New Testament*	
Esther	483–331 BC	Titus	62–64 AD
Job	Unknown BC	Philemon	60–62 AD
Psalms	1440–450 BC	Hebrews	67–70 AD
Proverbs	c. 971–686 BC	James	44–49 AD
Ecclesiastes	940–931 BC	1 Peter	62–65 AD
Song of Songs[58]	971–950 BC	2 Peter	67–68 AD
Isaiah	740–680 BC	1 John	85–95 AD
Jeremiah	627–570 BC	2 John	90–95 AD
Lamentations	586 BC	3 John	90–95 AD
Ezekiel	590–570 BC	Jude	65–70 AD
Daniel	536–530 BC	Revelation	94–96 AD
Hosea	750–710 BC		
Joel	835–796 BC		
Amos	c. 760–750 BC		
Obadiah	853–840 BC / 627–586 BC		
Jonah	c. 785–760 BC		
Micah	742-687 BC		
Nahum	c. 663–612 BC		
Habakkuk	615–588 BC		
Zephaniah	640–621 BC		
Haggai	c. 520 BC		
Zechariah	520–470 BC		
Malachi	433–424 BC		

In Chronological Order			
Old Testament		*New Testament*	
Unknown BC	Job	44–49 AD	James
1450–1405 BC	Genesis	49–50 AD	Galatians
1450–1405 BC	Exodus	50–65 AD	Matthew
1450–1405 BC	Leviticus	50–65 AD	Mark
1450–1405 BC	Numbers	51 AD	1 Thessalonians
1450–1405 BC	Deuteronomy	51–52 AD	2 Thessalonians
1440–450 BC	Psalms	55 AD	1 Corinthians

When Only God Knew

In Chronological Order			
Old Testament		*New Testament*	
c. 1405–1385 BC	Joshua	55–57 AD	2 Corinthians
c. 1375–1010 BC	Ruth	56–57 AD	Romans
c. 1043 BC	Judges	60–61 AD	Luke
971–950 BC	Song of Songs	60–62 AD	Ephesians
c. 971–686 BC	Proverbs	60–62 AD	Philippians
940–931 BC	Ecclesiastes	60–62 AD	Philemon
c. 931–722 BC	1 Samuel	60–62 AD	Colossians
931–722 BC	2 Samuel	62–64 AD	1 Timothy
853–586 BC	Obadiah	62–64 AD	Titus
835–796 BC	Joel	62–65 AD	1 Peter
c. 785–760 BC	Jonah	62–70 AD	Acts
c. 760–750 BC	Amos	65–70 AD	Jude
750–710 BC	Hosea	66–67 AD	2 Timothy
742–687 BC	Micah	67–68 AD	2 Peter
700–680 BC	Isaiah	67–70 AD	Hebrews
c. 663–612 BC	Nahum	80–90 AD	John
640–621 BC	Zephaniah	85–95 AD	1 John
627–570 BC	Jeremiah	90–95 AD	2 John
615–588 BC	Habakkuk	90–95 AD	3 John
590–570 BC	Ezekiel	94–96 AD	Revelation
586 BC	Lamentations		
c. 561–538 BC	1 Kings		
c. 561–538 BC	2 Kings		
c. 536–530 BC	Daniel		
520 BC	Haggai		
520–470 BC	Zechariah		
457–444 BC	Ezra		
450–430 BC	1 Chronicles		
450–430 BC	2 Chronicles		
483–331 BC	Esther		
433–424 BC	Malachi		
445–400 BC	Nehemiah		

B. Old Testament Reliability Generally

Written: 1450–400 BC

1. Leviticus—the Oldest Old Testament Text Ever Read

Written: 1450–1405 BC
Confirmed: 20th century AD (2300–3300 years later)

Scientists have only recently been able to read the oldest biblical text ever found, a charred scroll from the book of "Leviticus" which had been burned in a fire 1400 years ago.[59] The scroll had sat in an archaeologist's office (and was thought to be) impossible to read without destroying it.[60] The 2,000-year-old scroll had "been in the hands of archaeologists for decades," but it was believed that it was not "possible to read it, since it was too dangerous to open the charred and brittle scroll." That was until scientists began "using special imaging technology that can look into what's inside." When they did, they found "the earliest evidence of a biblical text in its standardised [sic] form," which came "from the Book of Leviticus" and "show the *first physical evidence* of a long-held belief that the Hebrew Bible that's in use today is more than 2,000 years old,"[61] i.e., that the book in the Bible entitled "Leviticus" had been accurately reproduced.

The reliability of the Old Testament, not just "Leviticus," had, however, already been re-confirmed when a Bedouin shepherd discovered the "Dead Sea Scrolls" in 1946.

2. The Dead Sea Scrolls

Fact Stated: 1450–400 BC (Dates Old Testament written)
Fact Confirmed: 20th century, particularly 1946–1956 AD
(2300–3500 years later)

"The discovery of the Dead Sea Scrolls was a watershed moment in biblical studies."[62] "Until 1948, the oldest manuscripts of the Old

Testament dated back to 895 AD."[63] That was until the discovery of the Dead Sea Scrolls, most of which were written between 150 BC and 70 AD.[64] Most of the Dead Sea Scrolls were, as discussed in more detail below, discovered between 1946 and 1956 by Bedouin shepherds and a team of archeologists, 2000 years after they were written,[65] and they have been very effective in confirming the accuracy of the Bible.

The discovery of the Dead Sea Scrolls began in 1946-1947 when a Bedouin shepherd found a small cave opening in the eastern Judaean Desert, the modern West Bank in Israel.[66] After lowering himself into the cave, he discovered several sealed jars which contained leather scrolls.[67] After the initial discovery, archaeologists searched other nearby caves between 1952 and 1956 and found ten other caves that contained thousands of ancient documents as well.[68] There were originally eleven scrolls; a twelfth scroll was discovered in February, 2017.[69] Various scholars have "estimated that the texts were upwards of 2,000 years old."[70]

Eventually, the scrolls were brought to a Syrian Orthodox Archbishop who recognized that they were written in Hebrew.[71] He had the scrolls examined by John Trevor at the American School of Oriental Research, who contacted the world's foremost Middle East archaeologist, Dr. William Albright, and together Trevor, Albright, other archaeologists, and others confirmed the antiquity of the scrolls and dated those they were considering back to between the first and second century BC.[72]

Fragments from every Old Testament book, except for the book of Esther, were discovered.[73] Cave 1, which was excavated in 1949, and cave 4, excavated in 1952, proved to be the most productive caves.[74] The oldest piece of biblical Hebrew (in the scrolls), a fragment from the book of Samuel,[75] was discovered in cave 4 and is now dated back to the third century BC.[76] One of the most significant discoveries was a well-preserved scroll of the entire book of Isaiah.[77]

With hundreds of manuscripts from every book, except Esther, the Dead Sea Scrolls have been a major key in assessing whether the Old Testament has been accurately preserved.[78] The Dead Sea Scrolls predated the oldest Jewish text from which the Old Testament had been taken by about one thousand years.[79] Scholars were anxious to see how the Dead Sea documents matched up with that Jewish text as a consequence of claims of critics and religious groups, such as Muslims and Mormons, that the content of the present-day Old Testament has been corrupted and is not well preserved.[80]

After years of careful study, the conclusion was reached that the Dead Sea Scrolls were almost identical with the oldest Jewish text from which the Old Testament had previously been derived, providing "valuable evidence that the Old Testament had been accurately and carefully preserved, that the Old Testament canon existed prior to the third century BC," and that the prophecies in the Old Testament which foretold of Christ "predated the birth of Christ" and predicted such events as "the rise of Persia, Greece, and Rome,"[81] long before they occurred. "The Dead Sea Scrolls, then, increase the confidence in the reliability of the Bible," i.e., that the Old Testament is a faithful transmission of the oldest known copies of those books.[82]

3. Jewish Scribes—Meticulous Reproduction

The conclusion that the Old Testament we have today is faithful to its original writing is further supported by what is known about the practices of the Jewish scribes who made copies of the Old Testament over time. The Jewish scribes conscientiously and meticulously rewrote the books of the Old Testament.

Scholars believe the Old Testament canon was closed earlier than 200 BC. Too, they believe the earliest biblical manuscripts were transmitted in the oral tradition. At some point, however, it was deemed critical that Scripture be written down to ensure its accuracy.

The Scriptures were so important to the nation of Israel, that a special class of scholars called Soferim (Hebrew: סֹיְרְפוֹם) developed during the Second Temple period. From about 500 BC to 100 AD, the primary task of these scribes was to preserve Israel's sacred traditions, which served as the foundation of the Jewish nation.[83]

Another author indicated that the Old Testament was first committed to writing "perhaps in the eighth to seventh centuries BC."[84]

When the care which the scribes took began is subject to some scholarly dispute. "Paul D. Wegner, professor of Old Testament studies at Gateway Seminary in Ontario, California," indicated that "during the Talmudic period (100 BC to AD 400), meticulous rule were developed to preserve the Old Testament text in synagogue scrolls."[85]

Another author states that the rules began to be developed with the Babylonian King Nebuchadnezzar II's siege of Jerusalem. The siege occurred in the sixth century BC.[86] After the siege, Jews, particularly the intelligentsia and Jewish society, were taken by force to Babylonia in what has been called the "Babylonian Captivity, also called Babylonian Exile."[87] Seventy years after Jerusalem was captured and the forced exile began, the captivity formally ended when Cyrus the Great, the Persian conqueror of Babylonia, gave the Jews permission to return to their homeland and Jerusalem.[88]

According to the Bible, Ezra, a religious "scribe skilled in the Law of Moses,"[89] recovered a copy of the Torah (Genesis, Exodus, Leviticus, Numbers, and Deuteronomy) and read it aloud to the whole nation,[90] probably in the fifth century BC. Beginning at that time, the Jewish scribes responsible for making copies of the Old Testament adopted the following process for creating copies of the Torah and eventually other books in the Old Testament to assure their reliability:

1. All materials had to be made according to strict specifications. They could only use clean kosher animal skins, both to write on and to bind manuscripts. Quills had to be made from the feathers of clean birds. The ink had to be black and prepared according to scribal specifications.

2. No word or even a letter could be written from memory. A scribe had to have another scroll open before him and pronounce every word out loud before copying it.

3. Every time before writing the name of God, a scribe had to reverently wipe his pen and wash his entire body and say, "I am writing the name of God for the holiness of His name."

4. Each column of writing could have no less than forty-eight and no more than sixty lines.

5. Every letter had to have some space around it. The letters, words, and paragraphs had to be counted, and the document became invalid if two letters touched each other. The middle paragraph, word, and letter had to correspond to those of the original document. If one letter touched another or if a letter was defective because of incorrect writing, a hole, a tear, or a smudge so that it could not be easily read, the scroll was invalidated.

6. Within thirty days of completion, an editor had to review the manuscript, count every letter and every word as a way of checking. The editor would also make sure that the middle word on each page of the copy was the same as the middle word on the manuscript being copied. If as many as three pages required corrections, the entire manuscript had to be redone.

7. The documents could be stored only in sacred places (synagogues, etc.).[91]

Such practices assure us today that each copy was trustworthy and that the Old Testament we have contains a reliable iteration of the Old Testament when it was first written.

4. Nuzi Tablets

Fact Stated: 1500 BC
Fact Confirmed: 20th century (over 3400 years later)

Twenty thousand ± cuneiform clay tablets were discovered shortly before World War II[92] at the ruins of Nuzi, east of the Tigris River, 3,500 years after they were written in approximately 1500 BC. As one author reported,

> Nuzi was a Hurrian[93] administrative center not far from the Hurrian capital at Kirkuk in northern Iraq. The Hurrians are equivalent to the Horites in the Old Testament, also called Hivites and Jebusites. Excavations were carried out at Nuzi by American teams from 1925 to 1933. The major find was more than 5,000 family and administrative archives spanning six generations, ca. 1450–1350 BC. They deal with the social, economic, religious and legal institutions of the Hurrians.[94]

The tablets tell of practices similar to those in Genesis such as adoption for childless couples (Gn 15:2), children by proxy (Gn 16; 21:1), inheritance rights (Gn 25:29), marriage arrangements (Gn 28 and levirate marriage (Gn 38; Dt 25:5). They also demonstrate the significance of the deathbed blessing (Gn 27; 48) and household gods (Gn 31:14–30). Some Nuzi tablets, called 'tablets of sistership,' have agreements in which a man adopted a woman as a sister. In the society of the Hurrians, a wife enjoyed both greater protection and a superior position when she also had the legal status of a sister. In such a case, two separate documents were drawn up, one for marriage and the other for sistership. This may explain why both Abraham (Gn 12:10 20:1) and Isaac (Gn 26:7) said their wives were their sisters. It is possible that they had previously adopted them to give them higher status, in accordance with the custom of the day.[95]

The Nuzi tablets reveal institutions, practices, and customs remarkably similar to those found in Genesis (written 1450–1405 BC).[96] Included among these customs was the description of the custom for a sterile wife to "provide a slave girl to her husband in order to beget a son,"[97] as the Bible reports Sarai (later Sarah) did for Abram (later Abraham) in Genesis 16.[98]

"This practice is also attested to in many [other] texts found by archaeologists. The Alalakh Texts [eighteenth century BC] and even the Code of Hammurabi all agree that procuring a son in this way was an accepted custom."[99]

5. Artifacts

In 1979, archaeologists made a discovery at the Ketef Hinnom site, a series of rock-hewn burial chambers located southwest of Jerusalem's old city, on the road to Bethlehem, that also confirms the reliability of the Old Testament. They discovered two silver plates with text written in Hebrew and believed to have been used as amulets in the seventh century BC, 2,700 years + earlier.[100] The text contained the priestly benediction from Numbers 6: 24–26 (written 1450–1405 BC) originally written over 3,000 years before the amulets were found. The silver plates said, "The lord bless you and keep you; the lord make his face shine upon you and be gracious to you; the lord turn His face toward you and give you peace."[101] "The inscriptions on the Ketef Hinnom Amulets, now displayed at the Israel Museum, are considered the oldest biblical text yet discovered."[102]

When Only God Knew

C. New Testament Reliability Generally

Written: 44–96 AD

The New Testament writers had completed their work within about sixty years after Jesus' crucifixion. Most New Testament books were written between AD 50 and 96 by the apostles or someone closely associated with them.[103]

As the above chart clearly shows, the New Testament books were completed within seventy years of Jesus' crucifixion, whether that occurred in 30 or 33 AD, a date as to which there is disagreement. This is important because it means there were plenty of people around when the New Testament documents were penned who could have contested the writings.[104] In other words, those who wrote the documents knew that if they were inaccurate, plenty of people would have pointed it out.[105] But there are no ancient documents dating to the first century, by the end of which all of the books of the New Testament had been written, that contest the facts reported in the New Testament writings.

1. Chart of Ancient Writings

Historians of the ancient world rely on writings left behind by various authors to determine what occurred and when. While scholars who have considered when ancient books were written must make judgments on when various ancient documents were written, and the number of ancient books, including the New Testament, which scholars have located changes over time, it should be noted that

> the New Testament is the best-attested book of the ancient world. The manuscript copies of most Greek and Latin authors can usually be counted on both hands, with some rising in the hundreds. Homer's writings are the second-most popular with less than 2500 copies of his Iliad and Odyssey combined. But

Homer pales in comparison with the New Testament.[106]

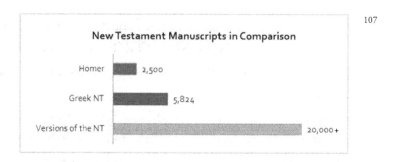

107

New Testament Manuscripts in Comparison

- Homer — 2,500
- Greek NT — 5,824
- Versions of the NT — 20,000+

Applying the standard that the more copies of original writings that remain and the closer in time of the copies to the original writing, the more confident historians can be that a writing is a reliable copy of an original document, the New Testament is, as can be seen from the following chart, the most contemporary of ancient documents with the most copies existing from the earliest time and, therefore, the most reliable historical document of the ancient world available to historians. The following chart is taken from various sources.

Author	Date Originally Written	Date of Earliest Copy Remaining	Approximate Time Span Between Original and Copy	Number of Copies Remaining
Aristophanes *Assorted Works*	488–385 BC	900 AD	1350 yrs. +	10
Aristotle *Assorted Works*	384–322 BC	1100 AD	1450 yrs. +	49
Caesar *Gallic Wars*	100–44 BC	900 AD	Fragment – 950 yrs. +	251
Demosthenes *Speeches*	300 BC	1100 AD	1400 yrs. +	444
Euripides *Tragedies*	480–406 BC	1100 AD	1550 yrs. +	330
Herodotus *The History of Herodotus*	480–425 BC	900 AD	1350 yrs. +	109

When Only God Knew

Author	Date Originally Written	Date of Earliest Copy Remaining	Approximate Time Span Between Original and Copy	Number of Copies Remaining
Homer *Iliad*	800–900 BC	400 BC	550 yrs. +	1900
Livy *History of Rome*	59 BC 17 AD	4th Century AD (Fragment) Mostly 10th Century AD	450 yrs. + 1050 yrs. +	473
New Testament *(In Greek)*	50–100 AD	2nd Century AD (circa 130 AD)	Fragment – 25 yrs. + Whole – 100 yrs. +	5856
New Testament *(All languages)*			Fragment – 25 yrs. + Whole – 100 yrs. +	23,986
Plato *Tetralogies*	400 BC	895–900 AD	1300–1400 yrs. +	238
Pliny, the Elder *Natural History*	49–79 AD	5th Century AD (Fragment) 14th–15th Century AD (Remainder)	450 yrs. + 1450 yrs. +	200
Sophocles *Plays (including Oedipus Rex)*	496–406 BC	3rd Century BC	750 yrs. +	226
Suetonius *The Twelve Caesars*	118–120 AD	9th Century AD	800 yrs. +	8 +
Tacitus *Annals*	circa 100 AD	850–1100 AD	750–1000 yrs. +	36
Thucydides *History*	460–400 BC	900 AD	1350 yrs. +	188

Over time, additional copies of the New Testament from the early centuries after Christ's crucifixion are being found, and the New Testament's currency is regularly re-confirmed. According to one writer, "there exist in various languages more than 25,000 manuscripts," as compared to the 23,986 indicated above; almost 6,000 of those texts are in Greek.[108] "The earliest New Testament manuscript in existence is dated to the beginning of the second century" AD (circa 114 AD, approximately eighty years after Jesus' crucifixion).

Scholars are still counting the number of ancient New Testament copies in languages other than Greek.[109] The number of New Testament manuscripts in Greek alone stands at 5856, according to the chart. To that number must be added another 10,000+ for Latin copies (which the NT began to be translated into in the second century), and several thousand more for Coptic, Syriac, Armenian, Ethiopic, Georgian, Arabic, Hebrew, and many other languages. Conservative estimates are that the New Testament weighs in at 20,000 to 25,000 manuscripts in these various languages. Scholars do not know for sure *because* they have not finished counting them all yet.

Twenty thousand to 25,000 New Testament manuscripts in these various languages is over ten times the 1900 manuscripts for Homer's *Iliad*, and Homer wrote the *Iliad* 900 years earlier. And the average New Testament manuscript is not some small scrap; the average is more than 450 pages long. In terms of sheer quantity of manuscripts, nothing in the ancient world comes close to the New Testament.[110]

As is plain from the chart, there are more existing copies of the New Testament ("NT") written closer in time to what happened in it than all other historical books of ancient times. That alone makes the New Testament a more reliable ancient history account than the other writings included in the chart. There are also thousands more New Testament Greek manuscripts, the language in which the New Testament was first written, than any other ancient writing.

The table illustrates that the Greek NT does extremely well with both the time gap (25–100 years) and the number of [original copies remaining] (5856), as compared to all the other documents in the table. But the situation is even better for the NT [due to all of the original copies of the New Testament remaining] in other languages.

One authority reported that there are over 2000 Armenian, almost 1000 Coptic, six Gothic, more than 600 Ethiopian, more than 10000 Latin, more than 350 Syriac, forty-three Georgian, and more than 4000 Slavic manuscript copies of the NT.

The only conclusion one can reasonably reach is that we (can) have more confidence in the textual transmission of the NT than in any other document of ancient history. To question the transmission accuracy of the NT texts we have today is to question all of ancient history.[111]

Specific examples of documents that have been discovered and were written close to the writing of the New Testament include, but are not limited to, the following:

- Rylands Papyrus—discovered 1920—a small fragment of the Gospel of John (written 80–90 AD) [measures 3.5" x 2.5"]—is the oldest universally accepted manuscript from the New Testament. It is dated to 125 AD, very close to the date of the event it describes, was found near the Nile River, a long way from its place of composition in Ephesus and describes Jesus's trial before Pilate.[112]
- Bodmer Papyrus II—discovered 1952 in Egypt and dated from 150–200 AD—contains most of John's gospel (written 80–90 AD).[113]

- Chester Beatty Papyri, three papyri dating from 200 AD, was acquired between 1931 and 1935, [over 1700 years later, and contains most of the New Testament [written 44–96 AD].[114]
- Codex Vaticanus, three papyri dating from 200 AD, is in the Vatican Library, was first inventoried in 1481 AD, [almost 1500 years after it was written,] and contains a nearly complete Bible.[115]
- Codex Sinaiticus, dated to 350 AD discovered in 1859 AD, contains a nearly complete New Testament and over half of the Old Testament (the earliest books of the Bible appear have been damaged).[116]

The New Testament is also far more internally consistent than are the other ancient writings identified in the chart. The agreement or consistency among preserved known Greek manuscripts of the New Testament "is rated as 99.5 percent."[117] The degree of difference is extraordinarily small, particularly when compared with other ancient texts.

"In spite of the number of authors, forty,[118] and the volume of writing, the Bible, when it comes to internal agreement, exceeds what one could expect from any other ancient document."[119] For example, Homer's Iliad written "sometime around 900 BC," does not have a single copy that is 100 percent in agreement with the others. On its website, Christian Apologetics and Research Ministry, rates the agreement among the copies of Homer's Iliad as only 95 percent.[120]

> If the critics of the Bible dismiss the New Testament as reliable information, then they must also dismiss the reliability of the writings of Plato, Aristotle, Caesar, Homer, and the other authors mentioned in the chart at the beginning of the paper. On the other hand, if the critics acknowledge the historicity and

writings of those other individuals, then they must also retain the historicity and writings of the New Testament authors; after all, the evidence for the New Testament's reliability is far greater than the others.[121]

2. Ancient Writers/Documents Discussing Gospel Facts

Facts Confirmed: 62 AD–116 AD

There are many ancient secular non-Christian writers and writings that confirm the reliability of the Bible. They discuss both Jesus and early Christians. Some, but not all, of them are discussed below.

Titus Flavius Josephus ("Josephus"), a Jew and a Roman citizen born in Jerusalem four years after the crucifixion of Jesus in the same city who lived from 37/38 AD through 100 AD,[122] worked under a couple of Roman emperors and wrote near the end of the first century AD. In *Testimonium Flavianum*, one of the most remarkable passages in *The Antiquities of the Jews*, which he wrote in 93 AD, Josephus confirms that Jesus existed when he said,

> At this time there was a wise man called Jesus, and his conduct was good, and he was known to be virtuous. Many people among the Jews and the other nations became his disciples. Pilate condemned him to be crucified and to die. But those who had become his disciples did not abandon his discipleship. They reported that he had appeared to them three days after his crucifixion and that he was alive. Accordingly, he was perhaps the Messiah, concerning whom the prophets have reported wonders. And the tribe of the Christians, so named after him, has not disappeared to this day.[123]

Because questions were raised about whether Josephus penned those exact words, one scholar reconstructed the text as follows:

> At this time there appeared Jesus, a wise man. For he was a doer of startling deeds, a teacher of the people who receive the truth with pleasure. And he gained a following both among many Jews and among many of Greek origin. And when Pilate, because of an accusation made by the leading men among us, condemned him to the cross, those who had loved him previously did not cease to do so. And up until this very day the tribe of Christians, named after him, has not died out.[124]

No matter which way the passage is read, however, it proves the existence of Jesus in the first century AD and that he was condemned to be crucified on the cross by Pilate. As one author said about the reconstructed text from Josephus,[125] Josephus

> also suggests that Jesus was innocent. A straightforward report would have told that Pilate executed the man from Nazareth because he was considered to be the king of the Jews. But instead of naming the accusation, the Jewish historian names the accusers. Since he usually delights in writing about the deserved punishment of rebels and pretenders, the fact that he does not inform us of the charge, means that he thought that Jesus was innocent.[126]

In chapter nine of book twenty of the Jewish Antiquities, Josephus again verifies the existence of Jesus when he discusses the death of James, the brother of Jesus, after the Sanhedrin assembled to judge "the brother of Jesus, who was called Christ, whose name was James."[127]

Pliny the Younger, whose full name was Gaius Plinius Caecilius Secundus, was a Roman governor who lived from 61–113 AD.[128] In 112 AD, Pliny the Younger wrote to Emperor Trajan concerning how to deal with Christians, who refused to worship the emperor or recant their faith and instead worshiped Jesus.[129]

Tacitus, a Roman historian and senator who lived from 55 to 117 AD, wrote his Annals in 116 AD in which he referred to Jesus, his execution by Pontius Pilate, and the existence of early Christians in Rome. It is one of the first mentions by a non-Christian source of Christianity, describing in one place Nero's persecution of the Christians for the Great Fire of Rome, which happened in 64 AD.[130]

Suetonius, the son of a Roman knight,[131] lived from 69 AD until after 122 AD[132] (perhaps until 140 AD)[133] and wrote in his Lives of the Twelve Caesars[134] in 112 AD about riots which broke out in the Jewish community in Rome under the emperor Claudius ("Tiberius Claudius Drusus Caesar"). Suetonius said of Claudius that "He banished from Rome all the Jews, who were continually making disturbances at the instigation of one Chrestus,"[135] meaning Jesus. The event was noted in Acts 18:2 (written 62–70 AD, NIV), which says, among other things, that "Claudius had ordered all Jews to leave Rome."

The Talmud, a series of Jewish religious documents, refers to Jesus using the term "Yeshu." "He is called 'Yeshu ha Notzri'/ Jesus the Nazarene."[136] These references probably date back to the second century.[137]

> These stories were recorded in the Talmud from the time of the Destruction of the Temple in 70 AD and, (according to the author of the statement,) are probably earlier records than the written Gospels of the New Testament. The oral tradition of these stories go

(sic) all the way back to the time that Jesus was teaching in Galilee.[138]

Talmud Sanhedrin 43a also says that "it is taught: On the eve of Passover they hung Yeshu," i.e., Jesus.[139]

While written by Jewish scholars who would not be favorable to the idea that Jesus was the prophesied Messiah and while not approving the full biblical story of Jesus, even the Jewish Talmud confirms that He was crucified in Jerusalem at the time of Passover as discussed in the Gospels of Matthew, Mark, Luke, and John.[140]

Mara (a Syrian Stoic): Around the time the Gospels of Matthew, Mark, Luke, and John were being written (50–90 AD), Mara (a Syrian Stoic) was imprisoned by the Romans. While imprisoned, Mara wrote a letter to his son, which most scholars date to shortly after 73 AD during the first century.[141] Written after the Jewish temple in Jerusalem was destroyed by the Romans in 70 AD and the Jews were massacred, taken as slaves, or dispersed from Jerusalem,[142] his letter said,

> What advantage did the Jews gain from executing their wise King? It was just after that that their kingdom was abolished. God justly avenged… the Jews, ruined and driven from their land, live in complete dispersion… Nor did the wise King die for good; He lived on in the teaching which He had given.[143]

Scholars also refer to the wise king's death as being a murder or an execution.[144] Another translation of the letter says,

> What else can we say, when the wise are forcibly dragged off by tyrants, their wisdom is captured by insults, and their minds are oppressed and without defense? …What advantage did the Jews gain from

executing their wise king? It was just after that their kingdom was abolished. God justly avenged… the Jews, desolate and driven from their own kingdom, live in complete dispersion. But Socrates is not dead, … nor is the wise king, because of the "new law" he laid down.[145]

Some scholars believe this describes the fall of Jerusalem as God's punishment for the crucifixion of Jesus in Jewish Jerusalem.

The Dead Sea scrolls: The Dead Sea Scrolls, most of which were written between 150 BC and 70 AD, as pointed out above, also show the language and customs of Jews of Jesus' time.

> "According to Henry Chadwick, (a British academic, theologian, Church of England priest, a former Dean of Christ Church Cathedral, Oxford and a leading historian of the early church,)[146] similar uses of languages and viewpoints recorded in the New Testament and the Dead Sea scrolls are valuable in showing that the New Testament portrays the first century period that it reports and is not a product of a later period."[147]

3. Destruction of the Temple in Jerusalem

Prophesied in the Bible: 50–61 AD
Confirmed: After the Temple Destroyed–70 AD

Many ancient writers, such as Josephus, the "contemporary Roman Jewish historian who fought alongside the Jewish people in the revolt,"[148] have reported on the revolt against Rome in 66 AD, which led to the destruction of the temple in and the city of Jerusalem by the Romans in 70 AD.[149] A bronze coin bearing the Hebrew phrase

"Freedom of Zion," and dating to the revolt against Rome in 66–70 AD, has been discovered at the Temple Mount Sifting Project[150] in Jerusalem.[151]

The date (70 AD) that the temple in Jerusalem was destroyed by Rome supports the conclusion that the facts stated in the New Testament were written soon after Jesus' crucifixion and are, therefore, very current and thus very historically reliable. Jerusalem was the civil and religious capital of the Jews and perhaps the most important city to the authors of the New Testament. Jerusalem was the center of Jewish culture and religion, to which all the New Testament authors at one time ascribed, and the temple in Jerusalem was its most significant edifice.

Still, there is no mention in the Gospels of Matthew, Mark, Luke, and John of the temple's destruction, as you would have expected if the Gospels were written later than 70 AD because the temple was the center of Jewish life in Jerusalem but perhaps more so because Jesus had predicted its destruction before He was crucified. Matthew 24:1–2 (NIV) (written 50–65 AD) says,

> Jesus left the temple and was walking away when his disciples came up to him to call his attention to its buildings. "Do you see all these things?" he asked. "Truly I tell you, not one stone here will be left on another; every one will be thrown down."

See also Luke 19: 42–44 (NIV) (written 60–61 AD), reporting that Jesus wept over Jerusalem as He approached it and saw it, prophesying its destruction, saying

> If you, even you, had only known on this day what would bring you peace—but now it is hidden from your eyes. The days will come upon you when your enemies will build an embankment against you and

When Only God Knew

encircle you and hem you in on every side. They will dash you to the ground, you and the children within your walls. They will not leave one stone on another, because you did not recognize the time of God's coming to you.

The Gospels of Matthew and Luke[152] record that Jesus prophesied that the temple in Jerusalem would be destroyed forty years before it was torn down. Jesus' destruction prophecy was reported by Matthew and Luke less than thirty years after Jesus died, i.e., in 50–65 AD and 60–61 AD, respectively, and ten to twenty years before the temple's actual destruction. Such a significant event as the destruction of the temple would have been historically important to the writers of the New Testament because, among other things, the destruction of the temple would have verified the prophecy which Jesus made prior to His crucifixion and forty years before it happened. The fact that the actual destruction of the temple in 70 AD was not reported anywhere in the New Testament supports the conclusion that the facts recorded in the New Testament were written within a very short time after Jesus' crucifixion, but in any event, mostly before the prophesied temple destruction took place in 70 AD.

That also supports the conclusion that the facts reported in the New Testament are reliable. Remember, the closer in time to an event that a record is made, the more likely it is to be accurate.

4. Historical Trustworthiness of Luke

The apostle Luke wrote the Gospel of Luke (60–61 AD) and Acts (62–70 AD). Luke "is the longest of the four gospels and the longest book in the New Testament"[153] and, "tells of the origins, birth, ministry, death, resurrection, and ascension of Jesus Christ."[154] Acts "is the fifth book of the New Testament; it tells of the founding of the Christian church and the spread of its message to the Roman Empire."[155] Together, Luke and Acts "account for 27.5 percent of the

New Testament, the largest contribution by a single author."[156]

"As a physician, Luke would have been trained as a careful observer, a quality that would have been invaluable in" writing Luke and Acts.[157] Luke is considered by many to be a very accomplished historian. William Mitchell Ramsay, also spelled Ramsey, who lived from 1851 to 1939[158] and was "one of the great archaeologists and topographers"[159] and a New Testament scholar,[160] wrote that Luke "is a historian of the first rank' and 'should be placed along with the very greatest of historians.'"[161] When he wrote, Luke acted as historians are expected to.

> First, he noted the consistent reporting of "those
> matters" (referring to existing reporting of New Tes-
> taments matters, including the reporting in the Gos-
> pels of Matthew and Mark, both written 50–65 AD).
> These writers drew up narratives that agreed with the
> teaching that circulated among the congregations at
> the time, for the writings were "even as they delivered
> them unto us."
>
> Second, Luke recognized the reliability of the
> narratives, for they were based on eyewitness testi-
> mony.
>
> Third, the works were further validated by the fact
> that the eyewitnesses themselves had been changed
> by what they "saw and heard" (cf. Acts 4:20). There-
> fore, they were "ministers of the word."
>
> Fourth, Luke indicated that the things Jesus
> Christ "did and taught" (see Acts 1:1) were "fulfilled
> among us." These events were not in the distant past;
> they were still capable of demonstrable proof—the
> evidence was fresh at hand (cf. 1 Cor. 15:5–8).

When Only God Knew

A. T. Robertson observed, "Luke writes after the close of Christ's earthly ministry and yet it is not in the dim past."

> With these familiar facts before his audience, Luke seized on the precedent for writing about the historical roots of Christianity. Significant interest abounded concerning Jesus of Nazareth, and Luke knew that additional good could be accomplished by supplementing the current literature with a more comprehensive work while thorough verification was still possible.[162]

Luke's reliability as a historian has been confirmed on other occasions. As an example, for a long time—for 1700 years through the middle of the eighteenth century AD—many skeptical scholars thought Luke made up the term "politarch," which he used to describe the leaders of Thessalonica in Acts 17.[163] But a politarch really "was a Hellenistic and Roman-era Macedonian title for an elected governor (archon) of a city."[164]

> Acts 17:6, 8 (written 62–70 AD) mention the "rulers of the city" of Thessalonica, who beat and imprisoned Paul and Silas. Luke, the inspired writer of Acts, is a most careful historian. Different cities/districts used specific words to designate their rulers. Here Luke uses the word "politarch" [πολιτάρχης], which was a "very rare title for magistrates."[165]

Luke was accurate in describing the rulers of Thessalonica as politarchs. A "Politarch" inscription existed on the inside of (the Vardar arch), the arch spanning the Via Egnatia, a road into Thessalonica, at its western gate entrance to Thessalonica, until 1876 when the gate was torn down.[166] Its translation was first published in Milan, Italy, in

1740 on page DXCV of volume II of the *Novus Thesaurus Inscriptionum*.[167] It confirmed Luke's reference to politarchs and the accuracy of Luke as a historian. There are now more than sixty known inscriptions that mention politarchs, three-fourths from the Macedonian area of Greece, with about half from Thessalonica itself.[168]

Church historian Philip Schaff, in a section entitled "The Acts and Secular History," wrote:

> The "politarchs" of Thessalonica, 17:6, 8 (Greek text: τοὺς πολιτάρχας, i.e., τοὺς ἄρχοντας τῶν πολιτῶν, praefectos civitatis, the rulers of the city).
>
> This was a very rare title for magistrates and might easily be confounded with the more usual designation "poliarchs." But Luke's accuracy has been confirmed by an inscription still legible on an archway in Thessalonica, giving the names of seven "politarchs" who governed before the visit of Paul.[169]

For all those reasons, we can rely on the facts Luke related in the Gospel of Luke and the book of Acts, which include the crucifixion and resurrection of Jesus. They are "of the first rank."

5. Eye-Witness Accounts

The Bible is full of eyewitness accounts. While the veracity of eye-witness accounts has come under recent challenge across America,[170] there are at least two reasons why New Testament eyewitness accounts are different and support the reliability of the New Testament.

First, as discussed in more detail in chapter 4, apostles, eyewitnesses who lived with Jesus for three years, died horrible deaths[171] while refusing to deny the truth of what they had witnessed as described in the New Testament. In addition, those eyewitnesses reported that hundreds of people saw Jesus after He was raised from the dead,[172] who could have been confronted about what they saw, but there is no record that any witnesses of the risen Jesus denied that they saw Him alive after His crucifixion. Such resurrection would be of keen interest to the Jewish and Roman leaders, whom one would have thought would have the incentive to disprove what the eyewitnesses are reported to have seen.

Second, the eyewitnesses to Jesus' life in the New Testament were more than casual observers of what happened. They were His students and were more focused on what they saw of Him and of what they were told by Him. As one author, very familiar with eye-witness testimony, said,

> Most eyewitnesses [that the author] interviewed in [his] casework had no idea they would later be called into a jury trial to testify about what they heard or observed. As a result, they sometimes regret not paying better attention when they had the opportunity. But the disciples of Jesus had a distinct advantage over modern eyewitnesses in this regard. They were *students* of Jesus. Unlike spontaneous, unprepared witnesses of a crime, the disciples were desperately attentive to the words and actions of Jesus, and [that author imagined] their attention to detail became even more focused with each miraculous event. For this reason, the authors of the gospels became excellent eyewitnesses and recognized the importance of their testimony very early.
>
> While Jesus walked here on earth, His followers studied and learned from His actions and words. They were often mesmerized, confused and challenged by what they saw and heard. In spite of this, Jesus taught them and occasionally sent them out on their own. They memorized His teaching and relied on his wisdom when they weren't with Him.[173]

For a thorough rebuttal of skepticism about the authenticity of the Gospels of Matthew, Mark, Luke, and John, the reader may want to read *Apologetics: Were the Gospels Written While the Eyewitnesses Were Still Alive?* Published by Timothy Paul Jones on May 5, 2015.[174]

6. Other Reasons to Rely on the New Testament

There are several other reasons we can rely on the New Testament with the highest degree of confidence.

First, the early days of Christianity produced reliable copies. Copyists in the first several centuries of the Church were not rank amateurs, as some suggest. For the most part, they were professional scribes who took their work as seriously as their reputations.

Scribes were paid by the line, and they were not necessarily Christians. And when we consider the surviving Greek Old Testament manuscripts, it is very difficult to find manuscripts in which a scribe changed the text.

Mistakes in early papyrus copies are mostly misspellings, which are fixed in the next generation of copies. And because there are so many copies to compare—some 2.5 million manuscript pages—it would have been virtually impossible for any person, or any group or collaborators, to tamper with one manuscript without rewriting all the copies in circulation across the known world at the time.

Second, textual variants in these copies do not change their meaning or message. Dan Wallace, executive director of The Center for the Study of New Testament Manuscripts, says there are two key questions to ask with respect to textual variants. First, is the variant meaningful? In other words, does it change the meaning of the text? Second, is it viable? That is, does is possibly represent the original?

Wallace notes that a mere 0.2 percent of textual variants in ancient New Testament documents are both meaningful and viable, and 70 percent of those are merely spelling differences. Out of some 20,000 lines of ancient text, only forty lines are in doubt, and none of these involves a significant Christian teaching. Wallace notes that even Bart Ehrman, author of numerous books denying the reliability of Scripture, is forced to acknowledge that truth.

> Even the two greatest variants—the last twelve vers-es of Mark's Gospel[175] and the story of the woman caught in adultery in the Gospel of John[176]—do not undermine the teachings of Jesus or the record of the early church. It does not change the Biblical fact that Jesus still forgives sins and does so despite the fact the earliest transcripts do not contain Mark 16:9–20 (ESV) (written 50–65 AD), which discusses Jesus' post-resurrection appearances, and the ending of Mark seems to draw from the writings of Luke.
>
> …
>
> The implications for the New Testament are profound. If the Gospels and other New Testament books were written in the mid-to-late first century, and if they survived at least 150 years, then there is continuity between the (originals) and the earli-est manuscript copies, which date to the second and third centuries. In support of this view, Evans cites the writing of church father Tertullian in AD 190 as he responds to heretics who changed Paul's letters. Tertullian notes that Paul's originals still exist and may be consulted.[177]

As is plain from the above, the Bible we have today, both the Old and New Testament, are extraordinarily reliable copies of those books as they were when they were originally penned. Based on the prem-ises in this chapter and the previous two chapters, it is now time for the reader to weigh.

PART II

Archaeology/Anthropology/ History Prove the Bible's Accuracy

Archaeology is "the scientific study of material remains (such as fossil relics, artifacts, and monuments) of past human life and activities."[178] Anthropology is "the science of human beings; *especially*: the study of human beings and their ancestors through time and space and in relation to physical character, environmental and social relations, and culture."[179] History is "a branch of knowledge that records and explains past events."[180] History is discerned both from recorded, or written information made contemporaneously with the historical event and later, and discovered later most often using archaeological and anthropological tools. All three support the accuracy of the Bible.

"At the turn of the twentieth century, skeptics viewed the Bible as myth rather than real world history."[181] Additionally, many archaeologists undertook their "scientific" study of acts with the assumption that facts reported in the Bible are not reliable—just myth—for the purpose of disproving the historicity of the Bible, rather than undertaking their study with the purpose of following the facts to whatever truth they lead.

For the reliability of historical reports, historians rely, among other things, on writings left behind by various authors to determine what occurred in the ancient world.[182] The closer to an event that information is recorded and the more copies that exist of a writing describing the event, the more the information contained in the writing is considered reliable. As pointed out in Chapter 3 above, the Bible's New Testament is by far the most reliable ancient writing compared to other ancient writings. For the reasons pointed out in Chapter 3 above, the Old Testament is likewise also a reliable record of historical facts.

Recent archaeology supports the conclusion that the Bible contains accurate and reliable history. The Bible refers to hundreds of people, including but not limited to kings, places, including but not limited to cities, and events for which archaeological evidence has been uncovered.

And this is exactly what has been found.[183] As the online book *Archeological Evidence*[184] says,

> It would be extremely difficult for the honest skeptic to dispute the overwhelming archaeological support for the historical accuracy of both the Old and New Testaments. Numerous items discussed in the Bible such as nations, important people, customary practices, etc. have been verified by archaeological evidence. Bible critics have often been embarrassed by discoveries that corroborated Bible accounts they had previously deemed to be myth, such as the existence of the Hittites, King David, and Pontius Pilate, just to name a few. The noted Jewish archaeologist Nelson Glueck summed it up very well:
>
> *It may be stated categorically that no archeological discovery has ever controverted a single biblical reference. Scores of archeological findings have been made which confirm in clear outline or in exact detail historical statements in the Bible.*[185]
>
> When compared against secular accounts of history, the Bible always demonstrates amazing superiority. The noted biblical scholar R. D. Wilson, who

was fluent in forty-five ancient languages and dialects, meticulously analyzed twenty-nine kings from ten different nations, each of which had corroborating archaeological artifacts. Each king was mentioned in the Bible as well as documented by secular historians, thus offering a means of comparison. Wilson showed that the names as recorded in the Bible matched the artifacts perfectly... The Bible was also completely accurate in its chronological order of the kings.

One of the more overwhelming testimonies regarding the depth of archaeological evidence for the New Testament is in the account of the famous historian and archaeologist Sir William Ramsay. Ramsay was very skeptical of the accuracy of the New Testament, and he ventured to Asia minor over a century ago to refute its historicity. He especially took interest in Luke's accounts in the Gospel of Luke and the Book of Acts, which contained numerous geographical and historic references. Dig after dig the evidence without fail supported Luke's accounts. Governors mentioned by Luke that many historians never believe existed were confirmed by the evidence excavated by Ramsay's archaeological team. Without a single error, Luke was accurate in naming thirty-two countries, fifty-four cities, and nine islands. Ramsay became so overwhelmed with the evidence he eventually converted to Christianity. Ramsay finally had this to say,

I began with a mind unfavorable to it... but more recently I found myself brought into contact with the Book of Acts as an authority for the topography, antiquities, and society of Asia Minor. It was gradually borne upon me that in various details the narrative showed marvelous truth.

Luke is a historian of the first rank; not merely are his statements of fact trustworthy ... this author should be placed along with the very greatest historians.[186]

The classical historian A. N. Sherwin-White agrees with Ramsay's work regarding the Book of Acts

> Any attempt to reject its basic historicity even in matters of detail must now appear absurd. Roman historians have long taken it for granted.[187]

Archaeological discoveries ranging from evidence for the Tower of Babel, to Exodus, to the fallen Walls of Jericho, all the way to the tombs of contemporaries of St. Paul, have greatly enhanced the believability of the Bible. Though this vast archaeological evidence does not prove God wrote the Bible,[188] it surely must compel the honest skeptic to at least acknowledge its historical veracity. For the believer its yet another reassuring testimony to the reliability of the Bible. In the words of the University of Yale archaeologist Millar Burrows:

> … Archeological work has unquestionably strengthened confidence in the reliability of the scriptural record. More than one archeologist has found respect for the Bible increased by the experience of excavation in Palestine.[189]

Other historians and archaeologists confirm the reliability of the Bible as a historical narrative.[190] So, for example, Nelson Glueck, the noted Jewish archaeologist quoted above, also wrote "Scores of archaeological findings have been made which confirm in clear outline or exact detail historical statements in the Bible."[191]

Jonathan L. Reed, a professor of religion at the University of La Verne in La Verne, California, a director of the Sepphoris Acropolis Excavations in Israel and a leading authority on the archaeology of

When Only God Knew

early Christianity who excavated in Galilee since 1987,[192] comments that "[t]he many archaeological discoveries relating to people, places, or titles mentioned in Acts do lend credence to its historicity at one level; many of the specific details in Acts are factual."[193]

John McRay, an archaeologist and professor emeritus of New Testament at Wheaton College (Illinois) who supervised excavating teams in the Holy Land: Caesarea, Sepphoris, and Herodium and was an expert in the languages, cultures, geography, and history of Israel-Palestine,[194] wrote, "It should be remembered that only about two hundred sites out of the approximately five thousand sites in the Holy Land have been excavated."[195]

> [To state in more detail what Sir William Mitchell Ramsay, the famous historian and archaeologist discussed above, thought in finding] the archaeological evidence compelling: "I may fairly claim to have entered on this investigation without any prejudice in favour of the conclusion which I shall now attempt to justify to the reader. On the contrary, I began with a mind unfavourable to it for the ingenuity and apparent completeness of the Tubingen theory had at one time quite convinced me. It did not lie then in my line of life to investigate the subject minutely but more recently I found myself often brought in contact with the book of Acts as an authority for the topography antiquities and society of Asia Minor. It was gradually borne in upon me that in various details the narrative showed marvelous truth."[196]

Ancient historian Paul Barnett, a historian of antiquities, New Testament scholar and former Anglican bishop[197] concluded: "Archaeological findings have confirmed that the texts of the New Testament are from first to last historical and geographical in character."[198]

Care should be taken, however, not to use the statement: "Archaeology proves the Bible." In fact, such a claim would be putting archaeology above the Bible. What happens when seemingly assured results of archaeology are shown to be wrong after all? Very often, archaeology does endorse particular Bible events.[199] And some would say that in this way, it "proves the Bible." But such a statement should be taken with reservation because archaeology is the support, not the main foundation.

Thousands of facts in the Bible are not capable of verification because the evidence has long since been lost. However, it is remarkable that where confirmation is possible and has come to light, the Bible survives careful investigation in ways that are unique in all literature. Its superiority to attack, its capacity to withstand criticism and its amazing facility to be proved right are all staggering by any standards of scholarship. Seemingly assured results "disproving" the Bible has a habit of backfiring.[200]

Some examples of archaeological and anthropological discoveries and historical evidence which support the Bible's historical account follow. There are many others.

CHAPTER 4

People Named in the Bible

Various people are identified in the Bible. For hundreds or, in some cases, thousands of years, there were some who opined that many of those persons did not exist and/or that their biblical story was not true. The facts continuing to be uncovered by archaeologists and historians do not support their position. As time goes on, more and more people named in the Bible and the facts concerning them are being confirmed, from which there is assurance that these people lived and that their story was accurate. The following discusses some of them.

A. Old Testament

It took as long as 3500 years after the Bible had already reported the existence and impact on the ancient world of various individuals for their existence to be re-discovered by modern archaeology. Following are some of the persons who are named or whose story is told in the Old Testament for whom or which there is independent evidence of their existence or the events surrounding them.

1. Joseph

Fact Stated: Genesis and Exodus (written 1450–1405 BC)
Fact Confirmed: 20th century AD (3500 years later ±)

The story of the Exodus of the Jews from Egypt in the Bible begins with Joseph, who was sold into slavery into Egypt by his brothers out of their jealousy against and anger with Joseph. They sold Joseph into slavery because their father, Israel, who loved Joseph more than his brothers, made Joseph a robe of many colors and because Joseph told his brothers of a dream in which Joseph would rule over them.[201] The Bible then tells the story of how Joseph became the second most powerful man in Egypt and how he ruled over everyone in Egypt, including his brothers who had immigrated to Egypt due to famine.[202] According to Genesis and Exodus, Joseph's family, who were shepherds, settled in the land of Goshen.[203] The Bible also describes Joseph's last wish—for his bones to be taken back to the land of his forefathers, Abraham, Isaac, and Jacob when his people returned.[204] According to Exodus, Moses took Joseph's bones when the Israelites left Egypt.[205]

There is substantial proof outside the Bible that Joseph existed and became the second most powerful man in Egypt,[206] and the return of his bones to his ancestral lands is accurate.

A large city of Semites called Avaris, beneath the city of Ramses located in the Eastern Nile Delta in the land of Goshen[207] has been discovered.[208] Its discovery began in the mid-1960s.[209] It consists of houses that often had burial sites under the dwelling, a tradition of Ur of the Chaldees,[210] the place from which Abraham, Joseph's great grandfather, came.[211] Avaris was a town of foreigners that "had some sort of special status with Egyptian royalty."[212] This fits perfectly with Genesis 41:41, 47:6, 27. Pharaoh told Joseph in Genesis 41:41 (ESV) (written 1450–1405 BC), "See, I have set you over all the land of Egypt," and in Genesis 47:6 (ESV) (written 1450–1405 BC): "The land of Egypt is before you. Settle your father and brothers in the best of the land. Let them settle in the land of Goshen."

Genesis 47:27 (ESV) (written 1450–1405 BC) then says, "Thus Israel settled in the land of Egypt, in the land of Goshen. And they gained possessions in it, and were fruitful and multiplied exceedingly."

Numerous Semite settlements are found in Goshen.[213] There is also evidence that shepherds, as were the Israelites who came to Egypt,[214] lived in that area.[215]

When Only God Knew

There was also a large home, some have described as a palace, in Avaris built for a high-ranking Semite.[216] Joseph was such a high-ranking Semite.[217] This palace has twelve pillars and twelve tombs.[218] Jacob, Joseph's father, had twelve sons,[219] each of whom was the first of the twelve tribes of Israel.[220]

One of the tombs is in the shape of a pyramid.[221] This is significant as only persons of importance in Egypt, such as Joseph is in the Bible, were buried in pyramids.[222] Unlike the other tombs, however, the tomb in the pyramid was empty of bones,[223] consistent with the Biblical reports that Joseph wanted to be taken from Egypt when his people left and that his bones were taken from Egypt in the Exodus.[224]

Moreover, a statue of the person in the tomb is a Semite wearing a striped multi-colored robe,[225] such as Joseph wore.[226] The statue was excavated in 1991 AD and has been determined to have been sculpted around the time of the death of Joseph.[227]

The Egyptians were always careful to portray different things that showed the national background of the subjects of their paintings or statues, as well as their status in society. The person portrayed in this statue had a lighter skin than was used in portraying native Egyptians. He also had a flail held across his chest. The flail was meant to symbolize that he was a person with considerable authority, but not a pharaoh; pharaohs were shown with the double crown of Egypt and the "uraeus" or cobra's head on that crown. He was therefore an "Asiatic," Semitic person [Hebrew].

The mushroom hairstyle is also Semitic and non-Egyptian. An additional fragment of the shoulder with the flail features a clear multi-coloured coat design. The very coat that his father gave him that got him sold to Egypt became the symbol of his authority above them.[228]

2. Samson

Fact Stated: Judges 13–16 (written circa 1043 BC)
Fact Confirmed: 2012 AD (3000 years later ±)

Most of us know the story of Samson and Delilah told in the book of Judges in the Old Testament.[229] His story describes, among other things, his great strength, his love for Delilah, his seduction by her for money paid by the lords of the Philistines whom Samson had defeated in battle,[230] his having finally confided in Delilah that his strength came from his hair because his head had never been shaved, her treachery in shaving his head while he slept and informing the Philistines that he no longer had his strength, his capture and blinding by the Philistines, how he pulled down the pillars of their temple once his hair grew back and he regained his strength and that he and all the lords and 3000 men and women of the Philistines in their temple died as a result.

The accuracy of the Old Testament story of Samson, even his very existence, has been challenged over the years. "The historicity of this heroic account has been long debated among scholars. Indeed, many scholars seem hesitant to comment on the historicity of the Samson narratives at all."[231]

Some scholars have described his story as mythology, comparing Samson to Heracles, the Greek name for the mythological figure better known today as Hercules, his Roman name. According to mythology, Hercules fought and defeated a lion; according to the Bible, the Spirit of the Lord helped Samson defeated a young lion, tearing it apart.[232]

Scholars have taken the position that Samson was not an actual person. For example,

> [i]n the Talmudic period,[233] some seem to have denied that Samson was a historical figure, regarding him instead as a purely mythological personage. This

was viewed as heretical by the rabbis of the Talmud, and they attempted to refute this.[234]

Some authors have suggested that the Samson story "echoes in other myths and sacred traditions around the globe" "founded upon the constellations of the starry sky, and not upon actions that took place on earth among literal historical human beings" or identifying Samson with the sun.[235]

There is, however, relatively new support for the story that Samson killed a lion, as the Bible records. A "new find was announced that some archaeologists suspect supports the existence of Samson and the story of him killing a lion," i.e., a seal uncovered by Israeli archeologists on July 30, 2012.[236] "A small stone seal found [by Tel Aviv University archaeologists][237] recently in the excavations of Tel Beit Shemesh [approximately thirty kilometers or nineteen miles west of Jerusalem in Israel's Jerusalem District][238] could be the first archaeological evidence of the story of the biblical Samson."[239] It shows a man and a lion locked in combat.[240]

> The seal, measuring 1.5 centimeters, depicts a large animal next to a human figure. The seal was found in a level of excavation that dates to the eleventh century (BC) That was prior to the establishment of the Judean kingdom and is considered to be the period of the biblical judges—including Samson. Scholars say the scene shown on the artifact recalls the story in Judges of Samson fighting a lion.[241]

Further support for the accuracy of the lion story comes from the fact that the seal is dated to the eleventh or twelfth century BC, very close to the time that its account was recorded in the book of Judges written circa 1043 BC.

While the seal does not conclusively prove that Samson killed a lion with his bare hands,

> it strongly suggests that the story of Samson fighting the lion didn't start off as a mythical story of some distant past. When people first started telling it, Samson was either still alive or had only just recently died.[242]

That just might mean that, at the very least, he was strong enough and tough enough that the people around him were willing to believe it happened.[243]

Perhaps even more relevant to the accuracy of the story, however, is that "the seal was found in a home in Beth Shemesh, the city in which Samson is said to have been born and the place where he was buried" and is dated to "the century in which he's believed to have lived."[244] Additionally, support for the story comes from the fact that the "biblical city of Timna, where the Bible describes Samson's wife living, is located not far from Beit Shemesh," and he was on his way to his engagement party at her house when he confronted the lion.[245]

There is other proof that Samson's story in Judges is an accurate historical account. For example, the Philistine war with Israel really happened.

> At the core of Samson's story is the war between the Philistines and Israel. The Philistines, in the Bible, are treated as foreign oppressors with religions and values that, to the Israelites, seemed strange and blasphemous. That was what made a Samson a hero—while the Philistines dominated them, he was wild and strong enough to slaughter thousands of them.
>
> There's almost no question, at this point, that this war really happened. The five cities of the Philistines have all been turned into archaeological sites, and ev-

When Only God Knew

erything they left behind fits perfectly with the idea that they were the Israelites' mortal enemies.

The Philistines moved into the neighborhood in 1200 BC. At most, this was a hundred years before Samson was born. Based on the pottery they brought with them, they came from Aegea and they brought with them Greek Gods and customs that the Israelites would have seen as barbaric.

A massive, powerful army came with them, too. Even the Egyptians, whose military was far more powerful than the Israelites, kept records that describe the Philistines as a nearly unbeatable army that raided them from the sea.

When Samson supposedly lived, their violent new neighbors would have seemed like the worst people alive. They were foreign conquerors who still hadn't assimilated into the society around them. They ate animals the Israelites considered unclean, worshipped gods they considered evil, and some of their foreign ideas were starting to spread.[246]

In addition, that fact that Judges reports that he was blinded supports the accuracy of Samson's story.

Before the Philistines killed Samson, according to the Biblical version of the story, Samson's eyes were gouged out and he was forced to push a massive millstone, grinding corn.

This wasn't make-believe—this was a real punishment. The Hittites came up with it, and their records show that it worked pretty well exactly how its described in the story of Samson.

Hittite administrators sent out multiple letters with lists of captives who have been put to work in mill houses grinding corn. In most of these lists, there's a mark next to the captive's name—each one is either labeled "sighted" or "blinded."

Outside of the story of Samson, there isn't direct proof that the Philistines used it, but it's extremely likely. The Philistines conquered the Hittites around Samson's time and almost certainly picked up some of their ideas along the way.[247]

Finally, due to the construction of Philistine temples, pushing them down was physically possible, particularly for a strong man like Samson.

When you imagine it happening in a modern building, it seems a bit absurd. Recently, though, archaeologists have excavated real Philistine temples from around that time and, as it turns out, it's not as crazy as it might seem.

Philistine temples really were supported by two main pillars that made up the foundations of the building. If someone was able to knock those two pillars down, the roof really would have come crashing down on everyone inside.

Knocking them over wasn't as impossible as it might sound, either. The pillars were made out of cedar wood resting on stone support bases. It certainly wouldn't be easy to break through them, but it's hypothetically possible that one of the cedar poles could have been pushed free of the stone base.

They were close together, too. In the temple in the Philistine city of Gath,[248] the pillars were just two meters [just under 6 feet, 8 inches] apart—close enough that a tall man would have been able to stand between them and push against them both, just like in the story.[249]

The linguistic evidence in Judges also supports the accuracy of Samson's story.

The Hebrew text is very clear in its description of the actions of Samson. The text reads that Samson grasped the two middle pillars that supported the house of the temple, 'ehad kîmînô we'ehad bismo'lô (one with his right hand and one with his left). The pillar bases at Tell Qasile, (where one Philistine temple was unearthed), are about two m (seven ft) apart, well within the reach of a tall man. Therefore, the first part of the description of Samson's death is consistent with the excavated temple.

The text then reads that Samson 'bent powerfully' in his effort to dislodge the pillars. The Hebrew term natah (bend), while a common word, contains connotations of bending under a force or effort. Issachar bends his shoulder to the burden (Genesis 49:15, NIV) (written 1450–1405 BC). A wadi, riverbed, is said to bend or slope (Numbers 21:15, NASB) (written 1450–1405 BC).

The word used in conjunction with the term "bend" is bekoha, literally "in strength." The assumed root of the term is khh, meaning "the capacity to act." The term is an expression of potency and refers to the subject's capacity to produce. Moreover, the usual intent is to denote physical strength (Citation omitted).

It is noteworthy that the term khh occurs eight times in the book of Judges, with seven of the occurrences in chapter 16 (verses 5, 6, 9, 15, 17, 19, 30). While this term denotes the ability to do something, often the 'emphasis is on the lack of strength or the insufficiency of human strength in comparison to God.' One must observe that the first five occurrences in chapter 16 deal with Delilah looking for the secret of Samson's strength in order to render Samson helpless, and the sixth occurs with the loss of his strength after she cut his hair. The final occurrence, between the pillars, comes immediately following Samson's petition to the Lord for power. Herein Samson does not rely only upon his natural strength, but that which comes from God. This usage of the term seems to parallel that which is found in the Psalter. In the Psalter the term occurs in "isolated individual laments with reference to dissipated human might that occasions the pious to pray for God's assistance" (Citations omitted).

> The combination of these two terms denotes a powerful movement on the part of Samson. Such a surge of power would be consistent with the effort needed to dislodge the pillars from their bases, as they were held in place by the weight of the temple. Once the pillars were in motion Samson would have to continue dragging them off their bases.[250]

We then read that the temple fell upon the Philistine lords and onlookers. The Hebrew term napal (fall) occurs in the text. It has been argued that "besides the common physical action or occurrence of falling, a violent or accidental circumstance is often indicated…damage, death, or destruction are often designated" (Citation omitted). Clearly, this act was not an accident but a violent surge of power such as alluded to above. Possibly a better rendering of the term would be "fall in/collapse." If Samson dragged the pillars off their bases, the roof would collapse upon the Philistine lords. Once the main hall of the temple collapsed, the rest of the structure, being extremely unstable from the weight of the people and having its main supports lost, would collapse as well. Therefore, the narrative is perfectly consistent with the findings at Tell Qasile.[251]

When Only God Knew

3. The Hittites

Fact Stated: Genesis-Nehemiah (written 1450–400 BC)
Fact Confirmed: 20th century (3500 years later ±)

There are fifty-eight biblical passages that identify the Hittites.[252] They are first identified in Genesis[253] (written 1450–1405 BC) and last mentioned in Nehemiah[254] (written 445–400 BC). The Bible makes over forty references to the Hittite Empire.[255] As examples, Genesis 23 (written 1450–1405 BC) reports that Abraham buried Sarah in the Cave of Machpelah, which he purchased from Ephron the Hittite, and Second Samuel 11 (written 931–722 BC) tells of David's adultery with Bathsheba, the wife of Uriah the Hittite.

Yet, as recently as a little over a century ago, the Hittites were unknown outside of the Old Testament, and critics claimed that they were a figment of biblical imagination.[256] "Just another Bible myth," skeptics charged.[257] In 1906, however, archaeologists digging east of Ankara, Turkey, discovered the ruins of Hattusas, the ancient Hittite capital, at what is today called Boghazkoy, as well as its vast collection of Hittite historical records, which showed an empire flourishing in the mid-second millennium BC.[258] In 1906, Hugo Winckler uncovered a library of 10,000 clay tablets that fully documented the Hittite Empire and further confirmed the reliability of the Bible.[259] "In the past one hundred years, the archaeologist's spade has unearthed Hittite civilization: It has proved to be both large and important."[260]

4. Kings and Others in the Old Testament

Facts Stated: 2 Samuel to Esther (written 930–331 BC)
Facts Confirmed: 19th–21st century AD (2100–2900 years later ±)

There are many examples of archaeology supporting the existence of various kings and others reported in the Old Testament, many of whom were thought for a long time not to have existed at all.

a. King David

David, before and after he was king, is referred to in the Old Testament in many places.[261] "Until 1993, (however), there was no (non-biblical) proof of the existence of King David or even of Israel as a nation prior to Solomon."[262] The 1993 discovery of the Tel Dan inscription—writing on a ninth-century BC stone slab (or stela)—3000 + years after David was king changed all that;[263] it furnished non-Biblical historical evidence of his existence.[264] Then, "in 2005 Israeli archaeologist Eilat Mazar found King David's palace relying on the Bible as one of her many tools."[265]

David is not the only example of an Old Testament person or event in which some personage in the Bible was involved that has been verified by non-biblical evidence. For example, archaeology supports the history of conquests and rebellions described in the Bible, including those examples that follow.

b. King Sargon II of Assyria

Samaria fell to the Assyrians in 722 BC,[266] as reported in 2 Kings 17:5–6 (written circa 561–538 BC). For a long time, Bible critics questioned the existence of king Sargon of Assyria and challenged Isaiah 20:1 (written 700–680 BC), which refers to king Sargon of Assyria, because "they knew of no king named Sargon in lists of Assyrian kings; now Sargon's palace has been recovered at Khorsabad, including a wall inscription and a library record endorsing the battle against the Philistine city of Ashdod,"[267] also mentioned in Isaiah 20:1.[268] In fact, Sargon II, who invaded Israel, "deported 27,290 Israelites from their homeland and re-settled them" in the Assyrian Empire.[269] Those facts confirm 2 Kings 17:6 (NIV) (written circa 561–538 BC) which says that in "the ninth year of Hoshea, the king of Assyria captured Samaria and deported the Israelites to Assyria [and] settled them in Halah, in Gozan on the Habor River and in the towns of the Medes," and is further supported by other material evidence. At various Mesopotamian sites, archaeologists have unearthed

When Only God Knew

examples of ostraca (pottery fragments with writing on their surface) listing Israelite names.[270]

c. Pharaoh Shishak

Another example of conquest supported by non-biblical evidence is found in 1 Kings 14 (written circa 561–538 BC) and 2 Chronicles 12 (written 450–430 BC), which describe "Pharaoh Shishak's conquest of Judah in the fifth year of the reign of King Rehoboam... and how Solomon's temple in Jerusalem was robbed of its treasures," a victory that is "commemorated in hieroglyphic wall carvings on the Temple of Amon at Thebes."[271]

d. Mesha, the king of Moab

2 Kings 3 (written circa 561–538 BC) reports that Mesha, the king of Moab, rebelled against the king of Israel following the death of Ahab; a "three-foot stone slab, also called the Mesha Stele, discovered in 1868,[272] confirms that Mesha, the king of Moab, existed and confirms the revolt by claiming triumph over Ahab's family" in approximately 850 BC.[273]

e. Uzziah, king of the Southern Kingdom of Judah

According to Second Chronicles (written 450–430 BC), Uzziah, king of the Southern Kingdom of Judah, was stricken with leprosy before he died.[274] Second Chronicles 26:16-19 (NIV) (written 450–430 BC) says,

> But after Uzziah became powerful, his pride led to his downfall. He was unfaithful to the Lord his God, and entered the temple of the Lord to burn incense on the altar of incense. Azariah the priest with eighty other courageous priests of the Lord followed him in. They confronted King Uzziah and said, "It is not right for you, Uzziah, to burn incense to the Lord. That is for the priests, the descendants of Aaron, who

have been consecrated to burn incense. Leave the sanctuary, for you have been unfaithful; and you will not be honored by the Lord God."

Uzziah, who had a censer in his hand ready to burn incense, became angry. While he was raging at the priests in their presence before the incense altar in the Lord's temple, leprosy broke out on his forehead.

Uziah's stone burial plaque was discovered on the Mount of Olives in 1931, over 2,500 years after he died, and it reads, as would be expected of someone who died of leprosy: "Here were brought the bones of Uzziah, king of Judah. Do not open."[275]

f. Assyrian King Esarhaddon

Finally, an interesting fact respecting Esarhaddon, king of the Neo-Assyrian Empire who rebuilt Babylon after his father had destroyed it,[276] who lived from in the seventh century BC and is not named in the Quran, but only in the Bible, is that, because the so-called "Islamic State," after it seized Mosul, blew up a shrine believed to mark the tomb of the prophet Jonah and dug deep tunnels underneath it, archaeologists have discovered that the "Islamic State" revealed an untouched 600 BC palace with a marble cuneiform inscription relating to King Esarhaddon, thereby further confirming the historicity of the Bible.[277]

The evidence goes on and on. Other biblical personages of many different ethnicities, including the following, and their reported events have likewise been confirmed by relatively recent archaeological discoveries:[278]

When Only God Knew

Name	Who was he?	When (BC)	Where in the Bible?
Egyptians			
So (Osorkon IV)	Pharaoh	730 – 715	2 Kings 17:4
Tirhakah (Taharqa)	Pharaoh	690 – 664	2 Kings 19:9, etc.
Necho II (Neco II)	Pharaoh	610 – 595	2 Chronicles 35:20,[279] etc.
Hophra (Apries)	Pharaoh	589 – 570	Jeremiah 44:30[280]
Aram-Damascans			
Hadadezer	King	Early ninth century to 844/842	1 Kings 11:23, etc.
Ben-hadad, son of Hadadezer	King	844/842	2 Kings 6:24, etc.
Hazael	King	844/842 – c. 800	1 Kings 19:15, etc.
Ben-hadad, son of Hazael	King	Early eighth century	2 Kings 13:3, etc.
Rezin	King	Mid-eighth century to 732	2 Kings 15:37, etc.
Israelites from the Northern Kingdom of Israel			
Omri	King	884 – 873	1 Kings 16:16, etc.
Ahab	King	873 – 852	1 Kings 16:28, etc.
Jehu	King	842/841 – 815/814	1 Kings 19:16, 2 Kings 9-10
Joash (Jehoash)	King	805 – 790	2 Kings 13:9, etc.
Jeroboam II	King	790 – 750/749	2 Kings 13:13, etc.
Menahem	King	749 – 738	2 Kings 15:14, etc.
Pekah	King	750(?) – 732/731	2 Kings 15:25, etc.
Hoshea	King	732/731 – 722	2 Kings 15:30, etc.
Sanballat "I"	Governor of Samaria under Persian rule	Circa. mid-fifth century	Nehemiah 2:10,[281] etc.

Name	Who was he?	When (BC)	Where in the Bible?
Israelites from the Southern Kingdom of Judah			
Ahaz (Jehoahaz)	King	742/741 – 726	2 Kings 15:38, etc.
Manasseh	King	697/696 – 642/641	2 Kings 20:21, etc.
Hilkiah	High priest during Josiah's reign	Within 640/639 – 609	2 Kings 22:4, etc.
Shaphan	Scribe during Josiah's reign	Within 640/639 – 609	2 Kings 22:3, etc.
Azariah	High priest during Josiah's reign	Within 640/639 – 609	1 Chronicles 5:39, etc.
Gemariah	Official during Jehoiakim's reign	Within 609 – 598	Jeremiah 36:10, etc.
Jehoiachin (Jeconiah or Coniah)	King	598 – 597	2 Kings 24:6, etc.
Shelemiah	Father of Jehucal the royal official	Late seventh century	Jeremiah 37:3, etc.
Jehucal (Jucal)	Official during Zedekiah's reign	Within 597 – 586	Jeremiah 37:3, etc.
Pashhur	Father of Gedaliah the royal official	Late seventh century	Jeremiah 38:1
Gedaliah	Official during Zedekiah's reign	Within 597 – 586	Jeremiah 38:1

When Only God Knew

Name	Who was he?	When (BC)	Where in the Bible?
Assyrians			
Tiglath-pileser III (Pul)	King	744 – 727	2 Kings 15:19, etc.
Shalmaneser V	King	726 – 722	2 Kings 17:3, etc.
Sennacherib[282]	King	704 – 681	2 Kings 18:13, etc.
Adrammelech (Ardamullissu or Arad-mullissu)	Son and assassin of Sennacherib	Early seventh century	2 Kings 19:37, etc.
Esarhaddon	King	680 – 669	2 Kings 19:37, etc.
Babylonians			
Mero-dach-baladan II	King	721 – 710 and 703	2 Kings 20:12, etc.
Nebuchadnezzar II	King	604 – 562	2 Kings 24:1, etc.
Nebo-sarsekim	Official of Nebuchadnez-zar II	Early sixth century	Jeremiah 39:3
Nergal-sharezer	Officer of Nebuchadnez-zar II	Early sixth century	Jeremiah 39:3
Nebuzaradan	A chief officer of Nebuchad-nezzar II	Early sixth century	2 Kings 25:8, etc. & Jeremiah 39:9, etc.
Evil-merodach (Awel Marduk or Amel Marduk)	King	561 – 560	2 Kings 25:27, etc.
Belshazzar	Son and co-regent of Nabonidus	Circa 543? – 540	Daniel 5:1,[283] etc.

Name	Who was he?	When (BC)	Where in the Bible?
Persians			
Cyrus II (Cyrus the Great)	King	559 – 530	2 Chronicles 36:22, etc.
Darius I (Darius the Great)	King	520 – 486	Ezra 4:5,[284] etc.
Tattenai	Provincial governor of Trans-Euphrates	Late sixth to early fifth century	Ezra 5:3, etc.
Xerxes I (Ahasuerus)	King	486 – 465	Esther 1:1,[285] etc.
Artaxerxes I Longimanus	King	465 – 425/424	Ezra 4:7, etc.
Darius II Nothus	King	425/424 – 405/404	Nehemiah 12:22

B. New Testament

Although the existence and activities of New Testament individuals were often confirmed by ancient writers or historians, it sometimes took thousands of years after the Bible had already reported the existence and impact on the ancient world of various individuals in the New Testament for their existence to be re-discovered by modern archaeology. The following describes independent evidence of the existence of some of the persons who are named in the New Testament and the events surrounding them.

1. First of All, Jesus, and then the Early Christians

Eyewitness Reports: New Testament (written 50–96 AD)
Fact Confirmed: 50–96 AD through 2nd century AD

"Jesus' reality—His historicity—is the foundation of Christianity."[286]
In addition to what was stated in Chapter 3, there is a lot of evidence

that Jesus lived, was crucified, died, and was raised from the grave as described in the New Testament. There is also substantial evidence respecting who the early Christians were and that were willing to and did die because they knew who Jesus was and what He did.

The Gospels of Matthew, Mark, Luke, and John and the book of Acts report eyewitness accounts of how Jesus lived and died and about Him after He rose from the grave. The remainder of the New Testament contains numerous accounts as to what He did while He was alive, what He taught, and how early Christians lived their lives as a consequence. There is also secular proof of those facts.

a. Martyred Apostles

"In the Bible, fourteen people are considered apostles—the original members of the Twelve Disciples, plus Matthias (who was chosen to replace Judas Iscariot [who committed suicide after betraying Jesus]), and Paul (the apostle to the Gentiles)."[287] Jesus' original disciples, all of whom except for Judas Iscariot became apostles, were "Simon (who is called Peter) and his brother Andrew; James son of Zebedee, and his brother John; Philip and Bartholomew; Thomas and Matthew the tax collector; James son of Alphaeus, and Thaddaeus; Simon the Zealot and Judas Iscariot, who betrayed him."[288]

> Only two of their deaths are recorded in the Bible (James, John's brother and the son of Zebedee, and Judas Iscariot). Most of what we know about the other apostles' deaths come from ancient Christian writers and church tradition, and there are often multiple accounts of where and how they died.[289]

What we do know, however, is that all but one, John, or perhaps two if you consider one of the many alternative narratives regarding the death of Simon the Zealot, of the apostles who lived with Jesus for three years died horrible deaths,[290] as did Matthias and as did Paul who heard Jesus' voice as he was traveling to Damascus to persecute Christian believers.[291] While we know that their deaths, except for the death of John who died of old age, and perhaps Simon the Zealot as discussed below, were brutal and happened as a consequence of their preaching what Jesus did and who He was, their deaths are not always supported by eyewitness accounts as many of the apostles died in foreign lands.

Even though they died horrible deaths, we do know that they refused to deny the truth of what they saw and lived as described primarily in the Gospels of Matthew, Mark, Luke, and John and in the book of Acts (written 50–96 AD). They all died knowing, and many are reported as preaching as they died that Jesus died on the cross and that they saw Him alive afterward, affirming that Jesus rose from the grave. Not one recanted. If it had all been a hoax, someone would have said so.

i. Andrew

One article, citing National Geographic, said,

> According to fifteenth Century religious historian Dorman Newman, Andrew—the brother of Peter—went to Patras in western Greece in 69 AD, where the Roman proconsul Aegeates debated religion with him. Aegeates tried to convince Andrew to forsake Christianity, so that he would not have to torture and execute him. But when that didn't work, apparently he decided to give Andrew the full treatment. Andrew was scourged, and then tied rather than nailed to a cross, so that he would suffer for a longer time before dying.[292]

Another article said,

Andrew was martyred by crucifixion in the Greek city of Patras around 60 AD. Like his brother, Peter [as discussed below], Andrew didn't consider himself worthy to die in the same way as Jesus, and so he was bound—not nailed—to a cross which was hung in an X shape instead of a T. For this reason, an X-shaped cross is sometimes referred to as Saint Andrew's Cross.[293]

"Andrew lived for two days, during which he preached to passers-by."[294]

ii. Bartholomew

"A number of scholars believe that he was the only one of the twelve disciples who came from royal blood, or noble birth."[295]

Bartholomew's name appears with every list of the disciples (Matthew 10:3; Mark 3:18; Luke 6:14; Acts 1:13). This was not a first name, however; it was his second name. His first name probably was Nathanael, whom Jesus called "An Israelite indeed, in whom there is no guile" (John 1:47).[296]

"Some sources simply say he was martyred, while others say he was skinned alive and beheaded."[297] One legend claims he was flayed to death by a whip in Armenia while being crucified upside down.[298] Another claims that he preached in India, where he died by being flayed alive with knives.[299]

iii. James

There are three "James" mentioned in the New Testament. Only two, James, the brother of John and the son of Zebedee, and James, the son of Alphaeus, were apostles.[300] The third, known as James the Just, was related to Jesus and will also be discussed below. There seems to be some confusion among various writers as to how each James died.[301] Regardless of how they died, all three men died horrible deaths without denying that they had personal knowledge that Jesus lived, died, and was resurrected.

The apostle James, John's brother and the son of Zebedee, was the first apostle to be martyred.[302] The death of James was recorded in the book of Acts.[303] He was killed with a sword by beheading on the order of King Herod Agrippa I of Judea, sometime between 41 and 44 AD, about eleven years after the death of Christ, in a general persecution of the early church.[304] Herod Agrippa "may have been motivated toward this persecution by zealous Pharisees (like Paul, before his conversion to Christianity), who sought to suppress the Jews who taught that Jesus was resurrected from the dead."[305]

One non-biblical story associated with the death of James that was reported by various early Christian church leaders has to do with the conversion of a Roman officer who guarded James as he was being condemned to death.

> The Roman officer who guarded James watched amazed as James defended his faith at trial. Later, the officer walked with James to the place of execution. Overcome by conviction, the Roman officer declared his new faith to the judge and knelt beside James to accept beheading as a Christian.[306]

"James the Just was an important leader in the early church,"[307] but he was not an apostle. He was either the brother or cousin of Jesus.[308] Tradition tells us that James the Just was pushed from the pinnacle of the temple at which he was preaching,[309] probably in 62 AD.[310] He was thrown down over one hundred feet by the scribes and Pharisees from the same pinnacle as to which the New Testament reports Satan had taken Jesus during his temptation.[311] Because he lived after the fall and rose to his knees and began to pray for his persecutors, he was then stoned, and his brains dashed out with a fuller's club.[312]

James, the son of Alphaeus, also called James the Lesser, was the second apostle named James.[313] How James, the son of Alphaeus, died depends on whether or not you confuse him as the same person as James the Just (the brother or cousin of Jesus),[314] which for some commentators has been the case. That confusion may be because "in art, James son of Alphaeus is typically portrayed with a fuller's club, reflecting the church's (early) assumption that he was the same person as James the Just."[315] As pointed out above, that seems to be historically inaccurate as reflected in the books of Matthew, Mark, Luke, and Acts, the last two written by Luke who William Mitchell Ramsay, "one of the great archaeologists and topographers"[316] and a New Testament scholar,[317] described as "a historian of the first rank' (who) 'should be placed along with the very greatest of historians.'"[318] Tradition "claims James son of Alphaeus preached in Egypt" where he "was crucified in the city of Ostrakine."[319]

Whichever account of the deaths of the three James is accurate, they each died painful deaths without denying that Jesus lived, what He did, and who He was.

iv. Matthew

Historians have concluded that Jesus was crucified sometime between 31 and 33 AD. Matthew lived many years after Jesus' crucifixion, writing the book of Acts as late as 70 AD. "Matthew, like most of the apostles late in their lives, became a missionary and was arrested in Ethiopia. It was there that he was staked or impaled to the earth by spears and then beheaded."[320]

v. Matthias

The apostle chosen to replace Judas Iscariot was either stoned while hanging on a cross or beheaded or stoned and then beheaded.[321]

vi. Paul, formerly known as Saul

Paul, formerly known as Saul, who later became an apostle of Christ, was an educated Jew who spent his early life persecuting Christians.[322] According to Acts and Paul's account, he was on his way to Damascus to continue that persecution when suddenly a light from heaven shown on him, he heard the voice of Jesus, and he was struck blind for three days, which led to his conversion to Christianity.[323] While Luke wrote most of the New Testament by volume in two books, Luke and Acts, Paul's letters to various early Christian churches constitute the most books in the New Testament written by any author.[324] Traditionally, Paul is credited with writing Romans, 1 Corinthians, 2 Corinthians, Galatians, Ephesians, Philippians, Colossians, 1 Thessalonians, 2 Thessalonians, 1 Timothy, 2 Timothy, Titus, Philemon and Hebrews,[325] all letters—epistles—to Christian communities throughout the Roman Empire.

> Even historians debate the exact date or manner in which Paul died, but it is almost universally accepted that he was martyred. Based on historical events of the day, it is likely that Paul was beheaded, [after being tortured],[326] possibly around the same time that Peter was crucified [by Emperor Nero] "in the Neronian persecution" after the Great Fire of Rome.[327]

Yet he, too, never denied his faith or the fact that he stopped persecuting Christians after having heard the voice of Jesus.

vii. Peter

"Simon, also known as Peter, was one of the most prominent disciples of Jesus Christ, and one of the most important leaders of the early Christian church (Catholic tradition even claims he was the first pope), so it shouldn't come as a surprise that he suffered a fate similar to Jesus.'"[328] Peter died thirty-three to thirty-seven years after the death of Christ, sometime between 64 and 68 AD.[329] He was crucified by Emperor Nero "in the Neronian persecution"[330] "after the Great Fire of Rome, which [Nero] famously blamed Christians for starting."[331] "But, feeling unworthy to be crucified in the same manner as Jesus, his Savior, Peter requested to be crucified upside down, on an inverted cross, which he was."[332]

viii. Philip

The reports of how the apostle Philip died vary. "One source suggests he was hung until dead, another suggests crucifixion during his ministry in Egypt."[333] Other tradition says Philip was martyred by being tortured and crucified at Hierapolis in Phrygia, the name for that part of the western plateau of Asia Minor where the ancient Phyrigian Anatolian kingdom (twelfth-seventh century BC) had once ruled.[334] "Others claim he was beheaded in Hierapolis."[335] Some claim that he was both crucified and then beheaded.[336]

One commentator reported that "according to most historians, Philip's death was exceedingly cruel. He was impaled by iron hooks in his ankles and hung upside down to die."[337]

Another said, "When Philip continued to preach from the cross, the crowd released his brother. Philip, however, refused to be released, so he died on the cross."[338]

ix. Simon the Zealot

"There are numerous accounts of Simon the Zealot's death, but the earliest records didn't come until centuries after his death."[339] According to Ryan Nelson in *How Did the Apostles Die? What We Actually Know*, [340]

> In the fifth century, Moses of Chorene, a fifth century AD priest and bishop, to whom is attributed the work, History of Armenia,[341] wrote that Simon the Zealot was martyred in the Kingdom of Iberia, a

name given by the ancient Greeks and Romans to the ancient Georgian kingdom of Kartli (fourth century BC-fifth century AD) corresponding roughly to the eastern and southern parts of the present-day Georgia."[342]

The Golden Legend, a book "depicting the lives of the saints in an array of factual and fictional stories," and "perhaps the most widely read book, after the Bible, during the late Middle Ages," "compiled around 1260 by Jacobus de Voragine, a scholarly friar and later archbishop of Genoa,"[343] says he was martyred in Persia in 65 AD.

Ethiopian Christians believe he was crucified in Samaria.

Another account says he was crucified in 61 AD in Britain.

In the sixteenth century, Justus Lipsius, the Latin name for Joest Lips, a "Flemish humanist, classical scholar, and moral and political theorist" who lived from 1547 through 1606,[344] claimed he was sawed in half.

Eastern tradition claims he died of old age in Edessa.[345]

One "Catholic website also alleged Simon the Zealot died in Edessa but was crucified."[346] "So maybe he was a martyr. And maybe not. But he probably was."[347]

x. *Thaddeus or Jude*

"The apostle Jude, who wrote the next to the last book in the New Testament by the same name (in 65–70 AD), went all the way to Persia and it was there that he was crucified."[348] One church tradition holds that Thaddeus founded a church at Edessa, Persia, and was killed by arrows during his crucifixion.[349]

When Only God Knew

xi. Thomas

Thomas, known as doubting Thomas, was the apostle who said he would not believe that Jesus had risen from the grave, unless he saw the crucifixion "nail marks in His hands and put (his) finger where the nails were, and put (his) hand into His side."[350] After Jesus appeared to him and Thomas saw the scars on Jesus' hands and put his finger in Jesus' side,[351] Thomas preached the Gospel message until He was martyred.

"The earlier traditions, as believed in the fourth century, say he preached in Parthia or Persia and was finally buried at Edessa. The later traditions carry him farther east (as far as India)."[352] His martyrdom, wherever it occurred, was by a lance.[353] He was probably "martyred in Mylapore, India, where he was stabbed with spears" on July 3, 72 AD.[354]

b. John

John the apostle was the son of Zebedee and the younger brother of the apostle James.[355] John outlived all of the disciples, despite being sentenced to death, boiled in oil, and drinking poison, and exile to the island of Patmos, dying of old age at Ephesus, perhaps about 98 AD, but certainly, sometime between 89 AD and 120 AD.[356] Ephesus was "an ancient Greek city on the coast of Ionia, three kilometers southwest of present-day Selçuk in İzmir Province, Turkey."[357]

c. Ancient Secular Writers

Many non-Christian writers who lived after Jesus in the ancient world were critical when they wrote accounts about Him and His followers. What many of those writers said is discussed in Chapter 3 of this book as proof of the New Testament's reliability, and the reader may recognize some repetition. Even so, ancient non-Christian writers support both the reliability of the Bible and the existence of Jesus and, so, are included here.

One such writer was Flavius Josephus, a Jewish historian who lived between 38 and 100 AD.[358] He mentioned Jesus in book 18, chapter 3, paragraph 3 of *The Antiquities of the Jews* written in 93 AD, and suggested that Jesus may have been more than just a man when he said,[359]

> Now there was about this time Jesus, a wise man, if it be lawful to call him a man; for he was a doer of wonderful works, a teacher of such men as receive the truth with pleasure. He drew over to him both many of the Jews and many of the Gentiles. He was [the] Christ. And when Pilate, at the suggestion of the principal men amongst us, had condemned him to the cross, those that loved him at the first did not forsake him; for he appeared to them alive again the third day; as the divine prophets had foretold these and ten thousand other wonderful things concerning him. And the tribe of Christians, so named from him, are not extinct at this day.[360]

Josephus also talks about Jesus when he mentions James, who he describes as Jesus' brother, in book 20, chapter 9 of *The Antiquities of the Jews*.[361]

Lucian of Samosata, a second-century Greek philosopher, writer, satirist, and rhetorician, who lived circa 120 AD until sometime after 180 AD,[362] also confirmed Jesus' existence and described the early Christian church when he said,

> The Christians, you know, worship a man to this day—the distinguished personage who introduced their novel rites, and was crucified on that account... You see, these misguided creatures start with the general conviction that they are immortal for all time,

When Only God Knew

which explains the contempt of death and voluntary self-devotion which are so common among them; and then it was impressed on them by their original lawgiver that they are all brothers, from the moment that they are converted, and deny the gods of Greece, and worship the crucified sage, and live after his laws. All this they take quite on faith, with the result that they despise all worldly goods alike, regarding them merely as common property.[363]

Though Lucian opposed Christianity, he acknowledges that Jesus existed, was crucified, and that Christians worship Him.

Mara Bar-Serapion (a Syrian Stoic), who was imprisoned by the Romans, wrote a letter to his son after the Jewish temple was destroyed in 70 AD in which he spoke about the death of Jesus and others, and said,

> What advantage did the Athenians gain from putting Socrates to death? Famine and plague came upon them as a judgment for their crime. What advantage did the men of Samos gain from burning Pythagoras? In a moment their land was covered with sand. What advantage did the Jews gain from executing their wise King? It was just after that their Kingdom was abolished. God justly avenged these three wise men: the Athenians died of hunger; the Samians were overwhelmed by the sea; the Jews, ruined and driven from their land, live in complete dispersion. But Socrates did not die for good; he lived on in the teaching of Plato. Pythagoras did not die for good; he lived on in the statue of Hera. Nor did the wise King die for good; He lived on in the teaching which He had given.[364]

The "Wise King" referred to Jesus, who was crucified less than four decades before the temple in Jerusalem was destroyed by the Romans in 70 AD.[365]

Gaius Plinius Caecilius Secundus, known as Pliny the Younger, a Roman governor in the Roman province of Bithynia (modern-day Turkey),[366] lived from 61 or 62–112 or 113 AD.[367] In 112 AD, he wrote to Emperor Trajan because he was "faced with a dilemma" concerning how to deal with Christians, who refused to worship the emperor and instead worshiped Jesus.[368] The letters mark "the first time the Roman government recognized Christianity as a religion separate from Judaism."[369] In his Epistles, Book X, Letter 96, written less than a hundred years after Jesus' crucifixion, he confirmed the early Christians' knowledge of the existence of Jesus and who He was and described how they lived in response to that knowledge when Pliny the Younger said.

> They [the Christians] were in the habit of meeting on a certain fixed day before it was light, when they sang in alternate verses a hymn to Christ, as to a god, and bound themselves by a solemn oath, not to any wicked deeds, but never to commit any fraud, theft or adultery, never to falsify their word, nor deny a trust when they should be called upon to deliver it up; after which it was their custom to separate, and then reassemble to partake of food—but food of an ordinary and innocent kind.[370]

Suetonius, whose full name was Gaius Suetonius Ranquillus (circa 71–135 AD), also a Roman historian, wrote in his *Lives of the Twelve Caesars* in 120 AD about riots which broke out in the Jewish community in Rome under the emperor Claudius and said, "because they were constantly rioting at the instigation of *Chrestus*" and "since the Jews constantly made disturbance at the instigation of *Chrestus* (Christ), (Claudius) expelled them from Rome."[371]

Tacitus, another Roman historian who lived from circa 55 AD to about 117 AD, discusses the Great Fire in Rome under Nero, who blamed the fire on the Christians living in Rome, reaffirms the existence and crucifixion of "Christus," Jesus, and confirms the early Christians willingness to die for Christ in his *Annals*:

> Consequently, to get rid of the report, Nero fastened the guilt and inflicted the most exquisite tortures on a class hated for their abominations, called Christians by the populace. Christus, from whom the name had its origin, suffered the extreme penalty during the reign of Tiberius at the hands of one of our procurators, Pontius Pilatus, and a most mischievous superstition, thus checked for the moment, again broke out not only in Judaea, the first source of the evil, but even in Rome, where all things hideous and shameful from every part of the world find their centre and become popular. Accordingly, an arrest was first made of all who pleaded guilty; then, upon their information, an immense multitude was convicted, not so much of the crime of firing the city, as of hatred against mankind. Mockery of every sort was added to their deaths. Covered with the skins of beasts, they were torn by dogs and perished, or were nailed to crosses, or were doomed to the flames and burnt, to serve as a nightly illumination, when daylight had expired.[372]

Tacitus' writings confirm the existence of Jesus as well as the spread of Christianity at an early date. Several other details that he mentions line up with the New Testament:

1. Christ's public ministry began during the reign of Tiberius Caesar.[373]
2. Pontius Pilate was governor of Judea at the time of Christ's death.[374]
3. Jesus was put to death as a criminal.[375]

Thallus, a Samaritan-born Roman historian who wrote on the history of the Ancient Near East,[376] "wrote a three-volume history of the Mediterranean world from before the Trojan War to the 167th Olympiad, circa 112–109 BC."[377] His writings are only found as citations by others.[378] Sextus Julius Africanus ("Julius Africanus" or "Africanus"), a Christian traveler who lived from about 160–240 AD and historian of the late second and early third centuries[379] and the first Christian historian known to produce a universal chronology,[380] who wrote about quoted Thallus' account of an eclipse of the sun in 221 AD.

> On the whole world there pressed a fearful darkness, and the rocks were rent by an earthquake, and many places in Judea and other districts were thrown down. Thallos calls this darkness an eclipse of the sun in the third book of histories, without reason it seems to me.[381]

This appears to be a reference to the eclipse at the crucifixion reported in Luke 23:44–45 (ESV) (written 60–61 AD) which said, "It was now about the sixth hour, and there was darkness over the whole land until the ninth hour, while the sun's light failed."

While the quotation from Thallus, a pagan Roman historian,[382] expresses doubts about the darkness that was reported at Jesus' death, his doubts are not supportable scientifically because Jesus was crucified at Passover,[383] which occurs only at the time of a full moon and "a solar eclipse can occur only at new moon."[384] Because it is not possible for a solar eclipse to occur at a full moon, a reasonable conclusion to be drawn from that is that Thallus' mentioning of the eclipse was describing the one at Jesus' crucifixion.

The Jewish Rabbi, Eliezer, who did not believe that Jesus was the predicted Old Testament messiah, is believed to have said the following in the last decade of the first century around 90 AD, thereby, while using the pejorative term "Balaam" to express his contempt for and disapproval of Jesus, confirming Jesus' existence.

> Balaam looked forth and saw that there was a man, born of woman, who should rise up and seek to make himself God, and to cause the whole world to go astray. Therefore God gave the power to the voice of Balaam that all the peoples of the world might hear, and thus he spoke. Give heed that ye go not astray after that man; for it is written, God is not man that he should lie. And if he says that he is God he is a liar, and he will deceive and say that he depart and comes again at the end. He says and he shall not perform.[385]

Don Stewart, an internationally recognized Christian apologist and speaker,[386] opines that "though Rabbi Eliezer does not name the person under consideration, it is obviously Jesus" and that "he confirms that fact that Jesus claimed to be God as well as Jesus' promise that He would come again."[387]

The Talmud, a collection of Jewish writings constituting its religious and civil law completed by 500 AD, states:

> On the eve of Passover they hung Yeshu [of Nazareth] and the crier went forth for forty days beforehand declaring that "Yeshu [Yeshu of Nazareth] is going to be stoned for practicing witchcraft, for enticing and leading Israel astray. Anyone who knows something

to clear him should come forth and exonerate him."
But no one had anything exonerating for him and
they hung him on the eve of Passover[388]

This reference also confirms that Jesus' death took place at the
time of the Passover.[389]

2. John the Baptist

Fact Stated: Deuteronomy (written 1450–1405 BC).
Matthew, Mark, Luke, and John (written 50–90 AD)
Fact Confirmed: 100 AD, at the latest

John the Baptist preceded Jesus, preaching and baptizing in the wilderness of Judea.[390] The Bible not only discusses John the Baptist and his ministry,[391] but some parts of the Old Testament also appear to predict his birth and ministry.[392]

Josephus, the Jewish historian who lived between 38 and 100 AD,[393] mentions John the Baptist and Herod, who beheaded him,[394] in book 18, ch. 5, par. 2 of The Antiquities of the Jews written in 93 AD, when he says,[395]

> Now some of the Jews thought that the destruction
> of Herod's army came from God, and that very justly,
> as a punishment of what he did against John, that
> was called the Baptist: for Herod slew him, who was
> a good man, and commanded the Jews to exercise
> virtue, both as to righteousness towards one another,
> and piety towards God, and so to come to baptism;
> for that the washing [with water] would be acceptable to him, if they made use of it, not in order to the
> putting away [or the remission] of some sins [only],
> but for the purification of the body; supposing still
> that the soul was thoroughly purified beforehand by
> righteousness.

When Only God Knew

Note: Although there is no reason for doubting this quote since Greek manuscripts all agree with the quote, nonetheless, some commentators have challenged the reliability of Josephus' accounts because they seem too favorable regarding Christ, and the writings of Josephus were transmitted primarily through the Christian community.

3. Caiaphas

Fact Stated: Matthew, Luke, and John (written 50–90 AD)
Fact Confirmed: 1990–1994 AD (1900 years later ±)

Caiaphas, the Jewish high priest in Jerusalem who indicted Jesus before Pontius Pilate on Good Friday, was identified in several books of the Bible as part of the Jewish leadership in Jerusalem who plotted to kill Jesus.[396] His bones were the first bones of a biblical personality ever discovered; they were discovered in the Peace Forest of Jerusalem south of the temple area between 1990 and 1994 in an ossuary, a highly ornate limestone box appropriate for a man of high standing.[397]

4. Pontius Pilate

Fact Stated: Matthew, Mark, Luke, John, Acts and 1 Timothy
(written 50–90 AD)
Fact Confirmed: 1st century AD
Re-Confirmed: 1961 AD (over 1800 years later)

Pontius Pilate is referred to in the Bible as the Roman governor who was instrumental in Jesus' crucifixion,[398] but his very existence had not too long ago been questioned by "scholars."[399] The archeological record, however, establishes that he was the fifth governor of Roman Judea; he was appointed by the emperor Tiberius in 26 AD and suspended by L. Vitellius, the Roman governor of Syria, in 37 AD, after slaughtering a number of Samaritans at Mt. Gerizim,[400] "one of the two mountains in the immediate vicinity of the West Bank city of Nablus" (commonly equated in early Christian literature with ancient Shechem),[401] "approximately 49 kilometers (30 mi) north of Jerusalem, (approximately 63 kilometers (39 mi) by road)."[402]

Pilate is also mentioned by Flavius Josephus, a first-century Jewish historian, who included references to Jesus and the Origins of Christianity in his Antiquities of the Jews written around 93–94 AD,[403] and Tacitus, a Roman politician and historian who lived from 56–117 AD and was hostile to Christianity,[404] both of whom have been previously discussed.

Evidence for the existence of Pilate was also discovered in an inscription after Italian excavations at Caesarea Maritima in 1961.[405] Caesarea Maritima, "also known as Caesarea Palestinae, was an ancient city in the Sharon Plain on the coast of the Mediterranean, now in ruins and included in an Israeli national park."[406] Antonio Frova, director of the excavations, found a dedicatory stone that bore a three-line inscription: *Tiberieum/[Pon]tius Pilatus/Praef]ectus Iuda(e-ae)*,[407] that is "Tiberius (the Roman emperor of the period)/Pontius Pilate/Prefect of Judea."[408] This find was highly valued because no other evidence of Pilate was known at the time it was discovered.[409] The inscription not only confirms the historicity of Pilate, but it also clarifies the title that he bore as governor.

Since 1961, a number of Pilate coins have been found.[410] Today, Pontius Pilate coins minted by Pilate in the seventeenth year of the reign of Tiberias—or AD 30–31, near the death and resurrection of Jesus—names his office as "procurator" and can be found in the British Museum.[411]

5. Gallio, Proconsul of Achaia

Fact Stated: Acts (written 62–70 AD)
Fact Confirmed: 1905 AD (1850 years later ±)

Acts 18:12 (NIV) (written 62–70 AD) describes an attack on Paul, who wrote much of the New Testament. It says, "While Gallio was proconsul of Achaia, the Jews of Corinth made a united attack on Paul and brought him to the place of judgment." A decree of Clau-

When Only God Knew

dius found at Delphi (Greece) in 52 AD was addressed to L. Iunius Gallio, the proconsul of Achaia while Paul was in Corinth, and supports the conclusion that Gallio was the proconsul of Achaia the previous year.[412] "The Delphi (Gallio) inscription—discovered 1905, now in Delphi Museum in Greece—fixed the date of Gallio's service as proconsul as 51–52 AD, providing a way of dating the events in Acts 18:12–17 and much of Paul's ministry.[413]

6. Quirinius, a Governor of Syria

Fact Stated: Luke (written 60–61 AD)
Fact Confirmed: 1912 AD (1850 years later ±)

In Luke 2:1–2 (NIV) (written 60–61 AD), Luke said,

> "In those days, Caesar Augustus issued a decree that a census should be taken of the entire Roman world (This was the first census that took place while Quirinius was governor of Syria)."

For many years, skeptics of the Bible's accuracy used that passage, which described Quirinius as governor of Syria before the death of Herod I when Caesar Augustus ordered that a census be taken, to argue Luke had made a historical error.[414] While the controversy as to the accuracy of Luke's reference in Luke 2:1–2 (written 60-61 AD) to Quirinius as governor of Syria before the death of Herod I still rages, it has, however, received substantial scholarly[415] and even inscriptional support in the Quirinius inscription discovered in Antioch in 1912 by William Mitchell Ramsay, the archaeologist, topographer and New Testament scholar, and J.G.C. Andersen, an archaeologist who specialized in the study of Asia minor and was, among other things, lecturer and reader in Roman epigraphy and Camden professor of ancient history, all at Oxford University.[416]

Moreover,

Publius Sulpicius Quirinius [or Cyrenius in the Greek] was a well-known Roman official who lived ca. 51 BC–AD 21. He is mentioned by numerous ancient authors, including Josephus, Suetonius, Pliny the Elder, Cassius Dio, Tacitus, Strabo, and Caesar Augustus himself.[417]

7. Lysanias, Tetrarch of Abilene

Fact Stated: Luke (written 60–61 AD)
Fact Confirmed: 1737 AD (over 1650 years later)

Luke 3:1 (written 60–61 AD) names Lysanias as the tetrarch of Abilene when Jesus was alive. For years scholars said this was an error that proved Luke was wrong, arguing that it was common knowledge that Lysanias was not a tetrarch but the ruler of Chalcis about fifty years earlier than what Luke described.[418]

Abila is a city that lies about three miles south of the Yarmuk River, the modern border between Jordan and Syria, and was a part of the Decapolis, a group of ten cities (Abila, Damascus, Dion, Gerasa, Gadara, HipposPella, Philadelphia, Raphana and Scythopolis) that formed a Hellenistic or Greco-Roman confederation or league located south of the Sea of Galilee in the Transjordan in ancient times.[419] An archaeological inscription from 14 to circa 29–37 AD found in Abila in 1737 AD[420] said that Lysanias was the tetrarch in Abila near Damascus at the time that Luke said he was.[421] That archaeological inscription confirmed the accuracy of Luke's account in Luke 3:1. It turns out that there had been two people named Lysanias, and Luke had accurately recorded the facts.

8. Publius, Chief Official of Malta

Fact Stated: Acts (written 62–70 AD)
Fact Confirmed: Circa 1747 AD (almost 1700 years later ±)

Acts 28:7 (NIV) (written 62–70 AD), says "There was an estate nearby (where the shipwrecked Paul, Luke and 274 others landed) that belonged to Publius, the chief official of the island," referring to Malta.[422] In the English Standard Version, the Greek is translated that there "were lands belonging to the *chief man* of the island, named Publius" (Emphasis added).

"At one time some scholars thought Luke (the writer of Acts who accompanied Paul on Paul's fourth missionary journey which shipwrecked on Malta) made an error in referencing Publius' title as the "chief man of the island."[423] This so-called error was again among the very general and disproven skepticism about Luke's accuracy as a historian. The reader may want to return to the "Historical Trustworthiness of Luke" section in chapter 3 above.

Subsequent archaeology has proven challenges to Luke's accurate reporting of Publius as the chief man or chief official were wrong, and Luke is continuously shown to have been historically accurate in his description. Inscriptions "were eventually found that verified Luke accurately recorded Publius' title."[424] This is the story.

"In AD 60, the Acts of the apostles records that Saint Paul was shipwrecked on an island named Melite, which, (according to Wikipedia), many Bible scholars and Maltese conflate with Malta," but which the evidence shows really was Malta as stated in the English translations of Acts.[425]

> There were 276 people on board the sailing vessel Paul, and the Apostle Luke, was on during his fourth missionary journey. The ship ran into bad weather near Malta and was torn apart by the rough seas and wind of the Mediterranean Sea.[426]

As a consequence, Paul and Luke were shipwrecked on Malta. While they were in Malta, an important official named Publius hosted the apostles and others for three days.[427]

The exact words "chief man" have been found in "inscriptions as a title of an official in Malta."[428]

> [T]wo inscriptions—one in Greek, the other in Latin—have been found at Cavite Vecchia, in which that apparently official title occurs. An inscription found in Malta designates the governor of the island by the same title.[429]

The Latin inscription was discovered in 1747 AD and uses the term "Mel Primus" to refer to the chief of the Maltese.

9. Sergius Paulus, a Proconsul

Fact Stated: Acts (written 62–70 AD)
Fact Confirmed: 1877 AD (1800 years later ±)

In Acts 13:7 (ESV) (written 62–70 AD), Luke describes Sergio Paulus, a proconsul in Cyprus,[430] summoning Barnabas and Saul ("Paul") "to hear the Word of God." For a long time, Luke's use of the "proconsul" title for Sergius Paulus was challenged as inaccurate. History again met that challenge.

> According to Strabo, a first century BC and first century AD geographer and historian, Cyprus was a senatorial province during the Roman Empire in the 1st century AD, meaning that the senate appointed a *proconsul* to rule the island each year. Ancient Roman records, such as the writings of Cicero, also demonstrate that the religious center of Paphos was selected as the capital of Roman Cyprus. The city of Paphos,

When Only God Knew

as the book of Acts indicates, is located on the far west side of the island of Cyprus and archaeological excavations indicate that a substantial Hellenistic city existed there during the 1st century AD. This city functioned as the Roman seat of power where the *proconsul* would have been situated during his term of office.

Multiple inscriptions contain the name Sergius Paulus appear to portray the man as a person of prominence in the Roman Empire during the first century AD. A Greek inscription discovered at Soloi in Cyprus, north of Paphos, mentions a *proconsul* named Paulus during the 1st century AD (*IGR III*, 930). A portion of the inscription translates as "He also altered the senate by means of assessors during the time of the proconsul Paulus."

Although the text only mentions the Paulus part of his name, it does specify him as the proconsul. Of linguistic significance is the fact that Luke, the author of Acts, uses the Greek term *anthupatos* to designate the position of Sergius Paulus as *proconsul* (Acts 13:7). This Greek term is the equivalent of the Latin term *proconsul* (*A Greek-English Lexicon* by Liddell, Scott, Jones, and McKenzie.). In ca. 22 BC, Caesar Augustus made Cyprus a senatorial province which meant one would expect to find a *proconsul* there rather than a *prefect*, such as in Judaea Province where Pontius Pilatus is called a *prefect* and Luke uses different Greek terminology to designate this. Further, mention of the thirteenth year of Caesar Claudius places the date of the inscription in the early fifties AD and necessitates that the proconsul Paulus referred to as being in power at an earlier time than the inscription had ruled on Cyprus prior to the early fifties AD.[431]

There have been other archaeological discoveries confirming Luke's description of Sergius Paulus as proconsul of Cyprus. The first "two of these discoveries, (discussed below), are from the Island of Cyprus and were found by a veteran of the Civil war by the name of General Louis di Cesnola," who "would later be named the first curator of the Metropolitan Museum in New York."[432] The discoveries are:

1. The first inscription "found at the city of Silo in 1877 just a short distance north of Paphos, mentioned by Luke in the book of Acts, just before Paul's encounter with Sergius Paulus. The inscription mentions 'the proconsul Paulus' and dates to around 54 AD during the reign of (Emperor) Claudius."[433]

2. The second inscription from "Kythraia (Chytri), located in Northern Cyprus, (makes) reference to a 'Quintus Sergius' whose last name is missing from the inscription, but could possibly be Paulus. The inscription, found on a blue marble slab indicates that this man must have lived during the reign of either Claudius, Gaius, or Tiberius Caesar. One translation of the inscription which is located in the Metropolitan Museum reads:"

CLAUDIUS CAESAR SABASTOA
… QUINTUS SERGIUS PAULUS"[434]

3. A boundary stone of Claudius mentioning Sergius "discovered at Rome in 1887. It records the appointment (AD 47) of the Curators of the banks and the channel of the river Tiber, one of whom was Sergius. Since Paul's journey to Cyprus is usually dated to the first half of the 40s (AD) (and some scholars date his visit even earlier),

it is thought Sergius may have first served three years as Proconsul at Cyprus, then returned to Rome, where he was appointed curator."[435]

4. The name L. Sergius Paulus was also found in 1912 on an inscription in present-day Turkey at Pisidian Antioch, a major military and administration base for the Romans.[436]

Luke's historical reporting of biblical persons alive during his time has been consistently confirmed. The people on whom he reported were real people.

CHAPTER 5

Places in the Bible

There are many places in the Bible whose existence or location has been questioned by skeptics. Again, relatively recent archaeology has proven that they existed. The relative recentness of that rediscovery supports a conclusion that God intended to use places reported in the Bible but lost to history—for a time since the writing of the Bible—to prove His existence. The following discusses some of those places.

A. Old Testament

1. Cities

Fact Stated: Old Testament (written 1450–424 BC)
Fact Confirmed: 19th and 20th centuries AD (2500–3350 years later ±)

For centuries, archaeologists have looked for cities identified in the Bible, some of which were thought for a long time by some skeptics not to have existed. Those archaeologists have only relatively recently found many of those cities.

a. Babylon

Babylon "is referenced 280 times in the Bible, from Genesis to Revelation."[437] According to Jack Zavada,[438] it is "referred to by many names in the Bible,"[439] some of which he names as follows:

- Land of the Chaldeans (Ezekiel 12:13; written 590–570 BC)
- Land of Shinar (Daniel 1:2; written 536–530 BC)

- Land of Shinar (Zechariah 5:11; written 520–470 BC)
- Desert of the Sea (Isaiah 21:1, 9, KJV; written 740–680 BC)
- Lady of kingdoms (Isaiah 47:1–5, KJV; written 740–680 BC)
- Land of Merathaim (Jeremiah 50:21; written 627–570 BC)
- Sheshach (Jeremiah 25:12, 26, KJV; written 627–570 BC)[440]

Daniel 4:29–30 (NIV) (written 536–530 BC) says of Babylonian King, Nebuchadnezzar II,[441] "as the king was walking on the roof of the royal palace of Babylon, he said, 'Is not this the great Babylon, which I have built by my mighty power and for the glory of my majesty?'"

While Babylon is now one of the cities of the ancient world with which people today are very familiar, Babylon and its beauty have not always been known. The splendor of Babylon "was unknown to modern historians until it was confirmed by the German professor Koldewey,[442] who excavated Babylon approximately one hundred years ago,"[443] 2400 ± years after Daniel was written. "Historians (now) believe Babylon was the first ancient city to exceed 200,000 people."[444]

b. Ur of the Chaldees

Critics in the 1800s denied the existence of Abraham's[445] hometown, Ur of the Chaldees, referred to in Genesis 11:31 (written 1450–1405 BC). That was until Sir Leonard Woolley's[446] systematic excavations from 1922 to 1934 uncovered the immense ziggurat or temple tower at Ur near the mouth of the Euphrates in Mesopotamia.[447] Mesopotamia is a region located on the banks of the Tigris and Euphrates Rivers, which now lies in the modern-day Middle East. The region corresponds to most parts of modern-day Iraq as well as parts of Iran, Kuwait, Syria, and Turkey.[448]

We now know that Ur was the largest city of Shinar or northern Chaldea in Mesopotamia and the principal commercial and political center of the country but was, except for its cemetery, abandoned about 500 BC.[449]

c. Sodom and Gomorrah

Likewise,

> Genesis 19 describes the destruction of the cities of Sodom and Gomorrah as a result of the deviant behavior and sins of their inhabitants. A group of archaeologists believes they've uncovered the ruins of the ancient city of Sodom, located in Tall el Hammam, east of the Jordan river. The dates of the site are consistent with the early historical period of the Bible. The city is estimated to have been occupied between 3500 and 1540 BC.
>
> The site is considerably larger compared to other sites in the region. Its location isn't the only reason why it seems to be the ancient city of Sodom. Archaeologists believe that the city was abandoned suddenly toward the end of the Middle Bronze Age, which fits the Biblical picture of Sodom being suddenly destroyed.[450]

"Biblical archaeologist Ron Wyatt discovered the ruins of Sodom and Gomorrah southeast of the Dead Sea in 1989."[451] The discovery of the two cities proves that they were in existence ninety to one hundred and thirty-five years after the description of their destruction in Genesis.

d. Other Cities

Many other large and small cities mentioned in the Bible have also now been excavated, also demonstrating that the Old Testament is a historically accurate document.[452] For example, Arad,[453] Beersheba,[454] Bethel,[455] Bethshemesh,[456] Beth Shean or Bethshan,[457] Dan (also called Laish),[458] Gezer;[459] Gibeah,[460] Haran,[461] Hazor,[462] Hesbon,[463] Jericho,[464] Lachish,[465] Megiddo,[466] Nineveh,[467] Shechem,[468] Shiloh,[469] and Susa[470] have all been found.[471] "Such geographical markers are extremely significant in demonstrating that fact, not fantasy, is intended in the Old Testament historical narratives."[472]

2. Tower of Babel

Fact Stated: Genesis 11 (written 1450–1405 BC)
Fact Confirmed: 19th century (over 3200 years later)

As discussed in *Evidence for Bible's Tower of Babel Discovered*,[473] and by others:

> "Biblical scholars have long debated whether the Tower of Babel really existed. Now, a remarkable stone tablet never before shown on film appears to settle that question," the *Smithsonian* magazine says, featuring a video on its website.
>
> The tablet, which dates to about 600 BC, is from the private collection of Norwegian businessman Martin Schøyen,[474] and it includes the clearest image ever found of the Great Ziggurat of Babylon, according to Andrew George, professor of Babylonian history at the University of London, who also says in the video that it carries an illustration which

looks like a pyramid-like structure, with a depiction of King Nebuchadnezzar II,[475] the ruler of Babylon from 605–562 BC.

The Schøyen Collection says on its website that the ziggurat in Babylon was originally built around the time of Hammurabi 1792–1750 BC. "The restoration and enlargement began under Nabopolassar, the first king of the Neo-Babylonian Empire, ruling from November 626—August 605 BC,[476] and was finished after forty-three years of work under Nebuchadnezzar II, 604–562 BC."

It adds, "Here we have for the first time an illustration contemporary with Nebuchadnezzar II's restoring and enlargement of the Tower of Babel, and with a caption making the identity absolutely sure. We also have the building plans, as well as a short account of the reconstruction process. The text also mentions the restoration of the E-ur-imin-anki ziggurat in Borsippa, once believed by some scholars to be the Tower of Babel."[477]

The tablet "was discovered over a century ago" and "offers conclusive evidence that the tower of Babel was real."[478] Until that discovery, "our knowledge of the Tower of Babel has been based on (written accounts) in Genesis 11:1–9, and of Herodotus:[479] *The Histories* I:178-182, with the measurement of the first two stages, and a Seleucid[480] tablet of 229 BC (Louvre AO 6555), giving the sizes of the stages."[481]

B. New Testament

1. Cities

Cities mentioned in the New Testament, some of which had been mentioned in the Old Testament, were "abandoned and forgotten for many centuries,"[482] were destroyed with some but not all being subsequently rebuilt or became so inconsequential to the nations in which they were located that proof of the accuracy of their biblical history had to be rediscovered. For a while, many cities were lost to geography or history, but they have now been excavated and studied, demonstrating that the New Testament is historically accurate and can be relied on. The cities include but are not necessarily limited to Bethsaida, Capernaum, Chorazin, Ephesus, Gaza, Joppa, and Nazareth.

2. Cities of Bethsaida, Capernaum, and Chorazin

Jesus spent most of his ministry in what has been called "The Evangelical Triangle." This is a small geographic area containing the area between the biblical cities of Capernaum, Korazin, also spelled Chorazin and Korazim, and Bethsaida.[483]

According to the Gospels of Matthew and Luke (written 50–65 AD), Jesus cursed those three cities because their citizens had heard His message and had probably seen more miracles more often than the citizens of other cities, but they refused to understand who He was. Matthew 11:20–24 (NIV) (written 50–65 AD)[484] says:

> Then Jesus began to denounce the towns in which most of his miracles had been performed, because they did not repent. "Woe to you, Chorazin! Woe to you, Bethsaida! For if the miracles that were performed in you had been performed in Tyre and

When Only God Knew

Sidon,[485] they would have repented long ago in sack-cloth and ashes. But I tell you, it will be more bearable for Tyre and Sidon on the day of judgment than for you. And you, Capernaum, will you be lifted to the heavens? No, you will go down to Hades. For if the miracles that were performed in you had been performed in Sodom, it would have remained to this day. But I tell you that it will be more bearable for Sodom on the day of judgment than for you."

"Although it obviously happened some generations after Jesus, it is, (for instance), interesting that the descendants of (the people in Corazin) would allow a Medusa to be built right into their synagogue wall," betraying "an assimilation with the Greek and pagan practices of the time."[486] In Greek mythology, Medusa was "the most famous of the (three) monster figures known as Gorgons" and "was usually represented as a winged female creature having a head of hair consisting of snakes."[487] According to Greek mythology, "anyone who looked directly at Medusa was turned to stone,"[488] certainly not the message Jesus taught.

For centuries, the locations of Bethsaida, Capernaum, and Chorazin were lost. Here is what happened in them and how they were found.

a. Bethsaida

Fact Stated: Matthew, Mark, Luke, and John (written 50–90 AD)
Fact Confirmed: 2017 AD (1900 years later ±)

Bethsaida is referred to in all four of the Gospels: Matthew, Mark, Luke, and John.[489] Pliny the Elder,[490] "in his Natural History (written 49–79 AD), places Bethsaida on the eastern side of the Sea of Galilee," "near the place where the Jordan enters the Sea of Galilee."[491] It was six miles from Capernaum,[492] which is one of the "cursed' cities described above and discussed below.

Bethsaida played a very significant role in Jesus' ministry. John 1:44 (written 80–90 AD, tells us that Bethsaida was the hometown of the apostles Peter, Andrew, and Philip).[493] The apostle Philip introduced Jesus to the apostle Bartholomew, also known as Nathanael, to whom Jesus confirmed He was the Son of God.[494]

According to Mark 8:22–25 (written 50–65 AD), Jesus restored a blind man's sight just outside Bethsaida. As reported in Luke 9:10–17 (written 60–61 AD), in a desolate place near Bethsaida, Jesus miraculously feeds five thousand men, in addition to the women and children, who followed Him to Bethsaida, from five loaves of bread and two fish. According to Mark 6:45–52 (written 50–65 AD) and John 6:16–20 (written 80–90 AD), after the miracle of the loaves and fishes, the boat with His disciples was in the Sea of Galilee on the way to the other side of Bethsaida and nearby Capernaum, both in the Evangelical Triangle, when Jesus walked on water to assure them that He would keep them safe.

At "about the time Jesus was crucified, the local ruler Herod the Great's[495] son Philip, raised the fishing village of Bethsaida to the status of a city and named it Bethsaida Julias (in honour of the wife of the Emperor Augustus)."[496] "Bethsaida Julias contained both Gentile (Syrian) and Jewish populations, and it apparently continued to exist after the Jewish Revolt in AD 66–74, but declined in the third century and was probably destroyed by the Assyrian invasion in the 8th century" AD.[497]

"Archaeologists tend to agree that the capital of the kingdom of Geshur[498] was situated at et-Tell, a place… sometimes identified with the town of Bethsaida."[499] "The first excavations of the site were conducted in 1987–1989, by the Golan Research Institute,"[500] "While there has been controversy respecting where Bethsaida was located, on August 7, 2017, it was reported that archaeologists say they may have located the lost Biblical city of Bethsaida-Julias."[501] Excavations indicate that the settlement was founded in the 10th century" BC.[502]

b. Capernaum

Fact Stated: Matthew, Mark, Luke, and John (written 50–90 AD)
Fact Confirmed: 1838 AD (1700 years later ±)

Capernaum is, like Bethsaida, also referred to in all four of the Gospels, Matthew, Mark, Luke, and John[503] and was one of the three cities which Matthew 11:20–24 (written 50–65 AD) reports Jesus cursed. In the New Testament, it is mentioned sixteen times.[504]

The Bible says that Jesus lived and ministered in Capernaum,[505] having moved there after the people of Nazareth, where He grew up, rejected Him.[506] It was reported to have been the hometown of the tax collector, Matthew the apostle.[507] It was around Capernaum that Jesus chose several of His apostles: Peter and his brother, Andrew,[508] John and James, the sons of Zebedee,[509] and Matthew, the tax collector.[510]

According to the New Testament, "Jesus performed more miracles and preached more sermons in and around Capernaum than at any other place during His entire ministry."[511] For instance, He drove an unclean spirit from a man at the synagogue in Capernaum where he was preaching.[512] After leaving the synagogue, Jesus healed Simon's, i.e., Peter's mother-in-law.[513] After healing Peter's mother-in-law, Luke, the "historian of the first rank," according to Sir William Mitchell Ramsay,[514] reported that Jesus healed many other sick and demon-possessed people.[515] As pointed out above, according to Mark 6:45–52 (written 50–65 AD) and John 6:16–20 (written 80–90 AD), after the miracle of the loaves and fishes near Bethsaida, the boat with His disciples was in the Sea of Galilee on the way to nearby Capernaum and the other side of Bethsaida, both in the Evangelical Triangle, when Jesus walked on water to assure them that He would keep them safe.

Capernaum continued to exist for many years (after it was cursed it did not take) part in the rebellions that occurred in the first and second centuries, and for hundreds of years, Jews who believed in Jesus and non-Jews who believed in Jesus lived together. It wasn't until the Muslim era, in the middle of the eighth century (AD), that Capernaum was destroyed, probably in the big earthquake of 749 AD.[516]

"After lying buried for centuries, the ruins of Capernaum were discovered in 1838."[517]

In 1838, American explorer Edward Robinson discovered ruins which he identified as those of a synagogue but did not relate this to ancient Capernaum. In 1866, Charles William Wilson[518] identified the location (then known as Tel Hum) as Capernaum.[519]

From the archaeological discoveries, we now have modern-day evidence that Capernaum was "located on the northern shore of the Sea of Galilee."[520] "The excavations revealed that the site was established at the beginning of the Hasmonean period,[521] roughly in the second century BC, and abandoned in the eleventh century" AD.[522]

c. Chorazin

Fact Stated: Mathew and Luke (written 50–65 AD)
Fact Confirmed: 1869 AD + (1800 years later +)

Chorazin, also spelled Korazin and Korazim, was, along with Bethsaida and Capernaum, in what has become known as the "Evangelical Triangle," "because most of Jesus' teachings and miracles occurred there."[523] "Residents of Chorazin lived within sight of Bethsaida and Capernaum."[524] Chorazin is about two and one-half miles north of Capernaum.[525] As pointed out above, "all three—more likely villages than cities—incurred Jesus' condemnation ("Woe to you, Chorazin!") because their people did not accept His teachings and repent."[526]

When Only God Knew

While it is in "the "Evangelical Triangle, Chorazin is only mentioned in the New Testament twice and both times was due to the curse that Jesus put on it."[527]

Chorazin was described by Eusebius around 330 AD as being in ruins, apparently following an earthquake.[528] Eusebius of Caesarea, also called Eusebius Pamphili, lived in the fourth century AD and was a Christian bishop and historian "whose account of the first centuries of Christianity, in his Ecclesiastical History, is (considered) a landmark in Christian historiography."[529]

According to one author, life returned to Chorazin over the next one hundred years after that destruction, when the synagogue was rebuilt, "until the eighth century; settlement was resumed in the thirteenth century and a small population remained until the beginning of the twentieth century, when the site was abandoned."[530] According to another author, "during the third century AD, the city became uninhabited."[531] Still, another author says,

> From what's left today, researchers revealed that the destruction of Chorazin was most probably caused by an earthquake that took place sometime in the fourth century AD. Further evidence suggested that the town was reborn again in the fifth century.[532]

In any event,

> [t]he first archaeological work on the city began in the nineteenth century. The synagogue in Chorazin was discovered as a result of a survey conducted by the Palestine Exploration Fund[533] in 1869. In 1905–07 excavations on the city were begun and work was resumed at different times, continuing on as late as 1980–84.

Surprisingly, Chorazin's archaeological remains have yielded no evidence of first century (time of Jesus) settlement on the present site. An abundance of coins and other information date the current site clearly to the third and fourth centuries AD. However, potsherds gathered nearby may indicate that the biblical city of Jesus' day lies somewhere in the immediate area.[534]

That being said, "some archaeological evidence found just outside of Chorazin point to a first-century settlement, a find that led some to believe that this might have been the original location of Chorazin."[535]

3. Cities of Ephesus, Joppa, and Nazareth

Ephesus, Gaza, and Joppa all played significant roles in spreading Christianity. Each of those important cities was at one time destroyed, and much of their history has had to be rediscovered.

a. Ephesus

Fact Stated: Acts and Ephesians (written 60–70 AD)
Fact Confirmed: 1869 AD (1800 years later ±)

Ephesus has been described by the Encyclopedia Britannica as "the most important Greek city in Ionian Asia Minor."[536] Ephesus played a major role in the Bible. Yet, for hundreds of years before its pagan temple was unearthed, no one had seen it.

Ephesus was an ancient Greek city founded as a colony of Athens in the tenth century BC on the coast of Ionia, the ancient region comprising the central west coast of Anatolia (now in Turkey).[537] It "had one of the most advanced aqueduct systems in the ancient world, with at least six aqueducts of various sizes supplying different areas of the city."[538]

"During the Classical Greek era, it was (also) one of the twelve cities of the Ionian League"[539] and "flourished after it came under the control of the Roman Republic in 129 BC," approximately one hundred years before the Roman Republic became the Roman Empire.[540] "The city was famed for the nearby Temple of Artemis, (the Artemiseum), (completed around 550 BC), one of the Seven Wonders of the Ancient World"[541] built to worship Artemis, the daughter of Zeus and the mythological Greek "goddess of wild animals, the hunt, and vegetation and of chastity and childbirth, who was identified by the Romans with Diana."[542] Under the first Roman Emperor Augustus, who never claimed the title for himself but, nevertheless, reigned from either 31 BC (after Augustus' naval victory at Actium over Mark Antony),[543] or 27 BC, until his death in 14 AD.[544] Ephesus became "the first city of the Roman province of Asia."[545]

Ephesus, where the apostle Paul ministered and to whom he wrote the Ephesians epistle and to whom John wrote in Revelation, played a very significant role in the spread of Christianity and in early church history from the 50s AD; it is mentioned eighteen times in the Bible.[546]

From AD 52–54, the apostle Paul lived in Ephesus, working with the congregation and apparently organizing missionary activity into the hinterlands. Initially, according to the Acts of the Apostles, Paul attended the Jewish synagogue in Ephesus, but after three months he became frustrated with the stubbornness or hardness of heart of some of the Jews, and moved his base to the school of Tyrannus (Acts 19:9)… Paul introduced about twelve men to the 'baptism with the Holy Spirit' who had previously only experienced the baptism of John the Baptist (Acts 19:1–7). Later a silversmith named Demetrios stirred up a mob against Paul, saying that he was endangering the livelihood of those making silver Artemis shrines (Acts 19:23–41).[547]

"According to local belief, Ephesus was the last home of the Virgin, Mary, who was lodged near the city by St. John and died there."[548] The city was the site of several fifth-century Christian Councils.[549]

Though prominent in the ancient world, the city was, however, done by both barbarians and by nature.

> It was destroyed by the Goths in 263 AD, and although rebuilt, the city's importance as a commercial centre declined as the harbour was slowly silted. It was partially destroyed by an earthquake in AD 614.[550]
>
> By the early Middle Ages the city was no longer useful as a port and fell into decline. Late Byzantine Ephesus, conquered by the Seljuqs, also spelled Seljuks,[551] in 1090, was merely a small town. After brief splendour in the fourteenth century, even this was deserted, and the true site of the Artemiseum remained unsuspected until 1869.[552]
>
> Big earthquakes and malarial mosquitoes finally finished Ephesus sometime between the 6th and 10th century. The site was completely abandoned after the 14th century. After it was abandoned, it was covered naturally in time and most of the city was buried by dust and dirt.[553]

As pointed out above, Acts 19:23–41 (written 62–70 AD) describes how Paul's preaching caused a reduction in the sale of "silver shrines of Artemis," i.e., idols, and that he "was shouted down by a mob who wanted their commerce in idols to the mythological Greek goddess of wild animals, the hunt, and vegetation and of chastity and

When Only God Knew

childbirth" for whom the Artemiseum had been built and around which much of Ephesus' commerce revolved, to continue.

Ephesus, in particular the Artemisium, was uncovered and is now additional evidence of the biblical references to both. In 1858, John Turtle Wood, an English architect, engineer, and archaeologist who lived from 1821 to 1890,[554] "received a commission to design railway stations" in Turkey, when he became interested in the remains of the Artemisium, "which had completely disappeared from view about 500 years previously," but which was had been important to Christian history.

> In 1863, Wood relinquished his commission and began the search. The British Museum granted him a permit and a small allowance for expenses in return for the property rights in any antiquities he might discover in Ephesus.[555]

While "working at Ephesus for the British Museum between 1863 and 1874," he "struck a corner of the Artemiseum" in May 1869 which "exposed to view not only the scanty remains of the latest edifice (built after 350 BC) but the platform below it of an earlier temple of identical size and plan subsequently found to be that of the 6th century" BC,[556] and where "since further expected discoveries were not made (his) excavations stopped in 1874."[557]

> In 1895 German archaeologist Otto Benndorf, financed by a 10,000 guilder donation made by Austrian Karl Mautner Ritter von Markhof,[558] resumed excavations. In 1898 Benndorf founded the Austrian Archaeological Institute, which plays a leading role in Ephesus today.[559]

Ephesus is now "one of the largest Roman archaeological sites in the eastern Mediterranean;" "the visible ruins still give some idea of the city's original splendour."[560]

b. Joppa

Fact Stated: Old Testament (written 1405–430 BC);
Acts (written 62–70 AD)
Fact Confirmed: 1903 AD (1850–3300 years later ±)

Joppa is mentioned four times in the Old Testament and ten times in the New Testament, all in Acts.[561]

According to legend, Joppa was built after the Flood by Japheth, one of Noah's sons, who named it after himself.[562] It "is the biblical name for present-day Jaffa, a port city on the Mediterranean Sea in Israel" "located about thirty miles south of Caesarea and is now surrounded by the modern city of Tel Aviv, the largest metropolitan region in Israel."[563] Jaffa was formally merged with Tel Aviv in 1950.[564] It "is one of the oldest seaport cities in Israel, with a history that goes back" to somewhere between 4500 and 5000 BC.[565] One author described it as one of the oldest ports on earth.[566] "Joppa flourished on the ancient trade route that connected Egypt in the south and Syria in the east; with her natural harbor, Joppa grew into a rich trade center that linked Europe, Africa, and Asia.."[567]

According to the Bible, much happened in Joppa.

In the Old Testament, it was from Joppa that Jonah fled from the Lord's command to go to Nineveh to witness to evil-doers by attempting to go to Tarshish. Jonah 1:1–3 (NIV) (written 785–760 BC) says,

> The word of the LORD came to Jonah son of Amittai: "Go to the great city of Nineveh and preach against it, because its wickedness has come up before me." But Jonah ran away from the LORD and headed for Tarshish. He went down to Joppa, where he found

a ship bound for that port. After paying the fare, he went aboard and sailed for Tarshish to flee from the LORD.

Joppa had been included in the inheritance of the Tribe of Dan apportioned at Shiloh as they were entering the promised land.[568] Joppa "became one of Solomon's main harbors for trade and security."[569] According to 2 Chronicles 2:1, 8, and 16 (written 450–430 BC) and Ezra 3:6–7 (written 457–444 BC), Joppa was the port where cedars cut down in Lebanon were delivered for the building of the temple by Solomon in Jerusalem.

In the New Testament, Peter came to Joppa and raised Tabitha, also called Dorcas, from the dead.[570] After doing that, he stayed in Joppa with Simon the tanner for many days.[571] Peter was in Joppa when he had his vision that Jesus came to save all men, Jews, and Gentiles alike.[572]

Because of her prime location, however, Joppa "was sacked and rebuilt more than almost any other city in Israel," beginning at least as early as the fifteenth century BC by Egypt.[573] It was conquered twenty-two times,[574] by Egyptians, Assyrians, Babylonians, Phoenicians, Philistines, Israelites, Persians, Greeks, Maccabeans, Seleucids, Herod, Romans, Crusaders, "Mongols, Mamluks, Ottoman (Turks), French, British and—just before the state of Israel was declared in 1948—by Zionist militias,"[575] and by such notable historical figures as Alexander the Great, Richard the Lionheart, Muslim sultan Saladin, Louis IX of France, Napoleon and General Edmund Allenby,[576] who led the British Egyptian Expeditionary Force to victory in Palestine and Syria in 1917 and 1918.[577]

After the Maccabees defeated the (Greek) Seleucids around 163 BC, … the Greeks in Joppa retaliated by drowning 200 Jews (there). This cost them the port and their boats when Judas Maccabee burned it all…

The control of the city's port brought in substantial shipping wealth for Israel.[578]

"After Pompey[579] conquered Israel in 63 BC and took Joppa, a succession of victors took it again beginning with Herod in 39 BC, then Cleopatra and Mark Anthony in 32 BC, and finally Julius Caesar when he defeated the lovers two years later, giving it to Herod."[580]

Herod used the vast income of Jaffa to build the improved seaport of Caesarea as a thank you, which gave him even more money to build his palaces and temples in Israel. Once Caesarea was fully functional, Jaffa waned in importance, but still provided a natural seaport. During the Great Revolt against the Romans, Joppa was a major center of unrest. The Jewish rebels attacked the Roman ships here, so the Syrian proconsul Cestius Gallus destroyed it in 66 AD and killed 8,400 inhabitants. It was rebuilt and then utterly destroyed again by Vespasian[581] in 66 AD.[582]

In Arab times, the harbor of Caesarea oozed full of mud and so once more the natural harbor of Jaffa prospered. But it soon became the center of wars between the Crusaders and the Arabs, until finally in 1268 it was conquered by Sultan Baybars who stripped it of timber and marble for his new Cairo mosque. Less than a century later his successors purposely destroyed the harbor and the city to deny any new Crusaders a foothold in the Holy Land.[583]

"But again it was rebuilt. Jaffa was destroyed by Napoleon" in 1799, not leaving a single person alive in Jaffa.[584] "During Israel's War of Independence, much of Jaffa was destroyed."[585] "In 1965, a process of reconstruction began."[586]

When Only God Knew

Through archaeology and historical records, we know that the above facts are accurate and that Joppa was a large city with a long history and would be the kind of place that a disciple, such as Peter, would have gone to spread the Gospel of Christ. "During the spring of 1903, the first archaeological excavation in Jaffa was carried out in an area east of the old city, directed by G. A. Barton, director of the American School of Archaeology in Jerusalem (later renamed the American Schools of Oriental Research)."[587] "The tel[588] of Jaffa has been excavated during several digs in the last century, but never in its entirety."[589]

> From the oldest archaeological layers it becomes clear that Jaffa had a wall and gates, and a rampart leading up to the gates. These were destroyed at the beginning of the thirteenth century BC around the time when the Philistines would have conquered the city. On one of the doorjambs of the Bronze Age gates is an inscription with the name Ramses II, the Egyptian Pharaoh.
>
> From the Greek era dates an inscription which says that Ptolemy IV ruled Israel from Egypt, and coins were found with the Greek name of Jaffa, "Joppa."
>
> Near to the sea an excavation uncovered a three-roomed catacomb under a private house. Inside there was a burial cave, containing several graves from the Persian until the Byzantine periods. Some have finely carved stone doors.
>
> In the Jewish cemetery at Abu Kabir [Giv'at Herzl] there are many graves as well, dating from the Late Roman times until the Byzantine era, which give an impression of the Jewish community of the Mishnaic-Talmudic period. The cemetery was already dug

out in the nineteenth century by a French archaeologist. Tombstones bear inscriptions in Hebrew, Aramaic and Greek. Two additional burial caves were discovered in 1991.[590]

"The majority of excavations in Jaffa are salvage in nature and are conducted by the Israel Antiquities Authority since the 1990s."[591]

c. Nazareth

Fact Stated: Matthew, Mark, Luke, John, Acts (written 50–90 AD)
Fact Confirmed: 2009 AD (1900 years later ±)

Some skeptics have claimed that Nazareth, where the New Testament reports Jesus came from, did not exist during the time of Jesus.[592] Those skeptics have again been proven to be wrong, at least twice. The Israel Antiquities Authority announced it found a Nazareth house in 2009 with artifacts from the first century,[593] and archaeologists found a first-century synagogue inscription at Caesarea proving Nazareth existed.[594]

4. Pool of Bethesda

Fact Stated: John (written 80–90 AD)
Fact Confirmed: 19th century AD (1700 years later ±)

John 5:2 (written 80–90 AD) describes a pool called Bethesda, "which has five colonnades" or porticos. It was lost to history for almost two millennia. The Pool of Bethesda was discovered in the ninth century AD.[595] Before that discovery, having five porticos was considered an unusual feature and caused "many skeptical scholars to say the pool and the story of Jesus healing the paralytic were mythical."[596] The discovery of a pool with the five colonnades or porticos is additional support for the reliability of the New Testament.

When Only God Knew

5. Pool of Siloam

Fact Stated: John (written 80–90 AD)
Fact Confirmed: 2004 AD (1920 years later ±)

In John 9: 6–11 (ESV) (written 80–90 AD), John reports a blind man whom Jesus healed saying,

> As Jesus went along, he saw a man blind from birth. His disciples asked him, "Rabbi, who sinned, this man or his parents, that he was born blind?" "Neither this man nor his parents sinned," said Jesus, "but this happened so that the works of God might be displayed in him. As long as it is day, we must do the works of him who sent me. Night is coming, when no one can work. While I am in the world, I am the light of the world." After saying this, he spit on the ground, made some mud with the saliva, and put it on the man's eyes. "Go," he told him, "wash in the Pool of Siloam" [this word means "Sent"]. So the man went and washed, and came home seeing.

The Pool of Siloam was discovered in 2004 and contained coins found showing the pool was in use during the life of Jesus.[597]

6. Capernaum Synagogue

Fact Stated: Mark and John (written 50–90 AD)
Fact Confirmed: 1969 AD (1900 years later ±)

Mark 1:21 (written 50–65 AD) and John 6:59 (written 80–90 AD) report on Jesus and some of His disciples going to Capernaum and Jesus' teaching in its synagogue on the Sabbath. Excavation of the Capernaum Synagogue began in 1969, and underneath a fourth-century synagogue, the first-century synagogue in which Jesus taught was located.[598]

CHAPTER 6

Historical Events in the Bible

Various events are described in the Bible. For, in some cases, thousands of years, there were some who opined that events did not happen, often calling them mythology. Facts uncovered by archaeologists, scientists, and historians do not support those critical narratives, however. As time goes on, more and more events are being confirmed from which there is assurance that these events occurred and that their story was accurate. This chapter contains some of the proofs for Old and New Testament events uncovered relatively re cently. As in prior chapters, this chapter does not contain all that has been recently confirmed.

A. Old Testament

1. The Flood

Fact Stated: Genesis (written 1450–1405 BC)
Fact Confirmed: 1928–1929 AD (3300 years later ±)

Genesis 6:14–15 (NIV) (written 1450–1405 BC) says God told Noah:

> So make yourself an ark of cypress wood; make rooms in it and coat it with pitch inside and out. This is how you are to build it: The ark is to be three hundred cubits long, fifty cubits wide and thirty cubits high.

The flood which covered the earth discussed in Genesis chapter 6 (written 1450–1405 BC) beginning at verse 9 might be subject to challenge, except for the fact that other civilizations also report such a flood. For example,

> Mesopotamians, Egyptians, and Greeks all report a flood in primordial times. A Sumerian king list from c. 2100 BC divides itself into two categories: those kings who ruled before a great flood and those who ruled after it. One of the earliest examples of Sumero-Akkadian-Babylonian literature, the Gilgamesh Epic, describes a great flood sent as punishment by the gods, with humanity saved only when the pious Utnapishtim [aka, "the Mesopotamian Noah"] builds a ship and saves the animal world thereon. A later Greek counterpart, the story of Deucalion and Phyrra, tells of a couple who survived a great flood sent by an angry Zeus. Taking refuge atop Mount Parnassus [aka, "the Greek Ararat"], they supposedly repopulated the earth by heaving stones behind them that sprang into human beings.[599]

There is additional evidence of the flood,

> During the 1928–1929 excavation season in southern Mesopotamia [present-day Iraq], British archaeologist Leonard Woolley[600] uncovered three meters [10 ft] of waterborne sediment in the ancient city of Ur.[601] Woolley interpreted this as evidence of the biblical flood. The layer was dated to 4000 to 3500 BC. Similar evidence has been found at many other sites in the region, but not all of them are consistent with the dates of the layer found by Woolley.[602]

Even though there are other flood stories, by comparing the specifics, scientific reliability, internal consistency, the correspondence to the secular records, and the existence of common elements among the flood traditions around the world, the Genesis account is a more acceptable accurate historical record.[603]

2. Migration of Abraham and the Nomadic Way of Life

Fact Stated: Genesis (written 1450–1405 BC)
Fact Confirmed: 1922–1934 AD (3300 years later ±)

According to Genesis, Abraham traveled from Ur of the Chaldeans, his home, into Canaan,[604] the Promised Land in the Bible.[605] On his way to Canaan, the promised land, the Bible records that Abraham migrated through numerous places.[606]

> Early critics in the 1800s denied the existence of Abraham's hometown, Ur of the Chaldees [Genesis 11:31]. This continued until Sir Leonard Woolley's systematic excavations from 1922–34 uncovered the immense ziggurat or temple tower at Ur near the mouth of the Euphrates in Mesopotamia. The name "Abraham" appears in Mesopotamian records, and the various nationalities the patriarch encountered, as recorded in Genesis, are entirely consistent with the peoples known at that time and place.[607]

Semitic tribes at the time of Abraham were continually moving into and out of Mesopotamia.[608] Abraham's trek into the promised land along a route up the Euphrates valley to Haran in southern Anatolia, which has also been identified and excavated, and then down through Syria to Canaan is geographically accurate.[609] Using that Fertile Crescent route was the only way to travel successfully from Mesopotamia to the Mediterranean in those days.[610]

Nothing in the Genesis account contradicts the nomadic way of life with flocks and herds that was characteristic of life in the nineteenth or eighteenth centuries BC.[611] The agreements and contracts of the time, such as finding a bride from members of the same tribe and other customs, are well known elsewhere in the ancient Near East.[612] To argue that the patriarchs did not exist because their names have not been found archaeologically is merely an argument from silence—the weakest form of argumentation that can be used.[613] As fair-minded historians put it, "Absence of evidence is not necessarily evidence of absence."[614]

3. Jewish Life Before the Exodus and Moses' Miracles in Egypt

Fact Stated: Exodus (written 1450–1405 BC)
Fact Confirmed: 19th century (3300 years later ±)

There is skepticism among liberal scholars respecting whether God's plagues and Moses' miracles took place and as to the Jews living in Egypt for four hundred years before their exodus from Egypt described in Exodus. There is, however, substantial proof outside the Bible that the stories of Jews living in Egypt and that Moses' miracles, as told in Exodus,[615] are accurate.

Many secular Egyptologists and archaeologists deny the evidence for the Exodus, some by insisting that the Bible places the exodus in Exodus in the thirteenth century BC because Exodus 1:11 (written 1450–1405 BC) states that the Jews built Pithom and Ramses, which they say could not have occurred until the thirteenth century BC. Since the first buildings in those cities actually appeared two centuries earlier,[616] however, they are mistaken about that the date of the exodus in the Bible. The evidence that the first buildings in Pithom and Ramses appeared in the fifteenth century BC is consistent with the date that Exodus was written between 1450 and 1405 BC.

There is additional proof that the Jews made bricks for buildings in Pithom and Ramses. Exodus chapter 5 reports that, after Pharoah got angry with Moses and the Jews who were making bricks, he told his taskmasters over the Jews to stop supplying them with straw to make the bricks. Exodus 5:1–12 (NIV) says that, after Moses and Aaron went to the elders of the Israelites in Egypt,

> After Moses returned to Egypt from his exile, and he and Aaron "brought together all the elders of the Israelites," and Aaron told them everything the LORD had said to Moses and he also performed signs before the people, and they believed, Moses and Aaron went to Pharaoh and said, "This is what the LORD, the God of Israel, says: 'Let my people go, so that they may hold a festival to me in the wilderness.'" Pharaoh said, "Who is the LORD, that I should obey him and let Israel go? I do not know the LORD and I will not let Israel go." Then they said, "The God of the Hebrews has met with us. Now let us take a three-day journey into the wilderness to offer sacrifices to the LORD our God, or he may strike us with plagues or with the sword." But the king of Egypt said, "Moses and Aaron, why are you taking the people away from their labor? Get back to your work!" Then Pharaoh said, "Look, the people of the land are now numerous, and you are stopping them from working." That same day Pharaoh gave this order to the slave drivers and overseers in charge of the people: "You are no longer to supply the people with straw for making bricks; let them go and gather their own straw. But require them to make the same number of bricks as before; don't reduce the quota. They are lazy; that is why they are crying out, 'Let us go and sacrifice to our God.' Make the work harder for the people so that they keep working and pay no attention to lies."

Then the slave drivers and the overseers went out and said to the people, "This is what Pharaoh says: 'I will not give you any more straw. Go and get your own straw wherever you can find it, but your work will not be reduced at all.'" So the people scattered all over Egypt to gather stubble to use for straw.

Three thousand three hundred years later, evidence that the Jews made bricks just as reported in Exodus was discovered.

In 1883, the treasure or store cities of Pithom and Raamses were unearthed. The lower courses of the walls were made of the usual sun-dried mud bricks in which chopped up straw had been mixed for binding the clay together and strengthening it. In the middle courses, the bricks lacked straw, but contained stubble and roots of the grain crop, which the labourers had put in to take the place of straw. It appeared that they had put in whatever they could find.[617]

Then there are the plagues reported in Exodus. There are considered to be ten plagues against the Egyptians recorded in Exodus 7–12. They were:

1. the Nile River being turned into blood,
2. the plague of frogs,
3. the plague of gnats,
4. the plague of flies,
5. the plague which killed all Egyptian cattle and sheep,
6. the plague of boils,
7. the plague of hail and fire,
8. the plague of locusts,

When Only God Knew

9. the plague of darkness and

10. the death of firstborn man and beast.

There is evidence that the plagues are a historical event.

There are ninety ± Egyptian texts which contain parallels to Exodus.[618] For example, an Egyptian scribe named Ipuwer, an eyewitness to the Exodus plagues,[619] gave what appears to be an eyewitness account of disaster in Egypt that supports the biblical Exodus account.[620] Below is a comparison with the Exodus account of excerpts taken from this ancient Egyptian text,[621] the Ipuwer Papyrus, acquired by the Museum of Leiden in the Netherlands in 1828.[622] While there is some confusion among scholars as to when the Ipuwer Papyrus was written (ranging from 2050 BC, too early for the Exodus story, to a copy from around 1400 BC),[623] passages in the Ipuwer Papyrus are very similar to the Exodus story as shown in the following chart:

The Ipuwer Papyrus Account Paragraph ("¶")	Exodus (NIV) Chapter and Verse
¶2:56 "Plague is throughout the land. Blood is everywhere."	7:21 … Blood was everywhere in Egypt."
¶2:10 "Men shrink from tasting and thirst after water."	7:21, 24 The fish in the Nile died, and the river smelled so bad that the Egyptians could not drink its water. And all the Egyptians dug along the Nile to get drinking water, because they could not drink the water of the river.
¶2:10 "The river is blood." ¶7:20 "…all the waters that were in the river were turned to blood."	7:19–20 The Lord said to Moses, "Tell Aaron, 'Take your staff and stretch out your hand over the waters of Egypt—over the streams and canals, over the ponds and all the reservoirs—and they will turn to blood.' Blood will be everywhere in Egypt, even in vessels of wood and stone." Moses and Aaron did just as the Lord had commanded. He raised his staff in the presence of Pharaoh and his officials and struck the water of the Nile, and all the water was changed into blood.
2:10 "Forsooth, gates, columns and walls are consumed by fire."	9:23–24 "…fire ran down to the earth… there was hail, and fire flashing continually in the midst of the hail."

This kind of contemporary written comparison is evidence of the accuracy of the Exodus account, which in turn, is proof of the existence of God. The reader may want to research the other evidence for the Exodus, including other passages from the Ipuwer Papyrus.

Despite the proof described above, there are some who say that all the plagues in Exodus could be explained as the result of natural events. Maybe so, but that does not explain why those events happened just at the time that they did. It is unlikely that they all came when they did as just a matter of dumb luck for Moses and the Israelites.

Weighing all the evidence clearly supports the conclusion that Israelites were living the life described in Exodus at the time described and that the plagues happened and came from God.

4. The Exodus of the Israelites from Egypt

Fact Stated: Exodus (written 1450–1405 BC)
Fact Confirmed: 21st century AD (3400 years later ±)

There is also skepticism among liberal scholars respecting whether the exodus in Exodus took place. That the exodus described in the Bible occurred was authenticated shortly after the turn of the twenty-first century. As stated in the article, "Exodus Evidence: An Egyptologist Looks at Biblical History" from the May/June 2016 issue of *Biblical Archaeology Review*, evidence is presented that generally supports a thirteenth-century BC. Exodus during the Ramesside Period, when Egypt's 19th Dynasty ruled.[624]

> The article examines Egyptian texts, artifacts and archaeological sites, which demonstrate that the Bible recounts accurate memories from the thirteenth century BC. For instance, the names of three places that appear in the Biblical account of Israel's Exodus from Egypt correspond to Egyptian place names from the Ramesside Period [thirteenth-eleventh centuries BC]. The Bible recounts that, as slaves, the Israelites were forced to build the store-cities of Pithom and Ramses. After the ten plagues, the Israelites left Egypt and famously crossed the Yam Suph [often translated Red Sea or Reed Sea), whose waters were miraculously parted for them. The Biblical names Pithom,

Ramses and Yam Suph [often translated Red Sea or Reed Sea] correspond to the Egyptian place names Pi-Ramesse, Pi-Atum and [Pa-]Tjuf. These three place names appear together in Egyptian texts only from the Ramesside Period. The name Pi-Ramesse went out of use by the beginning of Egypt's Third Intermediate Period, which began around 1085 BC, and does not reappear until much later.[625]

5. Parting of the Red Sea and Drowning of Pharaoh's Army

Fact Stated: Exodus 14:5–9, 15–18, 21–29 (written 1450–1405 BC)
Fact Confirmed: 21st century AD (3400 years later ±)

Exodus 14:5–9, 15–18, 21–29 (NIV) (written 1450–1405 BC) says,

When the king of Egypt was told that the people had fled, Pharaoh and his officials changed their minds about them and said, "What have we done? We have let the Israelites go and have lost their services!" So he had his chariot made ready and took his army with him. He took six hundred of the best chariots, along with all the other chariots of Egypt, with officers over all of them. The Lord hardened the heart of Pharaoh king of Egypt, so that he pursued the Israelites, who were marching out boldly. The Egyptians—all Pharaoh's horses and chariots, horsemen and troops—pursued the Israelites and overtook them…

Then the Lord said to Moses, "Why are you crying out to me? Tell the Israelites to move on. Raise your staff and stretch out your hand over the sea to divide the water so that the Israelites can go through

When Only God Knew

the sea on dry ground. I will harden the hearts of the Egyptians so that they will go in after them. And I will gain glory through Pharaoh and all his army, through his chariots and his horsemen. The Egyptians will know that I am the Lord when I gain glory through Pharaoh, his chariots and his horsemen."

...

Then Moses stretched out his hand over the sea, and all that night the Lord drove the sea back with a strong east wind and turned it into dry land. The waters were divided, and the Israelites went through the sea on dry ground, with a wall of water on their right and on their left. The Egyptians pursued them, and all Pharaoh's horses and chariots and horsemen followed them into the sea. During the last watch of the night the Lord looked down from the pillar of fire and cloud at the Egyptian army and threw it into confusion. He jammed the wheels of their chariots so that they had difficulty driving. And the Egyptians said, "Let's get away from the Israelites! The Lord is fighting for them against Egypt." Then the Lord said to Moses, "Stretch out your hand over the sea so that the waters may flow back over the Egyptians and their chariots and horsemen." Moses stretched out his hand over the sea, and at daybreak the sea went back to its place. The Egyptians were fleeing toward it, and the Lord swept them into the sea. The water flowed back and covered the chariots and horsemen—the entire army of Pharaoh that had followed the Israelites into the sea. Not one of them survived. But the Israelites went through the sea on dry ground, with a wall of water on their right and on their left.

Recent evidence supports the biblical report of the splitting of the Red Sea and the drowning of pharaoh's army. In June, 2003, two Bible enthusiasts who dove the waters of the Red Sea were interviewed and reported that they believed they had found and photographed a chariot wheel and a chariot cab.[626]

As Joe Kovacs in *Chariots in Red Sea: 'Irrefutable Evidence'*, also reported in 2012, "Michael Rood, a Hebrew-roots teacher, has produced a video proffering evidence" that the reported find "is absolutely correct."[627] The DVD "documents the work of numerous researchers from the U.S. and overseas who have probed an underwater land bridge between a beachhead at Nuweiba, Egypt, and what is today Saudi Arabia," using "cameras mounted on remote-controlled submarines [which] revealed coral-encrusted chariot parts, horse and human remains strewn like battlefield wreckage on the bottom of the Red Sea," the literal translation of "yam suph," the Hebrew term for the Red Sea.[628] As reported by Kovacs, "'Even a novice can readily see that these are not natural coral formations,' Rood said, showing a variety of circular shapes he insists are chariot wheels, some with axles still intact."

> Rood also explained giant pillars which have been found on both sides of the crossing to mark the event. One was discovered eroded on the Egyptian shore by the late American archaeologist Ron Wyatt. Later, another was located on the Arabian side with "the legible remains of ancient paleo-Hebrew inscriptions." He says the words for pharaoh, death, Egypt, King Solomon and the sacred name of God, YHWH, are all present on the second pillar. "King Solomon, the wisest man who ever lived, knew exactly where the children of Israel made their escape just 500 years before, and so he established pillars to memorialize the yam suph crossing," said [Michael

When Only God Knew

Rood, an author, historian, teacher, broadcaster, and life-long student of the Bible].

[Rood also] points out the depth of water would make it impossible for a crossing to have taken place anywhere with the exception of the shallow land bridge at Nuweiba. "If the water were to be removed, it would still be impossible to cross this chasm which is as deep and wide as the Grand Canyon in Arizona," Rood said. "But," he added, "at the beach where Israel camped, an underwater land bridge gently slopes at a six-degree angle, levels out at about 900 feet, and then gradually rises to meet the western shore of Midian."[629]

Yet again, despite the proof described above, there are some who say that the splitting of the Red Sea described in Exodus could be explained as the result of a natural event—a theory that would not be accepted as evidence in American courtrooms. One researcher has theorized that the parting could have occurred due to a weather event.[630] According to that theorist, the weather event could have been a coastal effect called a "wind setdown." In a "wind setdown." strong winds—a little over sixty miles per hour—create a "push" on coastal water, which, in one location, creates a storm surge that could cause the parting of a body of water in another location, so much so that a bridge or pathway of dry land is revealed that could be crossed by a group of people.[631]

There are several problems with this theory. First, that same theorist admits that his theory only works if such an event had not occurred for a crossing of the Red Sea. This theorist says that the crossing could have occurred at the "Reed Sea," which he claims to be a better translation of the original Hebrew in Exodus.[632] There are some "scholars" who agree.[633] According to their theories, the Red Sea, or sea of reeds, in Exodus could have referred to "a large lake close to the

Red Sea, which has since dried up due to the Suez Canal," the Gulf of Eilat, which is referred to as the yam suph in the Books of Kings (1 Kings 9:26)," "a former coastal lagoon fed by a branch of the Nile," "a large lagoon on the north coast of the Sinai Peninsula "or, more specifically, Lake of Tanis which "would have been to the north of the modern day Red Sea in the Eastern Nile Delta region, just south of the Mediterranean Sea."[634]

So, these "scholars" have no idea where the crossing took place.

There are other reasons to question each theory that the sea crossed in Exodus was not the Red Sea. One problem with that theory is that the Hebrew term, Yam Suph, used in Exodus for the body of water that was crossed, has been translated the Red Sea for millennia. But you may say, "So what?"

And the answer is that the greater weight of the evidence supports the crossing was at the Red Sea.

First, the northern route crossing theory does not explain how in June, 2003, two Bible enthusiasts who dove the waters of the Red Sea were able to report that they believed they had found and photographed a chariot wheel and a chariot cab, as discussed above. It also does not explain the report by Joe Kovacs in Chariots in Red Sea: Irrefutable Evidence, in 2012, discussed above, respecting the video produced by Michael Rood[635] that "documents the work of numerous researchers from the US and overseas who have probed an underwater land bridge between a beachhead at Nuweiba, Egypt, and what is today Saudi Arabia," using "cameras mounted on remote-controlled submarines which revealed coral-encrusted chariot parts, horse and human remains strewn like battlefield wreckage on the bottom of the Red Sea."

Second, there is other evidence for the proposition that "Red Sea" is the proper translation.

One Hebrew scholar, who studied in depth the translation of the Hebrew term, Yam Suph, used in Exodus, disagrees that the sea in Exodus can be translated as either the Red Sea or the Reed Sea. The

When Only God Knew

term Yam Suph he translates as the "Sea of Storm."[636] Certainly, there were storms on the Red Sea.

Another problem with these theories of a northern cross over into the Sinai Peninsula by the Israelites is that they contradict the evidence from other passages recorded in Exodus. Exodus 14:1–3 (NIV) says, "Then the Lord said to Moses, 'Tell the Israelites to turn back and encamp near Pi Hahiroth, between Migdol and the sea. They are to encamp by the sea, directly opposite Baal Zephon.'"

While archaeologists do not know for certain where Pi Hahiroth, Migdol, or Baal Zephon are, the passage says the Israelites encamped between those cities and "the sea," and not a lagoon or lake to the north.

Other evidence in and outside the Bible also indicates that those cities are near the Red Sea, and that is where the Israelites crossed. Exodus 13:17–18 (NIV) says,

> When Pharaoh let the people go, God did not lead them on the road through the Philistine country, though that was shorter. For God said, "If they face war, they might change their minds and return to Egypt." So God led the people around by the desert road toward the Red Sea.

According to Genesis 21:34 (NIV), over 400 hundred years before the exodus, "Abraham stayed in the land of the Philistines." Eventually, the Philistines, a powerful seafaring warlike people, would inhabit a strip of land along the Mediterranean Sea in the Sinai Peninsula 25–30 miles long along the Mediterranean Sea and 12–15 miles wide parallel to the Nile River.[637] The Sinai Peninsula lies between the Mediterranean Sea to the north and the Red Sea to the south.[638]

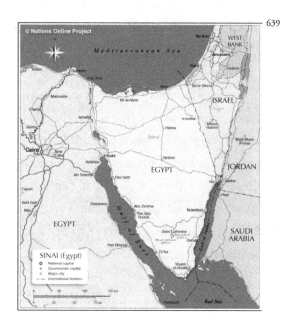

The distance from the Mediterranean Sea to the modern-day city of Suez on the very northern tip of the Red Sea is approximately eighty-five miles.[640] Goshen, where the Jews lived, is "located in the northeastern Nile Delta region of Egypt."[641] The Nile Delta also borders the Mediterranean Sea. The northern Nile Delta sat directly across the Nile from the Philistine territory.

Exodus 13:17–18 supports the conclusion that the Israelites did not take the shorter routes directly from Goshen to the Sinai Peninsula suggested by those that theorize that they did not cross through the Red Sea. That makes sense. If the Israelites had gone more directly from Goshen in the northeastern Nile Delta region into the Sinai Peninsula, they would have been more likely to run into the Philistines than if they took a longer indirect route from Goshen to the Red Sea. There is an estimate that the Israelites may have traveled as much as 500 kilometers (over 310 miles) to get to the point where they crossed through the Red Sea.[642] A crossing point that required that much travel from Goshen is likely to have put the Israelites on the east side of the Red Sea at least seventy or more safer miles past the territory of the Philistines in the Sinai Peninsula on the other

When Only God Knew

side of the Nile. That would have more likely protected them from the threat of Philistine aggression than if they crossed into the Sinai Peninsula using any more northern route.

It would have been wise for the Israelites to cross over into the Sinai Peninsula as far from the Philistines as possible because crossing at more northern points would have put the newly freed militarily untrained Israelites, men but also women and children numbering about three million altogether, in danger of entering areas controlled by or of concern to the powerful and warlike Philistines. It is, consequently, unlikely that, as theorists suggest, the Israelites crossed over into the Sinai Peninsula over or through

1. any coastal lagoon fed by a branch of the Nile,
2. any lagoon on the north coast of the Sinai Peninsula or
3. any lake to the north of the modern-day Red Sea in the Eastern Nile Delta region, just south of the Mediterranean,[643]

all of which would have put them at greater risk of entering territory controlled by or of concern to the Philistines or of catching Philistine attention. By going from Goshen, where the Jews lived, to the Red Sea and then crossing into the Sinai Peninsula, the Israelites would have been more likely not to run into Philistines.[644]

Then there was the army of Pharaoh, which contained "six hundred chosen chariots and all the other chariots of Egypt with officers over them all," which was destroyed when the water crashed back down on them. *See* Exodus 14:6–7, 26–28 (ESV). Proof that such happened in the Red Sea is discussed above. Lagoons and lakes that would have existed during the exodus have vanished, many because they were drained because of or to build the Suez Canal, which was officially completed in 1869.[645] Consequently, it is not known for sure how deep the lagoons and lakes that would have existed during the exodus were. That being said, the destruction of the pharaoh's army is not as likely to have happened if the water was in a shallow lagoon or lake, such as one found at Tanis in 2009,[646] than if the water was in a deeper body of water such as the Red Sea.

In addition, again, these theories do not explain why, no matter where it happened, the water was split just at the time that it was. It is, still again, unlikely that it happened just as a matter of dumb luck for Moses and the Israelites just as they needed to get away from pharaoh's army.

Weighing all the evidence clearly supports the conclusion that the Bible is accurate, and the Red Sea was split at the precise time that the Israelites needed it to be to be saved from the pharaoh's army and that that was done by God.

6. Jericho's Fall

Fact Stated: Joshua (written 1405–1385 BC)
Fact Confirmed: 20th century AD (3300 years later +)

According to Joshua 6 (written 1405–1385 BC), after the Israelites marched around Jericho once a day for six days, on the seventh day they circled the city seven times, and on the seventh time around, priests blew their trumpets, the people shouted, and the walls fell down.[647] The Bible then says that when the walls collapsed, the Israelites stormed the city and set it on fire.[648]

There have been those who have taken the position that the fall of Jericho reported in the Bible never occurred. For example, "when Dame Kathleen Kenyon excavated at Jericho in the 1950s, she claimed not to have found any collapsed walls or even evidence of a living city at Jericho during the time of Joshua's invasion—i.e., nothing for him to conquer.[649] She did, however, find what she described as an earlier Jericho that around 1550 BC, according to her one hundred years before the Joshua story, was subject to a violent conquest with fallen walls and a burnt ash layer a yard thick, indicating destruction by fire.[650] Skeptics saw that as solid evidence that Joshua's conquest of Jericho must have been folklore."[651]

Despite the skeptics, however, archaeologist Bryant G. Wood, editor of *Bible and Spade*[652] pointed out that three major expeditions to the site, including Kenyons, "uncovered abundant evidence to support the Biblical account."[653] As Wood showed, "John Garstang (1930–1936) and Kathleen Kenyon (1952–1958) both dug at Jericho for six seasons and a German excavation directed by Ernst Sellin and Carl Watzinger dug for three," and "all found abundant evidence of the city's destruction by fire in a layer related to the Biblical date of 1400 BC."[654] In September 1997, Dr. Wood visited Jericho and determined that even skeptics had found the same evidence uncovered in the earlier excavations, which fit the Biblical story perfectly.[655] He also concluded that Kenyon had misdated her finds and that the destruction of Jericho actually took place in the 1400s BC [mere decades before Joshua was written] when Joshua was very much around.[656] Wood based his chronology respecting the Kenyon find on stratigraphy,[657] pottery types, carbon-14 dating,[658] and other evidence, including collapsed walls, to show "archaeological confirmation of the biblical detail" for the fall of Jericho.[659]

Just more evidence to be weighed by the reader.

7. Hezekiah's Defense of Jerusalem/ Hezekiah's Tunnel

Fact Stated: 2 Kings (circa 561–538 BC)
Fact Confirmed: 1838 AD (2400 years later ±)

Archaeology 2400 years after the biblical report also supports a biblically described engineering feat by Hezekiah, the king of the Southern Kingdom of Judah from 721 to 686 BC who feared a siege by the Assyrian king, Sennacherib.[660] Second Kings 20:20 (written circa 561–538 BC) (NIV) says, "As for the other events of Hezekiah's reign, all his achievements and how he made the pool and the tunnel by which he brought water into the city, are they not written in the book of the annals of the kings of Judah?" King Hezekiah "preserved Jerusalem's water supply by cutting [or completing] a tunnel through

1,750 feet of solid rock from the Gihon Spring to the Pool of Siloam inside the city walls."[661]

"The tunnel was first described in modern times by Franciscus Quaresmius in 1625," and "it was later explored in 1838 by the American biblical scholar Edward Robinson."[662] "At the Siloam end of the tunnel, an inscription, presently in the archaeological museum at Istanbul, Turkey, celebrates this remarkable accomplishment; the tunnel is probably the only biblical site that has not changed its appearance in 2,700 years."[663]

8. Assyrian Invasions

Fact Stated: 2 Kings and 1 Chronicles (written circa 561–430 BC)
Fact Confirmed: 20th century AD (2500 years later ±)

The Bible reports several invasions by the Assyrians of Judah.[664] For example, 2 Kings 15:17–20 says,

> In the thirty-ninth year of Azariah king of Judah, Menahem son of Gadi became king of Israel, and he reigned in Samaria ten years. He did evil in the eyes of the Lord. During his entire reign he did not turn away from the sins of Jeroboam son of Nebat, which he had caused Israel to commit.
>
> Then Pul king of Assyria invaded the land…

According to 2 Kings 17:3–6,

> Shalmaneser king of Assyria came up to attack Hoshea, who had been Shalmaneser's vassal and had paid him tribute. But the king of Assyria discovered that Hoshea was a traitor, for he had sent envoys to So king of Egypt, and he no longer paid tribute to the king of Assyria, as he had done year by year. There-

fore Shalmaneser seized him and put him in prison. The king of Assyria invaded the entire land, marched against Samaria and laid siege to it for three years. In the ninth year of Hoshea, the king of Assyria captured Samaria and deported the Israelites to Assyria.

Second Kings 20:1 describes an attack on Judah at the direction of the Assyrian King Sargon, which had been prophesized by Isaiah when the book with his name was written between 740 and 680 BC 2 Kings 20:1 says, in part, "the year that the supreme commander, sent by Sargon king of Assyria, came to Ashdod and attacked and captured it."

These reports were first confirmed 2500 years after they were reported in the Bible by expeditions in 1932–1938, 1966–68, 1974, and 1987 when archaeologists at the site of Lachish, the second most important city in Judah after Jerusalem, uncovered artifacts from Assyrian invasions.[665]

Samaria fell to the Assyrians in 722 BC. Assyrian records claim that King Sargon II captured 27,290 prisoners and took them into exile to different locations, including Halah and Habor and other places under Assyrian control.

This account is confirmed in 2 Kings 17:6 and further supported by material evidence. At these Mesopotamian sites, archaeologists have unearthed examples of ostraca [pottery fragments with writing on their surface].

In 701 BC, the Assyrian king Sennacherib invaded Judah. Many cities fell to the invading army, including the southern city of Lachish mentioned in 2 Kings 18:13–17. After a siege, the city was captured by the Assyrians, and several archaeological finds are consistent with this event.

At the site of Lachish, archaeologists have uncovered arrowheads, a siege ramp, a counter-ramp, the crest of a helmet, and a chain used by the defenders against the siege ram. At the site of the ancient Assyrian city of Nineveh [northern Iraq], a relief sculpture depicting the capture of Lachish was retrieved from the palace of Sennacherib.[666]

Two thousand five hundred years and confirmation of what we already knew from the Bible.

B. New Testament

1. The Life of Jesus

Fact Stated: Matthew, Mark, Luke, and John (written 50–90 AD)
Fact Confirmed: No evidence denying

The Gospels of Matthew, Mark, Luke, and John and the Book of Acts in the Bible contain eye-witness accounts of how Jesus lived, died, and rose from the grave. Apostles who lived with Jesus for three years died horrible deaths-including by impaling, beheading, crucifixion, flaying, and being thrown to their deaths—never denying that Jesus lived as the Bible said that he did, that he did the many miracles which the Bible describes and that they saw him alive after he died on the cross. They died after hundreds of people saw Jesus after he was raised from the dead,[667] as described in the Book of Acts, and could have been confronted about what they saw.

There is no record that any witnesses of the risen Jesus denied that they saw Him alive after his crucifixion. Except for Judas, who betrayed Jesus and committed suicide, eleven apostles, including one that took Judas' place, were martyred; only one (John) died of old age. Not one recanted. If it had all been a hoax, someone would likely have said so.

The martyred disciples were:[668]

- **Andrew:** Church tradition says Andrew was crucified on a Crux Decussata, or X-shaped cross, to which he was tied to prolong his death after being beaten severely by seven soldiers. He preached to his tormentors for two days until he died.
- **Bartholomew:** Legend claims he was flayed to death by a whip in Armenia crucified upside down.
- **James:** He was the first apostle to be martyred. He was killed with the sword by beheading on order of King Herod Agrippa I of Judea, about AD 44 and about eleven years after the death of Christ, in a general persecution of the early church. The Roman officer who guarded James watched, amazed as James defended his faith at trial. Later the officer walked with James to the place of execution. Overcome by conviction, the Roman officer declared his new faith to the judge and knelt beside James to accept beheading as a Christian.
- **James the son of Alphaeus, also called James the Lesser:** According to tradition, he was thrown down over one hundred feet from the southeast pinnacle of the temple in Jerusalem by the scribes and Pharisees, the same pinnacle where Satan had taken Jesus during the Temptation. When he lived, he was then stoned, and his brains dashed out with a fuller's club.
- **Matthew:** Legend has it that he died a martyr in Ethiopia. He was killed by a sword wound in 60–70 AD.
- **Matthias:** The apostle chosen to replace Judas Iscariot was either stoned while hanging on a cross or beheaded.

- **Peter:** He died thirty-three/thirty-four years after the death of Christ. Legend has it that the Romans were going to crucify Peter, but he told them he was not worthy to be executed in the same manner as Jesus; so he was crucified upside down on a Crux Decussata or X-shaped cross.
- **Philip:** Tradition says Philip was martyred at Hierapolis in Phrygia, in Asia Minor, where he was tortured and crucified.
- **Simon the Zealot:** Church tradition says that he spread the gospel in Egypt and was either beaten to death with sticks or crucified in Persia.
- **Thaddeus or Jude:** Church tradition holds that Thaddeus founded a church at Edessa, Persia, and was crucified there as a martyr. He was killed by arrows.
- **Thomas:** Tradition holds that he carried the gospel to the east and was martyred in Persia or India by a lance.
- **John** outlived all of the disciples, despite being sentenced to death, boiled in oil, and drinking poison and exile, dying of old age at Ephesus, perhaps about 98 AD, but sometime between 89 and 120 AD.

2. Jesus' Miracles Witnessed by Thousands

Fact Stated: Matthew, Mark, Luke, and John (written 50–90 AD)
Facts: No evidence denying

The multitude of miracles which Jesus performed is contained primarily in the Gospels of Matthew (written 50–65 AD), Mark (written 50–65 AD), John (written 80–90 AD), and Luke, "a historian of the first rank" who "should be placed along with the very greatest of historians,"[669] whose Gospel was written 60–61 AD. Sometimes thousands of people, many of whom, including children, would have been alive at the writing of some of the gospels twenty to thirty-five years after the miracles occurred, witnessed the miracle. Sometimes only a few witnessed a miracle.

Whether there were thousands or just a few witnesses to a miracle, there is no report of any witness ever coming forward to deny the reported miracles, including Jesus' disciples who died the horrific deaths described before and including Pharisees and Jewish elders who had a strong and stubborn theological disbelief in Jesus' deity as the Son of God and had reason to challenge Jesus' miracles to discredit Jesus and what is written in the New Testament.

The following passages discuss Jesus' unchallenged miracles:

a. Turning water into wine at a wedding witnessed by Jesus' disciples, including John, Jesus' mother and the host, servants, and guests at the wedding.

(Jesus' first miracle of turning water into wine at a wedding.)

On the third day a wedding took place at Cana in Galilee. Jesus' mother was there, and Jesus and his disciples had also been invited to the wedding. When the wine was gone, Jesus' mother said to him, "They have no more wine."

"Woman, why do you involve me?" Jesus replied. "My hour has not yet come."

His mother said to the servants, "Do whatever he tells you."

Nearby stood six stone water jars, the kind used by the Jews for ceremonial washing, each holding from twenty to thirty gallons.

Jesus said to the servants, "Fill the jars with water"; so they filled them to the brim.

Then he told them, "Now draw some out and take it to the master of the banquet."

They did so, and the master of the banquet tasted the water that had been turned into wine. He did not realize where it had come from, though the servants who had drawn the water knew. Then he called the bridegroom aside and said, "Everyone brings out the choice wine first and then the cheaper wine after the guests have had too much to drink; but you have saved the best till now."

John 2:1–11 (NIV)

What Jesus did here in Cana of Galilee was the first of the signs through which he revealed his glory; and his disciples believed in him.

b. Healing of a royal official's son witnessed by Jesus' disciples, including John, the royal official's and his son and servants.

(Jesus' second miracle of healing of a royal official's son.)

Once more he visited Cana in Galilee, where he had turned the water into wine. And there was a certain royal official whose son lay sick at Capernaum. When this man heard that Jesus had arrived in Galilee from Judea, he went to him and begged him to come and heal his son, who was close to death.

"Unless you people see signs and wonders," Jesus told him, "you will never believe."

The royal official said, "Sir, come down before my child dies."

"Go," Jesus replied, "your son will live."

The man took Jesus at his word and departed. While he was still on the way, his servants met him with the news that his boy was living. When he inquired as to the time when his son got better, they said to him, "Yesterday, at one in the afternoon, the fever left him."

Then the father realized that this was the exact time at which Jesus had said to him, "Your son will live." So he and his whole household believed.

This was the second sign Jesus performed after coming from Judea to Galilee.

John 4:46–54 (NIV)

c. Healing a twelve-year discharge of blood witnessed by Jesus' disciples and the healed woman.

(The miracle of healing the woman with the twelve-year-long discharge of blood.)

While he was saying this, a synagogue leader came and knelt before him and said, "My daughter has just died. But come and put your hand on her, and she will live." Jesus got up and went with him, and so did his disciples.

Just then a woman who had been subject to bleeding for twelve years came up behind him and touched the edge of his cloak. She said to herself, "If I only touch his cloak, I will be healed."

Jesus turned and saw her. "Take heart, daughter," he said, "your faith has healed you." And the woman was healed at that moment.

Matthew 9:18–22 (NIV)

And a woman was there who had been subject to bleeding for twelve years. She had suffered a great deal under the care of many doctors and had spent all she had, yet instead of getting better she grew worse. When she heard about Jesus, she came up behind him in the crowd and touched his cloak, because she thought, "If I just touch his clothes, I will be healed." Immediately her bleeding stopped and she felt in her body that she was freed from her suffering.

At once Jesus realized that power had gone out from him. He turned around in the crowd and asked, "Who touched my clothes?"

"You see the people crowding against you," his disciples answered, "and yet you can ask, 'Who touched me?'"

But Jesus kept looking around to see who had done it. Then the woman, knowing what had happened to her, came and fell at his feet and, trembling with fear, told him the whole truth. He said to her, "Daughter, your faith has healed you. Go in peace and be freed from your suffering."

Mark 5:25–34 (NIV)

Now when Jesus returned, a crowd welcomed him, for they were all expecting him. Then a man named Jairus, a synagogue leader, came and fell at Jesus' feet, pleading with him to come to his house because his only daughter, a girl of about twelve, was dying.

As Jesus was on his way, the crowds almost crushed him. And a woman was there who had been subject to bleeding for twelve years,[a] but no one could heal her. She came up behind him and touched

When Only God Knew

the edge of his cloak, and immediately her bleeding stopped.

"Who touched me?" Jesus asked.

When they all denied it, Peter said, "Master, the people are crowding and pressing against you."

But Jesus said, "Someone touched me; I know that power has gone out from me."

Then the woman, seeing that she could not go unnoticed, came trembling and fell at his feet. In the presence of all the people, she told why she had touched him and how she had been instantly healed. Then he said to her, "Daughter, your faith has healed you. Go in peace."

Luke 8:40–48 (NIV)

d. Healing the synagogue leader's dead or dying daughter witnessed by Jesus' disciples, the synagogue leader, members of his household, and his daughter and reported throughout the synagogue leader's district.

(The miracle of healing the synagogue leader's dead or dying daughter.)

While he was saying this, a synagogue leader came and knelt before him and said, "My daughter has just died. But come and put your hand on her, and she will live." Jesus got up and went with him, and so did his disciples.

When Jesus entered the synagogue leader's house and saw the noisy crowd and people playing pipes, he said, "Go away. The girl is not dead but asleep." But they laughed at him. After the crowd had been put outside, he went in and took the girl by the hand,

and she got up. News of this spread through all that region.

Matthew 9:18–19, 23–26 (NIV)

e. Healing two blind men witnessed by Jesus' disciples, the blind men and reported throughout the blind men's district.

(The miracle of healing two blind men.)

As Jesus went on from [healing the synagogue leader's daughter], two blind men followed him, calling out, "Have mercy on us, Son of David!"

When he had gone indoors, the blind men came to him, and he asked them, "Do you believe that I am able to do this?"

"Yes, Lord," they replied.

Then he touched their eyes and said, "According to your faith, let it be done to you"; and their sight was restored. Jesus warned them sternly, "See that no one knows about this." But they went out and spread the news about him all over that region.

Matthew 9:27–31 (NIV)

f. Healing a demon-possessed man unable to speak witnessed by Jesus' disciples, including Matthew, the mute man, and those who brought the man to Jesus and known to the Pharisees.

(The miracle of healing a demon-possessed man unable to speak.)

While [the healed blind men were going out and spreading the news about Jesus having healed them] a man who was demon-possessed and could not talk was brought to Jesus. And when the demon was driven out, the man who had been mute spoke. The crowd was amazed and said, "Nothing like this has ever been seen in Israel."

But the Pharisees said, "It is by the prince of demons that he drives out demons."

Matthew 9:32–34 (NIV)

g. Healing the sick and feeding five thousand men, besides women and children, from only five loaves of bread and two fish witnessed by over five thousand people, including Jesus' disciples.

(The miracle of healing the sick and feeding five thousand men, besides women and children, from only five loaves of bread and two fish.)

When Jesus heard that John the Baptist had been beheaded in prison, he withdrew by boat privately to a solitary place. Hearing of this, the crowds followed him on foot from the towns. When Jesus landed and saw a large crowd, he had compassion on them and healed their sick.

As evening approached, the disciples came to him and said, "This is a remote place, and it's already getting late. Send the crowds away, so they can go to the villages and buy themselves some food."

Jesus replied, "They do not need to go away. You give them something to eat."

"We have here only five loaves of bread and two fish," they answered.

"Bring them here to me," he said. And he directed the people to sit down on the grass. Taking the five loaves and the two fish and looking up to heaven, he gave thanks and broke the loaves. Then he gave them to the disciples, and the disciples gave them to the people. They all ate and were satisfied, and the disciples picked up twelve basketfuls of broken pieces that were left over. The number of those who ate was about five thousand men, besides women and children.

Matthew 14:13–21 (NIV)

(The miracle of feeding five thousand men, besides women and children, from only five loaves of bread and two fish.)

Some time after Jesus had explained to his disciples who He was, Jesus crossed to the far shore of the Sea of Galilee [that is, the Sea of Tiberias], and a great crowd of people followed him because they saw the signs he had performed by healing the sick. Then Jesus went up on a mountainside and sat down with his disciples. The Jewish Passover Festival was near.

When Jesus looked up and saw a great crowd coming toward him, he said to Philip, "Where shall we buy bread for these people to eat?" He asked this only to test him, for he already had in mind what he was going to do.

Philip answered him, "It would take more than half a year's wages to buy enough bread for each one to have a bite!"

Another of his disciples, Andrew, Simon Peter's brother, spoke up, "Here is a boy with five small barley loaves and two small fish, but how far will they go among so many?"

Jesus said, "Have the people sit down." There was plenty of grass in that place, and they sat down [about five thousand men were there]. Jesus then took the loaves, gave thanks, and distributed to those who were seated as much as they wanted. He did the same with the fish.

When they had all had enough to eat, he said to his disciples, "Gather the pieces that are left over. Let nothing be wasted." So they gathered them and filled twelve baskets with the pieces of the five barley loaves left over by those who had eaten.

John 6:1–13 (NIV)

h. Walking on water and calming the storm witnessed by Jesus' disciples.

(The miracle of Jesus' walking on water and calming the storm.)

Immediately after feeding the five thousand men, besides women and children, Jesus made the disciples get into the boat and go on ahead of him to the other side, while he dismissed the crowd. After he had dismissed them, he went up on a mountainside by himself to pray. Later that night, he was there alone, and the boat was already a considerable distance from land, buffeted by the waves because the wind was against it. Shortly before dawn Jesus went out to them, walking on the lake. When the disciples saw him walking on the lake, they were terrified. "It's a ghost," they said, and cried out in fear. But Jesus immediately said to them: "Take courage! It is I. Don't be afraid." "Lord, if it's you," Peter replied, "tell me to come to you on the water." "Come," he said. Then Peter got down out of the boat, walked on the water and came toward Jesus. But when he saw the wind, he was afraid and, beginning to sink, cried out, "Lord, save me!" Immediately Jesus reached out his hand and caught him. "You of little faith," he said, "why did you doubt?" And when they climbed into the boat, the wind died down. Then those who were in the boat worshiped him, saying, "Truly you are the Son of God."

Matthew 14:22–33 (NIV)

i. Healing the daughter of a Canaanite woman witnessed by Jesus' disciples, the woman, and her daughter.

(The miracle of healing the daughter of a Canaanite woman.)

Leaving a place where the Jewish Pharisees and Jewish elders challenged Him because his disciples had broken the tradition of the elders, Jesus withdrew to the region of Tyre and Sidon. A Canaanite woman from that vicinity came to him, crying out, "Lord, Son of David, have mercy on me! My daughter is demon-possessed and suffering terribly."

Jesus did not answer a word. So his disciples came to him and urged him, "Send her away, for she keeps crying out after us."

He answered, "I was sent only to the lost sheep of Israel."

The woman came and knelt before him. "Lord, help me!" she said.

When Only God Knew

He replied, "It is not right to take the children's bread and toss it to the dogs."

"Yes it is, Lord," she said. "Even the dogs eat the crumbs that fall from their master's table."

Then Jesus said to her, "Woman, you have great faith! Your request is granted." And her daughter was healed at that moment.

Matthew 15:21–28 (NIV)

j. Healing the lame, the blind, the cripple, the mute, and many others and feeding four thousand men, besides women and children, from seven loaves of bread and a few small fish witnessed by over four thousand people, including Jesus' disciples.

(The miracle of healing the lame, the blind, the cripple, the mute, and many others and feeding four thousand men, besides women and children, from seven loaves of bread and a few small fish.)

After healing the Canaanite woman's daughter Jesus, went along the Sea of Galilee. Then he went up on a mountainside and sat down. Great crowds came to him, bringing the lame, the blind, the crippled, the mute and many others, and laid them at his feet; and he healed them. The people were amazed when they saw the mute speaking, the crippled made well, the lame walking and the blind seeing. And they praised the God of Israel.

Jesus called his disciples to him and said, "I have compassion for these people; they have already been with me three days and have nothing to eat. I do not want to send them away hungry, or they may collapse on the way."

His disciples answered, "Where could we get enough bread in this remote place to feed such a crowd?"

"How many loaves do you have?" Jesus asked.

"Seven," they replied, "and a few small fish."

He told the crowd to sit down on the ground. Then he took the seven loaves and the fish, and when he had given thanks, he broke them and gave them to the disciples, and they in turn to the people. They all ate and were satisfied. Afterward the disciples picked up seven basketfuls of broken pieces that were left over. The number of those who ate was four thousand men, besides women and children.

Matthew 15:29–38 (NIV)

(The miracle of feeding four thousand men, besides women and children, from seven loaves of bread and a few small fish.)

During those days another large crowd gathered. Since they had nothing to eat, Jesus called his disciples to him and said, "I have compassion for these people; they have already been with me three days and have nothing to eat. If I send them home hungry, they will collapse on the way, because some of them have come a long distance."

His disciples answered, "But where in this remote place can anyone get enough bread to feed them?"

"How many loaves do you have?" Jesus asked.

"Seven," they replied.

When Only God Knew

He told the crowd to sit down on the ground. When he had taken the seven loaves and given thanks, he broke them and gave them to his disciples to distribute to the people, and they did so. They had a few small fish as well; he gave thanks for them also and told the disciples to distribute them. The people ate and were satisfied. Afterward the disciples picked up seven basketfuls of broken pieces that were left over. About four thousand were present.

Mark 8:1–9 (NIV)

k. Paying taxes with a coin from a fish's mouth witnessed by the Apostle Peter and probably Matthew

(The miracle of paying taxes with a coin from a fish's mouth.)

After Jesus and his disciples arrived in Capernaum,[670] the collectors of the two-drachma temple tax came to Peter and asked, "Doesn't your teacher pay the temple tax?"

"Yes, he does," he replied.

When Peter came into the house, Jesus was the first to speak. "What do you think, Simon?" he asked. "From whom do the kings of the earth collect duty and taxes—from their own children or from others?"

"From others," Peter answered.

"Then the children are exempt," Jesus said to him. "But so that we may not cause offense, go to the lake and throw out your line. Take the first fish you catch; open its mouth and you will find a four-drachma coin. Take it and give it to them for my tax and yours."

Matthew 17:24–27 (NIV)

1. Healing a demon-possessed man in the synagogue witnessed by the Apostles, Simon also called Peter, Andrew, Peter's brother, and John and James, the sons of Zebedee, the demon-possessed man and those in the synagogue and known by people in the "whole region of Galilee."

(The miracle of healing a demon-possessed man in the synagogue.)

Jesus, and the Apostles, Peter, Andrew, John and James, went to Capernaum, and when the Sabbath came, Jesus went into the synagogue and began to teach. The people were amazed at his teaching, because he taught them as one who had authority, not as the teachers of the law. Just then a man in their synagogue who was possessed by an impure spirit cried out, "What do you want with us, Jesus of Nazareth? Have you come to destroy us? I know who you are—the Holy One of God!"

"Be quiet!" said Jesus sternly. "Come out of him!" The impure spirit shook the man violently and came out of him with a shriek.

The people were all so amazed that they asked each other, "What is this? A new teaching—and with authority! He even gives orders to impure spirits and they obey him." News about him spread quickly over the whole region of Galilee.

Mark 1:21–28 (NIV)

When Only God Knew

m. Healing others, including Peter's mother-in-law, witnessed by the Apostles, Simon, Andrew, John, and James, those healed, including but not limited to Peter's mother-in-law, and the whole town where Peter's mother-in-law lived.

(The miracle of healing others, including Peter's mother-in-law.)

As soon as they left the synagogue, they went with James and John to the home of Simon and Andrew. Simon's mother-in-law was in bed with a fever, and they immediately told Jesus about her. So he went to her, took her hand, and helped her up. The fever left her, and she began to wait on them.

That evening after sunset the people brought to Jesus all the sick and demon-possessed. The whole town gathered at the door, and Jesus healed many who had various diseases. He also drove out many demons, but he would not let the demons speak because they knew who he was.

Mark 1:29–34 (NIV)

n. Curing a man of leprosy witnessed by the cured man, probably Peter and at least some of Jesus' other disciples and known to the cured man's priest and to so many others to whom the cured man spread the news that "Jesus could no longer enter a town openly."

(The miracle of curing a man of leprosy.)

A man with leprosy came to him and begged him on his knees, "If you are willing, you can make me clean."

Jesus was indignant. He reached out his hand and touched the man. "I am willing," he said. "Be clean!" Immediately the leprosy left him and he was cleansed.

Jesus sent him away at once with a strong warning: "See that you don't tell this to anyone. But go, show yourself to the priest and offer the sacrifices that Moses commanded for your cleansing, as a testimony to them." Instead he went out and began to talk freely, spreading the news. As a result, Jesus could no longer enter a town openly but stayed outside in lonely places. Yet the people still came to him from everywhere.

Mark 1:40–45 (NIV)

o. Healing a paralyzed man witnessed by the paralyzed man, his friends who brought the man to Jesus, some teachers of the law, other residents of Capernaum (probably "in such large numbers that there was no room left" in the house where the man was healed) and most probably some or all of his disciples.

(The miracle of healing a paralyzed man.)

A few days after Jesus cured the man with leprosy when Jesus again entered Capernaum, the people heard that he had come home. They gathered in such large numbers that there was no room left, not even outside the door, and he preached the word to them. Some men came, bringing to him a paralyzed man, carried by four of them. Since they could not get him to Jesus because of the crowd, they made an opening in the roof above Jesus by digging through it and

When Only God Knew

then lowered the mat the man was lying on. When Jesus saw their faith, he said to the paralyzed man, "Son, your sins are forgiven."

Now some teachers of the law were sitting there, thinking to themselves, "Why does this fellow talk like that? He's blaspheming! Who can forgive sins but God alone?" Immediately Jesus knew in his spirit that this was what they were thinking in their hearts, and he said to them, "Why are you thinking these things? Which is easier: to say to this paralyzed man, 'Your sins are forgiven,' or to say, 'Get up, take your mat and walk'? But I want you to know that the Son of Man has authority on earth to forgive sins." So he said to the man, "I tell you, get up, take your mat and go home." He got up, took his mat and walked out in full view of them all. This amazed everyone and they praised God, saying, "We have never seen anything like this!"

Mark 2:1–12 (NIV)

p. Calming a storm witnessed by Jesus' disciples and perhaps others out in boats.

(The miracle of calming a storm.)

That day after Jesus explained parables to his disciples, including the parable of the mustard seed, when evening came, he said to his disciples, "Let us go over to the other side." Leaving the crowd behind, they took him along, just as he was, in the boat. There were also other boats with him. A furious squall came up, and the waves broke over the boat, so that it was nearly swamped. Jesus was in the stern, sleeping on a cushion. The disciples woke him and said to him, "Teacher, don't you care if we drown?"

He got up, rebuked the wind and said to the waves, "Quiet! Be still!" Then the wind died down and it was completely calm.

He said to his disciples, "Why are you so afraid? Do you still have no faith?"

They were terrified and asked each other, "Who is this? Even the wind and the waves obey him!"

Mark 4:35–41, NIV

q. Drowning demons which Jesus caused to flee from a demon-possessed man witnessed by Jesus' disciples, the demon-possessed man and herdsmen and reported to many others.

(The miracle of drowning demons which Jesus caused to flee from a demon-possessed man.)

Jesus and His disciples went across the lake to the region of the Gerasenes.[671] When Jesus got out of the boat, a man with an impure spirit came from the tombs to meet him. This man lived in the tombs, and no one could bind him anymore, not even with a chain. For he had often been chained hand and foot, but he tore the chains apart and broke the irons on his feet. No one was strong enough to subdue him. Night and day among the tombs and in the hills he would cry out and cut himself with stones.

When he saw Jesus from a distance, he ran and fell on his knees in front of him. He shouted at the top of his voice, "What do you want with me, Jesus, Son of the Most High God? In God's name don't torture me!" For Jesus had said to him, "Come out of this man, you impure spirit!"

Then Jesus asked him, "What is your name?"

"My name is Legion," he replied, "for we are many." And he begged Jesus again and again not to send them out of the area.

A large herd of pigs was feeding on the nearby hillside. The demons begged Jesus, "Send us among the pigs; allow us to go into them." He gave them permission, and the impure spirits came out and went into the pigs. The herd, about two thousand in number, rushed down the steep bank into the lake and were drowned.

Those tending the pigs ran off and reported this in the town and countryside, and the people went out to see what had happened. When they came to Jesus, they saw the man who had been possessed by the legion of demons, sitting there, dressed and in his right mind; and they were afraid. Those who had seen it told the people what had happened to the demon-possessed man—and told about the pigs as well.

Mark 5:1–16 (NIV)

Jesus and his disciples sailed to the region of the Gerasenes, which is across the lake from Galilee. When Jesus stepped ashore, he was met by a demon-possessed man from the town. For a long time this man had not worn clothes or lived in a house, but had lived in the tombs. When he saw Jesus, he cried out and fell at his feet, shouting at the top of his voice, "What do you want with me, Jesus, Son of the Most High God? I beg you, don't torture me!" For Jesus had commanded the impure spirit to come out of the man. Many times it had seized him, and though he was chained hand and foot and kept under guard, he had broken his chains and had been driven by the demon into solitary places.

Jesus asked him, "What is your name?"

"Legion," he replied, because many demons had gone into him. And they begged Jesus repeatedly not to order them to go into the Abyss.

A large herd of pigs was feeding there on the hillside. The demons begged Jesus to let them go into the pigs, and he gave them permission. When the demons came out of the man, they went into the pigs, and the herd rushed down the steep bank into the lake and was drowned.

When those tending the pigs saw what had happened, they ran off and reported this in the town and countryside, and the people went out to see what had happened. When they came to Jesus, they found the man from whom the demons had gone out, sitting at Jesus' feet, dressed and in his right mind; and they were afraid. Those who had seen it told the people how the demon-possessed man had been cured. Then all the people of the region of the Gerasenes asked Jesus to leave them, because they were overcome with fear. So he got into the boat and left.

The man from whom the demons had gone out begged to go with him, but Jesus sent him away, saying, "Return home and tell how much God has done for you." So the man went away and told all over town how much Jesus had done for him.

Luke 8:26–39 (NIV)

r. Healing the dying daughter of Jairus, a synagogue leader, witnessed by Jesus' disciples, the synagogue leader, his wife, members of the child's household, and his daughter and reported throughout the synagogue leader's district.

(The miracle of healing the dying daughter of Jairus, a synagogue leader.)

Then one of the synagogue leaders, named Jairus, came, and when he saw Jesus, he fell at his feet. He pleaded earnestly with him, "My little daughter is dying. Please come and put your hands on her so that she will be healed and live." So Jesus went with him. A large crowd followed and pressed around him… While Jesus was still speaking, some people came from the house of Jairus, the synagogue leader. "Your daughter is dead," they said. "Why bother the teacher anymore?"

Overhearing what they said, Jesus told him, "Don't be afraid; just believe."

He did not let anyone follow him except Peter, James and John the brother of James. When they came to the home of the synagogue leader, Jesus saw a commotion, with people crying and wailing loudly. He went in and said to them, "Why all this commotion and wailing? The child is not dead but asleep." But they laughed at him.

After he put them all out, he took the child's father and mother and the disciples who were with him, and went in where the child was. He took her by the hand and said to her, "Talitha koum!" [which means "Little girl, I say to you, get up!"]. Immediately the girl stood up and began to walk around (she was twelve years old). At this they were completely astonished. He gave strict orders not to let anyone know about this, and told them to give her something to eat.

Mark 5:22–24, 35–43 (NIV)

Now when Jesus returned, a crowd welcomed him, for they were all expecting him. Then a man named Jairus, a synagogue leader, came and fell at Jesus' feet, pleading with him to come to his house because his only daughter, a girl of about twelve, was dying.

...

While Jesus was still speaking, someone came from the house of Jairus, the synagogue leader. "Your daughter is dead," he said. "Don't bother the teacher anymore." Hearing this, Jesus said to Jairus, "Don't be afraid; just believe, and she will be healed." When he arrived at the house of Jairus, he did not let anyone go in with him except Peter, John and James, and the child's father and mother. Meanwhile, all the people were wailing and mourning for her. "Stop wailing," Jesus said. "She is not dead but asleep."

They laughed at him, knowing that she was dead. But he took her by the hand and said, "My child, get up!" Her spirit returned, and at once she stood up. Then Jesus told them to give her something to eat.

Luke 8:40–42, 49–55 (NIV)

s. Healing the deaf and dumb man witnessed by the deaf and dumb man, people who brought the man to Jesus and some of Jesus' disciples and reported to others near where the miracle occurred.

(The miracle of healing the deaf and dumb man.)

Then Jesus left the vicinity of Tyre and went through Sidon, down to the Sea of Galilee and into the region of the Decapolis.[672] There some people brought to him a man who was deaf and could hardly talk, and they begged Jesus to place his hand on him.

After he took him aside, away from the crowd, Jesus put his fingers into the man's ears. Then he spit and touched the man's tongue. He looked up to heaven and with a deep sigh said to him, "Ephphatha!" [which means "Be opened!"]. At this, the man's ears were opened, his tongue was loosened and he began to speak plainly.

Jesus commanded them not to tell anyone. But the more he did so, the more they kept talking about it. People were overwhelmed with amazement. "He has done everything well," they said. "He even makes the deaf hear and the mute speak."

Mark 7:31–37 (NIV)

t. Healing the blind man in Bethsaida witnessed by Jesus' disciples, the blind man and, apparently, people who were where the healing took place.

(The miracle of healing the blind man in Bethsaida.) [673]

They, [Jesus and His disciples], came to Bethsaida, and some people brought a blind man and begged Jesus to touch him. He took the blind man by the hand and led him outside the village. When he had spit on the man's eyes and put his hands on him, Jesus asked, "Do you see anything?"

He looked up and said, "I see people; they look like trees walking around."

Once more Jesus put his hands on the man's eyes. Then his eyes were opened, his sight was restored, and he saw everything clearly.

Mark 8:22–25 (NIV)

u. Jesus' transfiguration witnessed by Peter, James, and John.

(The miracle of Jesus' transfiguration.)

After six days Jesus took Peter, James and John with him and led them up a high mountain, where they were all alone. There he was transfigured before them. His clothes became dazzling white, whiter than anyone in the world could bleach them. And there appeared before them Elijah and Moses, who were talking with Jesus.

Peter said to Jesus, "Rabbi, it is good for us to be here. Let us put up three shelters—one for you,

When Only God Knew

one for Moses and one for Elijah." (He did not know what to say, they were so frightened).

Then a cloud appeared and covered them, and a voice came from the cloud: "This is my Son, whom I love. Listen to him!"

Suddenly, when they looked around, they no longer saw anyone with them except Jesus.

As they were coming down the mountain, Jesus gave them orders not to tell anyone what they had seen until the Son of Man had risen from the dead. They kept the matter to themselves, discussing what "rising from the dead" meant.

Mark 9:2–10 (NIV)

v. Casting out from a boy of a spirit that caused the boy to be unable to speak and to injure himself witnessed by the disciples, the boy, his father, a large crowd around them, and the teachers of the law.

(The miracle of casting out from a boy of a spirit that caused the boy to be unable to speak and to injure himself.)

When [Jesus, Peter, James and John came from the mountain at which Jesus was transfigured] to the other disciples, they saw a large crowd around them and the teachers of the law arguing with them. As soon as all the people saw Jesus, they were overwhelmed with wonder and ran to greet him.

"What are you arguing with them about?" he asked.

A man in the crowd answered, "Teacher, I brought you my son, who is possessed by a spirit that has robbed him of speech. Whenever it seizes him, it throws him to the ground. He foams at the mouth, gnashes his teeth and becomes rigid. I asked your disciples to drive out the spirit, but they could not."

"You unbelieving generation," Jesus replied, "how long shall I stay with you? How long shall I put up with you? Bring the boy to me."

So they brought him. When the spirit saw Jesus, it immediately threw the boy into a convulsion. He fell to the ground and rolled around, foaming at the mouth. Jesus asked the boy's father, "How long has he been like this?"

"From childhood," he answered. "It has often thrown him into fire or water to kill him. But if you can do anything, take pity on us and help us."

"'If you can'?" said Jesus. "Everything is possible for one who believes."

Immediately the boy's father exclaimed, "I do believe; help me overcome my unbelief!"

When Jesus saw that a crowd was running to the scene, he rebuked the impure spirit. "You deaf and mute spirit," he said, "I command you, come out of him and never enter him again."

The spirit shrieked, convulsed him violently and came out. The boy looked so much like a corpse that many said, "He's dead." But Jesus took him by the hand and lifted him to his feet, and he stood up.

Mark 9:14–27 (NIV)

When Only God Knew

w. Healing the blind beggar witnessed by Jesus' disciples and a large crowd.

(The miracle of healing the blind beggar, Bartimaeus.)

Then they came to Jericho. As Jesus and his disciples, together with a large crowd, were leaving the city, a blind man, Bartimaeus [which means "son of Timaeus"], was sitting by the roadside begging. When he heard that it was Jesus of Nazareth, he began to shout, "Jesus, Son of David, have mercy on me!" Many rebuked him and told him to be quiet, but he shouted all the more, "Son of David, have mercy on me!"

Jesus stopped and said, "Call him."

So they called to the blind man, "Cheer up! On your feet! He's calling you." Throwing his cloak aside, he jumped to his feet and came to Jesus.

"What do you want me to do for you?" Jesus asked him.

The blind man said, "Rabbi, I want to see."

"Go," said Jesus, "your faith has healed you." Immediately he received his sight and followed Jesus along the road.

Mark 10:46–52 (NIV)

x. Catching fish where none had been caught witnessed by Peter, James, and John.

(The miracle of catching fish where none had been caught.)

One day as Jesus was standing by the Lake of Gennesaret,[674] the people were crowding around him and listening to the word of God. He saw at the water's edge two boats, left there by the fishermen, who were washing their nets. He got into one of the boats, the one belonging to Simon, and asked him to put out a little from shore. Then he sat down and taught the people from the boat.

When he had finished speaking, he said to Simon, "Put out into deep water, and let down the nets for a catch." Simon answered, "Master, we've worked hard all night and haven't caught anything. But because you say so, I will let down the nets." When they had done so, they caught such a large number of fish that their nets began to break. So they signaled their partners in the other boat to come and help them, and they came and filled both boats so full that they began to sink. When Simon Peter saw this, he fell at Jesus' knees and said, "Go away from me, Lord; I am a sinful man!" For he and all his companions were astonished at the catch of fish they had taken, and so were James and John, the sons of Zebedee, Simon's partners.

Then Jesus said to Simon, "Don't be afraid; from now on you will fish for people." So they pulled their boats up on shore, left everything and followed him.

Luke 5:1–11 (NIV)

When Only God Knew

y. Healing a man with the shriveled hand in the synagogue witnessed by the man, Pharisees and the teachers of the law, and others in the synagogue.

(The miracle of healing a man with the shriveled hand in the synagogue.)

On another Sabbath he, [Jesus], went into the synagogue and was teaching, and a man was there whose right hand was shriveled. The Pharisees and the teachers of the law were looking for a reason to accuse Jesus, so they watched him closely to see if he would heal on the Sabbath. But Jesus knew what they were thinking and said to the man with the shriveled hand, "Get up and stand in front of everyone." So he got up and stood there.

Then Jesus said to them, "I ask you, which is lawful on the Sabbath: to do good or to do evil, to save life or to destroy it?"

He looked around at them all, and then said to the man, "Stretch out your hand." He did so, and his hand was completely restored.

Luke 6:6–10 (NIV)

z. Healing a centurion's deathly ill servant witnessed by the centurion, his servant, Jewish elders, and, apparently, the crowd following Jesus to the centurion's house.

(The miracle of healing a centurion's deathly ill servant.)

When Jesus had finished [speaking about building a house on the rock] to the people who were listening, he entered Capernaum. There a centurion's servant, whom his master valued highly, was sick and about to die. The centurion heard of Jesus and sent some elders of the Jews to him, asking him to come and heal his servant. When they came to Jesus, they pleaded earnestly with him, "This man deserves to have you do this, because he loves our nation and has built our synagogue." So Jesus went with them.

He was not far from the house when the centurion sent friends to say to him: "Lord, don't trouble yourself, for I do not deserve to have you come under my roof. That is why I did not even consider myself worthy to come to you. But say the word, and my servant will be healed. For I myself am a man under authority, with soldiers under me. I tell this one, 'Go,' and he goes; and that one, 'Come,' and he comes. I say to my servant, 'Do this,' and he does it."

When Jesus heard this, he was amazed at him, and turning to the crowd following him, he said, "I tell you, I have not found such great faith even in Israel." Then the men who had been sent returned to the house and found the servant well.

Luke 7:1–10 (NIV)

aa. Raising a widow's dead son witnessed by Jesus' disciples, a large crowd, including the bearers of the son's bed, the widow and her son.

(The miracle of raising a widow's dead son.)

Soon afterward, Jesus went to a town called Nain, and his disciples and a large crowd went along with him. As he approached the town gate, a dead person was being carried out—the only son of his mother, and she was a widow. And a large crowd from the town was with her. When the Lord saw her, his heart went out to her and he said, "Don't cry."

Then he went up and touched the bier they were carrying him on, and the bearers stood still. He said, "Young man, I say to you, get up!" The dead man sat up and began to talk, and Jesus gave him back to his mother.

Luke 7:11–16 (NIV)

ab. Healing the man with dropsy witnessed by Pharisees and experts in the law.

(The miracle of healing the man with dropsy.)

One Sabbath, when Jesus went to eat in the house of a prominent Pharisee, he was being carefully watched. There in front of him was a man suffering from abnormal swelling of his body. Jesus asked the Pharisees and experts in the law, "Is it lawful to heal on the Sabbath or not?" But they remained silent. So taking hold of the man, he healed him and sent him on his way.

Then he asked them, "If one of you has a child or an ox that falls into a well on the Sabbath day, will you not immediately pull it out?" And they had nothing to say.

Luke 14:1–6 (NIV)

ac. Cleansing ten lepers witnessed by the ten lepers and reported to their priests.

(The miracle of cleansing ten lepers.)

Now on his way to Jerusalem, Jesus traveled along the border between Samaria and Galilee. As he was going into a village, ten men who had leprosy met him. They stood at a distance and called out in a loud voice, "Jesus, Master, have pity on us!" When he saw them, he said, "Go, show yourselves to the priests." And as they went, they were cleansed.

Luke 17:11–14 (NIV)

ad. Healing Malchus' severed ear witnessed by Jesus' disciples, including Judas Iscariot, Malchus and the chief priests and officers of the temple and the Jewish elders who had come to arrest him as to whom there is no report that it did not happen.

(The miracle of healing Malchus' ear.)

While he was still speaking [to his disciples after Jesus prayed at the Mount of Olives just before his arrest by the Jewish authorities], a crowd came up, and the man who was called Judas, one of the Twelve, was leading them. He approached Jesus to kiss him, but Jesus asked him, "Judas, are you betraying the Son of Man with a kiss?" When Jesus' followers saw what was going to happen, they said, "Lord, should we strike with our swords?" And one of them struck the servant of the high priest, cutting off his right ear. But Jesus answered, "No more of this!" And he touched the man's ear and healed him.

Luke 22:47–51 (NIV)

When Only God Knew

ae. Healing the man at the Bethesda pool who had been an invalid for thirty-eight years witnessed by at least John, Jewish leaders, the man who was healed, and other disabled people who waited at the pool for healing.

(The miracle of healing the man at the Bethesda pool who had been an invalid for thirty-eight years.)

Some time later, Jesus went up to Jerusalem for one of the Jewish festivals. Now there is in Jerusalem near the Sheep Gate a pool, which in Aramaic is called Bethesda and which is surrounded by five covered colonnades. Here a great number of disabled people used to lie—the blind, the lame, the paralyzed. One who was there had been an invalid for thirty-eight years. When Jesus saw him lying there and learned that he had been in this condition for a long time, he asked him, "Do you want to get well?"

"Sir," the invalid replied, "I have no one to help me into the pool when the water is stirred. While I am trying to get in, someone else goes down ahead of me." Then Jesus said to him, "Get up! Pick up your mat and walk." At once the man was cured; he picked up his mat and walked. The day on which this took place was a Sabbath, and so the Jewish leaders said to the man who had been healed, "It is the Sabbath; the law forbids you to carry your mat."

But he replied, "The man who made me well said to me, 'Pick up your mat and walk.'" So they asked him, "Who is this fellow who told you to pick it up and walk?" The man who was healed had no idea who it was, for Jesus had slipped away into the crowd that was there. Later Jesus found him at the temple and said to him, "See, you are well again. Stop sinning or something worse may happen to you." The man went away and told the Jewish leaders that it was Jesus who had made him well.

John 5:1–15 (NIV)

af. Healing the man born blind witnessed by Jesus' disciples, including John, the man, his parents and neighbors, those who had formerly seen him blind and begging and investigated by the Pharisees.

(The miracle of healing the man born blind.)

As Jesus went along, he saw a man blind from birth. His disciples asked him, "Rabbi, who sinned, this man or his parents, that he was born blind?"

"Neither this man nor his parents sinned," said Jesus, "but this happened so that the works of God might be displayed in him. As long as it is day, we must do the works of him who sent me. Night is coming, when no one can work. While I am in the world, I am the light of the world."

After saying this, he spit on the ground, made some mud with the saliva, and put it on the man's eyes. "Go," he told him, "wash in the Pool of Siloam" [this word means "Sent"]. So the man went and washed, and came home seeing. His neighbors and those who had formerly seen him begging asked, "Isn't this the same man who used to sit and beg?" Some claimed that he was.

Others said, "No, he only looks like him." But he himself insisted, "I am the man." "How then were your eyes opened?" they asked. He replied, "The man

When Only God Knew

they call Jesus made some mud and put it on my eyes. He told me to go to Siloam and wash. So I went and washed, and then I could see."

"Where is this man?" they asked him. "I don't know," he said.

They brought to the Pharisees the man who had been blind. Now the day on which Jesus had made the mud and opened the man's eyes was a Sabbath. Therefore the Pharisees also asked him how he had received his sight. "He put mud on my eyes," the man replied, "and I washed, and now I see."

Some of the Pharisees said, "This man is not from God, for he does not keep the Sabbath." But others asked, "How can a sinner perform such signs?" So they were divided. Then they turned again to the blind man, "What have you to say about him? It was your eyes he opened." The man replied, "He is a prophet." They still did not believe that he had been blind and had received his sight until they sent for the man's parents. "Is this your son?" they asked. "Is this the one you say was born blind? How is it that now he can see?"

"We know he is our son," the parents answered, "and we know he was born blind. But how he can see now, or who opened his eyes, we don't know. Ask him. He is of age; he will speak for himself." His parents said this because they were afraid of the Jewish leaders, who already had decided that anyone who acknowledged that Jesus was the Messiah would be put out of the synagogue. That was why his parents said, "He is of age; ask him."

A second time they summoned the man who had been blind. "Give glory to God by telling the truth," they said. "We know this man is a sinner."

He replied, "Whether he is a sinner or not, I don't know. One thing I do know. I was blind but now I see!" Then they asked him, "What did he do to you? How did he open your eyes?" He answered, "I have told you already and you did not listen. Why do you want to hear it again? Do you want to become his disciples too?" Then they hurled insults at him and said, "You are this fellow's disciple! We are disciples of Moses! We know that God spoke to Moses, but as for this fellow, we don't even know where he comes from." The man answered, "Now that is remarkable! You don't know where he comes from, yet he opened my eyes. We know that God does not listen to sinners. He listens to the godly person who does his will. Nobody has ever heard of opening the eyes of a man born blind. If this man were not from God, he could do nothing."

John 9:1–32 (NIV)

ag. Raising Lazarus from the dead witnessed by Jesus' disciples, including John, Lazarus, Mary, and Martha, Lazarus' sisters, and Jews who had come to Martha and Mary to comfort them and reported to the Pharisees who had plotted to kill Jesus.

(The miracle of raising Lazarus from the dead.)

Now a man named Lazarus was sick. He was from Bethany, the village of Mary and her sister Martha. [This Mary, whose brother Lazarus now lay sick, was

When Only God Knew

the same one who poured perfume on the Lord and wiped his feet with her hair]. So the sisters sent word to Jesus, "Lord, the one you love is sick."

When he heard this, Jesus said, "This sickness will not end in death. No, it is for God's glory so that God's Son may be glorified through it." Now Jesus loved Martha and her sister and Lazarus. So when he heard that Lazarus was sick, he stayed where he was two more days, and then he said to his disciples, "Let us go back to Judea." "But Rabbi," they said, "a short while ago the Jews there tried to stone you, and yet you are going back?" Jesus answered, "Are there not twelve hours of daylight? Anyone who walks in the daytime will not stumble, for they see by this world's light. It is when a person walks at night that they stumble, for they have no light."

After he had said this, he went on to tell them, "Our friend Lazarus has fallen asleep; but I am going there to wake him up."

His disciples replied, "Lord, if he sleeps, he will get better." Jesus had been speaking of his death, but his disciples thought he meant natural sleep.

So then he told them plainly, "Lazarus is dead, and for your sake I am glad I was not there, so that you may believe. But let us go to him."

Then Thomas [also known as Didymus] said to the rest of the disciples, "Let us also go, that we may die with him."

On his arrival, Jesus found that Lazarus had already been in the tomb for four days. Now Bethany was less than two miles[b] from Jerusalem, and many Jews had come to Martha and Mary to comfort them in the loss of their brother. When Martha heard that

Jesus was coming, she went out to meet him, but Mary stayed at home.

"Lord," Martha said to Jesus, "if you had been here, my brother would not have died. But I know that even now God will give you whatever you ask."

Jesus said to her, "Your brother will rise again."

Martha answered, "I know he will rise again in the resurrection at the last day." Jesus said to her, "I am the resurrection and the life. The one who believes in me will live, even though they die; and whoever lives by believing in me will never die. Do you believe this?"

"Yes, Lord," she replied, "I believe that you are the Messiah, the Son of God, who is to come into the world."

After she had said this, she went back and called her sister Mary aside. "The Teacher is here," she said, "and is asking for you." When Mary heard this, she got up quickly and went to him. Now Jesus had not yet entered the village, but was still at the place where Martha had met him. When the Jews who had been with Mary in the house, comforting her, noticed how quickly she got up and went out, they followed her, supposing she was going to the tomb to mourn there.

When Mary reached the place where Jesus was and saw him, she fell at his feet and said, "Lord, if you had been here, my brother would not have died."

When Jesus saw her weeping, and the Jews who had come along with her also weeping, he was deeply moved in spirit and troubled. "Where have you laid him?" he asked.

"Come and see, Lord," they replied. Jesus wept. Then the Jews said, "See how he loved him!" But some of them said, "Could not he who opened the eyes of the blind man have kept this man from dying?"

Jesus, once more deeply moved, came to the tomb. It was a cave with a stone laid across the entrance. "Take away the stone," he said.

"But, Lord," said Martha, the sister of the dead man, "by this time there is a bad odor, for he has been there four days." Then Jesus said, "Did I not tell you that if you believe, you will see the glory of God?" So they took away the stone. Then Jesus looked up and said, "Father, I thank you that you have heard me. I knew that you always hear me, but I said this for the benefit of the people standing here, that they may believe that you sent me."

When he had said this, Jesus called in a loud voice, "Lazarus, come out!" The dead man came out, his hands and feet wrapped with strips of linen, and a cloth around his face. Jesus said to them, "Take off the grave clothes and let him go." Therefore many of the Jews who had come to visit Mary, and had seen what Jesus did, believed in him. But some of them went to the Pharisees and told them what Jesus had done.

John 11:1–46 (NIV)

ah. The second miracle of catching fish witnessed by Jesus' disciples.

[According to John 20:30–31, after] "Jesus performed many other signs in the presence of his disciples, which are not recorded in" the Book of John),

Jesus appeared again to his disciples, by the Sea of Galilee. It happened this way: Simon Peter, Thomas [also known as Didymus], Nathanael from Cana in Galilee, the sons of Zebedee, and two other disciples were together. "I'm going out to fish," Simon Peter told them, and they said, "We'll go with you." So they went out and got into the boat, but that night they caught nothing.

Early in the morning, Jesus stood on the shore, but the disciples did not realize that it was Jesus. He called out to them, "Friends, haven't you any fish?" "No," they answered. He said, "Throw your net on the right side of the boat and you will find some." When they did, they were unable to haul the net in because of the large number of fish. Then the disciple whom Jesus loved said to Peter, "It is the Lord!" As soon as Simon Peter heard him say, "It is the Lord," he wrapped his outer garment around him [for he had taken it off] and jumped into the water. The other disciples followed in the boat, towing the net full of fish, for they were not far from shore, about a hundred yards.[c] When they landed, they saw a fire of burning coals there with fish on it, and some bread. Jesus said to them, "Bring some of the fish you have just caught." So Simon Peter climbed back into the boat and dragged the net ashore. It was full of large fish, 153, but even with so many the net was not torn. Jesus said to them, "Come and have breakfast." None of the disciples dared ask him, "Who are you?" They knew it was the Lord.

John 21:1–12 (NIV)

When Only God Knew

So many miracles, so many witnesses, many of whom would, presumably, have been alive well past the writing of most of the Gospels, so much reason for the Jewish leaders to disprove the miracles, but there is no report that any of the thousands of witnesses to those miracles ever denied that they occurred.

3. Crucifixion of Jesus

Fact Stated: Matthew, Mark, Luke, and John (written 50–90 AD)
Fact Confirmed: 1968 AD (1900 years later ±)

Psalm 22:16–17 (written 1440–450 BC) is understood to be prophesying that when Jesus will be crucified, his hands and feet will be pierced with nails.[675] Psalm 22:16 (NIV) says, "Dogs surround me, a pack of villains encircles me; they pierce my hands and my feet."

The Gospels of Luke and John support the historical conclusion that the story of Jesus' hands and feet were pierced with nails. In John 20:25–28, we see Doubting Thomas after the other disciples told him that they had seen Jesus:

> So the other disciples told him, "We have seen the Lord!" But he said to them, "Unless I see the nail marks in his hands and put my finger where the nails were, and put my hand into his side, I will not believe." A week later his disciples were in the house again, and Thomas was with them. Though the doors were locked, Jesus came and stood among them and said, "Peace be with you!" Then he said to Thomas, "Put your finger here; see my hands. Reach out your hand and put it into my side. Stop doubting and believe." Thomas said to him, "My Lord and my God!"
>
> John 20:25–28

Even before that, Jesus appeared to the disciples, and they saw the nail piercings. Luke 24:37–39 says,

They were startled and frightened, thinking they saw a ghost. He said to them, "Why are you troubled, and why do doubts rise in your minds? Look at my hands and my feet. It is I myself! Touch me and see; a ghost does not have flesh and bones, as you see I have."

Despite these historical reports, skeptics claimed it could not have happened because they said that Romans only tied criminals to the cross rather than used nails.[676] Skeptics also claimed crucified criminals were buried in mass graves.[677] Again they were proven wrong. The skeleton of a man excavated in 1968 "confirms the Bible's description of crucifixion by nails through the hands and feet and legs broken below the knee."[678] "This skeleton also confirms the fact Romans sometimes allowed crucifixion victims to be buried honorably ."[679]

4. Jesus' Resurrection

Fact Stated: Matthew, Mark, Luke, and John (written 50–90 AD)
Fact Confirmed: No evidence denying

a. Eyewitness Accounts

The Bible, the most contemporary and therefore reliable ancient history,[680] reports many persons who witnessed the death and resurrection of Jesus. One author reiterated the Bible report that[681]

there were many eyewitnesses at Jesus' death, including family, disciples, Romans and hostile accusers! They experienced three hours of darkness and a mighty earthquake that split rocks, opened graves and tore the curtain in the temple from top to bottom. Jesus' followers showed deep sorrow, and the crowds were silenced and beat their breasts. Had

When Only God Knew

these unusual events not occurred, as the biblical record states, few would have believed the account [*See, e.g.*, Matthew 27:45, 51–54; Mark 15:33, 38; Luke 23:44–45].

There was no doubt Jesus was dead in the mind of Pilate, the Roman centurion and two members of the ruling Jewish administration. Joseph of Arimathea asked Pilate to release the body of Jesus for burial. Pilate summoned the centurion for confirmation of Jesus' death. [The same soldier earlier acknowledged Christ as the "Son of God" at the time of His death]. Joseph and Nicodemus, both members of the Sanhedrin, buried Jesus' body before the beginning of the holy day [*See* Matthew 27:57–60; Mark 15:39, 42–46; Luke 23:50–54, John 19:38–42].

Chief priests met with Pilate to demand a guard on the tomb, apparently on the first holy day of Unleavened Bread. They sealed the tomb and set a watch. They had no doubt He was dead! [*See* Matthew 27:62–66].

Female relatives and followers of Jesus were convinced He was dead. They purchased spices and fragrant oils after the end of the holy day. These they prepared on the day before the weekly Sabbath and planned to add them to the myrrh and aloes used by Joseph and Nicodemus [*See* Luke 23:56, John 19:39].

After an earthquake, an angel descended to move the stone door covering the tomb. Women disciples had set out from home with spices early on the first day of the week while it was dark. Before they arrived, the guards froze with fear seeing the angel. Their later report to the chief priests would become a testimony of God's involvement [*See* Matthew 28:1–4; Mark 16:1–4; Luke 23:50–54; John 20:1].

Before sunrise, the women arrived and were surprised that the stone had been moved. Angels confirmed Jesus' resurrection and that He was going to Galilee as He had said some days before. The women were to go to the disciples and tell them He had risen [*See* Matthew 28:1–8; Mark 16:1–7; Luke 24:1–7; John 20:1–2].

The disciples did not believe the women who passed on the angels' message. Mary Magdalene told them that Jesus' body was gone [*See* Mark 16:9–11; Luke 24:8–11; John 20:11–18].

Peter and John ran to the tomb to see for themselves. John was apparently convinced by what he saw, while Peter wondered about it all [*See* Luke 24:12; John 20:3–9].

The resurrected Christ appeared first to Mary Magdalene near the tomb, and later to more women disciples. ... [*See* Mark 16:9; Luke 24:48; John 20:11–16; Acts 1:8, 21–22].

The disciples did not believe Mary when she told them Jesus appeared to her. In the meantime, Jesus appeared to a group of the women followers. He told them to tell His brethren to go to Galilee [*See* Matthew 28:5–10; Mark 16:9–11; Luke 24:8–11; John 20:11–18].

Jesus appeared to two disciples on the road to Emmaus. One is named as Cleopas. By expounding the prophecies about the Messiah from the Holy Scriptures and sharing a meal with them, Jesus helped them to understand that He was the resurrected Christ. They rushed back to the other disciples [*See* Mark 16:12–13; Luke 24:13–31].

The Emmaus disciples spoke to "the eleven," which is a reference to the apostles. But that doesn't mean all eleven apostles were present. …Thomas was not present [*See* Luke 24:13–35].

Jesus appeared, and they touched Him. As the two disciples told of their experience, Jesus appeared among them all and ate food to show He can appear in physical form. He showed them the wounds in His hands, feet and pierced side, which they touched. He rebuked them for not believing those He had appeared to already [*See* Matthew 28:16–20; Mark 16:14–18; Luke 24:36–49; John 20:19–23].

After eight days, Jesus appeared again—this time with Thomas present. John recounts that Jesus did many things in the presence of His disciples that convinced them He is the resurrected Christ [*See* John 20:26–29].

The disciples traveled to Galilee, where Jesus met them on a mountain. While in Galilee, He appeared to them by the shores of the Sea of Galilee. Jesus had already appeared to Peter three times [*See, e.g.,* Matthew 28:16–20; Luke 24:33–34].

Christ catches fishermen's attention. While waiting for Jesus to show Himself, Peter and six others decided to go to work, but didn't catch anything. Then Jesus miraculously filled their net with 153 large fish [*See* John 21:1–14].

More than 500 brethren saw Christ in Galilee, most of whom were still alive when Paul wrote 1 Corinthians 15:6 some thirty years later.

Disbelieving James and Jude: Initially, Jesus' brothers did not believe He was the Christ [John 7:3–5]. Although not directly recorded in the Gospels, Paul tells us that Jesus appeared to His half brother James. By the time the conference recorded in Acts 15 took place, James was the pastor of the congregation at Jerusalem. He had become a fervent follower of the risen Christ, along with at least one other brother, Jude [See, e.g., Mark 3:21, 31–35, 6:3; John 7:1–10; Acts 15:1–21; 1 Corinthians 15:7].

Additional disciples saw Christ: As mentioned by Paul, these may be those who, in addition to the twelve, made up the 120 disciples in the upper room on the Day of Pentecost, AD 31. As we have seen, there were over 500 other brethren who had already witnessed the resurrected Jesus in Galilee [See, e.g., 1 Corinthians 15:6].

The apostles returned to Jerusalem and continued to be instructed by Christ until the 40 days were finished [Acts 1:1–8]. He told them not to leave Jerusalem until they had received the Holy Spirit, which happened on Pentecost. Great growth came as a result of the miraculous signs and preaching of the apostles [See also, e.g., Luke 24:44–49].

Jesus' vicious enemy becomes [His] defender: Paul gave his own name as the final eyewitness. As a zealous Pharisee, he had violently persecuted Christians [Galatians 1:13–14; Acts 8:3]. He witnessed Stephen's martyrdom. On the way to Damascus to capture and throw believers into prison, he was struck blind when Christ appeared to him. Christ called him to a new life as a promoter of the faith he had tried to destroy. Paul implies he was taught by

When Only God Knew

the resurrected Christ in Arabia [Galatians 1:11–17]
[*See also* Acts 9:1–6; 18:9–10; 1 Corinthians 15:8–9].

So many people witnessed the resurrected Jesus, and still, there is no report of any witness or of any ancient historian contradicting Jesus' resurrection.

b. Additional Support for Jesus' Resurrection

Approaching the evidence from another direction shows that there are at least seven somewhat different reasons why the evidence shows that Christ did, indeed, rise from the dead:[682]

i. Proof of the Resurrection #1:
The Empty Tomb of Jesus

The empty tomb may be the strongest proof Jesus Christ rose from the dead. Two major theories have been advanced by unbelievers: someone stole Jesus' body, or the women and disciples went to the wrong tomb. The Jews and Romans had no motive to steal the body. Christ's apostles were too coward and would have had to overcome the Roman guards. The women who found the tomb empty had earlier watched Jesus being laid away; they knew where the correct tomb was. Even if they had gone to the wrong tomb, the Sanhedrin could have produced the body from the right tomb to stop the resurrection stories. Jesus' burial clothes were left neatly folded inside, hardly the act of hurrying grave robbers. Angels said Jesus had risen from the dead.

ii. Proof of the Resurrection #2:
The Holy Women Eyewitnesses

The holy women eyewitnesses are further proof that the Gospels are accurate historical records. If the accounts had been made up, no ancient author would have used women as witnesses to Christ's resurrection. Women were second-class citizens in Bible times; their testimony was not even allowed in court. Yet the Bible says the risen

Christ first appeared to Mary Magdalene and other holy women. Even the apostles did not believe Mary when she told them the tomb was empty. Jesus, who always had special respect for these women, honored them as the first eyewitnesses to His resurrection. The male Gospel writers had no choice but to report this embarrassing act of God's favor because that was how it happened.

iii. Proof of the Resurrection #3: Jesus' Apostles' New-Found Courage

After the crucifixion, Jesus' apostles hid behind locked doors, terrified they would be executed next. But something changed them from cowards to bold preachers. Anyone who understands human character knows people do not change that much without some major influence. That influence was seeing their Master bodily risen from the dead. Christ appeared to them in the locked room, on the shore of the Sea of Galilee, and on the Mount of Olives. After seeing Jesus alive, Peter and the others left the locked room and preached the risen Christ, unafraid of what would happen to them. They quit hiding because they knew the truth. They finally understood that Jesus is God incarnate, who saves people from sin.

iv. Proof of the Resurrection #4: Changed Lives of James and Others

Changed lives are yet another proof of the resurrection. James, the brother of Jesus, was openly skeptical that Jesus was the Messiah. Later, James became a courageous leader of the Jerusalem church, even being stoned to death for his faith. Why? The Bible says the risen Christ appeared to him. What a shock to see your own brother alive again after you knew He was dead. James and the apostles were effective missionaries because people could tell these men had touched and seen the risen Christ. With such zealous eyewitnesses, the early church exploded in growth, spreading west from Jerusalem to Rome and beyond. For 2,000 years, encounters with the resurrected Jesus have changed lives.

v. Proof of the Resurrection #5:
Large Crowd of Eyewitnesses

A large crowd of more than 500 eyewitnesses saw the risen Jesus Christ at the same time. The apostle Paul records this event in 1 Corinthians 15:6. He states that most of these men and women were still alive when he wrote this letter, about 55 AD. Undoubtedly, they told others about this miracle. Today, psychologists say it would be impossible for a large crowd of people to have had the same hallucination at once. Smaller groups also saw the risen Christ, such as the apostles and Cleopas and his companion. They all saw the same thing, and in the case of the apostles, they touched Jesus and watched Him eat food. The hallucination theory is further debunked because, after the ascension of Jesus into heaven, sightings of Him stopped.

vi. Proof of the Resurrection #6:
Conversion of Paul

The conversion of Paul records the most drastically changed life in the Bible. As Saul of Tarsus, he was an aggressive persecutor of the early church. When the risen Christ appeared to Paul on the Damascus Road, Paul became Christianity's most determined missionary. He endured five floggings, three beatings, three shipwrecks, a stoning, poverty, and years of ridicule. Finally, the Roman emperor Nero had Paul beheaded because the apostle refused to deny his faith in Jesus. What could make a person willingly accept—even welcome—such hardships? Christians believe the conversion of Paul came about because he encountered Jesus Christ, who had risen from the dead.

vii. Proof of the Resurrection #7:
They Died for Jesus

Countless people have died for Jesus, absolutely certain that the resurrection of Christ is a historical fact. Tradition says ten of the original apostles died as martyrs for Christ, as did the apostle Paul.

Hundreds, perhaps thousands, of early Christians died in the Roman arena and in prisons for their faith. Down through the centuries, thousands more have died for Jesus because they believed the resurrection is true. Even today, people suffer persecution because they have faith that Christ rose from the dead. An isolated group may give up their lives for a cult leader, but Christian martyrs have died in many lands for nearly 2,000 years, believing Jesus conquered death to give them eternal life.

5. The Miracle of Pentecost

Fact Stated: Acts (written 62–70 AD)
Fact: Never denied

Luke, the "historian of the first rank," wrote the book of Acts in which he reported another miracle which was witnessed by at least 120 people. That miracle was the infilling of the Holy Spirit in those 120± Christians in attendance in Jerusalem shortly after Jesus' resurrection, and their speaking in and understanding foreign tongues that they did not know but which was understood by all in attendance. Acts 1:15 and Acts 2:1–11 (NIV) says,

> In those days, after Jesus had been crucified and the disciples and Mary, the mother of Jesus, and other women were praying in Jerusalem just before the selection of Mathias to replace Judas Iscariot as a disciple, Peter stood up among the believers [a group numbering about a hundred and twenty].
>
> ...
>
> When the day of Pentecost came, they were all together in one place. Suddenly a sound like the blowing of a violent wind came from heaven and filled the whole house where they were sitting. They saw what seemed to be tongues of fire that separated and came to rest on each of them. All of them were filled with

When Only God Knew

the Holy Spirit and began to speak in other tongues as the Spirit enabled them.

Now there were staying in Jerusalem God-fearing Jews from every nation under heaven. When they heard this sound, a crowd came together in bewilderment, because each one heard their own language being spoken. Utterly amazed, they asked: "Aren't all these who are speaking Galileans? Then how is it that each of us hears them in our native language? Parthians, Medes and Elamites; residents of Mesopotamia, Judea and Cappadocia, Pontus and Asia, Phrygia and Pamphylia, Egypt and the parts of Libya near Cyrene; visitors from Rome [both Jews and converts to Judaism]; Cretans and Arabs—we hear them declaring the wonders of God in our own tongues!"

Although some of those who attended initially mocked what they perceived as being caused by "too much wine," *see* Acts 2:13. Peter made clear that what had happened was not the result of too much wine for two reasons. It was "only the third hour of the day," about three hours after dawn when the attendees began speaking and understanding tongues that were not their own;[683] more importantly, the pouring out of the Holy Spirit was fully in keeping with a prophecy in the Book of Joel written between 835 and 796 BC, approximately 800 years earlier, that God would pour out the Holy Spirit on men. *See* Acts 2:14–21.

In any event, other than the mockery of a few in attendance, not one of the 120± attendees later denied Pentecost, the pouring out of the Holy Spirit, and what they saw and heard that day—tongues of fire that separated resting on each of them and speaking and being heard in languages that were not native to them.

6. Paul's and Barnabas' Travels from Iconium to Lycaonia

Fact Stated: Acts (written 62–70 AD)
Fact Confirmed: 1910 AD (1840 years later ±)

In Acts 14:1–7, Luke writes that Paul and Barnabas fled Iconium[684] and entered the region of Lycaonia.[685] A century before Luke, Cicero had, however, written that Iconium was in the region of Lycaonia.[686] This made many scholars think Luke made a mistake—like saying someone left London and entered England.[687] Two matters of evidence overcome this skepticism of the accuracy of the passage in Acts written by Luke, which caused William Mitchell Ramsay, the archaeologist discussed in Chapter 3, to call Luke "a historian of the first rank" who "should be placed along with the very greatest of historians."

First was the discovery of a Phrygian Altar Inscription in 1910 by Ramsay, which was reported to show that the people of Iconium did not speak the Lycaonian language but the Phrygian and Greek languages.[688] This discovery by Ramsay has been considered confirmation that Acts 14 is accurate.[689]

It was not, however, just the discovery of that archaeological artifact that convinces reasonable people that the skepticism of Luke's accuracy in Acts has no foundation. Ancient literary texts are also convincing. One author, skeptical that the foregoing proved that Iconium was not in Lycaonia because Iconium did not speak the Lycaonian language, concluded that the language spoken in Iconium was not what convinced Ramsay. The author of *Biblical Archaeology 44: Iconium was not in Lycaonia*[690] said,

> What convinced Ramsay that Iconium was in Phrygia was not the discovery of an archaeological artifact, but ancient literary texts. He cites several sources in

The Bearing of Recent Discovery on the Trustworthiness of the New Testament:

- Xenophon identified Iconium as city of Phrygia in 394 BC (*Anabasis*).
- In AD 145, Pliny says Iconium was a Phrygian city.
- In AD 163, several Christians, including Justin Martyr, were put on trial in Rome for their Christian faith. One man at the trial—a slave named Hierax—was asked who his parents were. Hierax replied, "My earthly parents are dead; and I have been brought here (a slave) torn away from Iconium of Phrygia." This is the only report we have from a native of Iconium.
- Firmillian, bishop of Caesarea, is said to have attended a council in AD 232 at Iconium in Phrygia.

Apparently, it was not until AD 372, when Valens instituted a new province of Licaonia, that Iconium was included in that region. So, Iconium was not just a city in Phrygia for a few decades, but for hundreds of years.

Whether we rely on the Phrygian Altar Inscriptions discovered in 1910 by Ramsay or on the ancient texts, the proof is overwhelming that Luke's description in Acts—all of Acts including what happened at Pentecost and the location of Iconium—is reliable and accurate.

PART III

Principles of Science, Mathematics, Medicine, Mechanics, and Engineering and Related to Celestial Matters Affirm the Reliability of the Bible

Science is the "systematic knowledge of the physical or material world gained through observation and experimentation."[691] Science is also defined as "knowledge or a system of knowledge covering general truths or the operation of general laws especially as obtained and tested through the scientific method."[692]

The evidence to be weighed in this section is whether scientific principles described in the Bible, many only to be later confirmed, are sufficient for the reader to determine that the Bible is reliable. But the reader should not judge the scientific principles found in the Bible by the standards of a science book used by educators.

The Bible was not given to be a scientific textbook, obviously. You don't study the Bible to build a rocket. And the Bible doesn't use scientific language.

However, rest assured. The Bible never, never, never gives bad science. Not once in over sixteen hundred years in which this book was written does it give bad science. In fact, it is always ahead of science. There are things in the Bible, the Bible says were true, that we've just discovered a hundred years ago, two hundred years ago, three hundred years ago.[693]

As pointed out in the introduction, to his book *100 Years of Nobel Prizes*, which discusses Nobel Prize winners from 1901-2000, Baruch Aba Shalev, a geneticist and author, made us aware of the fact that only 11 percent of Nobel laureates claimed to be atheists or agnostics, and 91 percent of the winners for medicine, 93 percent of the winners for chemistry and 95 percent of the winners for physics did not.[694]

Johannes Kepler,[695] the famous German astronomer, once said, "Science is simply thinking God's thoughts after him."[696]

> In other words, God established the laws of physics and then we discover them. God established the laws of biology and we discover them. God established the laws of mathematics and we discover them. One of the reasons why we know the Bible can be trusted is because it's scientifically accurate. And the reason it's accurate is because the laws of the universe were invented by God. So he obviously understands them even in years past when we didn't. For thousands of years we've misunderstood different things.
>
> One thing about truth is it never changes. But one thing about science is it constantly changes. There's nothing more worthless than an obsolete science book. I guarantee you that the science book you had in the third grade is not being used in the third grade today. A lot of things in that book are no longer believed or even taught. Nothing is more worthless than a five-year-old computer book. You can find them in any garage sale and nobody wants them, because things get out of date so fast. Things that we once scientifically believed, we now know more about it. In fact, in medical science it happens all the time.[697]

Other well-known and well-respected scientists have similar opinions. Francis Bacon, considered the father of the scientific method, said,

> The glory of God is to conceal a thing, but the glory of the king is to find it out; as if, according to the innocent play of children, the Divine Majesty too delight to hide his works, to the end to have them found out, and as if kings could not obtain a greater honour than to be God's playfellows in that game.[698]
>
> Isaac Newton, one of the greatest scientists and mathematicians in recorded history, failed to find disbelief. From his masterwork the *Principia: Mathematical Principles of Natural Philosophy*: "He endures always and is present everywhere, and by existing always and everywhere he constitutes duration [time] and space. Since each and every particle of space is always, and each and every invisible moment of duration is everywhere, certainly the maker and lord of all things will not be never or nowhere... God is one and the same God always and everywhere. He is omnipresent not only virtually but also substantially; for active power cannot subsist without substance."[699]

Rene Descartes, a 17th century AD "creative mathematician of the first order, an important scientific thinker, and an original metaphysician,"[700] in his *Meditations on First Philosophy*, even said, "the certitude and truth of all science depends on the knowledge alone of the true God."[701]

Even modern science has not changed the opinion of most scientists about the existence of God; they "believe in God, not in spite of but in concert with modern science."[702] So, for instance,

- Robert Milliken, the "elementary particle physicist who won the 1923 Nobel Prize for work on the measurement of charged particles," argued in *Evolution in Science and Religion*, "for the non-contradictory nature of the two disciplines."

- Max Born, "influential in the development of quantum mechanics and who shared the 1954 Nobel Prize in physics, famously said that 'the dance of atoms, electrons, and nuclei, which in all its fury, is subject to God's eternal laws.'"

- "Michael Faraday, known for his unification of electricity and magnetism, when asked to speculate on life after death, said, 'Speculations? I have none. I am resting on certainties. I know in whom I have belief and am persuaded that He is able to keep that which I have committed unto him against that day.'"

- "Another pioneer of quantum physics, Erwin Schrödinger, rebuts the theory that science is inherently anti-theistic: 'A personal God cannot be encountered in a world picture that becomes accessible only at a price that everything personal is excluded from it; he's quoted in Paul Halpern's 2015 book *Einstein's Dice and Schrödingers Cat: Two Great Minds Battled Quantum Randomness to Create a Unified Theory of Physics*. 'We know that whenever God is experienced, it is an experience exactly as real as a direct sense impression, as real as one's own personality.'"

- "Astrophysicist Joseph Hooten Taylor, Jr., co-winner of the 1993 Nobel Prize in physics for discovering the first binary pulsar and opening the door to new studies in gravitational physics [said] 'A scientific discovery is also a religious discovery.' Taylor is quoted in *50 Nobel Laureates Who Believe in God* by Tihomir Dimitrov. 'There is no conflict between science and religion. Our knowledge

When Only God Knew

of God is made larger with every discovery we make about the world.'"[703]

As most scientists agree, the Bible and science are very consistent. It was, in part, in how long that it took us to discover the laws of physics, biology, mathematics other scientific principles after they were enunciated or referred to in the Bible that we can find comfort in relying on the Bible as accurate and as God-breathed.

Now I realize that some readers may suggest that the first Chapter of the book of Genesis contains an example of bad science. Referring to the theory of evolution,[704] some readers may take the position that the Bible's creation timeline is bad science. But, again, I ask that all the facts be weighed impartially and with an open mind before any conclusion is reached, respecting the reliability of the Bible even in the face of that theory. While I personally believe that there is no unreliable evidence in the Bible and that the Bible is not fallible, even if the reader should conclude that there are unsupported facts in the Bible, it should be remembered that in a courtroom, those unsupported facts would be weighed against all the facts supported in and by the Bible in reaching a conclusion about the Bible's reliability as a basis for accepting Jesus as one's Savior. Remember the scales on which evidence is to be balanced discussed in Chapter 1 to determine if the Bible is reliable by either a preponderance, clearly and convincingly or beyond any reasonable.

There are a number of very prestigious and thoughtful scientists who have determined that "the world is too complicated in all its parts and interconnections to be due to chance alone," as was concluded by Allan Sandage,[705] "a prominent astronomer who worked at Carnegie Observatories remembered by the scientific community because he determined the first reasonably accurate values for the Hubble constant, the age of the universe, and he also discovered the first quasar" who "had received numerous awards for his phenomenal scientific work including the Crafoord Prize (1991) and the Eddington Medal of the Royal Astronomical Society (1963)" and who lived from 1926-2010 but only converted to Christianity in 1963 "after studying the Bible for thirty-five years."[706]

So, as a trier of fact, you, the reader, should keep an open mind in considering the evidence of the Bible's scientific reliability, including whether the theory of evolution is any more reliable than the story of creation in the Bible. After all, science is not infallible, and "scientific" conclusions change. There are, for example, over three and a half miles of obsolete science books in the Louvre, the world-famous art museum and world-class library in Paris, France.[707]

> [S]tuff they thought was scientifically fact fifteen hundred years ago was disproven a thousand years ago. What we thought a thousand years ago was disproven seven hundred fifty years ago. And what we've thought for twenty-five years is disproven ten years ago. And what we thought ten years ago is now changed to today.
>
> In 1861, for example, there was a very famous book that came out called *Fifty-one Incontrovertible Proofs that the Bible is Scientifically Inaccurate.* It's a very famous book. Fifty-one incontrovertible scientific facts they "knew," in 1861, do not agree with the Bible caused the author to conclude that the Bible is scientifically inaccurate. The only problem is today, a hundred fifty years later, you can't find a single scientist on the planet who would agree with any one of those incontrovertible facts. They have all been disproven by science.[708]

Truth, however, does not change.[709] The facts in the Bible which support the truth of the Bible should be weighed even against modern skepticism as to some of the scientific facts in the Bible. For many years, scientific facts in the Bible were not believed until science later, and often only recently, proved them correct.

It has only been relatively recently from a historical viewpoint that the truth of many scientific principles described in the Old Testament referred to below have been confirmed. Such "Johnny-come-lately" confirmation of principles and guidelines is too often overlooked by those who rely on previously so-called unassailable scientific principles. One problem with so-called unassailable scientific principles is that they often continue to infect the ongoing narrative as to the Bible's accuracy, without the cure of later proven truth as to facts in the Bible.

For example, as Peter Stoner, a scientist who had been chairman of the mathematics and astronomy departments at Pasadena City College until 1953 and who then went to Westmont College in Santa Barbara, California, where he served as chairman of the science division and eventually professor emeritus of science, pointed out that

> Young's *General Astronomy*, published in 1898[, more or less only 60 years before Stoner served in his scientific academic posts], is full of errors. Yet, the Bible, written over 2,000 years ago is devoid of scientific error. For example, the shape of the earth is mentioned in Isaiah 40:22. Gravity can be found in Job 26:7. Ecclesiastes 1:6 mentions atmospheric circulation. A reference to ocean currents can be found in Psalm 8:8, and the hydraulic cycle is described in Ecclesiastes 1:7 and Isaiah 55:10. The second law of thermodynamics is outlined in Psalm 102:25–27 and Romans 8:21. And these are only a few examples of scientific truths written in the Scriptures long before they were "discovered" by scientists.[710]

scientific evidence in behalf of special creation. For example, he points out that science had previously taught that special creation was impossible because matter could not be destroyed or created. He then points out that atomic physics had now proved that energy can be turned into matter and matter into energy.

He then considers the order of creation as presented in Genesis 1:1–13. He presents argument after argument from a scientific viewpoint to sustain the order which Genesis chronicles. He then asks, "What chance did Moses have when writing the first chapter of Genesis of getting thirteen items all accurate and in satisfactory order?" His calculations conclude it would be one chance in 31,135,104,000,000,000,000,000 [1 in 31 x 1021]. He concludes, "Perhaps God wrote such an account in Genesis so that in these latter days, when science has greatly developed, we would be able to verify His account and know for a certainty that God created this planet and the life on it."[711]

Accurate scientific principles were originally penned in the Bible by men with no apparent experience, skills, knowledge, or education to reach the conclusion necessary to articulate the principles. That fact alone supports the conclusion that the source of the knowledge was not those who wrote them down, but, rather, a more knowledgeable source—the one who in the first place created the principles for a universe in which the principles worked and were needed. The evidence that biblically stated scientific facts were only later proven also supports the conclusion that there was intent in using Johnny-come-lately facts to overcome skepticism, and that also proves the reliability of the Bible.

CHAPTER 7

Biology, Zoology, Health and Medicine

A. Biology and Zoology [712]

"The concept of biology as a single coherent field arose in the nineteenth century AD."[713] It took as long as 3500 years after the Bible reported biological, zoological, health, and medical facts for their reliability to be confirmed by modern science.

1. Adam and Eve

Fact Stated: Genesis (written 1450–1405 BC)
Fact Confirmed: 21st century AD (3500 years later ⊥)

The Genesis account of creation asserts that all humans descended from the same parents, Adam and Eve. There is now considerable debate in the scientific community over recent genetic studies, which indicate that there is a common mother for us all.[714] The claim is sometimes called the Eve hypothesis.

This "Eve" is "the woman whose mtDNA[715] was ancestral to that in all living people."[716] There is disagreement as to when this common mother lived; some say as recently as 6,000 years ago, and some say 200,000 years ago.[717]

One unknown author who did not identify himself or herself argued against the scientific finding that genetic studies indicate that there is a common mother for us all. That author said, "that adhering to Biblical literalism [about all humans descending from a common mother and father] and following the written accounts of lineage from the Adam and Eve results in the conclusion that the earth is roughly 6,000–10,000 years old."[718] Maybe it does. But that is not an argument that would be heard in a court of law. First, it is a red herring designed to divert the reader from the truth of the scientific fact. More importantly, it is not evidence of the inaccuracy of the scientific finding. It is merely arguing from an already formed conclusion, which is not evidence.[719]

2. Chemical Nature of Flesh—From Dust to Dust

Fact Stated: Genesis (written 1450–1405 BC)
Fact Confirmed: 1669–20th century AD (3050–3300 years later ±)

Genesis 2:7 (NIV) (written 1450–1405 BC) says, "Then the Lord God formed a man from the dust of the ground and breathed into his nostrils the breath of life, and the man became a living being."

Ecclesiastes 3:20 (written 940–931 BC) supports the conclusion that God knew what He created and that it was from the "dust of the ground." At a time when there was no scientific basis for the "dust" principle, Ecclesiastes 3:20 (NIV) said, "All go to the same place; all come from dust, and to dust all return."

Science today supports the biblical principle that we are formed from the elements found in "dust" and that we will return to those elements when we die. Almost 99 percent of the mass of the human body is made up of six elements, oxygen, carbon, hydrogen, nitrogen, calcium, and phosphorus.[720] None of these six primary elements, except carbon, were discovered until almost the eighteenth century. That is over 2,500 years after Ecclesiastes was written and over 3,000 years after Genesis. Phosphorus was not discovered until 1669 AD, hydrogen not until 1766, nitrogen not until 1772, oxygen not until 1774, and calcium not until 1808.[721]

Researchers at NASA's Ames Research Center, almost 3000 years after Ecclesiastes was written, confirmed that every element in man can be found in the soil, prompting one of the scientists to say, "… the biblical scenario for the creation of life turns out to be not far off the mark."[722] The finding was more than not far off the mark; it was

When Only God Knew

a bullseye. Eleven common elements found in the human body and their percentage of total body weight are:

- Oxygen: 65.0%
- Carbon: 18.5%
- Hydrogen: 9.5%
- Nitrogen: 3.2%
- Calcium: 1.5%
- Phosphorus: .0%
- Potassium: .4%
- Sodium: .2%
- Chlorine: .2%
- Magnesium: .1%
- Sulfur: .04%[723]

The other trace elements (less than 0.01 percent) in the human body are boron, cadmium, chromium, cobalt, copper, fluorine, iodine, iron, manganese, molybdenum, selenium, silicon, tin, vanadium, and zinc.[724] Every one of those elements is found in the Earth's crust,[725] i.e., the Earth's dust. Except for sulfur, copper, iron, and tin, none of these other trace elements in the human body had been discovered by the ancient world.[726] That includes at the time that Genesis was written sometime between 1450 and 1405 BC and when Ecclesiastes was written sometime between 940 and 931 BC. The first of these other trace elements to be discovered was zinc in thirteenth century India; the last to be discovered was iodine, but not until 1811.[727]

It is remarkable that the discovery of the elements in the human body—dust—occurred so many centuries after Genesis was written in 1405–1450 BC and after Ecclesiastes was written in 940–931 BC. As late as the first century AD, 1000 years after Ecclesiastes was written, only ten chemical elements had been known (antimony, copper, gold, iron, lead, mercury, silver, sulfur, tin, and zinc).[728] The other elements in the human body were not discovered as part of the human body until:[729]

Element	Percentage of Human Body	Year Discovered
Boron	(less than 0.01%)	1808 AD
Cadmium	(less than 0.01%)	1817 AD
Calcium	1.5%	1879 AD
Carbon	18.5%	1694 AD +
Chlorine	.2%	1774 AD
Chromium	(less than 0.01%)	1774 AD
Cobalt	(less than 0.01%)	1751 AD
Fluorine	(less than 0.01%)	1886 AD
Hydrogen	9.5%	1776 AD
Iodine	(less than 0.01%)	1811 AD
Magnesium	.1%	1755 AD
Manganese	(less than 0.01%)	1774 AD
Molybdenum	(less than 0.01%)	1781 AD
Nitrogen	3.2%	1772 AD
Oxygen	65.0%	1774 AD
Phosphorus	1.0%	1669 AD
Potassium	.4%	1807–1808 AD
Selenium	(less than 0.01%)	1826 AD
Silicon	(less than 0.01%)	1824 AD
Sodium	.2%	1807 AD
Sulfur	.04%	1777 [730] AD
Vanadium	(less than 0.01%)	1797 AD
Zinc	(less than 0.01%)	1875 AD

How was it that the Bible accurately stated that the body came from dust and would return to dust when it took scientists 3,000 years to verify what elements made up the human body? How was it that the non-scientist authors of Genesis and Ecclesiastes knew that? The science at the time did not verify those statements. The most logical conclusion is that the knowledge came from God who had, in fact, "formed a man, Adam, from the dust of the ground."

3. Like-Kind Biology from and to Like-Kind Biology—Biogenesis

Fact Stated: Genesis (written 1450–1405 BC)
Fact Confirmed: 1859 AD (3300 years later ±)

A scientific principle "postulates the production of new living organisms from pre-existing life."[731] That principle is called biogenesis. Biogenesis encompasses the belief that complex living things come only from other living things by means of reproduction. That is, life does not spontaneously arise from non-living material.[732]

Long before there was scientific proof for biogenesis, however, the Bible described the development of living organisms from other living organisms (i.e., biogenesis) as part of God's creation process. The Bible described that each kind of living organism came from the same kind of living organism.

Genesis 1:11–12 (NIV) (written 1450–1405 BC) says,

> Then God said, "Let the land produce vegetation: seed-bearing plants and trees on the land that bear fruit with seed in it, according to their various kinds." And it was so. The land produced vegetation: plants bearing seed according to their kinds and trees bearing fruit with seed in it according to their kinds. And God saw that it was good.

Genesis 1:21 (NIV) (written 1450–1405 BC) says,

> So God created the great creatures of the sea and every living thing with which the water teems and that moves about in it, according to their kinds, and every winged bird according to its kind. And God saw that it was good.

Genesis 1:25 (NIV) (written 1450–1405 BC) says,

> God made the wild animals according to their kinds, the livestock according to their kinds, and all the creatures that move along the ground according to their kinds. And God saw that it was good.

As you can see, the phrase "according to their kinds" occurs repeatedly. That phrase stresses the reproductive integrity of each kind of animal and plant. Today we know this occurs because all these reproductive systems are programmed by their genetic codes.[733]

The principle that each is made according to its kind—biogenetically—did not always have intellectual support, however. An idea that "was first propounded by Aristotle[734] in Ancient Greece" was "that living things could spontaneously come into being from nonliving matter."[735] Aristotle called that "abiogenesis."[736] That was believed by "the Ancient Greeks" and by European intellectuals for 2000 years after Aristotle died.[737] As late as the seventeenth century AD, abiogenesis "was the dominant view, sanctioned alike by antiquity and by authority."[738]

The idea that reproduction was the result of spontaneous generation from inanimate matter is no longer a mainstream scientific principle. This idea of Aristotle, the great philosopher, is just no longer believable.

"Francesco Redi,[739] as far back as 1668, had set out to refute the idea of macroscopic spontaneous generation."[740] It was not until 1858, however, that a "scientist named Rudolf Virchow[741] came up with a counter-hypothesis, claiming that life can only come from life," i.e., biogenesis.[742] The very next year, 1859, the famous scientist, Louis Pasteur,[743] performed an experiment that "cemented the Law of Biogenesis"[744] which had been first referenced in the Bible in the fifteenth century BC Confirming the principle of biogenesis in

When Only God Knew

1864, "Pasteur finally announced the results of his scientific experiments."[745]

While the statements in Genesis (written 1450–1405 BC) "that each is made according to its kind" can be used to support creationism, this book does not intend to debate the proofs of creation versus the theory of evolution. As pointed out in the Introduction, one purpose of this book is for the reader to think about how often God knew something was true before mankind found proof of it. The reader can then reach his or her own conclusion whether God's knowledge of so many things before mankind's proof of them should cause one to believe the remainder of the biblical narrative, including that God exists and created the world. At the very least, how often God knew something was true before mankind found proof of it should cause the reader to want to delve more deeply into matters about which there is controversy.

So as to the Bible's "like-kind" statements, how was it that the Bible accurately stated the principle of biogenesis when it took scientists approximately 3,3000 years to verify it? How was it that Moses, believed to be the author of Genesis, knew that plants and animals were not spontaneously generated from inorganic matter when ancient thought claimed it was? The science at the time did not verify Moses' "like-kind" statements. Again, the most logical conclusion is that the knowledge came from someone who did know—the God who had, in fact, established that biological law.

4. Circumcision—Blood Clotting in Infants

Fact Stated: Genesis (written 1450–1405 BC)
Fact Confirmed: 1929 AD (3300 years later ±)

Genesis 17:12–13 (NIV) (written 1450–1405 BC) reports that Abraham was told that… he that is eight days old shall be circumcised among you, every man child in your generations, he that is born in the house, or bought with money of any stranger, which is not of thy seed.

He that is born in thy house, and he that is bought with thy money, must needs be circumcised: and my covenant shall be in your flesh for an everlasting covenant.

Why does the Bible say that circumcision was to take place on the eighth day and not the third or some other day? Was there something in the science of the human body, not generally known to mankind, that indicated that day was the best day?

Important to an understanding of the biblical requirement that circumcision on the eighth day after a boy is born is that fact that prothrombin, a protein, plays a significant role in blood clotting. The quantity of this protein in the body is directly affected by vitamin K. Vitamin K is necessary for the synthesis of prothrombin.[746] If vitamin K is deficient, there will be a prothrombin deficiency, and hemorrhaging may occur.

In "normal" infants, the level of prothrombin on the first day after birth is high, with a rapid fall on the second, to a lower level on the third and fourth, followed by a recovery by the sixth day.[747] By waiting eight days after birth, it is more likely that there will not be a prothrombin deficiency and that, consequently, hemorrhaging is less likely to occur.

> On the eighth day, the amount of prothrombin present actually is elevated above one-hundred percent of normal—and is the only day in the male's life in which this will be the case under normal conditions. If surgery is to be performed, day eight is the perfect day to do it. Vitamin K and prothrombin levels are at their peak.[748]

But prothrombin was not even guessed at until 1872. Vitamin K was not identified for approximately another sixty years.[749] "Vitamin K was discovered fortuitously in 1929… and was immediately

When Only God Knew

associated with blood coagulation."[750] That discovery was over 3,300 years after God required circumcision on the eighth day.

How did either Abraham, a nomadic sheepherder, or even Moses, a non-scientist who is thought to have written Genesis, know in the fifteenth century BC that it would be best to circumcise babies on the eighth day? Had to be God.

5. Life is in the Blood

Fact Stated: Leviticus and Deuteronomy (written 1450–1405 BC)
Fact Confirmed: 1616 AD at the earliest (3000 years later ±)

Leviticus 17:11 (NIV) says, "For the life of the flesh is in the blood." Leviticus 17:14 (ESV) likewise says, "For the life of every creature is its blood: its blood is its life." Deuteronomy 12:23 (ESV) also says that "the blood is the life." Both books were written between 1445 and 1405 BC.

Anyone at any time would have known that if someone lost too much blood, they would die. Still, it took 3,000 years before the truth of these Biblical passages was scientifically confirmed for those that did not have traumatic blood loss.

Today, we know that the blood carries oxygen and other gases, water, nourishment, and hormones to every cell, maintains the body's temperature, and removes the waste material of the body's cells.[751] "Without the circulatory system, the body would not be able to fight disease or maintain a stable internal environment—such as proper temperature."[752] It was not until 1616 AD, however, that William Harvey[753] discovered blood circulation and that it is the key factor to physical life.[754] In doing so, he confirmed what the Bible revealed 3,000 years earlier. The implications of his discovery were, however, not fully appreciated for another 250 or so years.

The principle that you need healthy blood to live a healthy life was not always known. Medical practice for almost 5,000 years until relatively recently included bloodletting. "Doctors" would often withdraw considerable quantities of blood from a patient in an attempt to cure or prevent illness and disease.[755] "The vast majority of medical scholars today, however,] agree that bloodletting harmed far more people than it helped."[756]

"In its infancy, bloodletting was accomplished via the most primitive methods, including using sharp thorns or animal teeth."[757] Over time in Europe, there were, in general, two kinds of bloodletting. One method was done by opening a vein and/or an artery. The other was done by scarification with cupping and leeches.[758] Scarification usually occurred by "scraping the skin with a cube-shaped brass box containing multiple small knives." The scarification was followed by cupping, which involved placing a dome-shaped glass over the skin and extracting the air by suction or prior heating; a leech would then be applied to the area to suck out the blood.[759]

> The practice of bloodletting began around 3000 years ago with the Egyptians, then continued with the Greeks and Romans, the Arabs and Asians, then spread through Europe during the Middle Ages and the Renaissance. It reached its peak in Europe in the nineteenth century.[760] ...[For example, this] therapy was very popular in Europe in the 1830s, especially France, where 5 to 6 million leeches per year were used in Paris alone and about 35 million in the country as a whole. By the late 1800s, however, enthusiasm for leech therapy had waned, but leeches are still used today in select situations.[761]

There was no apparent thought to the adverse effects of removing healthy blood from the human body.

Moderation in bloodletting was missing from much of the practice in the ancient world and in Europe in the Middle Ages. And few precautions before bloodletting were. So, "by medieval times, bloodletting was usually carried out by a barber-surgeon; the red and white of the barber's pole is a reminder of their earlier role, with the red standing for blood, white for bandages or tourniquet and the pole itself for the stick grasped by the patient to assist in dilating the arm veins."[762] The common practice was for a barber-surgeon to bleed a patient, with his young assistant collecting the blood in a bowl while an accompanying physician examined the patient's urine.[763]

Beginning in the nineteenth century AD, however, bloodletting declined; today, in Western medicine, it is used only for a few select conditions.[764] Today we know that not only is bloodletting ineffective for most diseases, but in most cases, it was extremely harmful to patients—to the life of the flesh in their blood.

While there was Jewish bloodletting, it was far more restrictive than the rest of the ancient and medieval world. Jewish society and bloodletters practiced bloodletting more in keeping with God's admonish that "the blood is the life."

> [Bloodletting] is frequently mentioned in the Talmud.[765] It was performed not by a physician but by a skilled functionary called *umman* or *gara*, whose status was less than that of a physician. The bloodletter is mentioned in various passages in the Talmud, both favorably and unfavorably [e.g., Tian. 21b; Kid. 82a]. Some of the directives about bloodletting in the Talmud relate to specific ailments [e.g., Git. 67b; Av. Zara. 29a], but most are in the realm of preventive medicine based on the belief that the regular removal of blood from the body was of hygienic value. Among the ten indispensable requirements of a town, in the absence of which "no scholar should reside there" [Sanh. 17b], is a bloodletter. According to the Talmud, *bloodletting is one of the things which should be applied in moderation* [Git. 70a], and, in practice, the amount of blood to be let varies with the subject's age.

Maimonides[766] [Yad, De'ot 4:18], though in general agreement, suggests, in addition, consideration of the subject's "blood richness" and physical vigor [*Pirkei Moshe*, 12]. *Many instructions are given in the Talmud with respect to diet and precautions to be taken both before and after bloodletting [e.g., Shab. 129a-b; Git. 70a; Ned. 54b; Av. Zar. 29a; et al.]. Maimonides advises moderation in blood-letting: "A man should not accustom himself to let blood regularly, nor should he do so unless he is in great need of it" [Yad, loc. cit.]. The views of the Talmud and of Maimonides provide a sharp contrast to those of the ancient and medieval world, where the practice of bloodletting was unrestricted.* In late Hebrew literature [e.g., the *Ozar ha-Ḥayyim* of *Jacob Ẓahalon* and the *Ma'aseh Tuviyyah* of Tobias b. Moses *Cohn] directions for bloodletting and cupping are also found.[767]

(Emphasis added).

It appears that Jewish society recognized the proposition that "the life of the flesh is in the blood," and was far more moderate in the practice than were others.

Moses is thought to have written the first five books of the Bible, whose principles are to this day followed by Jews and Christians. How did Moses know in the fifteenth century BC that life is in the blood, which led to Jewish moderation in bloodletting when it would be 3,000 years before blood circulation was discovered and medical science first understood that blood and its circulation is the key factor to physical life, and it would even be an additional 250 years before the practice of bloodletting would be discontinued? God.

When Only God Knew

6. One Blood—All Nations

Fact Stated: Acts (written 62–70 AD)
Fact Confirmed: 20th century AD (1800 years later ±)

In Acts 17:22–26 (KJV) (written 62–70 AD), Luke, the physician, tells us that Paul told the Greeks at the Areopagus[768] in Athens, Greece, that God made the blood of all men in every nation the same. Luke reported in Acts 17:26 (KJV) that Paul said that God "hath made of one blood all nations of men for to dwell on all the face of the earth."

Luke, the physician who was familiar with the human body, could have contradicted Paul's statement based on the medicine of the time. He did not. But the statement by Paul, not a physician, that the blood of men in all nations is the same would not be scientifically proven until the twentieth century.

Until recent times, it was believed there were significant differences in the genetics and blood of the various human races. But

> [s]cientists today agree that there is really only one biological race of humans. Geneticists have found that if we were to take any two people from anywhere in the world, the basic genetic differences between these two people would typically be around 0.2 percent, even if they came from the same people group.[769]

There is also no significant difference in blood type among the various races. At the end of the nineteenth century AD, Karl Landsteiner, a Viennese pathologist and later Nobel prizewinner,

> showed that human blood naturally occurred in three different 'types.' A fourth was discovered in 1902 by his colleagues, [Alfred von] Decastello and [Adriano] Sturli. These four blood types were later given the

names by which they are known today: A, B, O, and the fourth type, AB.[770]

It had, however, been previously "thought that in the three major races of man, blood groups varied" according to where one was from. It was thought that blood groups A were in Europe, blood groups B were in Asia, and finally, blood groups O were in South America.[771] Today we know that all those blood types can be found in every race, although the percentage of each blood type may vary from one ethnicity to another.[772]

In fact, current science also disputes the belief that diseases like sickle cell anemia are race-specific. For example, *Race and Gene Studies: What Differences Make a Difference?*[773] says,

> Doctors were long taught that sickle cell anemia was a genetic disease of the black race, a marker of their race. Yet sickle cell is found among peoples from central and western Africa, but not southern Africa. It is also carried by Turks, Yemenis, Indians, Greeks, and Sicilians. That's because sickle cell arose several thousand years ago as a mutation in one of the genes that codes for hemoglobin. The mutation soon spread to successive populations along the trade routes where malaria was common. It turns out that inheriting one sickle cell allele[774] confers resistance to malaria and thus provides a selective advantage in malarial regions [inheriting sickle cell alleles from both parents causes sickle-cell disease]. In other words, sickle cell… is a marker not of skin color or race but ancestry, or more precisely, having ancestors from where malaria was common.

Yet again, how did Paul, or Luke, who told the Acts Areopagus story, relate with confidence in the AD first century that all men were of one blood when it would be almost 2,000 years before science determined that to be the case?

7. The Seed of Life

Fact Stated: Genesis (written in 1450–1405 BC)
Fact Confirmed: 1660s and 1670s AD (3000 years later ±)

Genesis 3:15 (ASV) (written in 1450–1405 BC) reports God as saying to the serpent in the Garden of Eden after Adam and Eve ate of the forbidden fruit:

> And I will put enmity between thee and the woman,
> and between thy seed and her seed: he shall bruise
> thy head, and thou shalt bruise his heel.

This verse revealed that women possess the "seed of life," 3,000 years before it became accepted in the Western World.

As a consequence of speculations by Aristotle respecting the role of men and women in the childbearing process, it was not common knowledge until just a few centuries ago that women carried a seed of life, i.e., an egg, to be fertilized. "In the fourth century BC, Aristotle wrote that man contributed the form of humanity through his semen, while woman contributed only brute matter—a substance less pure and less sanctified than semen itself."[775] Aristotle speculated that women were passive recipients in the child-making process, and "his views remained popular until the fifteenth century" AD.[776] For millennia after Genesis was written, it was assumed that the woman only contributed a place for a baby to grow. It was widely and wrongly believed that only males possessed the "seed of life" and that women were nothing more than the depository—"a glorified incubator"[777]—in which the male's seed of life could grow into a human being.

The scientific identification of the key component seeds of sexual reproduction—eggs and sperm—first occurred during the 1660s and 1670s AD.[778] Eggs, one of the seeds for human life, was first discovered "over 3,000 years after Genesis," the first book of the Bible, described the seed of life.

As with his other biblical statements, which were only later proven, how did Moses know that women carried the seed of life so long before science proved it?

B. Medical Knowledge, Public Health and Well-Being in Ancient Times

1. Ancient Egyptian Medicine

Egyptian medicine was thought of as highly advanced for its time. Egyptian doctors were sought after by kings and queens from far-away lands because they were considered the best in the world. Even so, some of their practices were bizarre and most likely did more harm than good. For example,

> Lizard blood, dead mice, mud and moldy bread were all used as topical ointments and dressings, and women were sometimes dosed with horse saliva as a cure for an impaired libido. Most disgusting of all, Egyptian physicians used human and animal excrement as a cure-all remedy for diseases and injuries. According to 1500 BC's Ebers Papyrus,[779] donkey, dog, gazelle and fly dung were all celebrated for their healing properties and their ability to ward off bad spirits.[780]

The Papyrus Ebers is an ancient Egyptian medical document that contains over 842 remedies for illnesses and injuries, concoctions, and magical spells to alleviate suffering.[781] The papyrus dated back to about 1552 BC and was discovered by Georg Ebers in 1872–3.[782] Some of the other Egyptian "cures" are…

- Spells and magical cures and treatments.
- To prevent the immoderate crying of children, a mixture of the seeds of the plant Sheben with some fly-dirt.
- Focuses primarily on the uterus as the source of a woman's ailments and prescribing "fumigation of the womb" as a cure, accomplished by directing incense smoke or inserting incense into the woman's vagina.
- Testing for fertility by placing an onion or a clove of garlic in a woman's vagina.
- Contraception by insertion of crocodile dung into the vagina.
- Testing for pregnancy by soaking vegetation with a woman's urine; if the plants flourish, she is pregnant.
- To prevent the hair from turning grey, anoint it with the blood of a black calf that has been boiled in oil; or with the fat of a rattlesnake.
- When hair falls out apply a mixture of six fats, those of the horse, the hippopotamus, the crocodile, the cat, the snake, and the ibex.
- To strengthen hair, anoint with the tooth of a donkey crushed in honey.
- Animal drugs included lizards' blood, swine's teeth, putrid meat, stinking fat, moisture from pigs' ears, milk, goose grease, asses' hoofs, animal fats from various sources, excreta of various animals, including human beings, donkeys, antelopes, dogs, cats, and even flies.[783]

And, apart from the papyrus,

[t]he grave of several small children revealed that they had eaten skinned mice just prior to their deaths. The Egyptians believed that the life-giving Nile created mice because these animals emerged from cracks in the mud after the Nile receded each year.[784]

Several medical prescriptions contained animal dung, which might have useful molds and fermentation substances, but were also infested with bacteria and must have caused many serious infections.

As for reproduction, the Egyptians also wrongly thought the origin of semen was in the bones and that it simply passed through the testicles. Female internal anatomy was understood even less well. Anatomical naivety can be gleaned from the fact that, although the function of the womb was understood, it was erroneously thought to be directly connected to the alimentary canal. Thus, placing a clove of garlic in the vagina was supposed to test for fertility: if garlic could be detected on the breath of a woman then she was fertile; if not, then she was infertile.[785]

Even so, Moses, the writer of Genesis, Exodus, Leviticus, Numbers, and Deuteronomy, all written 1450–1405 BC, did not include any of those Egyptian "cures," "remedies," or "medical principles" anywhere in those books. They were not included even though Moses was the grandson of the pharaoh and "was educated in all the wisdom of the Egyptians." *See, e.g.,* Exodus 2:10 (written 1450–1405 BC); Acts 7:22 (written 62–70 AD).

The practices commanded in the Torah, [the first five books of the Bible, also] far exceeded medical

When Only God Knew

standards practiced as recently as 100 or so years ago. While we certainly learned to avoid skinned mice or the fat of an ibex, our medical knowledge was abysmal right up to the beginning of the twentieth century.[786]

Why are Egyptian medical principles—scientifically ignorant principles—conspicuously absent in the first five books of the Bible written by a man "educated in all the wisdom of the Egyptians?" In fact, the Torah (or law of Moses, i.e., the first five books of the Bible[787]—Genesis, Exodus, Leviticus, Numbers, and Deuteronomy) reveals advanced principles and knowledge about hygiene, quarantine, and sanitation far superior to that possessed by the Egyptians and other ancient societies of that day. It also far exceeded medical standards practiced as recently as 200 years ago.[788]

Where did Moses get this advanced medical information? Why have the Jewish practices—thousands of years old—only recently been proven to be reliable.

2. Dietary Guidelines

Fact Stated: Leviticus (written 1450–1405 BC)
Fact Confirmed: 20th century AD (3400 years later ±)

We like fish. We also like shrimp, crabs, lobsters, and pork. But are they good for us?

We now know that "fish is among the healthiest foods on the planet.," "loaded with important nutrients, such as protein and vitamin D," and "is also a great source of omega-3 fatty acids, which are incredibly important for [the human] body and brain."[789] We also, however, now know that shrimp and shellfish such as crabs and lobsters—bottom feeders—are not as healthy because they ingest toxins and waste from the bottom that can be harmful to the human body.[790]

While those facts have been proven by modern researchers, the Israelites were told that was the case 3,400 or so years ago. We like fish, but we also like shrimp and crabs. In Leviticus 11:9–12 (NIV) (written 1450–1405 BC), the Bible said,

> These you may eat, of all that are in the waters. Everything in the waters that has fins and scales, whether in the seas or in the rivers, you may eat. But anything in the seas or the rivers that does not have fins and scales, of the swarming creatures in the waters and of the living creatures that are in the waters, is detestable to you. You shall regard them as detestable; you shall not eat any of their flesh, and you shall detest their carcasses. Everything in the waters that does not have fins and scales is detestable to you.

God-breathed Scripture states that those sea creatures which do not have fins or scales, which include bottom feeders such as shrimp and shellfish, should be avoided.

Likewise, it was 3200 years after the Israelites were told not to eat pork[791] before trichinosis was discovered. Trichinosis is generally known to occur from eating undercooked pork. It was not discovered until 1835, when "two men by the name of Sir Richard Owen and Sir James Paget were working in the laboratory in London," and they "observed the mass of worms that lined the diaphragm" of a cadaver. Sir Owen reported the finding to the zoological society in London and provided its present-day name.[792]

Scientists are also beginning to understand how eating pork can cause other significant health problems. According to the US National Library of Medicine National Institutes of Health (Emphasis Added), Liver specialists, Drs. Amin A. Nanji and Samuel W. French found that there is a,

Correlation between cirrhosis[793] mortality and the product of both alcohol and pork consumption was highly significant [r = 0.98, p less than 0.001]. In countries with low alcohol consumption, no correlation was obtained between alcohol consumption and cirrhosis. However, a significant correlation was obtained between cirrhosis and pork. A similar relationship was seen in the ten Canadian provinces, where there was no correlation between cirrhosis mortality and alcohol consumption, but a significant correlation was obtained with pork.[794]

Another study published in 2017 concluded that "consumption of raw or undercooked pork meat and liver is the most common cause of hepatitis E infection in" Europe.[795]

Because it took science 3400 years to confirm what was said in Leviticus, the reader should ask why it took so long for science to catch up to the Bible's prohibitions?

3. Sanitary Practices

Fact Stated: Leviticus, Numbers, and Deuteronomy
(written 1450–1405 BC)
Fact Confirmed: 19th and 20th centuries AD (3300–3400 years later ±)

Leviticus 6:25–28 (ESV) (written 1450–1405 BC) (emphasis added) reports that God told Moses to

[s]peak to Aaron and his sons, saying, "This is the law of the sin offering. In the place where the burnt offering is killed shall the sin offering be killed before the LORD; it is most holy. The priest who offers it for sin shall eat it. In a holy place it shall be eaten, in the court of the tent of meeting. Whatever touches its flesh shall be holy, and when any of its blood is

splashed on a garment, you shall wash that on which it was splashed in a holy place. *And the earthenware vessel in which it is boiled shall be broken. But if it is boiled in a bronze vessel, that shall be scoured and rinsed in water."*

Leviticus 15:1–12 (ESV) (written 1450–1405 BC) says,

The Lord spoke to Moses and Aaron, saying, "Speak to the people of Israel and say to them, 'When any man has a discharge from his body, his discharge is unclean. And this is the law of his uncleanness for a discharge: whether his body runs with his discharge, or his body is blocked up by his discharge, it is his uncleanness. Every bed on which the one with the discharge lies shall be unclean, and everything on which he sits shall be unclean. And anyone who touches his bed shall wash his clothes and bathe himself in water and be unclean until the evening. And whoever sits on anything on which the one with the discharge has sat shall wash his clothes and bathe himself in water and be unclean until the evening. And whoever touches the body of the one with the discharge shall wash his clothes and bathe himself in water and be unclean until the evening. And if the one with the discharge spits on someone who is clean, then he shall wash his clothes and bathe himself in water and be unclean until the evening. And any saddle on which the one with the discharge rides shall be unclean. And whoever touches anything that was under him shall be unclean until the evening. And whoever carries such things shall wash his clothes and bathe himself in water and be unclean until the evening. Anyone whom the one with the discharge touches without having rinsed his hands in water shall wash his clothes and bathe himself in water and be unclean until the evening. And an earthenware vessel that the one with the discharge touches shall be broken, and every vessel of wood shall be rinsed in water.'"

Numbers 19:14–16 (ESV) (written 1450–1405 BC) says,

"This is the law when someone dies in a tent: everyone who comes into the tent and everyone who is in the tent shall be unclean seven days. And every open vessel that has no cover fastened on it is unclean. Whoever in the open field touches someone who was killed with a sword or who died naturally, or touches a human bone or a grave, shall be unclean seven days."

Deuteronomy 23:10–11 (ESV) (written 1445–1405 BC) says,

If any man among you becomes unclean because of a nocturnal emission, then he shall go outside the camp. He shall not come inside the camp, but when evening comes, he shall bathe himself in water, and as the sun sets, he may come inside the camp.

Long before germ theory[796] was understood, the Israelites were, for example, instructed

1. to sanitize themselves by washing themselves and/or their clothes in running water if any blood touched a garment, they had a bodily discharge, if they came in contact with another person's discharge, or if they had touched a dead

human or animal carcass;

2. to wash any uncovered vessels that were in the vicinity of a dead body;

3. to destroy any vessels if a dead carcass touched it;

4. to purify through either fire or running water items recovered during war;

5. to bury their human waste outside of camp, and

6. to burn the waste of their animals.[797]

Leviticus 6:25–28 is a clear commandment to discard used pottery that may be contaminated with bacteria while metal pots could be disinfected by scouring and rinsing in water. Doctors used to wash their hands in a bowl of water, leaving invisible germs on their hands, even though the Bible says specifically to wash hands under "running water." Even the idea that physicians and surgeons should wash their hands is only about 150 years old.[798]

Our medical knowledge was abysmal right up to the beginning of the twentieth century. It was not until then that medical science had a full understanding of the fact that most diseases are caused by infection from microscopic organisms. Accordingly, the medical value of sterilization, sanitation, and quarantines, discussed below, were virtually unappreciated.[799]

In the 1840s, puerperal or childbirth fever, a bacterial infection after childbirth, was taking the lives of up to 30 percent of women who gave birth in hospitals. Women who gave birth at home remained relatively unaffected. Ignaz Philipp Semmelweis (1818–65), a Hungarian obstetrician educated at the universities of Pest[800] and Vienna, was an assistant professor on the maternity ward of the Vienna General Hospital. He observed that women examined by student doctors who had not washed their hands after leaving the autopsy room had very high death rates. When a colleague who had received a scalpel cut died of infection, Semmelweis concluded that puerperal fever was septic and contagious and that he and the medical students carried "cadaverous particles" on their hands. He ordered students to wash their hands with chlorinated lime before examining patients. As a result, the maternal death rate was reduced from 12 percent to 1 percent in two years. Nevertheless, Semmelweis encountered strong opposition from hospital officials as some doctors were offended at the suggestion that they should wash their hands. They felt that their social status as gentlemen was inconsistent with the idea that their hands could be unclean.[801]

The existence of germs themselves was unknown until around 1890 AD. That was when Louis Pasteur demonstrated in his Germ Theory of Disease that most infectious diseases were caused by microorganisms originating from outside the body. While Pasteur was not the first to propose germ theory, he developed it and conducted experiments that clearly indicated its correctness and managed to convince most of Europe it was true. This new understanding of germs and their means of transmission led to improved sanitary standards that resulted in an enormous drop in the mortality rate.[802]

How was it that Moses,

1. a man educated in all the wisdom of the Egyptians, which did not include sanitary practices which are common today for protection against infection and
2. who wrote Leviticus, Numbers, and Deuteronomy in the fifteenth century BC, knew to tell the Israelites to take precautions, the reason for which would only be proven over 3,000 years later?

4. Quarantine Leprosy and Plague, etc.

Fact Stated: Leviticus (written 1450–1405 BC)
Fact Confirmed: 14th century AD to 1890 AD (2770–3300 years later ±)

Quarantine is of particular interest as of this writing due to the Coronavirus pandemic that began in late 2019. It has, however, been a concern of the Bible for over 3300 years. "There are numerous stories of quarantine in the Bible when people were told by God, primarily through Moses, to 'stay safe at home' during plagues and disease."[803] It was not a general concern to mankind in general for millennia after the Bible instructed the Israelites as to quarantine.

Perhaps the most famous quarantine in the Bible is described in Exodus 11:1–12:30. In those verses, God warns the Israelites to mark their door lintels with lamb's blood and to stay (quarantine) in their homes until a plague that will kill the firstborn in Egypt (the Passover plague) was completed. The Israelites marked their lintels, quarantined themselves until the plague was gone, and saved their firstborn.

There are other admonishments about quarantine in the Bible. Leviticus 13:31–33 (ESV) (written 1405–1450 BC), for example, says,

> And if the priest examines the itching disease and it appears no deeper than the skin and there is no black hair in it, then the priest shall shut up the person with the itching disease for seven days, and on the seventh day the priest shall examine the disease. If the itch has not spread, and there is in it no yellow hair, and the itch appears to be no deeper than the skin, then he shall shave himself, but the itch he shall not shave; and the priest shall shut up the person with the itching disease for another seven days.[804]

Various Bible translations[805] have translated the "itching disease" as "the plague of the scall," "the scabies infection," "the itchy spot," merely "disease" or "infection," "the scaly sore," "the infection of the scale" and the "sores." Whichever disease it was, and they may all be referring to same medical condition, one thing is clear. Temporary quarantine after diagnosis was required.

Quarantine was also required other times in the Bible. Numbers 31:19 (NIV) (written 1450–1405 BC) says, "Anyone who has killed

When Only God Knew

someone or touched someone who was killed must stay outside the camp seven days." Leviticus 13:2–5 (NIV) (written 1450–1405 BC) says,

> "When anyone has a swelling or a rash or a shiny spot on their skin that may be a defiling skin disease,[806] they must be brought to Aaron the priest or to one of his sons who is a priest. The priest is to examine the sore on the skin, and if the hair in the sore has turned white and the sore appears to be more than skin deep, it is a defiling skin disease. When the priest examines that person, he shall pronounce them ceremonially unclean. If the shiny spot on the skin is white but does not appear to be more than skin deep and the hair in it has not turned white, the priest is to isolate the affected person for seven days. On the seventh day the priest is to examine them, and if he sees that the sore is unchanged and has not spread in the skin, he is to isolate them.

Leprosy was particularly concerning to ancient people, such as the fifteenth century BC Israelites, and quarantine was one of the required remedies. In Numbers 5:2 (NIV) (written 1450–1405 BC), God said to Moses, "Command the Israelites to send away from the camp anyone who has a defiling skin disease, leprosy according to the King James Version, or a discharge of any kind, or who is ceremonially unclean because of a dead body." Leviticus 13:45–46 (NIV) (written 1450–1405 BC) (emphasis added) says,

> The leprous person who has the disease shall wear torn clothes and let the hair of his head hang loose, and he shall cover his upper lip and cry out, "Unclean, unclean."[46] He shall remain unclean as long as

he has the disease. He is unclean. *He shall live alone. His dwelling shall be outside the camp.*

Leviticus 13:50–52 (NIV) (written 1450–1405 BC) also describes the seven-day cleanliness post-quarantine evaluation model. Leprosy and plague are characterized by disfiguring skin sores, nerve damage, and progressive debilitation. Throughout history, few diseases have provoked more stigma than leprosy, unique in its ability to generate fear.[807] Leviticus 13:50–52 talks about how you are to treat materials that come into contact with someone who has contracted leprosy or plague. It says,

> And the priest shall examine the disease and shut up that which has the disease for seven days. Then he shall examine the disease on the seventh day. If the disease has spread in the garment, in the warp or the woof, or in the skin, whatever be the use of the skin, the disease is a persistent leprous disease; it is unclean. And he shall burn the garment, or the warp or the woof, the wool or the linen, or any article made of skin that is diseased, for it is a persistent leprous disease. It shall be burned in the fire.

The laws against leprosy in Leviticus 13 appear to be the first model of quarantine legislation.

The use of the term "leprosy" in Scripture seems to cover a wider range of infectious diseases (also called plague), and the quarantine legislation could get quite complicated (*see* Leviticus 13 and 14), the general rule being quarantine, sometimes for just seven days. Careful observation was then made to see if the plague was healed and if it was, the person was declared clean after a ceremony and a further seven days of quarantine living outside the camp. Infected garments were to be burned if the disease had spread after seven days.

Today we know that bacteria cause leprosy.[808] For millennia after Leviticus was written, however, good quarantine practices were often non-existent despite the clear Bible mandate.

> As pointed out above, there were already, however, very strict commands in the Bible about how to deal with leprosy [and other infectious diseases]. In fact, these laws include quarantining the patient [Leviticus 13], something that was unheard of at the time.[809]

Those strict commands about how to deal with leprosy and other infectious diseases would have saved lives during the Black Death.[810]

> In fact, "until [the twentieth century], all previous societies, except for the Israelites who followed God's medical laws regarding quarantine, kept infected patients in their homes—even after death, exposing family members and others to deadly disease. During the devastating Black Death or bubonic plague of the fourteenth century, patients who were sick or dead were kept in the same rooms as the rest of the family. People often wondered why the disease (which killed half of Europe and seemed unstoppable) was affecting so many people at one time. They attributed these epidemics to 'bad air' or 'evil spirits.' However, careful attention to the medical commands of God as revealed in Leviticus would have saved untold millions of lives. Arturo Castiglione wrote about the overwhelming importance of this biblical medical law, 'The laws against leprosy in Leviticus 13 may be regarded as the first model of a sanitary legislation' [Arturo Castiglione, *A History of Medicine...* 1941, p. 71]. Fortunately, the church fathers of Vienna finally

took the biblical injunctions to heart and commanded that those infected with the plague… be placed
outside the city in special medical quarantine compounds. Caregivers fed them until they either died
or survived the passage of the disease. Those who
died in homes or streets were instantly removed and
buried outside the city limits. These biblical sanitary
measures quickly brought the dreaded epidemic under control for the first time. Other cities and countries rapidly followed the medical practices of Vienna
until the Black Death was finally halted" [Jeffrey, pp.
149–150].[811]

One out of every four people died during the
black plague. Because we didn't understand germs.
We didn't understand contagion. And we didn't understand infection. And we didn't understand quar-
antining people. … Nobody understood quarantine
because nobody understood germs.[812]

"The practice of quarantine, as we know it, only began during the
fourteenth century in an effort to protect coastal cities from plague
epidemics,"[813] but, as pointed out above, it was not used generally, at
least at first, to deter the spread of the Black Death.

Quarantine had not been generally used because, as previously
stated, the existence of germs and their effect on human disease was
unknown until the end of the nineteenth century when Louis Pasteur demonstrated in his Germ Theory of Disease that most infectious diseases were caused by microorganisms originating from outside the body.[814]

But quarantine was first used, and then only in some places, over
2,700 years after Leviticus and Numbers were written by Moses, who
would have had no scientific or medical basis for understanding why

When Only God Knew

there should be quarantine. So, again, how did Moses know the value of quarantine in the fifteenth century BC?

5. Nebuchadnezzar, the Beast

Fact Stated: Daniel (written 536–530 BC)
Fact Confirmed: 19th century AD (2400 years later ±)

The Fourth Chapter of the Book of Daniel talks about how Nebuchadnezzar II, the Babylonian King, became a beast. That occurred after the prophet, Daniel, interpreted a dream which Nebuchadnezzar had, saying that Nebuchadnezzar would dwell with the beasts. The Book of Daniel describes how Nebuchadnezzar began acting like a beast immediately after he bragged about how great he was. Daniel 4:31–33 (NIV) (written 536–530 BC) says,

> Even as the words were on his lips, a voice came from heaven, "This is what is decreed for you, King Nebuchadnezzar: Your royal authority has been taken from you. You will be driven away from people and will live with the wild animals; you will eat grass like the ox. Seven times will pass by for you until you acknowledge that the Most High is sovereign over all kingdoms on earth and gives them to anyone he wishes." Immediately what had been said about Nebuchadnezzar was fulfilled. He was driven away from people and ate grass like the ox. His body was drenched with the dew of heaven until his hair grew like the feathers of an eagle and his nails like the claws of a bird.

According to verse 34 of Chapter 4 of Daniel, after the time had passed, Nebuchadnezzar's senses returned to him.

"Liberal critics generally united in a low view of this chapter" for some time, "finding the text itself suspect."[815] For centuries, medicine could not explain this condition. That is until medical science discovered such conditions as boanthropy, "a psychological disorder in which the sufferer believes he or she is a cow or ox" and "porphyria, a group of enzyme disorders that manifest with neurological symptoms including hallucinations, depression, anxiety, and paranoia."[816]

Nonetheless, Daniel had described the centuries-long skeptical liberally suspected symptoms for the condition in the sixth century BC. That was 2500 years, more or less, before the condition became the topic of scientific, medical, and psychological focus.

It took until 1889 for Dr. B. J. Stokvis[817] to publish the first case and clinical description of acute hepatic porphyria and accurately describe the clinical syndrome, "porphyria."[818] Boanthropy, on the other hand, "is such an unusual and uncommon disorder that there is not much research into it, let alone case studies,"[819] although it appears to be first discussed as a specific psychological condition in the late nineteenth century AD.

Daniel 4's description of Nebuchadnezzar's condition is but another example of how the Bible was ahead of medical and psychological science. The facts were reported by Daniel, a Jewish noble and a prophet taken into captivity by Nebuchadnezzar, 2500 years before science would provide a basis for concluding that there was a medical basis for such a condition. Was the proof delayed so that it could be used as another basis for proving that God is all-knowing?

6. Emotional Health Relates to Physical Health.

Fact Stated:
Proverbs, Psalms, Ecclesiastes and Isaiah (written 1449–680 BC), Matthew, John, Romans, 2 Corinthians, Colossians, James and 1 Peter (written 44–90 AD)
Fact Confirmed: 20th and 21st centuries AD (3000 years later ±)

It is now an accepted fact that a person's physical health is strongly correlated with his or her mental and spiritual health. The Bible revealed this to us over 2500 years ago, however. That revelation can be found in Proverbs written primarily by King Solomon[820] and other statements in the Bible.

Proverbs (written 971–686 BC) is full of statements confirming that a glad heart supports physical health. Proverbs 12:4 (NIV) says, "A wife of noble character is her husband's crown, but a disgraceful wife is like decay in his bones." Proverbs 14:30 (NIV) says, "A heart at peace gives life to the body, but envy rots the bones." Proverbs 15:30 (NIV) says, "Light in a messenger's eyes brings joy to the heart, and good news gives health to the bones." Proverbs 16:24 (NIV) says, "Gracious words are a honeycomb, sweet to the soul and healing to the bones." Proverbs 17:22 (NIV) says, "A cheerful heart is good medicine, but a crushed spirit dries up the bones."

The connection of a healthy emotional state with physical health has only recently begun to be scientifically verified. In an online article, "Exploring the Link Between Health and Happiness" published in *Psychology Today*[821] on February 13, 2019, the author said the following:

> It's common sense that it's difficult to feel happy when you are seriously ill. But do feelings of happiness help to prevent people from becoming sick, or help them to get better quicker? That's the question posed by a new field of research focused on the relationship between happiness and health. Researchers are creating better measures for happiness and using new statistical techniques that help to tease out whether happiness really makes a difference in health. In these types of studies, happiness doesn't just mean that burst of joy you get from a feel-good movie or when your favorite team wins a game. It also includes more general feelings of satisfaction and a sense of meaning and purpose in life. A new sys-

tematic review published [February 2019] in the *Annual Review of Public Health* looks at the entire body of evidence on happiness and health to answer the question, does happiness really lead to better health?

...

Here's what studies have found so far:

First, there is clear evidence demonstrating a link between happiness and a decreased risk of mortality. Essentially, people who report that they feel a stronger sense of well-being are less likely to die compared to those who do not. It's important to note that this analysis does not establish a cause-and-effect relationship, but it still provides broad evidence of a connection. Next, there is a range of prospective studies that show happiness is associated with a reduced risk of specific diseases including stroke, diabetes, high blood pressure, and arthritis. There is also some evidence that people with serious health conditions—including spinal cord injury, coronary artery disease, and heart failure—are likely to recover more quickly when they experience feelings of happiness.

Even as prestigious an institution as the Mayo Clinic recognizes that positive emotional health is good for physical health. An article written by its staff said, "Whether you're guffawing at a sitcom on TV or quietly giggling at a newspaper cartoon, laughing does you good. Laughter is a great form of stress relief, and that's no joke."[822]

Stress Relief from Laughter

A good sense of humor can't cure all ailments, but data is mounting about the positive things laughter can do.

Short-term benefits

A good laugh has great short-term effects. When you start to laugh, it doesn't just lighten your load mentally; it actually induces physical changes in your body. Laughter can:

- **Stimulate many organs.** Laughter enhances your intake of oxygen-rich air, stimulates your heart, lungs, and muscles, and increases the endorphins that are released by your brain.

- **Activate and relieve your stress response.** A rollicking laugh fires up and then cools down your stress response, and it can increase and then decrease your heart rate and blood pressure. The result? A good, relaxed feeling.

- **Soothe tension.** Laughter can also stimulate circulation and aid muscle relaxation, both of which can help reduce some of the physical symptoms of stress.

Long-term effects

Laughter isn't just a quick pick-me-up, though. It's also good for you over the long term. Laughter may:

- **Improve your immune system.** Negative thoughts manifest into chemical reactions that can affect your body by bringing more stress into your system and decreasing your immunity. By contrast, positive thoughts can actually release neuropeptides that help fight stress and potentially more serious illnesses.

- **Relieve pain.** Laughter may ease pain by causing the body to produce its own natural painkillers.

- **Increase personal satisfaction.** Laughter can also make it easier to cope with difficult situations. It also helps you connect with other people.
- **Improve your mood.** Many people experience depression, sometimes due to chronic illnesses. Laughter can help lessen your depression and anxiety and may make you feel happier.

> Laughter is the best medicine.
>
> Go ahead and give it a try. Turn the corners of your mouth up into a smile and then give a laugh, even if it feels a little forced. Once you've had your chuckle, take stock of how you're feeling. Are your muscles a little less tense? Do you feel more relaxed or buoyant? That's the natural wonder of laughing at work.[823]

Yet again, science is just catching up to the wisdom of the Bible, more than 2500 years after passages in the Bible were written. That also supports the conclusion that the Bible is reliable.

Having shown that the Bible is scientifically, medically, and psychologically reliable, respecting the fact that emotional happiness leads to physical health, then the Bible should also be reliable in describing what can make one emotionally happy and thereby healthy. The Bible tells us, in too many places in both the Old and the New Testaments to quote, how to be happy.

There are Old Testament Bible verses that tell us that happiness comes from God. For example, Nehemiah 8:10 (NIV) (written 445–400 BC) says, "Do not grieve, for the joy of the Lord is your strength." Psalms 1:1–3, 16:11, 19:8, 28:7 and 30:5 (NIV) (probably written, respectively, about 444, 1044, 1015, 1015 and 1017 BC)[824] say,

When Only God Knew

Blessed is the one who does not walk in step with the wicked or stand in the way that sinners take or sit in the company of mockers, but whose delight is in the law of the Lord, and who meditates on his law day and night. That person is like a tree planted by streams of water, which yields its fruit in season and whose leaf does not wither—whatever they do prospers.

Psalm 1:1–3 (NIV)

"You make known to me the path of life; you will fill me with joy in your presence, with eternal pleasures at your right hand."

Psalm 16:11 (NIV)

"The precepts of the Lord are right, giving joy to the heart. The commands of the Lord are radiant, giving light to the eyes."

Psalm 19:8 (NIV)

"The Lord is my strength and my shield; my heart trusts in him, and he helps me. My heart leaps for joy, and with my song I praise him."

Psalm 28:7 (NIV)

Those who look to him are radiant; their faces are never covered with shame. This poor man called, and the Lord heard him; he saved him out of all his troubles. The angel of the Lord encamps around those who fear him, and he delivers them. Taste and see that the Lord is good; blessed is the one who takes refuge in him.

Psalm 30:5 (NIV)

Proverbs 10:28 and 29:18 (NIV) (written 971–686 BC) say,

> "The prospect of the righteous is joy, but the hopes of the wicked come to nothing" (Proverbs 10:28, NIV), and "Where there is no revelation, people cast off restraint; but blessed is the one who heeds wisdom's instruction" (Proverbs 29:18, NIV).

Ecclesiastes 9:7 (NIV) (written 940–931 BC) says, "Go, eat your food with gladness, and drink your wine with a joyful heart, for God has already approved what you do." Isaiah 9:3 (NIV) (written 740–680 BC), in a prayer to God, says, "You have enlarged the nation and increased their joy; they rejoice before you as people rejoice at the harvest, as warriors rejoice when dividing the plunder."

There are also New Testament Bible verses that tell us that happiness comes from God. Matthew 25:21 (NIV) (written 50–65 AD) says,

> His master replied, 'Well done, good and faithful servant! You have been faithful with a few things; I will put you in charge of many things. Come and share your master's happiness!

In John 15:10–11 (NIV) (written 80–90 AD), Jesus said,

> If you keep my commands, you will remain in my love, just as I have kept my Father's commands and remain in his love. I have told you this so that my joy may be in you and that your joy may be complete.

John 16:24 (NIV) (written 80–90 AD) says, "Until now you have not asked for anything in my name. Ask and you will receive, and your joy will be complete." Romans 15:13 (NIV) (written 56–57

When Only God Knew

AD) also says, "May the God of hope fill you with all joy and peace as you trust in him, so that you may overflow with hope by the power of the Holy Spirit." 1 Peter 1:8–9 (NIV) (written 62–65 AD) likewise says,

> Though you have not seen him[, speaking of Jesus], you love him; and even though you do not see him now, you believe in him and are filled with an inexpressible and glorious joy, for you are receiving the end result of your faith, the salvation of your souls.

There are Old and New Testament Bible verses that tell us to turn difficult situations around and be emotionally happy in hard times. For example, Psalms 30:11 and 126:4–5 (NIV) (probably written, respectively, about 1017 and 536 BC),[825] James 1:2–4 (NIV) (written 44–49 AD), 2 Corinthians 8:1–2 (NIV) (written 55–57 AD) and Colossians 1:9–12 (NIV) (written 60–62 AD) say,

> "You, (Lord God), turned my wailing into dancing; you removed my sackcloth and clothed me with joy."
> Psalm 30:11 (NIV)

> "Restore our fortunes, Lord, like streams in the Negev. Those who sow with tears will reap with songs of joy."
> Psalm 126:4 (NIV)

> Consider it pure joy, my brothers and sisters, whenever you face trials of many kinds, because you know that the testing of your faith produces perseverance. Let perseverance finish its work so that you may be mature and complete, not lacking anything.
> James 1:2 (NIV)

And now, brothers and sisters, we want you to know about the grace that God has given the Macedonian churches. In the midst of a very severe trial, their overflowing joy and their extreme poverty welled up in rich generosity.

2 Corinthians 8:1 (NIV)

For this reason, since the day we heard about you, we have not stopped praying for you. We continually ask God to fill you with the knowledge of his will through all the wisdom and understanding that the Spirit gives, so that you may live a life worthy of the Lord and please him in every way: bearing fruit in every good work, growing in the knowledge of God, being strengthened with all power according to his glorious might so that you may have great endurance and patience, and giving joyful thanks to the Father, who has qualified you to share in the inheritance of his holy people in the kingdom of light.

Colossians 1:9–12 (NIV)

We not only know how emotional health and happiness lead to physical health, but the Bible tells us how to be happy. It tells us what will make us happy.

So, you would think that Christians would be happier, particularly if they heeded the biblical prescriptions for happiness. According to many published articles, they are. "Studies show that religiously active tend to be happier in their lives than their secular counterparts."[826] The titles of two articles support the proposition that Christians are happier and sum it up. They are "It Turns out, Regular Church-Goers Are Happier, a New Pew Study Finds," written by Michelle Darrisaw, and "Christians Happiest Among All Faith Groups, Survey Reveals," an article written by Stoyan Zaimov.[827]

CHAPTER 8

Natural Science, Mechanics, Mathematics and Engineering

It took as long as 3500 years after the Bible discussed various natural science, mechanical, mathematical, and engineering principles and zoological facts for their accuracy to be verified by modern science and archaeology. Below are discussions of some of those biblical principles, according to the part of the Bible in which they are found and when "modern" disciplines confirmed them.[828]

A. Natural Science

1. Dinosaurs and Dragons— Young Earth/Old Earth

Fact Stated: Genesis, Psalms, and Isaiah (written 1450–680 BC);
Job 40:15–24 (date of writing unknown, 2000 BC to the 5th century BC,
but believed by most to be the oldest book in the Bible)
Fact Confirmed: 19th to 21st century AD (3200–3400 years later ±)

It would take 3500 years ± after large animals were described in the Bible before the secular world would identify those animals in the nineteenth century—the animals we now know as dinosaurs. Paleontology, "the study of the history of life on Earth as based on fossils," which include dinosaur fossils, did not even begin as a formal science until the 1700s.[829] Once the first identification of a dinosaur occurred, however, others were rapidly located.

It is not the purpose of this book to enter the controversy over whether the Earth is young—just 6,000 years ±—or old—millions upon millions of years. While there are interpretations of evidence used to support each viewpoint, each viewpoint interprets the evidence differently and reaches different conclusions from it. This book's purpose is only to point out facts that were not or should not have been known to the authors of the Bible, which were only later substantiated.

Nonetheless, it is inevitable that any discussion of dinosaurs becomes embroiled in the debate as to the real age of the world. The reader may want to read other literature which discusses such earth-age topics as:

1. why there is so little sediment at the bottom of the oceans;
2. why layers of rock are bent and are not broken as might be expected if rock had been deposited millions of years ago;
3. why scientists have found soft tissue in animal fossils that should not be soft if the fossils had been deposited millions of years ago;
4. what has been called the faint sun paradox;
5. what the decaying Earth's magnetic field says about the age of the Earth;
6. why do rocks, which are supposed to be millions of years old, contain so much helium if all helium in them should have leaked out in less than 100,000 years;
7. why has carbon-14, a radioactive form of carbon with a half-life of less than 6000 years, been found in fossils that are supposed to be millions of years old;
8. why are there the number comets roaming around the universe if the universe is old;
9. why is there relatively little salt in the seas and
10. why is the DNA in what was thought to be bacteria millions of years old so like modern bacterial DNA?[830]

When Only God Knew

One should, however, keep in mind when considering whether the Earth is old or new that the people who wrote the Bible would not have been, under the "old" version of the Earth's age, alive when dinosaurs roamed the Earth, because in that version the Earth is millions of years old. Yet incredibly large animals are described in the Bible. These animals were supposed by some scientists to have died millions of years ago, well before those same scientists say that mankind first appeared on the Earth; how then did men know only thousands of years ago to write about them in the Bible as if they had only recently existed?

There is evidence to be weighed that supports the conclusion that dinosaurs were alive as recently as a few thousand, not millions, years ago. Books in the Bible, the earliest of which was written probably no later than 1405 BC, appear to speak of dinosaurs. As should be expected, this evidence begins with Genesis, the first book of the Bible, and is found in the book of Job, whose exact date is unknown but is believed to be the oldest book in the Bible.

Genesis 1:24–25 (NIV) (written 1450–1405 BC) says,

> And God said, "Let the land produce living creatures according to their kinds: the livestock, the creatures that move along the ground, and the wild animals, each according to its kind." And it was so. God made the wild animals according to their kinds, the livestock according to their kinds, and all the creatures that move along the ground according to their kinds. And God saw that it was good.

One of the moving creatures described in Genesis would be the dinosaur. We know dinosaurs existed; dinosaur fossils, dinosaur bones, and other proofs of dinosaurs have been found. The question is, when did dinosaurs first and last "move along the ground," New archaeological findings may be on the verge of extinguishing the "scientific" theory that they became extinct millions of years ago.

In 2021, the year this book was written, a well-respected Egyptologist and his team found proof that dinosaurs were used to build the pyramids. That would have been much more recently than when old Earth proponents thought they died off. This is another example of science/archaeology catching up to the biblical narrative.

Professor Nabir Ibn Al-Sammud, leading a team of archeologists from the University of Cairo, "has uncovered ancient papyri and a number of stone palettes dating back to 3,500 BC which could prove ancient Egyptians might have lived amongst dinosaurs."[831] "The papyri were written by men who participated in the building of the Great Pyramid, the tomb of the Pharaoh Khufu, and mention the use of 'beastly creatures' of 'enormous size.'"[832] The "claim would have been rapidly dismissed if it did not come from one of Egyptology's most eminent figures and has definitely come as a surprise to the scientific community."[833] The pyramid of Khufu, the Great Pyramid of Giza, was finished in 2560 BC,[834] less than 5,000 thousand years ago.

Other evidence supports the conclusion that the Bible described dinosaurs only a few thousand years ago. Job 40:15–24 (KJV) (date of writing unknown, 2000 BC to the fifth century BC, but believed by most to be the oldest book in the Bible) says,

> Behold now behemoth, which I made with thee; he eateth grass as an ox. Lo now, his strength is in his loins, and his force is in the navel of his belly. He moveth his tail like a cedar: the sinews of his stones are wrapped together His bones are as strong pieces of brass; his bones are like bars of iron. He is the chief of the ways of God: he that made him can make his sword to approach unto him. Surely the mountains bring him forth food, where all the beasts of the field

play. He lieth under the shady trees, in the covert of the reed, and fens. The shady trees cover him with their shadow; the willows of the brook compass him about. Behold, he drinketh up a river, and hasteth not: he trusteth that he can draw up Jordan into his mouth. He taketh it with his eyes: his nose pierceth through snares.

Doesn't that sound like Job is giving an eye-witness account of a very, very large dinosaur, perhaps an apatosaurus, brachiosaurus, or a brontosaurus?[835] Its tail is compared to a cedar tree. Its strength, and apparently its bulk, is in its loins. It is described as having the ability to drink up a river. No modern animal meets this description. Some commentators claim Job is describing a hippopotamus; others claim Job might be describing an elephant. However, neither a hippo's tail nor an elephant's tail is "like a cedar." They are more like small twigs in comparison. And neither can drink up a river or even looks like it could.

Job 41:12–34 (NIV) (date of writing unknown, 2000 BC to the fifth century BC, but believed by most to be the oldest book in the Bible) also says,

I will not fail to speak of Leviathan's limbs, its strength, and its graceful form. Who can strip off its outer coat? Who can penetrate its double coat of armor? Who dares open the doors of its mouth, ringed about with fearsome teeth? Its back has rows of shields tightly sealed together; each is so close to the next that no air can pass between. They are joined fast to one another; they cling together and cannot be parted. Its snorting throws out flashes of light; its eyes are like the rays of dawn. Flames stream from its mouth; sparks of fire shoot out. Smoke pours from its nostrils as from a boiling pot over burning reeds. Its breath sets coals ablaze, and flames dart from its mouth. Strength resides in its neck; dismay goes before it. The folds of its flesh are tightly joined; they are firm and immovable. Its chest is hard as rock, hard as a lower millstone. When it rises up, the mighty are terrified; they retreat before its thrashing. The sword that reaches it has no effect, nor does the spear or the dart or the javelin. Iron it treats like straw and bronze like rotten wood. Arrows do not make it flee; slingstones are like chaff to it. A club seems to it but a piece of straw; it laughs at the rattling of the lance. Its undersides are jagged potsherds, leaving a trail in the mud like a threshing sledge. It makes the depths churn like a boiling caldron and stirs up the sea like a pot of ointment. It leaves a glistening wake behind it; one would think the deep had white hair. Nothing on earth is its equal—a creature without fear. It looks down on all that are haughty; it is king over all that are proud.

This passage describes a very, very large animal. Could this be a fanciful description of a dinosaur? It describes a large animal that could breathe fire. How could this creature exist? Doesn't this description sound like a dragon? More about that later.

Other passages in the Bible also talk about leviathan. Psalms 104:25–26 (NIV) (probably written about 1015 BC)[836] says,

There is the sea, vast and spacious, teeming with creatures beyond number—living things both large and small. There the ships go to and fro, and Leviathan, which you formed to frolic there.

Isaiah 27:1 (NIV) (written 700–680 BC) says,

> In that day, the Lord will punish with his sword—
> his fierce, great and powerful sword—Leviathan the
> gliding serpent, Leviathan the coiling serpent; he will
> slay the monster of the sea.

The easiest explanation of Job 40:15–24, Job 41:12–34, Psalm 104:25–26, and Isaiah 27:1 is that the biblical descriptions of leviathans and behemoths better fits (sic) extinct dinosaurs than any other beast or mythical creature! Henry Morris[837] writes the following in this regard.

> The description of behemoth seems to fit perfectly what we know about such a land dinosaur as apatosaurus, for example, and leviathan fits what we know about some large marine reptiles, such as the plesiosaur or ichthyosaur, for example.[838]

Contrary to the apparent conclusion in *Leviathan—Behemoths—Mythical Animals in the Bible*,[839] however, the evidence, including the recent find by the Egyptologist, Professor Nabir Ibn Al-Sammud, and his team, supports the conclusion that these animals were not mythical but represented descriptions of animals within the memory of the writer of Job and/or his contemporaries. Of note is the fact that "nearly every ancient civilization has some sort of art depicting giant reptilian creatures."[840] Does that art represent memories of dinosaurs that existed more recently than millions of years ago? It is unlikely that the art represented something that existed millions of years before the artists lived. Logic suggests that it was based on very recent memory.

That is particularly true since no dinosaurs were identified by any name until after a large tooth was found and determined to have come from a large animal—a dinosaur—in 1822 AD,[841]

> In 1822, Mary Ann Mantell[842] became the first person to discover and correctly identify a strange bone as part of a large, unknown reptile. Her husband, Dr. Gideon Mantell, later named this creature an "Iguanodon." From that time forward, these forgotten animals were given names chosen by the people who rediscovered them.[843]

The first dinosaur to be described scientifically was Megalosaurus. This genus was named in 1824 AD.[844] The word dinosaur had not even been invented yet.

> It wasn't until 1841 that British scientist Richard Owen came to realize that such fossils were distinct from the teeth or bones of any living creature. The ancient animals were so different, in fact, that they deserved their own name. So Owen dubbed the group "Dinosauria," which means "terrible lizards."[845]

These scientific identifications were all 3200 years ± after Genesis was written and perhaps longer after Job described these large animals.

Understanding what the terms in Job, originally written in Hebrew, mean is important to this discussion. Before we do that, we should also indicate what else was said about the creation of sea creatures in the Bible.

First, Genesis 1:21 (NIV) (written 1450–1405 BC) also says,

When Only God Knew

So God created the great creatures of the sea and every living thing with which the water teems and that moves about in it, according to their kinds, and every winged bird according to its kind. And God saw that it was good.

Dinosaurs *appear to be* mentioned in the Bible by other names. The list of large animals in the Bible in the original Hebrew are tanniyn, behemowth, behema, and livyathan. In English, the last three are called behemoth and leviathan.[846] The word tanniyn has been translated as "dinosaur."[847]

But the term "dinosaur" was not first used until 1841,[848] over three thousand years *after* the Bible first referred to "tanniyn." It appears that translators of the Bible saw a natural connection between the term "tanniyn" and "dinosaur," which came into being 3200 years± after "tanniyn" was first used. In fact, the first use of the word "dinosaur" as translation of the word "tanniyn" was by Sir Richard Owen, a scientist.[849]

Now back to dragons as promised.

While conventional thinking is that Genesis 1:21 speaks of God creating whales, "[t]he Hebrew word *tan* (plural, tannin)" used in that passage has been translated as sea monster, dragon, whale, and serpent.[850] The word tanniyn can be found twenty-eight times in the Bible.[851] It is translated as monsters once, whale twice, serpent three times, but dragon twenty-one times.[852] Why dragons twenty-one times? Could it be that, like other extinct animals, dragons did exist at one time but are now extinct? There is some evidence that fire-breathing animals could exist, again as will be discussed below. It could also be that "dragon" was used as a word to describe large reptilian creatures,[853] which would support the proposition that dinosaurs were alive for men to see.

The first thing to consider about dragons is that there have been stories describing them for millennia in many different countries.

"Even with the endless variations of language and culture that people have created—not to mention every possible type of landscape and climate they've called home—time and again, our ancestors have" told dragon stories which most people have described as a conjured myth.[854] Those stories are usually described as part of a culture's mythology. The fact that nearly every major culture in the world has traditions about dragons, however, should give one pause to consider whether there is credible evidence supporting the possibility of their existence in the past, as described in the Bible.

> We encounter dragons in almost every ancient culture of the world. Dragons played an important role in the beliefs of our ancestors, and these creatures were depicted in a variety of ways.[855]

"In ancient China, [for example], the dragon was a highly significant creature that became a symbol of the Emperor, and his throne was sometimes called the Dragon Throne."[856] The dragon is one of the twelve animals in the Chinese zodiac and one of the twelve names for a Chinese year.[857]

In ancient Mesopotamia, Marduk, the ruler of the Mesopotamian gods, was described as a dragon.[858] Ancient Mesopotamia also has a story about Mušḫuššu, a dragon described as "a scaly animal with hind legs resembling the talons of an eagle, lion-like forelimbs, a long neck and tail, a horned head, a snake-like tongue, and a crest."[859] From Babylonia, we have the story of the Tiamat, "sometimes considered dragons."[860] Other Asian countries, including but not limited to Tibet, Indonesia, Malaya, Japan, Korea, Philippines, India, Persia, and Viet Nam, also have stories of dragons.[861]

But ancient Asia and the Middle East are not the only places that have dragon stories. Europe, North America, South America, aboriginal Australia, and Africa also tell dragon tales.[862]

When Only God Knew

Are the dragon stories really mythical? Why do so many cultures have dragon stories? Are the earliest dragon stories based on remembered animals? Or are they merely the result of a cultural exchange of information? Did all these different cultures independently come up with the same fiction about dragons?

The dragon stories are unlikely to have begun in the separate imaginations of so many different cultures. In addition, in an ancient world where communication and travel were limited, the stories are not too likely to be the mere result of a simple cultural exchange of information between far-flung countries, particularly between the Old World (Europe, Asia, and Africa) and the New World (North and South America).

Again, this book will not get into a debate about when man and animals first appeared on Earth. Even using conclusions supported by old Earth theory proponents will not, however, show that the idea of dragons had to be or even could have been the result of a cultural exchange of ideas. A reasonable evidentiary conclusion can be reached that men may have seen dragons, even using evidence from those who do not believe that could have happened, such as the migration of humans into the New World.

The secular version of the story of the migration of humans into North America supports the conclusion that dragon stories are not the result of exchanged information. The conclusions reached by some is that "13,000 years ago [or even 1,000 or 2,000 years before that], small bands of Stone Age hunters walked across a land bridge between eastern Siberia and western Alaska, eventually making their way down an ice-free inland corridor into the heart of North America."[863] Others reach the conclusion that humans first arrived in North America 30,000 years ago.[864] Whether one concludes that mankind migrated into North America 13,000, 15,000, or even 30,000 years ago, those conclusions, however, logically support a determination that dragon stories in North America were not the result of a cultural exchange of the dragon idea.

First, according to scientists the Bering Land Bridge over which humans would have migrated over 10,000 years ago from Asia to North America disappeared at the end of the last ice age which they say ended between 10,000 and 12,500 years ago.[865]

Second, China is believed to have "the longest continuous tradition of dragon stories," but it only dates back about 5,000 years, more or less.[866] Other dragon stories are traced by some back to approximately 4000 BC,[867] 6000 years ago ±.

So, if the ice age ended and the land bridge disappeared more than 10,000 years ago, how could any cultural exchange of the dragon idea have occurred between anyone in the ancient world 5–6000 years ago when, if the Bering Land Bridge disappeared between 10,000 and 12,500 years ago, humans had already been in North America for thousands of years?

So, are we left with the conclusion that there must be some eye-witness basis, in fact, for dragon tales? Can the dragon stories and the Job 41:19–24 description of Leviathan's snorting, throwing out flashes of light, with flames streaming/darting from its mouth, with sparks of fire shooting out and smoke pouring from its nostrils as from a boiling pot over burning reed and with breath that sets coals ablaze be accurate? Those biblical passages are in keeping with the dragon stories of numerous and diverse cultures.

After balancing the evidence, the conclusion that dragons existed seems to me to be the most logical. And there is additional evidence that any dragons described in the Bible may have actually been seen by the writer of Job and/or his contemporaries.

Another piece of evidence that should be weighed in deciding if dragons may have existed and been described in Job, Psalms, and Isaiah comes from the finding of a skull that was donated to the Children's Museum of Indianapolis in 2004 by three Sioux City, Iowa, residents who found it during a trip to the Hell Creek Formation in South Dakota.[868] Due to "its dragon-like head, horns, and teeth," the new species was dubbed Dracorex hogwartsia (after the Harry Potter series in which dragons play such a large role), because the "skull mixes spiky horns, bumps, and a long muzzle" and "is flat-headed."[869]

Still, another piece of evidence to be considered as to the existence of dragons is that the description of a dragon is very similar to the descriptions of dinosaurs. *See* pictures below. If dinosaurs existed, couldn't dragons build very much like them have also existed? One article pointed out the following:

> "The dragons of legend are strangely like actual creatures that have lived in the past. They are much like the great reptiles which inhabited the earth long before man is supposed to have appeared on earth. Dragons were generally evil and destructive. Every country had them in its mythology." [Knox, Wilson, "Dragon," *The World Book Encyclopedia*, vol. 5, 1973, p. 265]. The article on dragons in the *Encyclopaedia Britannica* [1949 edition] noted that dinosaurs were "astonishingly dragonlike," even though its author assumed that those ancients who believed in dragons did so "without the slightest knowledge" of dinosaurs. The truth is that the fathers of modern paleontology used the terms "dinosaur" and "dragon" interchangeably for quite some time.[870]

871

Perhaps the key statement in that article is that ancients who "believed in dragons did so 'without the slightest knowledge of dinosaurs," which scientists tell us disappeared from the Earth millions of years ago and which were first identified to the modern world in 1822. 1822 is millions of years after dinosaurs are supposed to have disappeared from the Earth and over 5,000 years after the ancient dragon stories were first told. Why did ancients describe a fire-breathing animal so close in description to dinosaurs, which we know existed but about which they had no knowledge unless they saw an animal—either a dinosaur or one that breathed fire. The dragon stories are proof that either dragons existed or that dinosaurs did long after dinosaurs are said to have become extinct or both.

But fire-breathing animals? Could not happen. Right? Wrong.

Despite the long and ancient history of dragon stories, some dismiss the dragon translation of "tannin" as fictitious because the leviathan is described as breathing fire. However, some creation scientists believe this could have happened. The creature would merely need glands to produce a chemical or a combination of chemicals that would combust when exposed to air or to other chemicals, an idea that is far from science fiction.

First, there are several chemical compounds and elements which when combined, are flammable or explosive. For instance, mixing

When Only God Knew

oxidizing agents (e.g., nitric acid) with reducing agents (e.g., hydrazine) may cause fires or explosions; sodium metal and other materials in water will flame or explode; iron sulfide when in contact with oxygen (air), is liable to ignite spontaneously; potassium added to water will explode because mixing any alkali metal with water will cause an explosion; mixing potassium chlorate, table sugar and sulfuric acid can result in fire.[873] Another chemical, chlorine trifluoride, first discovered in the 1930s, "easily reacts, sometimes explosively, with just about every known substance on Earth."[874]

The reader may ask, "So what if you can cause fire or even an explosion when you mix two chemicals, there is no animal that can mix two elements or chemical compounds, is there?" There is.

The bombardier beetle has the ability and does mix materials. Bombardier beetles have the "ability to synthesize and release rapid bursts of stinky, burning-hot liquid from their rear ends."[875] Bombardier beetles

> are most notable for the defense mechanism that gives them their name: when disturbed, they eject a hot noxious chemical spray from the tip of the abdomen with a popping sound. The spray is produced from a reaction between two chemical compounds, hydroquinone and hydrogen peroxide, which are stored in two reservoirs in the beetle's abdomen. When the aqueous solution of hydroquinones and hydrogen peroxide reaches the vestibule, catalysts facilitate the decomposition of the hydrogen peroxide and the oxidation of the hydroquinone. Heat from the reaction brings the mixture to near the boiling point of water and produces gas that drives the ejection.[876]

Who is to say that there could not have been and were not other creatures that had the ability to mix chemicals like the bombardier beetle? If "dragons" had the ability to store and mix chemicals, just like bombardier beetles do, or to expel chemicals, such as iron sulphide, into the air, which would then cause a fire, dragons could be described as "breathing fire." Likewise, if "dragons" had the ability to expel chemicals, such as chlorine trifluoride, so that they came into contact with some combustible material, dragons could "breath fire." Dragons could then be rightly described as snorting out flashes of light, with flames streaming/darting from their mouths, sparks of fire shooting out and smoke pouring from their nostrils, and as having breath that sets coals ablaze, just as described in Job 41:19–24, the oldest book in the Bible.

Readers should weigh the evidence for the existence of dinosaurs and/or dragons and decide for themselves. When added to all the other evidence of the reliability of biblical accounts, the story in Job is not so far-fetched a description of dinosaurs and/or dragons which were witnessed or remembered by Job, the author of Job, or his contemporaries.

2. Hydrothermal Vents

Fact Stated: Genesis (written 1450–1405 BC); Job 38:16 (NIV)
(date of writing unknown, 2000 BC to the 5th century BC,
but believed by most to be the oldest book in the Bible)
Fact Confirmed: 1977 AD (3900–3350 years later ±)

Ocean hydrothermal vents are described in two books of the Bible written before 1400 BC—more than 3,000 years before their discovery by science.

Genesis 7:11 (NIV) (written 1450–1405 BC) says,

> In the six hundredth year of Noah's life, on the seventeenth day of the second month—on that day, all the springs of the great deep burst forth, and the floodgates of the heavens were opened.

When Only God Knew

Job 38:16 (NIV) (date of writing unknown, 2000 BC to the fifth century BC, but believed by most to be the oldest book in the Bible) says, "Have you journeyed to the springs of the sea or walked in the recesses of the deep?"

But the existence of ocean hydrothermal vents was not discovered until 1977, 3350 or more years after they were described in the Bible by authors who could not have seen them. In February 1977, "Robert Ballard, a marine geologist at Woods Hole Oceanographic Institution (WHOI)," sitting on a research vessel "400 miles off the South American coast" discovered the vents after looking at photos "taken by cameras towed 8,000 feet [2,500 meters] below the surface." The pictures

> unveiled a discovery that would turn our understanding of life on Earth on its head: Warm water was drifting out of the seafloor along the Galápagos Rift.
>
> Ballard, along with a team of thirty marine geologists, geochemists, and geophysicists, had found the world's first known active hydrothermal vent. There were no biologists aboard—because no one had expected the second shocking discovery that came soon after: Life was thriving in the abyss. Foot-long clams and human-sized tube worms with tulip-looking heads made the already extraterrestrial landscape look, well, alien.[877]

How could the authors of Genesis and Job have described vents 8,000 feet below the surface of the ocean? They did not have the equipment to discover them. There may be an even more important question to be answered. Why did these biblical authors, 3,350 years before they would be found, describe vents 8,000 feet below the surface of the ocean whose later discovery would turn mankind's preconceived erroneous understanding of life on Earth on its head? Could it have been to get someone's attention?

3. Hydrology and Weather

Fact Stated: Job (NIV) (date of writing unknown, 2000 BC to the 5th century BC, but believed by most to be the oldest book in the Bible); Psalms, Ecclesiastes, Isaiah, Jeremiah, & Amos (written 1440 BC[878]–450 BC)

Fact Confirmed: 17th century AD (2100–3600 years later ±)

The circulation and conservation of the Earth's water is hydrology and is called the hydrologic cycle, which describes how weather works.

The water, or hydrologic, cycle describes the pilgrimage of water as water molecules make their way from the Earth's surface to the atmosphere and back again, in some cases to below the surface. This gigantic system, powered by energy from the Sun, is a continuous exchange of moisture between the oceans, the atmosphere and the land.[879]

This cycle describes how weather gives rain and snow needed to survive.

While not all river water flows into the oceans of the world,[880] the rivers of the world do dump billions of gallons of water into oceans and seas each day, year in and year out. The Amazon River alone pours almost 60 million gallons of water into the Atlantic Ocean every second.[881] Even "the Mississippi River, which is just one of thousands of rivers all over this planet, dumps over six million gallons of water per second into the Gulf of Mexico."[882]

> The storehouses for the vast majority of all water on Earth are the oceans. It is estimated that of the 332,500,000 cubic miles… of the world's water supply … is stored in oceans. That is about 96.5 percent of all Earth's water.[883]

When Only God Knew

The amount of water in the atmosphere at any moment in time is… a minute fraction of Earth's total water supply: if it were to completely rain out, atmospheric moisture would cover the Earth's surface to a depth of only 2.5 centimeters, less than an inch. However, far more water—in fact, some 495,000 cubic kilometers, almost 119,000 cubic miles or over 15 quadrillion cubic feet, of it—are cycled through the atmosphere every year. It is as if the entire amount of water in the air were removed and replenished nearly forty times a year.[884]

"Evaporation is the process of changing liquid water into water vapor," which is how water is transported "from the Earth's surface to the atmosphere."[885] "Condensation is the process by which water residing in the air changes from water vapor (a gas) to liquid water,"[886] "the reverse of evaporation."[887] *Atmospheric circulation* refers to "the general circulation of the Earth and regional movements of air."[888] While the process of evaporation and condensation may have been vaguely understood in the ancient world, how the processes worked together to produce our weather was not. "The first attempt to explain the global atmospheric circulation was" not until 1686 by Edmond Halley, an English astronomer, and mathematician.[889]

Yet, the Bible contains many descriptions of weather circulation, condensation, evaporation, and precipitation and how they work together to make weather. All the gathering and releasing of water was described in the Bible hundreds of years before the science of hydrology was started. The Bible includes reasonably complete descriptions of the hydrologic cycle—the worldwide processes of evaporation into the atmosphere, the atmospheric circulation of water, its condensation, and mankind's life-saving precipitation.

Job 36:27–28 (NIV) (date of writing unknown, 2000 BC to the fifth century BC, but believed by most to be the oldest book in the

Bible) says, "He draws up the drops of water, which distill as rain to the streams; the clouds pour down their moisture, and abundant showers fall on mankind."

Job 36:27–28 shows significant scientific insight. The drops of water become vapor through evaporation and then pour down as rain after condensing as water in the clouds.

Psalm 135:7 (NIV) (probably written around 950 BC) says, "He makes clouds rise from the ends of the earth; he sends lightning with the rain and brings out the wind from his storehouses."

Jeremiah 10:13 (NIV) (written 627–570 BC) says, "When he thunders, the waters in the heavens roar; he makes clouds rise from the ends of the earth."

Amos 9:6 (NIV) (written 750–760 BC) says, "he builds his lofty palace in the heavens and sets its foundation on the earth; he calls for the waters of the sea and pours them out over the face of the land—the Lord is his name."

Ecclesiastes 1:6–7 (NIV) (written 940–930 BC), describing atmospheric circulation and river/ocean exchange of water, says,

> Blowing toward the south, Then turning toward the north, The wind continues swirling along; And on its circular courses the wind returns. All the rivers flow into the sea, Yet the sea is not full. To the place where the rivers flow, There they flow again.

Describing evaporation, Psalms 135:7 (NASB) (probably written around 950 BC) says that God "causes the mist to ascend rise up from the ends of the earth." Discussing precipitation, Psalms 104:13 (NIV) (probably written about 1015 BC) says that God "waters the mountains from his upper chambers." Isaiah 55:10 (NIV) (written 740–680 BC), also discussing precipitation, says, "As the rain and the snow come down from heaven, and do not return to it without watering the earth and making it bud and flourish, so that it yields seed for the sower and bread for the eater."

Yet,

> [c]enturies after the Book of Job was written, Aristotle, the "ancient Greek philosopher and scientist who lived from 384 to 322 BC, one of the greatest intellectual figures of Western history,"[890] demonstrated only a vague understanding of this process. Though he recognized that rain came from clouds, he incorrectly postulated that air turned into water and vice versa.[891]

Ancient Greeks, as well as other civilizations of that time, often attributed weather changes and natural phenomena to the gods.[892] All occurrences of favorable or poor weather were thought to be a direct result of the intervention of gods. Even Aristotle, who lived in the fourth Century BC, is considered by some to be the founder of meteorology because he wrote *Meteorologica*, "a philosophical treatise that included theories about the formation of rain, clouds, hail, wind, thunder, lightning, and hurricanes,"[893] … tried to explain the weather through the interaction of the four elements: earth, fire, air, and water.[894]

Even the ancient Greeks who attempted a scientific explanation for weather were wrong about how weather works. They wrongly believed there to be a vast subterranean freshwater lake or many watery caverns that supplied the rivers with water through springs. Aristotle was closer to the mark when he described evaporation and condensation, but he still held to the idea of subterranean water being the main source of the supply. These theories came about largely because no one could believe that rainfall was sufficient to keep rivers flowing.[895]

"The earliest literature indicating an understanding of hydrological cycle was apparently around the third or fourth century BC."[896] Even that literature was well after each of those Bible verses was written hundreds of years before. But

> "[i]t wasn't until the 17th century[, particularly 1686, the year that Edmond Halley first attempted to explain the global atmospheric circulation, and 1674, respectively for the scientists named below], however, that the poetic notion of a finite water cycle was demonstrated in the Seine River basin by two French physicists, Edmé Mariotte and Pierre Perrault, who independently determined that the snowpack in the river's headwaters was more than sufficient to account for the river's discharge. These two studies marked the beginning of hydrology, the science of water, and also the hydrologic cycle."[897]

How did it come to happen that Job described the process at least 3200 years before those two scientists would prove that the water cycle was a fact, thus beginning the science of hydrology? Why was the answer to how weather worked not understood until the seventeenth century? Why, just prior to the Age of Reason, when men first began to really challenge the existence of God, were these particular statements in Job proven accurate?

When Only God Knew

B. Scientific Principles Related to End Times—Atomic Energy.

Fact Stated: 2 Peter and Revelation (written 67–96 AD)
Fact Confirmed: 1907 AD, at the earliest (1800 years later ±)

Does the Bible describe consequences from the use of atomic energy? Ernest Rutherford, who received the Nobel Prize in chemistry in 1908, is credited with first splitting the atom in 1917.[898] It would, however, take until 1938, another twenty years, before three Germans, Otto Hahn, Lise Meitner, and Fritz Strassman discovered the "crucial step in the long scientific journey that led to the development of nuclear technology as we understand it today."[899] That was "the discovery of nuclear fission,… the process upon which all nuclear technology depends,"[900] including the atomic bomb.

It would have been impossible for people in the first century and earlier to have known anything about the atom bomb or its effects. If the Bible does describe consequences which could come from the use of an atomic bomb, but the ability to split atoms to create atomic energy was not discovered until the twentieth century, how did the biblical authors have the knowledge to describe those consequences in the Bible? If the Bible does describe consequences from the use of atomic energy, why was it 2000 years or more after the consequence of atomic warfare were described in the Bible before atomic energy principles were first scientifically proven?

Second Peter 3:10–12 (NIV) (written 67–68 AD), (emphasis added) says,

> But the day of the Lord will come like a thief, and then *the heavens will pass away with a roar*, and the *heavenly bodies will be burned up and dissolved*, and the earth and the works that are done on it will be exposed.

Since all these things are thus to be dissolved, what sort of people ought you to be in lives of holiness and godliness, waiting for and hastening the coming of the day of God, because of which *the heavens will be set on fire* and dissolved, and the *heavenly bodies will melt as they burn*!

Even more to the point is the Bible book of Revelation. In Revelation, the apostle John describes his revelation, believed by Christians to be from the Holy Spirit, as to the destruction that will occur at end times. Revelation 6:12 (ESV) (emphasis added) says,

When he opened the sixth seal, I looked, and behold, there was a great earthquake, and *the sun became black as sackcloth, the full moon became like blood,*

Revelation 6:14 (ESV) says (emphasis added): "*The sky vanished like a scroll that is being rolled up,* and *every mountain and island was removed from its place.*"

Revelation 8:7–9 (NIV) (emphasis added) says,

The first angel sounded his trumpet, and there came *hail and fire mixed with blood, and it was hurled down on the earth. A third of the earth was burned up, a third of the trees were burned up, and all the green grass was burned up.* And the second angel sounded, and as it were a *great mountain burning with fire was cast into the sea: and the third part of the sea became blood;* And *the third part of the creatures which were in the sea, and had life, died; and the third part of the ships were destroyed.*

Revelation 16:8 (emphasis added) says, "The fourth angel poured out his bowl on the sun, and *the sun was allowed to scorch people with fire.*"

These passages in the Bible are the same descriptions which one would expect to be the effects from an atomic bomb, speaking about the sky burning up, the earth itself melting, mountains and islands moved from their place, and the inability of the atmosphere to block out harmful ultraviolet rays, resulting in severe burns. "Chemical reactions in the atmosphere will eat away Earth's ozone layer, which protects Earth's inhabitants from ultraviolet radiation," and "decreased UV protection may lead to more sunburns and skin cancers in people."[901]

Scientists describe the effects of atomic warfare in terms comparable to what John describes in Revelation in the first century AD. One study from *The 2020 Vision Campaign* predicted that atomic warfare in just one region of the world would "create large amounts of light-absorbing smoke," and "depending upon the total number of bombs dropped, the resulting flames could create 5 million tons of carbonaceous smoke particles," which "could blacken the sky."[902]

Another article discussing atomic warfare says,

> The detonation of some hundreds of atomic bombs would cause a nuclear winter, with disastrous impacts on the environment and human food resources. The ash and dust, transported by the atomic blasts into the higher layers of Earth's atmosphere, would form a cloud layer, making it impossible for sunlight and heat to reach the surface …Plants, no longer able to produce nutrients by photosynthesis, would quickly die off followed by the starving animals and finally humans.[903]

John's words are a picture of the consequences of a nuclear exchange. The consequences of a nuclear exchange have been understood for less than a century.

While John did not use terms like "nuclear weapons, ICBM's, or fractional orbital bombs," terms like "hail and fire" and "a great mountain burning with fire" are exactly what you would expect an first-century AD man to say, describing things he had no knowledge of in the only terms he knew to use.[904] Could it be that what John was really witnessing as his revelation from the Holy Spirit was an end-of-the-age-of-man nuclear holocaust? The effects he describes could be.

Whether the Earth will end or not according to Revelation, which Christians believe as described in the Bible, how could an first-century AD man such as John have so accurately described the effects of such destructive power as an atom bomb when ancient civilizations had never experienced such destruction? How could John so accurately describe those effects unless he received that description by a "revelation" from a knowledgeable source?

Some may theorize—without evidence—that alien visitors could have passed on such knowledge to John. But remember, theories are not evidence, as pointed out in chapter 1. Even proponents of such theories cannot logically explain how John acquired that knowledge when he did in the first century BC or why scientific knowledge of such destructive power would only happen after secular skepticism as to God's existence which could then be used to overcome that skepticism.

When Only God Knew

C. Mechanics, Engineering, and Physics

1. The Ark

Fact Stated: Genesis (written 1450–1405 BC)
Fact Confirmed: 1993 AD (3400 years later ±)

This section on mechanics, engineering, and physics may seem to be an unusual place to talk about Noah's ark from the Bible. It is not. As is plain from the biblical narrative quoted below and from the evidence available today, the ark was a feat of nautical engineering at a time when how a boat handles and its sailing abilities was not known and was likely not even a consideration, but its design was ideal for its purpose. It was a feat by a man, Noah, who had no apparent nautical, nautical engineering, or ship-building skills before he built the ark.

Again, the question to be answered here is how did someone with no nautical or ship-building skills know that the design of the ark would work at all, much less as well as it did, as described below. And again, the second question to be answered is why has the design of the ark only recently been determined to be ideal for its purpose?

Genesis 6:13–15 (NIV) (written 1450–1405 BC), thought by most to be written by Moses, who also had no apparent nautical experience, says,

> So God said to Noah, "I am going to put an end to all people, for the earth is filled with violence because of them. I am surely going to destroy both them and the earth. So make yourself an ark of cypress wood; make rooms in it and coat it with pitch inside and out. This is how you are to build it: The ark is to be three hundred cubits long, fifty cubits wide and thirty cubits high.

So how long is a cubit? "The actual length of a cubit varied between different ancient groups of people. Here are some samples from Egypt, Babylon, and ancient Israel:"

Culture	Length of Cubit in Inches
Hebrew	17.5 in
Egyptian	17.6 in
Babylonian Long	19.8 in
Hebrew Long	est. 20.4 in
Egyptian Long	20.6 in[905]

Using those measurements, the ark would have been between 437 feet 6 inches and 515 feet long, 72 feet 11 inches and 85 feet 9 and ½ inches wide, and 40 feet 9 inches and 51 feet 6 inches high.

The dimensions of Noah's Ark described in the Bible are ideal for stability.[906] "The scale of the Ark is huge yet remarkably realistic when compared to the largest wooden ships in history."[907] Its "proportions are even more amazing—they are just like a modern cargo ship," and "in fact, a 1993 Korean study was unable to find fault with the specifications."[908]

Noah's Ark was the focus of a major 1993 scientific study headed by Dr. Seon Hong at the world-class ship research center KRISO, based in Daejeon, South Korea [Dr. Hong was principal research scientist at the time]. Dr. Hong's team compared twelve hulls of different proportions to discover which design was most practical. No hull shape was found to significantly outperform the 4,300-year-old biblical design. In fact, the Ark's careful balance is easily lost if the proportions are modified, rendering the vessel either unstable, prone to fracture, or dangerously uncomfortable. The research team found that the proportions of Noah's Ark carefully balanced the conflicting demands of stability [resistance to capsizing], comfort ["seakeeping"], and strength. In fact, the Ark has the same proportions as a modern cargo ship. The study also confirmed that the Ark could handle waves as high as 100 ft [30 m]. Dr. Hong is now director general of the facility and claims "life came from the sea," obviously not the words of a creationist on a mission to promote the worldwide Flood.[909]

Although in extreme cases, tsunamis can exceed 100 feet, "most tsunamis are less than 10 feet high." [910] As you can see from the fact that the ark could handle waves as high as 100 ft, its dimensions made it almost impossible to capsize.

Other skeptics as to the ark's capacity for its biblical purpose have also determined that its dimensions work. According to Helen Thompson writing in Smithsonian Magazine, those skeptics asked themselves the question, "if one could hypothetically build an ark to the specifications outlined in the Bible, and actually cram two of every species on the boat, would it float, or would Noah have found himself in a Titanic-like scenario?"[911]

That's what four physics graduate students at the University of Leicester [in Leicester, England] wondered. As part of a special course that encourages the students to apply basic physics principles to more general questions, the team did the math and found that an ark full of animals in those dimensions could theoretically float. They recently published their research in a peer-reviewed, student-run publication, the *Journal of Physics Special Topics*.

> "You don't think of the Bible necessarily as a scientifically accurate source of information, so I guess we were quite surprised when we discovered it would work," said Thomas Morris, one of the students who worked on the project, in a statement.[912]

These scientific conclusions halfway around the globe from each other are remarkable considering that Genesis 16:13–15 was written between 1450 and 1405 BC, well before nautical stability was important to the design and construction of boats. To the contrary, from the very earliest times, ships have been built without consideration of the science behind the process but with consideration of "the taste of the ages."[913] As late as the 1600s AD, three millennia—3000 years—after Genesis 16:13–15 was written,

> [a]esthetics were given more importance than the actual construction of and function of a ship, neglecting vital characteristics such as stability and hull proportion. Even the drawings were made without the application of geometry and the line traces. The drawings of the ships were similar to those of fortresses and luxurious houses with elaborate decorations and designs.[914]

And yet, Genesis describes an ark that was able to withstand waves ten times the usual size of a tsunami.

Again, weigh the evidence in reaching a conclusion whether the Bible is reliable.

2. The Laws of Thermodynamics

Fact Stated: Genesis, Ecclesiastes, and Isaiah (written 1450–680 BC);
Hebrews (written 67–70 AD)
Fact Confirmed: 1824 AD at the earliest (2400–3200 years later ±)

"Thermodynamics can be summarized essentially as the science of energy," and how its principles govern our universe. [915] Much engineering technology is based on the truths of the Laws of Thermodynamics,[916] which "are invariable, i.e., unchanging and constant, [and without] exceptions."[917] "Though there are many important thermodynamic principles that govern the behavior of energy, perhaps the most critical and significant principles are the First and Second Laws of Thermodynamics."[918]

The first law of thermodynamics is that there is only a certain amount of energy in a closed system, such as the universe, and that no further energy can be created.[919] Matter cannot be "created or destroyed."[920] This principle is also known as the "conservation of energy principle" and "is considered to be the single most important and fundamental 'law of nature' presently known to science and is one of the most firmly established."[921]

The second law of thermodynamics, which builds on the first and is also irreversible, states that though there is a constant amount of energy in each system which is merely transforming into different states, "that energy is becoming less usable."[922]

These two principles were not confirmed until the nineteenth century, however.

"Lord Kelvin (formerly William Thomson)[, the Scottish engineer, mathematician, and physicist who was born in 1824 and died in 1907,] is the man often called the Father of Thermodynamics because of his articulation of the second law of thermodynamics in 1849."[923] The second law of thermodynamics was confirmed by Rudolph Clausius, who lived from 1822–1888.[924] Others, however, consider the father of thermodynamics to be Nicolas Léonard Sadi Carnot, a French physicist and engineer who lived from 1796 to 1832 because he published a book containing the first law of thermodynamics principles in 1824, his only book.[925] Then there is Julius Robert von Mayer, a German physician and physicist who lived from 1814 to 1878 and who first announced the first law of thermodynamics in 1841.[926]

While "the word 'thermodynamics' was originally used in a publication by Lord Kelvin"[927] and principles as to the first law of thermodynamics may have been first discussed in 1824 or 1841, "principles of thermodynamics have been in existence since the creation of the universe."[928] Those principles are talked about in the Bible thousands of years before the phenomena were scientifically proven.

Genesis 2:1–2 (NIV) (written 1450–1405 BC) supports the first law of thermodynamics that no further energy can be created. It says (emphasis added):

> Thus *the heavens and the earth were completed in all*
> *their vast array. By the seventh day God had finished*
> *the work he had been doing;* so on the seventh day he
> rested from all his work.

The Bible plainly says that "after the six days of Creation, the mass/matter/energy creation process was terminated."[929] That is a perfect description of the first law of thermodynamics which was proved 3,200 years, more or less, after the principle was stated in Genesis.

There are other biblical passages that support the first law of thermodynamics written millennia before the scientific principle was established. For instance, Ecclesiastes 3:14 (NIV) (written 940–931 BC) says (emphasis added), "I know that everything God does will endure forever; *nothing can be added to it, and nothing taken from it.*"

As for the second law of thermodynamics that energy is becoming less usable, Isaiah 51:6 (NIV) (written 740–680 BC) says (emphasis added), "Lift up your eyes to the heavens, look at the earth beneath; *the heavens will vanish like smoke, the earth will wear out like a garment.*" Hebrews 1:10–11 (NIV) (written 67–70 AD) likewise says (emphasis added):

> He also says, "In the beginning, Lord, you laid *the*
> *foundations of the earth, and the heavens* are the work
> of your hands. *They will perish,* but you remain; they
> *will all wear out like a garment.*"

Lord Kelvin, who articulated the second law of thermodynamics in 1849,[930] did not describe the gradual dissipation—wearing out—of energy until 2500 years ± after Isaiah and 1800 ± years after Hebrews was written.

For the implications of the laws of thermodynamics on creation, the reader may want to do further research, including reading such online articles as "God and the Laws of Thermodynamics: A Me-

When Only God Knew

chanical Engineer's Perspective" written by Dr. Jeff Miller, Ph.D. Miller's article makes clear that science and the story of creation are perfectly compatible. As Lord Kelvin, the nineteenth-century Scottish engineer, mathematician, and physicist, said,

> Science positively affirms Creative Power. It is not in dead matter that we live and move and have our being, but in the creating and directing Power which science compels us to accept as an article of belief… There is nothing between absolute scientific belief in a Creative Power, and the acceptance of the theory of a fortuitous concourse of atoms… Forty years ago I asked [Justus von] Liebig [a German chemist who is widely credited as one of the founders of organic chemistry],[931] walking somewhere in the country if he believed that the grass and flowers that we saw around us grew by mere chemical forces. He answered, "No, no more than I could believe that a book of botany describing them could grow by mere chemical forces".… Do not be afraid of being free thinkers! If you think strongly enough you will be forced by science to the belief in God, which is the foundation of all religion. You will find science not antagonistic but helpful to religion.[932]

The reader should weigh this statement and the statements of other scientists who have concluded that the Bible states scientific fact as evidence of the Bible's accuracy in the debate over the reliability of the Bible. Even if one discounts the credible evidence of scientists' statements as mere opinion, such does not discredit the evidence that these two fundamental principles appeared in the Bible at a time when they were not known to the authors who described them, and it does not discredit the fact that the biblical statements of the law of thermodynamics were only confirmed hundreds on hundreds of years after they made and that they can also be used to overcome skepticism as to the Bible's reliability.

D. Weight of Air

Fact Stated: Job (date of writing unknown, 2000 BC to the 5th century BC, but believed by most to be the oldest book in the Bible)
Fact Confirmed: 1643 AD (3400 years later ±)

Job 28:25 (ESV) says, "When he gave to the wind its weight and apportioned the waters by measure."

Job 28:25 says that air—the wind—has weight. It makes no exception for the varied conditions in which air's weight is measured.

"There is a subtle difference between realizing that air is a substance [as opposed to a void] and establishing that is has weight."[933] "The former was demonstrated by Empedocles," who lived from 490–430 BC.[934] There was no scientific proof for the proposition that air had weight until "the fact that air has weight was first well comprehended" in 1643 by Evangelista Torricelli, an "Italian physicist, and mathematician who invented the barometer and whose work in geometry aided in the eventual development of integral calculus."[935]

E. Television in the Bible?

Fact Stated: Matthew and Revelation (written 50–96 AD)
Fact Confirmed: 20th century AD (1900 years later ±)

The Bible contains passages that describe something being witnessed by mankind in a way that could be on television.

Matthew 24:30 (NIV) (written 50–65 AD) says,

> Then will appear the sign of the Son of Man in heaven. And then all the peoples of the earth will mourn

When Only God Knew

when they see the Son of Man coming on the clouds of heaven, with power and great glory.

Perhaps more to the point, Revelation 11:9–11 (NIV) (written 94–96 AD) (discussing the prophets who will be slain in Jerusalem) says,

> For three and a half days some from every people, tribe, language and nation will gaze on their bodies and refuse them burial. The inhabitants of the earth will gloat over them and will celebrate by sending each other gifts, because these two prophets had tormented those who live on the earth. But after the three and a half days the breath of life from God entered them, and they stood on their feet, and terror struck those who saw them.

Television, which did not exist when those passages were written, is a device that allows everyone on earth to see a single event. While there were scientific developments in the nineteenth century that led to the television, the television itself was not invented until the twentieth century.

From 1924 to 1925, "American Charles Jenkins and John Baird from Scotland each demonstrated the mechanical transmissions of images over wire circuits."[936] Charles Jenkins "invented a mechanical television system called Radiovision and claimed to have transmitted the earliest moving silhouette images on June 14, 1923;" John Baird "patented the idea of using arrays of transparent rods to transmit images for television" [937] and became "the first person to transmit moving silhouette images."[938] From 1926 to 1930, Baird operated "a television system with thirty lines of resolution system running at five frames per second."[939]

On April 7, 1927, "Bell Telephone and the US Department of Commerce conducted the first long-distance use of television that took place between Washington, DC, and New York City."[940] In that same year, Philo Farnsworth, the "American inventor who developed the first all-electronic television system,"[941] filed "for a patent on the first completely electronic television system, which he called the Image Dissector." In 1928, the United States Federal Radio Commission issued "the first television station license (W3XK) to Charles Jenkins."[942]

The reader should answer the question, How and why were Matthew 24:30 and Revelation 11:9–11 written during the AD first century when a device that would make possible the viewing of the events they describe would not be invented for another 1900 years, more or less?

CHAPTER 9

Celestial Events

The accurate description of "celestial events" in the Bible and the very recent proof of them support the reliability of the Bible. The God of "Christianity is shown to be the best explanation for origin and nature of the universe."[943]

It took thousands of years for science to catch up to statements in the Bible that revealed the nature of the universe and the Earth's position in and relationship to it. This chapter will discuss some of those revealed facts. "There are no facts, however, wrested from the intriguing mysteries of this strange, onrushing cosmos which can in any degree disprove the existence and intelligent activities of" God.[944]

As with the other chapters in this book, this chapter is neither designed nor intended to discuss/debate the young versus old earth viewpoint. It is, like other chapters, only designed to point out statements of scientific fact in the Bible which were only later proven to be accurate, so that the reader can weigh that evidence for themselves in determining whether the Bible is generally reliable and where it most likely came from.

Nonetheless, it is worthy to note that there is additional support, not discussed below for reasons of economy, for the proposition that God knew and was involved in developing scientific laws supporting mankind's existence and of the existence of the God of the Bible. One astrophysicist, Hugh Ross, "a former atheist turned Christian,"[945] "has listed thirty-five parameters that must each fall within a very narrow range in order to make life possible," including:[946]

- Strong nuclear force constant
- Weak nuclear force constant

- Gravitational force constant
- Electromagnetic force constant
- Ratio of electromagnetic force constant to gravitational force constant
- Ratio of electronic to proton mass
- Ratio of protons to electrons
- Expansion rate of the universe
- Entropy level of the universe
- Mass density of the universe
- Velocity of light
- Age of the universe
- Initial uniformity of radiation
- Fine structure constant
- Average distance between stars

See also Doug Powell, *Guide to Christian Apologetics*[947] at 52–56, for additional impact on what would happen if only one of thirty-five parameters fell outside the "very narrow range in order to make life possible" or the disastrous results that would happen if only one sixty-six parameters having "to do with our sun-planet-moon system" was not met.

Not entering directly into the debate as to whether the Earth is old or new does not, however, mean there is no evidence that the Earth was created. As a December 1976 Time Magazine article, for instance, said,[948]

> "Most cosmologists… scientists who study the structure and evolution of the universe, agree that the biblical account of creation, in imagining an initial void, may be uncannily close to the truth."

When Only God Knew

A. Universe

1. Time, Space, Matter, Power, and Motion

Fact Stated: Genesis (written 1450–1405 BC)
Fact Confirmed: 4th century BC–18th century AD
(1100–3100 years later ±)

Genesis 1:1–3 (NIV) (written 1450–1405 BC) says,

> In the beginning God created the heavens and the earth. Now the earth was formless and empty, darkness was over the surface of the deep, and the Spirit of God was hovering over the waters. And God said, "Let there be light," and there was light.

Most people read the very first verse in the Bible without giving it much thought. However, the author of Genesis verbalized the same sophisticated principles that scientists now use thousands of years later. Science expresses the universe in five terms: time, space, matter, power, and motion. So does Genesis 1 at verses 1 and 2, the first two sentences in the Bible. It says,[949] "In the beginning [time], God created [power] the heavens [space] and the earth [matter]… And the Spirit of God was hovering [motion] over the waters."

It was not until Aristotle, the ancient Greek philosopher and scientist who lived from 384–322 BC,[950] however, that the importance of motion was first appreciated and for the connection between both motion and time, and motion and matter to be realized.[951] That is 1,100 years after Genesis was written. From antiquity into the eighteenth century, science and philosophy denied that space and time are real entities.[952] That was 3,100 years, more or less, after Genesis first expressed the universe through time, space, matter, power, and motion. It took a long time for science to understand the nature of the universe.

2. The Big Bang Beginning

Fact Stated: Genesis (written 1450–1405 BC)
Fact Confirmed: 20th century AD (3400 years later ±)

The word "beginning" in Genesis 1:1–3 refers to the beginning of time. However, for many years scientists were convinced that the universe was infinite (without beginning and without end) and that time had always existed. The belief that the universe had no beginning directly contradicts Genesis 1:1–3. Again, scientifically proven facts—evidence—would later support the biblical narrative.

For thousands of years, scientists and philosophers believed that the universe had no beginning and no end. Aristotle, the "ancient Greek philosopher and scientist who lived from 384 to 322 BC, one of the greatest intellectual figures of Western history,"[953] believed, for example, "that, although space was finite [with only some undefined void existing beyond the outermost sphere of the heavens], time was infinite, and that the universe has always existed and will always exist."[954]

As recently as "one hundred years ago, many scientists believed that the universe was infinite and eternal, with no beginning and no end,"[955] that was until Albert Einstein first developed his general theory of relativity in 1915. "The first public announcement of Einstein's theory suddenly proclaimed the falsity of a basic [long-held] cosmological tenet, that the universe is infinite."[956] That announcement was the beginning of the end of the belief that the universe had no beginning.

The previously cited Time Magazine article, discussing development of the idea that the universe had a beginning and an end, added that when Astronomer Edwin Hubble in 1929, "used shifts in the spectral lines of light emanating from distant galaxies to calculate that the islands of stars are moving at tremendous speeds away from

When Only God Knew

the earth—and from each other—... [to] some scientists, this outward rush of the galaxies suggested an original cosmic explosion."[957]

That original cosmic explosion became known as the Big Bang theory. The Big Bang theory, now overwhelmingly accepted with little disagreement, supports the conclusion that the universe is not infinite and that it had a beginning.

> The big-bang theory is the dominant theory of the origin of the universe. In essence, this theory states that the universe began from an initial point or singularity, which [is theorized to have] expanded over billions of years to form the universe as we now know it.[958]

The Big Bang Theory "is widely accepted because it best fits the data" and "prevailed as the most widely accepted view."[959]

The term Big Bang theory was initially coined by an English astronomer, Fred Hoyle., on March 28, 1949,[960] but it had been in scientific development from the time that Einstein proposed his general theory of relativity in 1915. In 1922, Alexander Friedman, a Russian cosmologist, and mathematician, for example, found that "solutions to Albert Einstein's general relativity field equations resulted in an expanding universe."[961] Mankind continues to verify that the universe has a beginning and an end. For example, NASA launched the Cosmic Background Explorer (COBE), also referred to as Explorer 66, space mission from Vandenberg Air Force Base in California on November 18, 1989. The Explorer 66 space mission was designed to test the Big Bang theory as to the origin of the universe; it provided evidence that supported the idea that the universe had a beginning.[962]

Yet you might ask why is Einstein's general theory of relativity, which most of us, including me, do not understand, important to the discussion of Genesis 1:1–3? Because if the universe is not infinite and has a beginning, that supports the biblical report of a beginning to the universe, which was stated at a time when the writer of Genesis did not have the scientific knowledge to make the statement; that knowledge would only be later acquired by mankind.

How did the writer of Genesis know to state that there was a beginning to the universe when scientific and philosophical thought until hundreds and hundreds and hundreds of years later would be that the universe had no beginning? Why did it take hundreds and hundreds and hundreds of years to prove the accuracy of Genesis as to the universe's beginning?

If the universe had a beginning, as generally agreed by the scientific community, what caused the universe to begin? Scientists have explained what caused the Big Bang in various ways, some like others and some very different. Some of them follow:

1. The Big Bang happened when "the universe expanded from an initial state of high density and temperature,"[963] without explaining what caused the density, where the matter that became dense came from, or what caused the high temperature;

2. The Big Bang happened when "all of the energy in the universe—some of which would later become galaxies, stars, planets, and human beings—was concentrated into a tiny point, smaller than the nucleus of an atom," "matter that was born in the Big Bang" and "matter *and* space *and* time all began when that microscopic point suddenly expanded violently and exponentially,"[964] without explaining where that energy came from;

3. The Big Bang happened when "all the matter found in the universe today—including the matter in people, plants, animals, the earth, stars, and galaxies—was created at the very first moment of time, thought to be about 13 billion years ago," when "every speck of its energy [was] jammed into a very tiny point," and "this extremely

When Only God Knew

dense point exploded with unimaginable force, creating matter and propelling it outward to make the billions of galaxies of our vast universe,"[965] without explaining where that matter or energy came from;

4. The Big Bang happened "when a vanishingly small seed ballooned into the universe,"[966] without a good explanation where the small seed came from;

5. The Big Bang was the result of a supernova explosion ignited from a flame that self-generates its own turbulence, spontaneously accelerates, and transitions into detonation by applying the right amount of turbulence and mixing to an unconfined flame until it becomes self-perpetuating,[967] without any explanation as to what caused any such Big Bang flame, turbulence or mixing;

6. The Big Bang was due to all of the mass/matter in the universe being concentrated at a single point and then exploding into existence,[968] without explaining where the mass/matter came from;

7. The Big Bang happened because

> When the universe began, it was just hot, tiny particles mixed with light and energy. ... As everything expanded and took up more space, it cooled down. The tiny particles grouped together. They formed atoms. Then those atoms grouped together. Over lots of time, atoms came together to form stars and galaxies. The first stars created bigger atoms and groups of atoms. That led to more stars being born. At the same time, galaxies were crashing and grouping together. As new stars were being born and dying, then things like asteroids, comets, planets, and black holes formed,[969]

without any explanation where the hot, tiny particles, light, and energy came from or why they mixed and

8. "The Big Bang was an expansion of space, not like an explosion at all,"[970] which says there was no explosion, contradicting other theories as to the Big Bang.

Some scientists estimate that the number of stars in the universe range from 10,000,000,000,000,000,000,000 to 1,000,000,000,00 0,000,000,000,000.[971] No one knows for sure, and there could be more than that.[972] That count does not include the planets which orbit those stars. None of the explanations of the causes of the Big Bang satisfactorily explain, however, how or why so much mass and matter for so many stars and planets were or could be concentrated at a single point.

In short, and to say the least, it is clear that "astronomers aren't sure what caused the Big Bang."[973] Also, remember in weighing the facts, as pointed out in Chapter 1, theories or theoretical possibilities are not evidence.

But there is another reasonable explanation for what caused the Big Bang. That explanation is that the God of the Bible was responsible for the Big Bang. As one Christian physicist, Dr. Steven Ball said,

> The Big Bang theory does not leave God out of the picture since it is merely a scientific account of how our universe has dramatically changed since its infancy. The question of its ultimate cause strongly suggests a Creator with a definite purpose.[974]

Disagreeing with Nobel Laureate Stephen Hawking's conjecture of an unknown physics phenomenon which he theorized "in an attempt to remove the need for a Creator," Dr. Ball concludes that "it

When Only God Knew

remains difficult to avoid the implications of the Big Bang theory, namely that there was a beginning to this universe having a cause beyond the universe itself."[975] As Dr. Ball says, "attempts to rule out God as the originator of the incredible features of our universe do not find much support from the scientific evidence."[976]

Even some naysayers who do not believe in God agree that there is design in the universe. For example, "Stephen Hawking, considered the best-known scientist since Albert Einstein acknowledges,"

> The universe and the laws of physics seem to have been specifically designed for us. If any one of about forty physical qualities [of the universe] had more than slightly different values, life as we know it could not exist: either atoms would not be stable, or they wouldn't combine into molecules, or the stars wouldn't form the heavier elements, or the universe would collapse before life could develop, and so on…[977]

So, the question is, whose design?

There is other evidence that the facts related in Genesis 1:1–3 are accurate. The fact that so much else of the Bible is accurate, as discussed above, makes it reasonable to conclude that the creation story is also accurate. Due to the reliability of other evidence supporting the Bible's accuracy and reliability discussed elsewhere in this book, the conclusion that the cause of the universe's beginning and its design is God is reasonable.

As there is no reliable secular scientific conclusion respecting what caused the various components which led to the Big Bang, the evidence from the report in Genesis that God caused the universe to begin is far more reliable than the secular theories as to the cause of the Big Bang. As the apostle Paul said in Romans 1:20 (NIV),

For since the creation of the world God's invisible qualities—his eternal power and divine nature—have been clearly seen, being understood from what has been made, so that people are without excuse.

3. Expanding Universe

Fact Stated: Job (date of writing unknown, 2000 BC to the 5th century BC, but believed by most to be the oldest book in the Bible); Psalms, Isaiah, and Jeremiah (written 1440–570 BC)
Fact Confirmed: 1929 AD (at least 2400 years later ±)

The universe is also expanding.[978] That fact was, however, not discovered until 1929 by Edwin Hubble, an astronomer at Caltech in California,[979] over 2,000 years after it was first reported in the Bible.

The Bible stated that the universe is expanding many times. Stretching is defined as "act of expanding by lengthening or widening."[980] The Scriptures clearly tell us that God stretches out the heavens like a curtain. For example, Job 9:8 (NIV) (date of writing unknown, 2000 BC to the fifth century BC, but believed by most to be the oldest book in the Bible), says, "He alone stretches out the heavens."

As another example, Isaiah 40:22 (NIV) (written 700–680 BC) says, "He stretches out the heavens like a canopy, and spreads them out like a tent to live in." *See also, e.g.,* Psalms 104:2 (written 1440–450 BC), Isaiah 42:5, 44:24, 45:12,48:13 and 51:13 (written 740–680 BC) and Jeremiah 10:12, 51:15 and 51:15 (written 627–570 BC).

How did the biblical authors of Job, Isaiah, Psalms, and Jeremiah, none of whom appears to have been trained in astronomy, know that the heavens were being stretched? Why was that fact—the expanding universe—only recently discovered?

When Only God Knew

4. Number of Stars in the Heavens

Fact Stated: Genesis and Jeremiah (written 1450–570 BC)
Fact Confirmed: 1687 AD ± (2200–3100 years later ±)

Genesis 15:5 (NIV) (written 1450–1405 BC) says: "He, [meaning God], took him, [meaning Abraham], outside and said, 'Look up at the sky and count the stars—if indeed you can count them.'"

Jeremiah 33:22 (NIV) (written 627–570 BC) says: "I will make the descendants of David my servant and the Levites who minister before me as countless as the stars in the sky and as measureless as the sand on the seashore."

Even today, scientists admit they cannot physically count the stars and do not know how many stars there are. As the European Space Agency has said,[981]

> Have you ever looked up into the night sky and wondered just how many stars there are in space? This question has fascinated scientists as well as philosophers, musicians and dreamers throughout the ages. Look into the sky on a clear night, out of the glare of streetlights, and you will see a few thousand individual stars with your naked eyes. With even a modest amateur telescope, millions more will come into view. So how many stars are there in the Universe? It is easy to ask this question, but difficult for scientists to give a fair answer!

Stars are not scattered randomly through space, they are gathered together into vast groups known as galaxies. The Sun belongs to a galaxy called the Milky Way. Astronomers estimate there are about 100 thousand million stars in the Milky Way alone. Outside that, there are millions upon millions of other galaxies also!

It has been said that counting the stars in the Universe is like trying to count the number of sand grains on a beach on Earth. We might do that by measuring the surface area of the beach, and determining the average depth of the sand layer.

Before modern astronomy, astronomers counted the stars they could see with the naked eye. The estimates vary as to how many stars can be counted with the naked eye and depend on whether there is other light or haze, which makes it difficult to count them.

Considering all the stars visible in all directions around Earth, the upper end on the estimates seems to be about 10,000 visible stars. Other estimates place the number of stars visible to the eye alone—

surrounding the entire Earth—at more like 5,000. At any given time, half of Earth is in daylight. So only half the estimated number—say, between 5,000 and 2,500 stars—would be visible from Earth's night side.[983]

For "years it was the accepted science that there were about a thousand stars in the universe," "that they could be counted," and "that the number of stars were finite." [984] There were many scholars prior to Galileo, discussed below, who believed that the stars could be counted, and several attempts were made to do so. Many of these counts arrived at around 1,000 stars.[985]

How many stars were known prior to the invention of the telescope? The standard star catalogue in the Middle Ages was published by Ptolemy in Alexandria around 150 AD; entitled Ptolemy's *Almagest*, it contains 1028 star entries.[986]

> Claudius Ptolemy [c. 100–170 AD] is one of the most influential scholars of all time. While he is also the author of treatises on geography, optics and harmonics, his fame primarily stems from two works on the science of the stars, dealing with mathematical astronomy [the *Almagest*], [Ptolemy's star catalogue], and astrology [the *Tetrabiblos*]. The *Almagest* and the *Tetrabiblos* remained the fundamental texts on the science of the stars for some 1,500 years.[987]

The *Almagest*, Ptolemy's star catalogue, was the standard reference for all things "star" until the birth of modern astronomy.

Modern astronomy was born in Europe as a consequence of the scientific discoveries of Nicolaus Copernicus; "astronomy made no major advances in strife-torn medieval Europe."[988] Copernicus, who lived from 1473–1543 AD, was a "Polish astronomer who proposed that the planets have the Sun as the fixed point to which their motions are to be referred (and) that Earth is a planet which, besides orbiting the Sun annually, also turns once daily on its own axis."[989] What Copernicus did for astronomy is called the Copernican Revolution because it set the stage for how astronomy was done.[990]

"Many of the modern scientific concepts of observation, experimentation, and the testing of hypotheses through careful quantitative measurements were pioneered by Galileo Galilei, more commonly simply know as Galileo, who lived nearly a century after Copernicus."[991] Galileo, who lived from 1564 to 1642 AD, was an "Italian natural philosopher, astronomer, and mathematician who made fundamental contributions to the sciences of motion, astronomy, and strength of materials and to the development of the scientific method."[992] Even so, during Galileo's lifetime and for at least fifty years after his death notable astronomers were still trying to "count" stars.

There were, for example, three early versions of a star catalogue by Tycho Brahe, a Danish astronomer, completed in 1598, which catalogued 777 stars and then, after updating, 1004 stars.[993] As late as 1687, forty-five years after Galileo died, the *Catalogus Stellarum Fixarum* of Johannes Hevelius, a Polish astronomer who lived from 1611 to 1687, was published posthumously containing 1,564 stars based on his naked eye count.[994]

Men still cannot physically count the stars even though they are now able to see more stars with the aid of tools that were not available during biblical time.

> With a good pair of binoculars, that number jumps to about 200,000 since you can observe stars down to magnitude 9. A small telescope capable of resolving magnitude 13 stars will let you count up to 15 million stars. Large observatories could resolve billions of stars.[995]

When Only God Knew

As pointed out above, however, some scientists using sophisticated mathematics estimate that the number of stars in the universe range from 10,000,000,000,000,000,000,000 to 1,000,000,000,000,000, 000,000,000,[996] but it is only an estimation and not an actual counting of the stars. Mathematicians at the University of Hawaii tried to guess the number of grains of sand in the world, which the Bible says is also countless, by calculating the grains of sand in all the beaches of the earth: they came up with 7,500,000,000,000,000,000 grains, but even that number probably excluded the number of grains of sand in the world's deserts.[997]

Much like the grains of sand in the world, no scientist has been able to count all the stars in the universe. One scientist calls the attempt to determine the number of grains of sand in the world sands and the number of stars in the universe to be a "guestimate."[998]

So, how was it that the author of Genesis, written 1450–1405 at a time when astronomers were trying to "count" stars, knew that actually counting stars was impossible? Why have modern astronomers only recently admitted that they can only estimate/guestimate the number of stars even with their sophisticated instruments? What is the source of knowledge in Genesis as to the stars' incalculable numbers? What does that say about why science only recently confirmed that man cannot count the stars in the universe? Is there a reason for such recent confirmation of the account in Genesis that stars are incapable of being counted as mankind began and now passes through a period of skepticism as to the accuracy of the Bible? Just some food for thought.

5. Each Star Unique

Fact Stated: 1 Corinthians (written 55 AD)
Fact Confirmed: 19th century AD (1800 years later ±)

First Corinthians 15:41 (NIV) (written 55 AD) says, "The sun has one kind of splendor, the moon another and the stars another; and star differs from star in splendor."

A person living in the first century AD, when 1 Corinthians was written, would probably not claim that stars differ from one another. All stars look the same to the naked eye. Even though a telescope, they seem to be just points of light.

Yet when scientists and astronomers began to scientifically analyze the stars, they concluded that each is unique and different from all others. They reached that conclusion after developing instruments that could analyze each star's "light spectra." Light spectra are the sequences of "colors formed when a beam of white light is dispersed [as by passage through a prism] so that its component wavelengths [colors] are arranged in order."[999] "Sunlight, which looks white to us, is actually made up of a mixture of all the colors of the rainbow," but analysis of light spectra was not reported until the seventeenth century AD.[1000] By measuring each star's light spectra, astronomers have, for example, concluded that stars have different temperatures and brightness and are made up of different amounts of elements.

But there was no evidence that light even had different parts—spectra which would eventually be used to analyze the stars—until the seventeenth century AD.

In 1672, in the first paper that he submitted to the Royal Society, Sir Isaac Newton[1001] described an experiment in which he permitted sunlight to pass through a small hole and then through a prism. Newton found that sunlight, which looks white to us, is actually made up of a mixture of all the colors of the rainbow.[1002]

It would, however, not be until the latter half of the nineteenth century, before astronomers began to embrace two new techniques—spectroscopy and photography—to understand the chemical composition of stars.[1003] According to astronomer Neil deGrasse Tyson, it took until the late 1800s for astronomers to learn "that light from the universe could be analyzed with a prism, which allowed us to figure out all sorts of things about planets, stars, and galaxies, especially their chemical composition and whether they are in motion through space."[1004]

When Only God Knew

The fact that stars, in fact, differs from other stars in splendor, as the Bible says, was proven 1800 years after the Bible reported it. Really makes you think how it came to be stated in the Bible at a time when there were no instruments that could measure each star's "splendor" and why it has only been recently that the truth of the statement in 1 Corinthians has been proven.

6. *Singing Stars*

Fact Stated: Job (date of writing unknown, 2000 BC to the 5th century BC, but believed by most to be the oldest book in the Bible)

Fact Confirmed: 1932 AD (2300 to 3900 years later ±)

While the exact date of its writing is unknown, Job, believed to be the oldest book in the Bible, was written between 2000 BC and the fifth century BC Job 38:1–6 (NIV) says,

> Then the Lord spoke to Job out of the storm. He said: "Who is this that obscures my plans with words without knowledge? Brace yourself like a man; I will question you, and you shall answer me. "Where were you when I laid the earth's foundation? Tell me, if you understand. Who marked off its dimensions? Surely you know! Who stretched a measuring line across it? On what were its footings set, or who laid its cornerstone—*while the morning stars sang together* and all the angels shouted for joy.
>
> (Emphasis added).

Science has only recently discovered that stars emit radio waves, which can be received on earth. They sing.

> We can't hear it with our ears, but the stars in the sky are performing a concert, one that never stops. The biggest stars make the lowest, deepest sounds, like tu-

bas and double basses. Small stars have high-pitched voices, like celestial flutes. These virtuosos don't just play one "note" at a time, either—our own Sun has thousands of different sound waves bouncing around inside it at any given moment.[1005]

But that discovery that the stars gave off radio waves did not occur until 1932. That was when Karl Jansky, an American who worked for Bell Telephone Laboratories in the State of New Jersey, used instruments that he specially designed to capture radio waves emitted by stars in our galaxy, the Milky Way.[1006] The universe is full of objects besides stars that emit radio waves, including planets and moons.[1007] Sounds the stars can be heard online if one wants.[1008]

But it took science 2,300 to 3,900 years after the fact was reported in the Bible by an author who could not have known without help, even to begin to understand the truth that stars sing together. Why are we only recently learning that stars make music—sing?

B. The Earth and Its Place in and Relation to the Universe

1. The Earth Hangs in Space

Fact Stated: Job (date of writing unknown, 2000 BC to the 5th century BC, but believed by most to be the oldest book in the Bible)
Fact Confirmed: 16th century AD–1887 AD (2,000–3,900 years later ±)

Job 26:7 (NIV) says, "He, [God], spreads out the northern skies over empty space; he suspends the earth over nothing."

In ancient times, however, it was not understood that the Earth was suspended in space; it was believed by many cultures in many different places that the Earth sat on or was supported by something or someone.

When Only God Knew

[A]ccording to some, we are living on the back of a giant turtle. We might also be living on the back of an elephant or a serpent, but let's stick with turtles for now, because the Cosmic Turtle is the most widely recognized "belief" in this particular category.

The Great Turtle myth was first brought to the public's attention in the seventeenth century, after a man named Jasper Danckaerts[1009] learned of it from several tribes of Native Americans he encountered. The Native Americans, however, are not the only ones who believed that the world rested on the shell of a giant turtle, as the myth is also prevalent in Chinese and Indian culture.[1010]

"In the creation stories of the Lenape and Iroquois people, the Earth is created as soil and is piled on the back of a great sea turtle that continues to grow until it is carrying the entire world."[1011] Hindus believed that eight mighty elephants held up the earth and that when "one of them grew weary, it lowered and shook its head, causing" earthquakes. Ancient Greeks believe that a Titan,[1012] Atlas, was punished by Zeus, the king of the Greek Gods after the Titans lost a war with the Gods of Olympus by being required to hold up the earth on his shoulders for all eternity.[1013] The ancient Mayans believed "that the sky was held up by four mighty gods called Bacabs."[1014] "Other Maya believed that the sky was supported by four trees of different colors and species, with the green *ceiba*, or silk-cotton tree, at the centre."[1015]

Some people still believe that the Earth is being held up.[1016]

Additionally, until relatively recently, scientists commonly accepted that a substance called aether or ether occupied all of space,[1017] i.e., that space was not primarily empty. The idea that aether occupied all of space "was proposed by the Greek philosopher Aristotle," who lived from 384 to 322 BC, because it was believed that "empty" space was impossible.[1018] Aether was accepted as "the medium that carried light waves in space by eighteenth and nineteenth century scientists."[1019]

That was "until the Michelson-Morley experiment" in 1887, which could not detect aether in space and which was followed by other experiments confirming that space was not made up of that substance.[1020] The Michelson-Morley experiment was "performed in Germany in 1880–81 by the physicist A.A. Michelson," and "the test was later refined in 1887 by Michelson and Edward W. Morley in the United States."[1021] The conclusions of this experiment "shocked the scientific community by yielding results which implied the non-existence of ether."[1022] Following the Michelson-Morley experiment, scientists and physicists in the 1900s "had to build their theories and equations based on an assumption that there is no medium capable of propagating a wave in space."[1023]

In the sixteenth century AD, Nicolaus Copernicus, the Polish astronomer, had already proven scientifically that the Earth was suspended in space.

> Copernicus (1473–1543) was not the first person to claim that the Earth rotates around the Sun. In Western civilization, ancient Greek astronomer Aristarchus, who lived from 310 BC to 230 BC, on the Greek island of Samos in the Aegean Sea, is generally credited with being the first person to propose a Sun-centered astronomical hypothesis of the universe [heliocentric]. At that time, however, Aristarchus's heliocentrism gained few supporters, and 18 centuries would then pass before Renaissance astronomer Nicolaus Copernicus produced a fully predictive mathematical model of a heliocentric system.[1024]

When Only God Knew

Scientists no longer believe in the existence of the and now know that the nothingness and the hanging of the earth over it spoken of in the Bible four millennia ago is accurate. In what is probably the oldest book of the Bible, Job, written at a time and in an ancient culture that knew nothing about space or planets, asserted that God hung the earth on and over nothing, i.e., the earth free-floats in space.

So, the evidence for this truth in the Bible, other than the Bible itself, took 2,000 to 3,900 years to be accepted by the scientific community. Even then, the fact that the Earth was suspended in space was not based on an actual observation of that suspension. The first picture of the Earth showing it suspended in space was not taken until the twentieth century. "When astronauts first went into the space, they looked back at the Earth with human eyes for the first time,"[1025] seeing it hanging in space.

Of interest to this discussion is that the Bible tells us that Moses, the adopted as the son of Pharaoh's daughter credited by many with writing Job, was "educated in all the wisdom of the Egyptians" *See* Acts 7:22.

The adopted son of the daughter of an Egyptian king must have been trained in all the wisdom of Egypt. This is also in harmony with the tradition reported by Manethe, an Egyptian priest also known as Menotho who flourished around 300 BC and wrote a history of Egypt in Greek, which makes Moses a priest of Heliopolis, and therefore presupposes a priestly education.[1026]

> When it came to education, he probably had the finest tutors available in the land. We know for sure, from written records, that they had a great university, in its time comparable in esteem to an Oxford or a Harvard today. He would have been instructed in astronomy, chemistry, mathematics, engineering, music, and art.[1027]

In the ancient Egyptian religion, it was believed, among other things, that Geb, the god of the earth, was "the physical support of the world."[1028] Ancient Egyptians also believed that Shu, "the god of dry air, wind and the atmosphere," held up "Nut, the sky goddess, and his daughter, above his son the earth god Geb," and that "there were also pillars to help Shu lift up the sky."

Yet not once in Scripture, including the first four books, including Genesis, written by Moses, and Job, thought to be written by Moses, is there any description that the earth is held up as the Egyptians thought it was. Why? Because it's not true.

Who told the author of Job 26:7 in the Bible that God "spreads out the northern skies over empty space; he suspends the earth over nothing?" How did he know that? Why have scientists only recently found evidence to support that biblically stated fact?

2. The Hole in the North

Fact Stated: Job (date of writing unknown, 2000 BC to the 5th century BC, but believed by most to be the oldest book in the Bible)
Fact Confirmed: 1981 AD (2,300–4,000 years later ±)

Job 26:7 (NIV) (date of writing unknown, 2000 BC to the fifth century BC, but believed by most to be the oldest book in the Bible) also says, in part, "He spreads out the northern skies over empty space." Again, the truth of this statement that northern skies spread over empty space was not proven for thousands of years.

> The Boötes Void is a hole in the Universe that has been described as the "spookiest place ever" with good reason. Consider this; our cosmic backyard is populated by more than thirty galaxies, collectively known as the Local Group, spanning an area of around ten million light years. The Boötes Void, however, spans an area of around 300 million light years—and it contains only sixty known galaxies in

a volume of space that represents 0.27 percent of the diameter of the known Universe.

This is the largest void yet discovered, and it should have contained around 10,000 galaxies. To put this volume into some kind of perspective is almost impossible, so let's replace the average density of galaxies with a simple graph that represents galactic density as valleys and peaks. On such a graph, galaxies would show as the peaks of narrow, steeply tapering "towers." For instance, typical galaxies such as the Milky Way would be represented as a peak with about the same footprint and height as the Empire State Building, while even a modestly sized void would represent a three-foot-deep hole that is three times as big as Manhattan. On this scale, the Boötes Void would swallow most of the US Eastern Seaboard.[1029]

Since the Boötes Void spans an area of around 300 million light years and one light year measures about six trillion miles,[1030] the Boötes Void spans an area of around 1,800, 000, 000, 000, 000, 000, 000 miles.

Boötes is a "northern constellation,"[1031] i.e., seen from the northern hemisphere. The discovery of the Boötes Void was reported by Robert Kirshner and others in 1981, thousands of years after Job was written, as part of a survey of galactic wavelengths.[1032] "The Boötes void is so huge that its diameter is a whole 2 percent of the diameter of the observable universe."[1033]

How did the writer of Job know that there was a void over the northern hemisphere as much as 3,900 years ago, and why are scientists only very recently learning about it?

PART IV

Prophecy in the Bible

The evidence does not support the conclusion that prophets in the Bible were merely fortune-tellers, mediums, soothsayers, wizards, or crystal ball gazers who simply predicted the future or pretended to. First, most—if not all—of his prophecies were not fulfilled in a prophet's lifetime, and, consequently, the prophet had nothing to personally gain from a prophecy while he lived; prophecies were made such a long time before they would occur that there was nothing to be done during a prophet's lifetime to show they were accurate. Second, the evidence is clear that false prophets could suffer death for not being *biblically* prophetic, and so, a biblical prophet was focused on receiving a prophecy from God and not just stating some feeling that he might have. Third and most importantly, the evidence shows that a biblical prophet was invariably accurate, and his prophecies would later be proven to be as predicted.

> According to "The Encyclopedia of Biblical Prophecy" by J. Barton Payne, there are 1,239 prophecies in the Old Testament and 578 prophecies in the New Testament for a total of 1,817. These prophecies are contained in 8,352 of the Bible's verses. Since there are 31,124 verses in the Bible, the 8,352 verses that contain prophecy constitute 26.8 percent of the Bible's volume.[1034]

Because there are so many prophecies, it is beyond the scope, capacity, economy, and intent of this book to discuss all 1,239 prophecies in the Old Testament and 578 prophecies in the New Testament—1,817 total prophecies. Or the 8,352 prophetic verses in the Bible, in part because some have not yet happened despite most of them having already occurred. Only some will be discussed.

While that number may seem high to some readers, it is, however, accurate to say that prophetic verses in the Bible, which later come true, also support the conclusion that the Bible is God-breathed and accurate. If biblical prophecy comes to pass, it is reasonable to infer that it must have been put in the Bible for a reason. The most obvious reason is to show the reader the existence and all-knowing nature of God.

One of the most interesting things that has occurred as to biblical prophecy relatively recently is the calculation of the probability or odds that a prophecy, particularly one as to Jesus, when made would actually occur.

So, what is *probability*? Probability, also known as "odds," is a branch of mathematics that measures the likelihood that a given event will occur. To begin, let's look at some interesting "odds:"

- Being struck by lightning in a year = 7×10^5 or 1 in 700,000
- Being killed by lightning in a year = 2×10^6 or 1 in 2,000,000
- Becoming president = 1×10^7 or 1 in 10,000,000
- A meteorite landing on your house = 1.8×10^{14} or 1 in 180,000,000,000,000
- You will eventually die when you are born = 1 in 1^{1035}

For example, when odds are ten to one, something is far more likely to occur naturally than when the odds are ten to 1,000,000. Some of those calculations will also be discussed.

Peter Stoner,[1036] perhaps the first to calculate the odds that prophecies as to Jesus would come true, using what he described as conservative figures, has calculated that the odds of only eight of the aproximately one hundred prophecies as to Jesus coming true is 1 in 10, 000, 000, 000, 000, 000, 000, 000, 000, 000,[1037] which supports the conclusion that the prophecies come from a supernatural all-knowing and all-present being. To illustrate the meaning of this number, Peter Stoner,

> asked the reader to imagine filling the State of Texas knee deep in silver dollars. Include in this huge number one silver dollar with a black check mark on it. Then, turn a blindfolded person loose in this sea of silver dollars. The odds that the first coin he would pick up would be the one with the black check mark are the same as eight prophecies being fulfilled accidentally in the life of Jesus.[1038]

Stoner "calculated the odds of fulfilling forty-eight prophecies" out of at least sixty-one major prophecies as to Jesus as to Jesus, at one in 10, 000, 000, 000, 000, 000, 000, 000, 000, 000, 000, 000, 000, 000, 000, 000, 000, 000, 000, 000, 000, 000, 000, 000, 000, 000, 000, 000, 000, 000, 000, 000, 000, 000, 000, 000, 000, 000, 000, 000, 000, 000, 000, 000, 000, 000, 000, 000, 000, 000, 000, 000.[1039]

Others, including Peter Stoner's grandson, Don, have given interesting examples to assist the reader in visualizing the impact of the odds of prophecies occurring when made which the reader may want to read.[1040]

Peter Stoner's conclusions are also reliable. In the foreword to Stoner's book, *Science Speaks*, which discusses mathematical probabilities of Bible prophecy coming true,

H. Harold Hartzler, Ph.D., the Secretary-Treasurer to "American Scientific Affiliation" writes the following. "The manuscript SCIENCE SPEAKS has been carefully reviewed by a committee of the American Scientific Affiliation members... and Executive Council... and has been found, in general, to be dependable and accurate in regard to the scientific material presented. The mathematical analysis included is based upon principles of probability which are thoroughly sound and Professor Stoner has applied these principles in a proper and convincing way."[1041]

Also of interest is the fact that modern archaeology supports the accuracy of biblical prophecy.

Some, but not all, of the prophecies in the Bible, when they were made, when they were confirmed, and, as applicable, when they may have been reconfirmed, will be discussed in chapters 10 and 11.

Prophecies that predicted occurrences, often thousands of years before they happened, would be later proven to a world which Jesus, a carpenter from Nazarene, knew was and would be skeptical to the point of unbelief. As Luke reports,

He, (referring to Jesus), said to them, "How foolish you are, and how slow to believe all that the prophets have spoken! Did not the Messiah have to suffer these things and then enter his glory?" And beginning with Moses and all the Prophets, he explained to them what was said in all the Scriptures concerning himself.

See Luke 24:25–27 (NIV) (written 60–61 AD).

The author has determined that even more conservative odds that prophecies, when made, would happen are evidence that supports

When Only God Knew

the reliability of the Bible. The reader should decide for himself or herself if, as the Bible says in Isaiah 46:10 (NIV) (written 740–680 BC), God made "known the end from the beginning, from ancient times, what (was) still to come."

CHAPTER 10

Old Testament Prophecy Fulfilled in Old Testament Times

Peter Stoner calculates the probabilities of eleven Old Testament prophecies concerning Samaria, Gaza and Ashkelon, Jericho, Palestine, Moab and Ammon, Edom, and Babylon and the odds of prophecies being fulfilled that predicted,

a. the closing of the Eastern Gate of Jerusalem. *See* Ezekiel 44:1–3 (written in 590–570 BC and occurring in AD 1540–41 by order of Suleiman the Magnificent, a sultan of the Ottoman Empire),[1042]

b. the plowing of Mount Zion, Jerusalem becoming a heap of rubble, and the temple hill becoming a mound over-grown with thickets, i.e., the destruction of Jerusalem, *see* Micah 3:12 (written 742–687 BC and which first oc-curred about 730 BC, subsequently again in 586 BC by the Babylonians and by the Romans in AD 70 and again in AD 135),[1043] and

c. the enlargement of Jerusalem according to a prescribed pattern, *see* Jeremiah 31:38–40 (NIV) (written 627–570 BC), which says,

> "The days are coming," declares the LORD, "when this
> city will be rebuilt for me from the Tower of Hananel
> to the Corner Gate. The measuring line will stretch

from there straight to the hill of Gareb and then turn to Goah. The whole valley where dead bodies and ashes are thrown, and all the terraces out to the Kidron Valley on the east as far as the corner of the Horse Gate, will be holy to the LORD. The city will never again be uprooted or demolished."

The boundaries of Jerusalem are now much larger than they were in the sixth and seventh centuries BC when Jeremiah was written. "By the end of the First Temple period the First Temple was destroyed by the Babylonians in 586 BC, the walled city of Jerusalem covered 160 acres."[1044] As discussed below, Cyrus of Persia issued an order in 538 BC (thirty to ninety years, more or less, after Jeremiah was written), allowing exiled Jews to return to Jerusalem and rebuild it and the Jewish temple. "Since 1860, Jerusalem has grown far beyond the Old City's boundaries,"[1045] and it continues to grow, although it has not yet reached the boundaries prophesied in Jeremiah 31:38-40.

Stoner calculated the odds of all eleven prophecies happening, most of which have occurred, at 1 in 1, 000, 000, 000, 000, 000, 000, 000, 000, 000, 000, 000, 000, 000,-000, 000, 000, 000, 000, 000,-000, 000, a number beyond the realm of mere coincidental possibility.

A. Prophecy that the Israelites Would Have Their Own Country

Fact Stated: Genesis (written 1450–1405 BC)
Fact Confirmed: Joshua (written circa 1405–1385 BC)
(440 to 700 years later ±)

Genesis 15:18 (NIV) (written 1450–1405 BC) prophesied that the descendants of Abraham would rule the land between the Nile River and the Euphrates River, i.e., the Promised Land. It says, "On that day the Lord made a covenant with Abram and said, 'To your de-

When Only God Knew

scendants, I give this land, from the Wadi of Egypt to the great river, the Euphrates.'"

Before that would happen, however,

a. Isaac, Jacob (born sixty years after Isaac was born), and Joseph (born ninety-one years after Jacob was born) would be born, and Joseph would start serving in Egypt as overseer to the pharaoh at age thirty,[1046] be a ruler in Egypt second only to the pharaoh and live another eighty years to the age of 110,[1047]

b. the Jews would be slaves in Egypt for 400 years[1048] and

c. the Jews would spend forty years wandering in the wilderness before entering the Promised Land.[1049]

In Genesis (written 1450–1405 BC), the prophecy that the Jews would own the Promised Land was reconfirmed to Jacob, Abraham's grandson. Genesis (NIV) 35:9–12 says,

> After Jacob returned from Paddan Aram, God appeared to him again and blessed him. God said to him, "Your name is Jacob, but you will no longer be called Jacob; your name will be Israel." So he named him Israel.
>
> And God said to him, "I am God Almighty; be fruitful and increase in number. A nation and a community of nations will come from you, and kings will be among your descendants. The land I gave to Abraham and Isaac I also give to you, and I will give this land to your descendants after you."

See also Genesis 15:18 (written 1440–1405 BC) where the promise was made to Abraham and Genesis 26:2–4 (written 1440–1405 BC) where the promise was made to Isaac. And it would still be hundreds of years before what was prophesied to Jacob, afterward known as Israel, as to the Israelites owning the Promised Land would first happen.

While it is possible, as the articles cited in the notes suggest, that the 400-year enslavement may not have begun soon after Joseph died, what is nonetheless clear is that hundreds of years passed after the promise was made to Abraham, Isaac, and Jacob in Genesis that the Israelites would rule the Promised Land before they actually did. How did the writer of Genesis know that it would happen hundreds of years before it did?

B. Ezekiel Prophecies as to the City of Tyre and Other "Lesser" Prophecies

Fact Stated: Isaiah, Ezekiel, Joel, Amos, Zechariah (written 835–470 BC)
Fact Confirmed: Circa 332 BC (140 to 500 years later ±)

The people of Tyre along with the people of its neighbouring city of Sidon are generally called, "Phoenician." The principal cities of the Phoenicians were originally Byblos, Sidon and Tyre but they established colonies all along the north-African coast and as far west as Portugal and Spain. The cities of Byblos, Sidon and Tyre are located within the territory of modern Syria and Lebanon.

. . .

The people of Tyre became overly confident in their natural island defenses and overly proud of the wealth and beauty of their city. They developed a feeling of jealousy and rivalry toward Jerusalem and exulted over the misfortunes she faced and hoped to exploit them for commercial opportunity. For these reasons the prophet Ezekiel was inspired to prophecy against her:[1050]

Hundreds of years before its destruction, many prophets prophesied the destruction of the ancient city of Tyre. Isaiah said, "Wail, you ships of Tarshish! For Tyre is destroyed and left without house or harbor." *See* Isaiah 23:1 (NIV) (written 740–680 BC). The prophet Joel warned Tyre that it would be destroyed. In Joel 3:4 (NIV) (written 835–796 BC), he said,

> "Now what have you against me, Tyre and Sidon and all you regions of Philistia? Are you repaying me for something I have done? If you are paying me back, I will swiftly and speedily return on your own heads what you have done. For you took my silver and my gold and carried off my finest treasures to your temples.[a] You sold the people of Judah and Jerusalem to the Greeks, that you might send them far from their homeland.

Amos 1:9–10 (NIV) (written circa 760–750 BC) says the following:

> This is what the LORD says: "For three sins of Tyre, even for four, I will not relent. Because she sold whole communities of captives to Edom, disregarding a treaty of brotherhood, I will send fire on the walls of Tyre that will consume her fortresses."

Zechariah 9:4 (NIV) (written 520–470 BC) says that "the Lord will take away her possessions and destroy her power on the sea, and she will be consumed by fire."

Perhaps the most descriptive prophet of Tyre's destruction, however, was Ezekiel.

Ezekiel was born in Israel, the son of a Jewish priest, and that was where he began his career as a prophet.[1051] In Ezekiel 26:3–16

(NIV) (written 590–570 BC), Ezekiel prophesies concerning the city of Tyre, saying the following:

> Therefore this is what the Sovereign Lord says: I am against you, Tyre, and I will bring many nations against you, like the sea casting up its waves. They will destroy the walls of Tyre and pull down her towers; I will scrape away her rubble and make her a bare rock. Out in the sea she will become a place to spread fishnets, for I have spoken, declares the Sovereign Lord. She will become plunder for the nations, and her settlements on the mainland will be ravaged by the sword. Then they will know that I am the Lord.
>
> "For this is what the Sovereign Lord says: From the north I am going to bring against Tyre Nebuchadnezzar king of Babylon, king of kings, with horses and chariots, with horsemen and a great army. He will ravage your settlements on the mainland with the sword; he will set up siege works against you, build a ramp up to your walls and raise his shields against you. He will direct the blows of his battering rams against your walls and demolish your towers with his weapons. His horses will be so many that they will cover you with dust. Your walls will tremble at the noise of the warhorses, wagons and chariots when he enters your gates as men enter a city whose walls have been broken through. The hooves of his horses will trample all your streets; he will kill your people with the sword, and your strong pillars will fall to the ground. They will plunder your wealth and loot your merchandise; they will break down your walls and demolish your fine houses and throw your stones, timber and rubble into the sea. I will put an

end to your noisy songs, and the music of your harps will be heard no more. I will make you a bare rock, and you will become a place to spread fishnets. You will never be rebuilt, for I the Lord have spoken, declares the Sovereign Lord.

Peter Stoner's book, entitled *Prophetic Accuracy*, discusses this Ezekiel prophecy.[1052] As Stoner points out,[1053]

[f]our years after this prophecy was given, Nebuchadnezzar laid siege to Tyre. The siege lasted thirteen years. When the city finally fell in 573 BC, it was discovered that everything of value had been moved to a nearby island.

Two hundred and forty-one years later Alexander the Great arrived on the scene. Fearing that the fleet of Tyre might be used against his homeland, he decided to take the island where the city had been moved to. He accomplished this goal by building a causeway from the mainland to the island, and he did that by using all the building materials from the ruins of the old city.[1054] Neighboring cities were so frightened by Alexander's conquest that they immediately opened their gates to him. Ever since that time, Tyre has remained in ruins and is a place where fishermen spread their nets.

Thus, every detail of the prophecy was fulfilled exactly as predicted. Stoner calculated the odds of such a prophecy being fulfilled by chance as being 1 in 75,000,000.[1055]

C. Other Prophecies as to Assyria, Babylonia, and Persia

Fact Stated: Leviticus and Isaiah (written 1450–680 BC)
Fact Confirmed: 2 Chronicles and Ezra (written 457–430 BC)
(250–1000 years later ±)

Leviticus 26:40–43 (NIV) (written 1450–1405 BC) says,

> But if they will confess their sins and the sins of their ancestors—their unfaithfulness and their hostility toward me, which made me hostile toward them so that I sent them into the land of their enemies—then when their uncircumcised hearts are humbled and they pay for their sin, I will remember my covenant with Jacob and my covenant with Isaac and my covenant with Abraham, and I will remember the land. For the land will be deserted by them and will enjoy its sabbaths while it lies desolate without them. They will pay for their sins because they rejected my laws and abhorred my decrees.

Leviticus 26:40–43 prophesied that a Jewish diaspora would occur due to the Israelites "unfaithfulness and their hostility" toward God, which would cause God to send them "into the land of their enemies" as a consequence of their rejection of God's laws and decrees. From the Christian perspective, the most significant unfaithfulness and hostility by the Israelites toward God occurred when they and their leaders rejected Jesus and caused Him to be crucified merely thirty-five years prior to a diaspora which began in AD 70 and was only resolved in the nineteenth and twentieth centuries when Jews returned to their homeland and the Jewish State of Israel was eventually established, in 1948 as will be discussed in Chapter 11.

When Only God Knew

Nonetheless, there had been earlier Jewish diasporas that began in the eighth century BC.

> The first exile was the Assyrian exile, the expulsion from the Kingdom of Israel [Samaria] begun by Tiglath-Pileser III of Assyria[1056] in 733 BCE. This process was completed by Sargon II[1057] with the destruction of the kingdom in 722 BCE, concluding a three-year siege of Samaria begun by Shalmaneser V.[1058] The next experience of exile was the Babylonian captivity, in which portions of the population of the Kingdom of Judah were deported in 597 BC and again in 586 BC by the Neo-Babylonian Empire under the rule of Nebuchadnezzar II.[1059]

What is known as the Babylonian captivity began after the collapse of the Assyrian Empire by 610 BC due to Babylonian attacks.[1060]

The Babylonians invaded Jerusalem in 597 BC and captured it. A second attack led to Jerusalem's second defeat in 586 BC Captives from both campaigns were taken to Babylonia to mark the captivity of the Southern Kingdom.[1061] After the young new king of Babylon, Nebuchadnezzar II, defeated the Egyptians, he marched to Judah, the southern Jewish kingdom, "and took thousands of Hebrews back to Babylon;" "Nebuchadnezzar made two more attacks when he heard of rebellion in Judah," and "each time he took captives."[1062]

The Babylonian captivity ended when Cyrus, the Persian king, joined by the Medes, as prophesied in Isaiah 13:17 (written 740–680 BC), conquered Babylon in 539 BC, 200 years ± after it had been predicted.

The Persians defeated Babylonia in the way predicted by Isaiah, the Jewish prophet, in Isaiah 45:1 (NIV) (written 740–680 BC), 150 to 200 years before the event would occur. Isaiah 45:1 said, "This is what the LORD says to his anointed, to Cyrus, whose right hand I take hold of to subdue nations before him and to strip kings of their armor, to open doors before him *so that gates will not be shut.*" (Emphasis added).

As one historian reported,

> In a military engagement known as the Battle of Opis, Cyrus knew that they could never break the walls [of Babylon]. So he waited until the Babylonians had a national feast where they would be unsuspecting of an attack. There was one entrance in through [sic] the Euphrates River, where someone would have to hold their breath and swim until the other side, virtually impossible. Cyrus had his men divert the water until the water was only at hip length. Cyrus took control of the city with virtually no fight. Babylon then came under the control of the Persian Empire.[1063]

Cyrus' entry into Babylon was probably due to the fact that "[d]espite Babylon's remarkable defenses, which included moats, and walls that were more than 70-feet thick and 300-feet high, and 250 watchtowers,"[1064] the Babylonians had, without realizing the danger on the riverside of Babylon, failed to make "fast all the street gates which gave access to the river."[1065] Another historian tells a different version as to why the gates on the river were open, however. According to that historian, "the *Cyrus Cylinder* says that the people opened their gates for Cyrus and greeted him as a liberator,"[1066] a different version as to how entry into Babylon by the invading Persians was accomplished which may be questionable as the "Cyrus Cylinder is a political and probably self-serving document issued by Cyrus the Great" which was created in 539 BC, "when he took Babylon."[1067]

In either case, however, as prophesied, Babylon was conquered because its gates were not shut as they should have been.

When Only God Knew

The Jews returned to Jerusalem after Cyrus, the Persian king, conquered Babylon. As 2 Chronicles 36:22–23 (NIV) says,

> In the first year of Cyrus king of Persia, in order to fulfill the word of the Lord spoken by Jeremiah, the Lord moved the heart of Cyrus king of Persia to make a proclamation throughout his realm and also to put it in writing: "This is what Cyrus king of Persia says: "'The Lord, the God of heaven, has given me all the kingdoms of the earth and he has appointed me to build a temple for him at Jerusalem in Judah. Any of his people among you may go up, and may the Lord their God be with them.'"

See also Ezra 1:1–4 (NIV) (written 457–444 BC), which says,

> In the first year of Cyrus king of Persia, in order to fulfill the word of the LORD spoken by Jeremiah, the LORD moved the heart of Cyrus king of Persia to make a proclamation throughout his realm and also to put it in writing: "This is what Cyrus king of Persia says: "'The LORD, the God of heaven, has given me all the kingdoms of the earth and he has appointed me to build a temple for him at Jerusalem in Judah. Any of his people among you may go up to Jerusalem in Judah and build the temple of the LORD, the God of Israel, the God who is in Jerusalem, and may their God be with them. And in any locality where survivors may now be living, the people are to provide them with silver and gold, with goods and livestock, and with freewill offerings for the temple of God in Jerusalem.'"

As one author succinctly put it,

> During ancient times, 10 of the 12 Tribes of Israel were decimated by the Assyrians. And the Babylonians later persecuted what was left of the people of Israel. But, instead of assimilating or perishing, some of the people eventually returned to their homeland and recover (sic) their way of life.
>
> The recovery was very complete, complete enough that Jerusalem again had been restored as the center of Jewish life. And the followers of Jesus were able to begin a process in Jerusalem by which Christianity later spread throughout the world.[1068]

As pointed out in chapter 11, the Jews would be disbursed abruptly in 70 AD and would not return to Israel for about another 1900 years.

D. Other Prophecies as to Persia

Fact Stated: Leviticus, Isaiah, and Jeremiah (written 1450–570 BC)
Fact Confirmed: 2 Chronicles and Ezra (written 457–430 BC)
(140–1020 years later ±)
Fact Re-confirmed: 1879 AD (2450–3300 years later ±)

Despite the custom of the time to slay or enslave all captives after battle, Leviticus 26:44 (NIV) (written 1450–1405 BC) prophesied that the people of Israel would not be destroyed during any captivity, which includes the Babylonian captivity described above. It says,

> Yet in spite of this, when they are in the land of their enemies, I will not reject them or abhor them so as to destroy them completely, breaking my covenant with them. I am the LORD their God.

When Only God Knew

Isaiah 44:28 (NIV) (written 700–680 BC) says, "who says of Cyrus, [1069] 'He is my shepherd and will accomplish all that I please; he will say of Jerusalem,' 'Let it be rebuilt,' and of the temple, 'Let its foundations be laid.'" And so it was. *See also* 2 Chronicles 36:22–23 (NIV) and Ezra 1:1–4 (NIV), quoted above.

According to the Encyclopaedia Britannica, Cyrus issued an order in 538 BC, from 140 to 200 years ± after Isaiah was written, allowing exiled Jews to return to Jerusalem and rebuild the Jewish temple, which was completed in 515 BC.[1070]

The prophet Jeremiah had also prophesied, closer in time to when it would happen than Isaiah's prophecy, that Cyrus would allow the Jews to return to their homeland to rebuild their temple. Jeremiah 29:10 (NASB) (written 627–570 BC) says, "For this is what the Lord says, 'When seventy years have been completed for Babylon, I will visit you and fulfill My good word to you, to bring you back to this place.'"

Cyrus' policy of religious tolerance and allowing the Jews to rebuild their temple has been reconfirmed by the discovery of a nine-inch clay cylinder in March 1879,[1071] at least 2,500 years after Isaiah was written and over 2,400 years after Cyrus allowed the return. The nine-inch clay cylinder reports Cyrus's victory over Babylonia in 539 BC and his subsequent policy of permitting Babylonian captives to return to their homes and rebuild their temples."[1072]

CHAPTER 11

Old and New Testimony Prophecies Fulfilled in New Testament and Modern Times

A. Old Testimony Prophecies about Jesus Fulfilled in New Testament Times

Biblical scholars have calculated that there are hundreds if not thousands of Old Testament prophecies that predict the coming of Christ and events in his life. Not all of them will be discussed. Focus will be on the top eight according to most scholars, and others will be touched on only briefly, again as a matter of economy.

Before we do that, one author on the subject has asked us to do an imaginary but helpful exercise prior to starting to think about the accuracy of the Old Testament writings about Jesus "and the equally astonishing unlikelihood of them all coming to pass" in order to understand the impact of those prophecies.

> Imagine that in Waco, Texas, ancient scrolls are uncovered which were written 600 to 1,000 years ago. Some were written before the discovery of America by Columbus, and all were written before the American Revolution. The scrolls predict that someone in our generation will be born who is of the direct lineage of George Washington. This person would be descended from a long line of important founders of America, all of whom were known to be from Virginia. The scrolls further reveal that the person

would be born in Tarrant County, Texas in the town of Azle. Miraculously, his mother would be a virgin. At the time of his birth, dignitaries from other countries would mysteriously know about him and would come to worship him and present him with precious gifts, believing he was a special envoy from God.

In addition, our imaginary prophecies would also reveal that as a result of this child being born, local ruling tyrants would make an attempt to murder him.[1073] This would result in the deaths of many other innocent children whose mothers would weep over their loss. To protect this special child from the tyrants, his father would take him to another country, later bringing him back. This future child would grow up to lead a religious revolution.

Now, imagine that all this came to be true in our lifetime, fulfilling the predictions of these centuries-old scrolls. As astronomically unlikely as the creation, preservation and fulfillment of these written prophecies might seem, this is a fair parallel to what we have in the ancient Hebrew Scripture prophecies about Jesus![1074]

1. Prophecy as to Where Jesus Will Be Born

Fact Stated: Micah (written 742–687 BC)
Fact Confirmed: Matthew, Luke, and John (written 50–90 AD)
(740–830 years later ±)

The prophet Micah, who "prophesied from approximately 737 to 696 BC,"[1075] prophesied that Jesus would be born in the city of Bethlehem. Micah 5:2 (NIV) (written 742–687 BC) says,

But as for you, Bethlehem Ephrathah, too little to be among the clans of Judah, from you one will go forth for me to be ruler in Israel. His goings forth are from long ago, from the days of eternity.

The fact that Jesus was born in Bethlehem was confirmed by the apostles Matthew, Luke, and John, who reported on his birth. In Matthew 2:1–2 (written 50–65 AD). Matthew says,

Now when Jesus was born in Bethlehem of Judaea in the days of Herod the king, behold, there came wise men from the east to Jerusalem,

Saying, Where is he that is born King of the Jews? for we have seen his star in the east, and are come to worship him.

See also Matthew 2:5, 6, 8, 16 (written 50–65 AD), Luke 2:4, 15 (written 60–61 AD) and John 7:42 (written 80–90 AD). The unsubstantiated premise that Jesus may have been born in any other place than Bethlehem in Judea has been successfully debunked by scholars.[1076]

Keeping in mind that "[t]he average population of Bethlehem from the time of Micah to [1958 when Stoner made his calculations] divided by the average population of the earth during the same period = 7,150/2,000,000,000," the odds of this prophecy coming true at the time that it was made was 2.8 in 1,000,000.[1077]

2. John the Baptist Will Minister before Jesus Begins His Ministry

Fact Stated: Isaiah and Malachi (written 740–424 BC)
Fact Confirmed: Matthew, Mark, Luke, and John (written 50–90 AD)
(470–830 years later ±)

Malachi 3:1 (NIV) (written 433–424 BC), written by the prophet

Malachi who may have "prophesied sometime between 445 BC and 425 BC to the people of Jerusalem,"[1078] said,

> I will send my messenger, who will prepare the way before me. Then suddenly the Lord you are seeking will come to His temple; the messenger of the covenant, whom you desire, will come," says the LORD Almighty.

Even earlier than that, Isaiah, the "Jewish prophet who lived during the eighth century BC,"[1079] said,

> A voice of one calling: "In the wilderness prepare the way for the Lord; make straight in the desert a highway for our God. Every valley shall be raised up, every mountain and hill made low; the rough ground shall become level, the rugged places a plain. And the glory of the Lord will be revealed, and all people will see it together.

Isaiah 40:3–5 (NIV) (written 740–680 BC).

500 to 700 ± years after Isaiah was written, the Gospels of Matthew, Mark, and Luke talk about the ministry of John the Baptist, the son of Zacharias, before the beginning of Jesus' ministry.

a. John the Baptist Preaches and Precedes Jesus

See, e.g., Matthew 3:1–2 (NIV) (written 50–65 AD), which says,

> In those days John the Baptist came, preaching in the wilderness of Judea and saying, "Repent, for the kingdom of heaven has come near."

See also Mark 1:1–6 (NIV) (written 50–65 AD), which says,

The beginning of the good news about Jesus the Messiah, the Son of God, as it is written in Isaiah the prophet: "I will send my messenger ahead of you, who will prepare your way" "a voice of one calling in the wilderness, 'Prepare the way for the Lord, make straight paths for him.'"

And so John the Baptist appeared in the wilderness, preaching a baptism of repentance for the forgiveness of sins. The whole Judean countryside and all the people of Jerusalem went out to him. Confessing their sins, they were baptized by him in the Jordan River. John wore clothing made of camel's hair, with a leather belt around his waist, and he ate locusts and wild honey. And this was his message: "After me comes the one more powerful than I, the straps of whose sandals I am not worthy to stoop down and untie. I baptize you with water, but he will baptize you with the Holy Spirit."

See also Luke 3:1–2 (NIV) (written 60–61 AD), which says,

In the fifteenth year of the reign of Tiberius Caesar—when Pontius Pilate was governor of Judea, Herod tetrarch of Galilee, his brother Philip tetrarch of Iturea and Traconitis, and Lysanias tetrarch of Abilene—during the high-priesthood of Annas and Caiaphas, the word of God came to John son of Zechariah in the wilderness.

See also John 1:19–30 NIV (written 80–90 AD), which says,

Now this was John's testimony when the Jewish leaders in Jerusalem sent priests and Levites to ask him who he was. He did not fail to confess, but confessed freely, "I am not the Messiah."

They asked him, "Then who are you? Are you Elijah?"

He said, "I am not."

"Are you the Prophet?"

He answered, "No."

Finally they said, "Who are you? Give us an answer to take back to those who sent us. What do you say about yourself?"

John replied in the words of Isaiah the prophet, "I am the voice of one calling in the wilderness, 'Make straight the way for the Lord.'"

Now the Pharisees who had been sent questioned him, "Why then do you baptize if you are not the Messiah, nor Elijah, nor the Prophet?"

"I baptize with water," John replied, "but among you stands one you do not know. He is the one who comes after me, the straps of whose sandals I am not worthy to untie."

This all happened at Bethany on the other side of the Jordan, where John was baptizing.

The next day John saw Jesus coming toward him and said, "Look, the Lamb of God, who takes away the sin of the world! This is the one I meant when I said, 'A man who comes after me has surpassed me because he was before me.'"

b. John the Baptist is an Answer to Prophecy

See, e.g., Matthew 3:3 (NIV) (written 50–65 AD), which says,

This is he who was spoken of through the prophet Isaiah:

"A voice of one calling in the wilderness, 'Prepare the way for the Lord, make straight paths for him.'"

See also Luke 3:4–6 (NIV) (written 60–61 AD), which says,

As it is written in the book of the words of Isaiah the prophet:

"A voice of one calling in the wilderness, 'Prepare the way for the Lord, make straight paths for him. Every valley shall be filled in, every mountain and hill made low. The crooked roads shall become straight, the rough ways smooth. And all people will see God's salvation.'"

We know from not only the Bible that John the Baptists existed. John the Baptist is, for instance, mentioned by Josephus, the Jewish historian; in the first century AD,[1080] Stoner has estimated that only one man in 1,000 men has had a forerunner to prepare his way as John the Baptist did for Jesus.[1081]

3. Jesus Will Enter Jerusalem as a King Riding on a Donkey

Fact Stated: Zechariah (written 520–470 BC)
Fact Confirmed: Matthew, Mark, Luke, and John (written 50–90 AD)
(520–610 years later ±)

Zechariah[1082] 9:9 (NIV) (written 520–470 BC) says, "Rejoice greatly, Daughter Zion! Shout, Daughter Jerusalem! See, your king comes to you, righteous and victorious, lowly and riding on a donkey, on a colt, the foal of a donkey."

Though Jesus entered Jerusalem on many prior occasions, the apostles Matthew, Mark, Luke, and John, writing 610 to 520 years after Zechariah, all confirmed with the same facts Jesus' last entry into Jerusalem as being on a donkey. Jesus' "final entry into Jerusalem, before his crucifixion, had a unique significance," because he "was triumphantly arriving as a humble King of peace; historically, entering a city on a donkey signified entry in peace, rather than a conquering king arriving on a horse."[1083]

Matthew 21:1–5 (NIV) (written 50–65 AD) says,

> As they approached Jerusalem and came to Bethphage on the Mount of Olives, Jesus sent two disciples, saying to them, "Go to the village ahead of you, and at once you will find a donkey tied there, with her colt by her. Untie them and bring them to me. If anyone says anything to you, say that the Lord needs them, and he will send them right away."
>
> This took place to fulfill what was spoken through the prophet:
> *"Say to Daughter Zion,*
> *'See, your king comes to you,*
> *gentle and riding on a donkey,*
> *and on a colt, the foal of a donkey.*

Mark 11:1–7 (NIV) (written 50 –65 AD) says,

> As they approached Jerusalem and came to Bethphage and Bethany at the Mount of Olives, Jesus sent two of his disciples, saying to them, "Go to the village ahead of you, and just as you enter it, you will find a colt tied there, which no one has ever ridden. Untie it and bring it here. If anyone asks you, 'Why are you doing this?' say, 'The Lord needs it and will send it back here shortly.'"

They went and found a colt outside in the street, tied at a doorway. As they untied it, some people standing there asked, "What are you doing, untying that colt?" They answered as Jesus had told them to, and the people let them go. When they brought the colt to Jesus and threw their cloaks over it, he sat on it.

Luke 19:28–35 (NIV) (written 60–61 AD) says,

After Jesus had said this, he went on ahead, going up to Jerusalem. As he approached Bethphage and Bethany at the hill called the Mount of Olives, he sent two of his disciples, saying to them, "Go to the village ahead of you, and as you enter it, you will find a colt tied there, which no one has ever ridden. Untie it and bring it here. If anyone asks you, 'Why are you untying it?' say, 'The Lord needs it.'" Those who were sent ahead went and found it just as he had told them. As they were untying the colt, its owners asked them, "Why are you untying the colt?"

They replied, "The Lord needs it." They brought it to Jesus, threw their cloaks on the colt and put Jesus on it.

Finally, John 12:14–16 (NIV) (written 80–90 AD) says,

Jesus found a young donkey and sat on it, as it is written: "Do not be afraid, Daughter Zion; see, your king is coming, seated on a donkey's colt."

At first his disciples did not understand all this. Only after Jesus was glorified did they realize that these things had been written about him and that these things had been done to him.

Peter Stoner, using conservative numbers for how many men have entered Jerusalem as a ruler riding on a donkey, estimated that only one in one hundred did.[1084] That figure is, in this author's opinion, far too conservative.

4. Jesus Will Be Betrayed by Judas, a Friend, and Suffer Wounds in His Hands

Fact Stated: Psalms and Zechariah (written 1440–470 BC)
Fact Confirmed: Matthew, Mark, Luke, and John (written 50–90 AD)
(530–1520 years later ±)

In Psalm 41:9 (NIV) (written 1440–450 BC), King David prophesied about the betrayal of Jesus, saying that "even my close friend in whom I trusted, who ate my bread, has lifted his heel against me." In Zechariah 13:6 (KJV) (written 520–470 BC), the prophet Zechariah, who had been told by God to play the role of an actor in a drama and pretended to be the future Messiah in that drama,[1085] likewise says, "And one shall say unto him, What are these wounds in thine hands? Then he shall answer, Those with which I was wounded in the house of my friends."

Judas was an apostle and a friend of and a person trusted by Jesus. Judas Iscariot was a handpicked disciple of Jesus Christ. Jesus trusted him so much, he was made treasurer of the apostolic evangelistic team by Jesus Himself.[1086]

Even so, Judas betrayed Jesus as reported hundreds of years after it was prophesied. Matthew 10:2–4 (NIV) (written 50–65 AD) says,

These are the names of the twelve apostles: first, Simon [who is called Peter] and his brother Andrew; James son of Zebedee, and his brother John; Philip and Bartholomew; Thomas and Matthew the tax collector; James son of Alphaeus, and Thaddaeus; Simon the Zealot and Judas Iscariot, who betrayed him.

Matthew 26:14 (NIV) (written 50–65 AD) says, "Then one of the Twelve—the one called Judas Iscariot—went to the chief priests." Matthew 26:16 (NIV) (written 50–65 AD) says, "From then on Judas watched for an opportunity to hand Him over." Yet when Jesus prophesied that one of His apostle followers would betray Him, Judas acted as if he could not be the one. Matthew 26:24–25 (NIV) (written 50–65 AD) says,

> The Son of Man will go just as it is written about him. But woe to that man who betrays the Son of Man! It would be better for him if he had not been born."
>
> Then Judas, the one who would betray him, said, "Surely you don't mean me, Rabbi?" Jesus answered, "You have said so."

See also Matthew 27:47–49 (written 50–65 AD), Mark 3:19, 14:10, 43–45 (written 50–65 AD), Luke 6:16, 22:1–4, 47–48 (written 60–61 AD) and John 6:71, 12:4, 13:21–26 (written 80–90 AD).

No one known to the author has denied that Judas betrayed Jesus.

And the New Testament supports that Jesus was pierced through his hands by the nails when He was crucified. See also Matthew (written 50–65 AD), (written 50–65 AD), Luke 24:39–40 (written 60–61 AD), and John 20:20, 24–28 (written 80–90 AD). Such has also been shown to be anatomically not only possible but the likely way Jesus was crucified.[1087]

Starting with the proposition that questions "how many, the world over has been betrayed by a friend, resulting in wounds in his hands," Stoner estimates very, very, very conservatively only 1 in 1,000.[1088]

5. Jesus Will Be Betrayed for Thirty Pieces of Silver

Fact Stated: Zechariah (written 520–470 BC)
Fact Confirmed: Matthew (written 50–65 AD) (520–585 years later ±)

Matthew 26:14–16 (NIV) (written 50–65 AD) says,

> Then one of the Twelve—the one called Judas Iscariot—went to the chief priests and asked, "What are you willing to give me if I deliver him over to you?" So they counted out for him thirty pieces of silver. From then on Judas watched for an opportunity to hand him over.

Matthew 27:3 (NIV) (written 50–65 AD) confirms the amount Judas received. It says, "When Judas, who had betrayed him, saw that Jesus was condemned, he was seized with remorse and returned the thirty pieces of silver to the chief priests and the elders."

That Judas would betray Jesus for thirty pieces of silver, however, had been prophesied by Zechariah over 500 hundred years before it happened. *See* Zechariah 11:4–14 (NIV) (written 520–470 BC). How did the prophet know half a millennium before that the betrayal of Jesus would be for *silver*, not shekels, commonly used Jewish coinage, and for exactly *thirty* pieces of it?

Again starting with a very conservative question that "of the people who have been betrayed, one in how many has been betrayed for exactly thirty pieces of silver," Stoner again estimates very very very conservatively only 1 in 1,000.[1089] I would estimate that the odds against it happening would be much higher.

6. The Betrayal Money Paid to Judas Will Be Used to Purchase a Potter's Field

Fact Stated: Zechariah (written 520–470 BC)
Fact Confirmed: Matthew (written 50–65 AD) (520–585 years later ±)

A potter's field is "a public burial place for paupers, unknown persons, and criminals."[1090] According to scholars, "The earliest known reference to a potter's field is from the Gospel of Matthew."[1091]

And yet, five hundred years before the Gospel of Matthew was written, Zechariah 11:13 (NIV) (written 520–470 BC) predicted that the thirty pieces of silver given to Judas to betray Jesus would be used to buy a potter's field. Zechariah 11:13 says, "And the LORD said to me, 'Throw it to the potter'—the handsome price at which they valued me! So I took the thirty pieces of silver and threw them to the potter at the house of the LORD."

Matthew 27:3–8 confirms that the silver given to Judas was used to buy a potter's field when it says,

> When Judas, who had betrayed him, saw that Jesus was condemned, he was seized with remorse and returned the thirty pieces of silver to the chief priests and the elders. "I have sinned," he said, "for I have betrayed innocent blood."
>
> "What is that to us?" they replied. "That's your responsibility."
>
> So Judas threw the money into the temple and left. Then he went away and hanged himself.
>
> The chief priests picked up the coins and said, "It is against the law to put this into the treasury, since it is blood money." So they decided to use the money to buy the potter's field as a burial place for foreigners. That is why it has been called the Field of Blood to this day.

How did Zechariah know well before the term "potter's field" was ever used that the silver paid to Judas would be thrown to the potter? Stoner estimates that the odds are 1 in 100,000 that one man "after receiving a bribe for the betrayal of a friend, would return the money, had it refused, and then experienced it being used to buy a potter's field."[1092]

7. Jesus Will Remain Silent While He is Afflicted

Fact Stated: Isaiah (written 740–680 BC)
Fact Confirmed: Matthew, Mark, and Luke (written 50–65 AD)
(730–805 years later ±)

Pontius Pilate, who would order Jesus crucified, found no guilt in Jesus and no reason to put Him to death and saw no evil having been done by Him *See* Mark 15:14 (written 50–65 AD); Luke 23:4, 14–16 (written 60–61 AD). Pilate even wrote to the Roman Emperor concerning Jesus and His crucifixion.

> Pontius Pilate on Jesus: "And these are the things which I lately had in my mind to report, which Jesus accomplished on the Sabbath. And other signs greater than these he did, so that I have perceived that the wonderful works done by him are greater than can be done by the gods whom we worship."[1093]

When Jesus stood before Pontius Pilate, who appeared inclined not to crucify Him at first, Jesus did not, however, defend himself. *See* Matthew27:12–14 (ESV) (written 50–65 AD), which says,

> But when Jesus was accused by the chief priests and elders, he gave no answer. Then Pilate said to Jesus, "Do you not hear how many things they testify against you?" But he gave him no answer, not even

When Only God Knew

to a single charge, so that the governor was greatly amazed.

Luke 23:9 (NIV) (written 60–61 AD) says that Pilate "plied (Jesus) with many questions, but Jesus gave him no answer." *See also* Mark 15:4–5 (written 50–65 AD).

Over 700 hundred years before Jesus did not answer Pilate's questions to defend Himself, Isaiah prophesied Jesus' refusal to answer questions. Isaiah 53:7 (NIV) (written 740–680 BC) says about Jesus that "He was oppressed, and he was afflicted, yet he opened not his mouth; like a lamb that is led to the slaughter, and like a sheep that before its shearers is silent, so he opened not his mouth."

It is interesting to note that the term "affliction" in the Bible has "no fewer than 11 Hebrew words in the Old Testament and three Greek words in the New Testament."[1094] The term "affliction" has historically been defined to include "mental distress" or "a state of pain, distress, or grief."[1095] Even today, affliction includes a state of "distress, or grief; misery" or a cause of mental pain or persecution.[1096] Without a doubt, Jesus, charged with crimes He did not commit, was persecuted and would have been distressed and grieving and perhaps in misery for what was being done to Him.

Peter Stoner estimated in 1958, over sixty years ago and again overly conservatively, that only one innocent man in a 1,000 would make no defense of himself.[1097]

8. Jesus Will Die after Having His Hands, Feet, and Side Pierced

Fact Stated: Psalms and Zechariah (written 1440–450 BC)
Fact Confirmed: Matthew, Mark, Luke, John, Acts, Galatians and Revelation (written 50–96 AD) (500–1540 years later ±)

Psalm 22:16 (NIV) (written 1440–450 BC) says, "Dogs surround me, meaning Jesus,], a pack of villains encircles me; they pierce my hands and my feet."

Zechariah 12:10 (NIV) (written 520–470 BC) says, in part, talking about the Messiah to come, "They will look on me, meaning Jesus,], the one they have pierced." Zechariah 13:6 (KJV) (written 520–470 BC) says, also in part, "And one shall say unto him, 'What are these wounds in thine hands?'"

There is no doubt that Jesus was crucified. It is made clear several times in the New Testament. *See, e.g.,* Matthew 20:19, 27:31, 35 (written 50–65 AD), Mark 15:14, 15, 20, 27 (written 50–65 AD), Luke 23:21, 32 (written 60–61 AD), John 19:6, 15, 23 (written 80–90 AD), Acts 2:36 (written 62–70 AD), Galatians 3:1 (written 49–50 AD) and Revelation 11:8. (written 94–96 AD). Even Pontus Pilate reported that he had Jesus crucified.[1098]

There has, however, sometimes been controversy as to whether that meant that His hands and feet were pierced because in some places and at some times criminals had been tied to the cross. The evidence clearly supports the conclusion, however, that His feet and His hands were pierced as had been predicted by Isaiah.

One very comprehensive study done by John C. Robinson in 2002 "demonstrated that the use of nails for crucifixion was prevalent during the time of Jesus and in his area and is helpful in supporting the historicity of the gospels."[1099] Others have reached the same conclusion, i.e., that Jesus hands and feet were pierced for His crucifixion.[1100]

There is also eyewitness testimony to Jesus' hands and feet being pierced. Luke, the excellent historian, reported the following:

> While the apostles were talking about how Jesus was seen on the road to a village called Emmaus after his resurrection, Jesus himself stood among them and said to them, "Peace be with you." They were startled and frightened, thinking they saw a ghost. He said to them, "Why are you troubled, and why do doubts rise in your minds? Look at my hands and my feet. It

When Only God Knew

is I myself! Touch me and see; a ghost does not have flesh and bones, as you see I have." When he had said this, he showed them his hands and feet.

Luke 24:36–40 (NIV) (written 60–61 AD)

The apostle John also confirmed that Jesus' hands, feet, and side were pierced and shared a story about how Thomas, the disciple for whom the disparaging phrase Doubting Thomas was named, would question whether who the other disciples had seen was really Jesus. After His first appearance after His resurrection, John 20:19–28 (NIV) says He appeared to His disciples. John says,

> On the evening of that first day of the week, when the disciples were together, with the doors locked for fear of the Jewish leaders, Jesus came and stood among them and said, 'Peace be with you!' After he said this, he showed them his hands and side. The disciples were overjoyed when they saw the Lord.
>
> Again Jesus said, 'Peace be with you! As the Father has sent me, I am sending you.' And with that he breathed on them and said, 'Receive the Holy Spirit. If you forgive anyone's sins, their sins are forgiven; if you do not forgive them, they are not forgiven.' Now Thomas [also known as Didymus], one of the Twelve, was not with the disciples when Jesus came. So the other disciples told him, 'We have seen the Lord!' But he said to them, 'Unless I see the nail marks in his hands and put my finger where the nails were, and put my hand into his side, I will not believe.'
>
> A week later his disciples were in the house again, and Thomas was with them. Though the doors were locked, Jesus came and stood among them and said,

'Peace be with you!' Then he said to Thomas, 'Put your finger here; see my hands. Reach out your hand and put it into my side. Stop doubting and believe.'

Thomas said to him, 'My Lord and my God!'

Stoner estimated that only one man in 10,000, since the time of David, has been crucified.[1101] As pointed out in Part IV above,

> [m]ultiplying all eight of these probabilities together produces a number [rounded off] of $1 \times 10.^{28}$ Dividing this number by an estimate of the number of people who have lived since the time of these prophecies [88 billion] produces a probability of all eight prophecies being fulfilled accidentally in the life of one person. That probability is 1in 10^{17} or 1 in 100,000,000,000,000,000. That's one in one hundred quadrillions![1102]

9. Other Prophecies about Jesus

But those are not the only prophecies as to Jesus that would come true. There are about 100 prophecies in all that have. With each additional proven prophecy, the odds increase that someone with superior knowledge—all-knowing and all present knowledge—knew the truth and stated the truth to be confirmed later as further proof of His existence.

So, for example, the Bible also prophesizes that

a. Jesus Will Perform Miracles

Fact Stated: Isaiah (written 740–680 BC)
Fact Confirmed: Matthew, Mark, Luke and John (written 50–90 AD)
(730–830 years later ±)

Isaiah 35:5–6 (NIV) (written 74–680 BC) prophesied that Jesus

When Only God Knew

would open the eyes of the blind, unstop the ears of the deaf and cause the lame to leap like a deer and the mute to shout for joy. That Jesus performed these miracles, as had been prophesied almost a thousand years before, is confirmed throughout the Gospels of Matthew. Mark, Luke, and John (written 50–90 AD). *See, e.g.*, Matthew 15:29–31 (Written 50–65 AD) where he performed miracles in front of a large crowd. There is no testimony, written record—no evidence—none—that Jesus did not perform miracles which Isaiah prophesied He would; thousands are reported as having witnessed them.

The first-century Jewish historian, Josephus, referred "to Jesus' miraculous works."[1103] Even "Julian the Apostate (Roman Emperor from 361–363 AD), who was an enemy of Christianity," confirmed that Jesus did "a very great work to heal the lame and the blind."[1104]

b. Jesus Will Be Forsaken on the Cross Despite His Anguish

Fact Stated: Psalms (written 1440–450 BC)
Fact Confirmed: Matthew and Mark (written 50–65 AD)
(500–1505 years later ±)

Psalm 22:1 (NIV) (written 1440–450 BC) says, "My God, my God, why have you forsaken me? Why are you so far from saving me, so far from my cries of anguish?"

Hundreds of years later, this prophecy was fulfilled as noted in Matthew 27:46 (NIV) (written 50–65 AD), which says,

> "From noon until three in the afternoon darkness came over all the land. About three in the afternoon Jesus cried out in a loud voice, "*Eli, Eli, lema sabachthani?*" [which means "My God, my God, why have you forsaken me?"].

Hundreds of years later, the fulfillment of this prophecy was also noted in Mark 15:34 (NIV) (written 50–65 AD), which says,

> At noon, darkness came over the whole land until three in the afternoon. And at three in the afternoon Jesus cried out in a loud voice, "*Eloi, Eloi, lema sabachthani?*" [which means "My God, my God, why have you forsaken me?"].

c. Jesus Will Be Given Gall and Vinegar on the Cross

Fact Stated: Psalms (written 1440–450 BC)
Fact Confirmed: Matthew, Mark, Luke and John (written 50–90 AD)
(500–1530 years later ±)

Psalm 69:21 (NIV) (written 1440–450 BC) says, "They put gall in Jesus' food and gave Jesus vinegar for his thirst." That this prophecy came true was confirmed hundreds of years later in Matthew 27:34, 48 (NIV) (written 50–65 AD), which says,

> There the soldiers guarding the cross offered Jesus wine to drink, mixed with gall; but after tasting it, he refused to drink it.
>
> ...
>
> Immediately one of them ran and got a sponge. He filled it with wine vinegar, put it on a staff, and offered it to Jesus to drink.

Mark 15:22–23, 36 (NIV) (written 50–65 AD), likewise says,

> They brought Jesus to the place called Golgotha [which means "the place of the skull]." Then [the

soldiers guarding the cross] offered him wine mixed with myrrh, but he did not take it.

...

Someone ran, filled a sponge with wine vinegar, put it on a staff, and offered it to Jesus to drink.

In Luke 23:36 (NIV) (written 60–61 AD), it says, "The soldiers also came up and mocked him. They offered him wine vinegar."

And in John 19:29 (NIV) (written 80–90 AD) it says, "A jar of wine vinegar was there, [so the soldiers guarding the cross] soaked a sponge in it, put the sponge on a stalk of the hyssop plant, and lifted it to Jesus' lips."

Jesus was offered vinegar "made of light wine rendered acid, the common drink of Roman soldiers 'mingled with gall,' or, according to Mark 15:23, "mingled with myrrh."[1105] How could the Psalmist know hundreds of years before it happened that anyone would offer Jesus gall and vinegar?

d. Jesus Will Be Beaten on the Way to Be Crucified

Fact Stated: Isaiah (written 700–680 BC)
Fact Confirmed: Matthew, Mark and Luke (written 50–61 AD)
(730–760 years later ±)

Isaiah 50:6 (NIV) (written 700–680 BC) prophesied that Jesus would offer his "back to those who beat [him], [his] cheeks to those who pulled out [his] beard; [he] did not hide [his] face from mocking and spitting. Isaiah 52:14 and 53:3 say,

Just as there were many who were appalled at him— his appearance was so disfigured beyond that of any human being and his form marred beyond human likeness—

...

He was despised and rejected by mankind, a man of suffering and familiar with pain. Like one from whom people hide their faces, he was despised, and we held him in low esteem.

That prophecy was fulfilled. *See* Matthew 26:67, 27:26–30 (NIV) (written 50–65 AD), which says,

> Then they spit in his face and struck him with their fists [when Jesus was arrested]. Others slapped him.
>
> ...
>
> Then he, Pontius Pilate, released Barabbas to them. But he had Jesus flogged, and handed him over to be crucified.
>
> Then the governor's soldiers took Jesus into the Praetorium and gathered the whole company of soldiers around him. They stripped him and put a scarlet robe on him, and then twisted together a crown of thorns and set it on his head. They put a staff in his right hand. Then they knelt in front of him and mocked him. "Hail, king of the Jews!" they said. They spit on him, and took the staff and struck him on the head again and again.

Mark 14:5, 15:15–19 (NIV) (written 50–65 AD) says,

> Then some began to spit at him; they blindfolded him, struck him with their fists, and said, "Prophesy!" And the guards took him and beat him.
>
> Wanting to satisfy the crowd, Pilate released Barabbas to them. He had Jesus flogged, and handed him over to be crucified.

The soldiers led Jesus away into the palace [that is, the Praetorium] and called together the whole company of soldiers. They put a purple robe on him, then twisted together a crown of thorns and set it on him. And they began to call out to him, "Hail, king of the Jews!" Again and again they struck him on the head with a staff and spit on him. Falling on their knees, they paid homage to him.

And Luke 22:63 (NIV) (written 60–61 AD), which says, "The men who were guarding Jesus began mocking and beating him."

e. Jesus' Clothes Would Be Divided among the Soldiers Who Guard Him on the Cross by Casting Lots

Fact Stated: Psalms (written 1440–450 BC)
Fact Confirmed: Matthew, Mark, Luke, and John (written 50–90 AD)
(500–1530 years later ±)

Psalm 22:16–18 (NIV) (written 1440–450 BC) says about Jesus that

Dogs surround me; a pack of villains encircles me; they pierce my hands and my feet. All my bones are on display; people stare and gloat over me. They divide my clothes among them and cast lots for my garment.

We don't know, really, what the lots were that were cast to guide decision-making at times in the Bible. Some researchers believe sticks of different lengths were used, or flat stones flipped like coins. While the Bible does not give specifics about the actual lots, the practice of casting lots seems akin to the modern-day flipping a coin.[1106]

That His clothes were divided by His guards at His crucifixion after casting lots is, however, reported in Matthew 27:35 (written

50–65 AD), Mark 15:24 (written 50–65 AD), Luke 23:34 (written 60–61 AD), John 19:23–24 (written 80–90 AD).

f. Jesus Would Die with the Wicked and Be Buried in a Rich Man's Grave

Fact Stated: Isaiah (written 700–680 BC)
Fact Confirmed: Matthew, Mark, Luke, and John (written 50–90 AD)
(730–790 years later ±)

According to Isaiah 53:9 (NIV) (written 700–680 BC), Jesus "was assigned a grave with the wicked and with the rich in his death, though he had done no violence, nor was any deceit in his mouth."

This prophecy was also fulfilled according to Matthew 27:38, 57–60 (NIV) (written 50–65 AD), which says,

> Two rebels were crucified with him, one on his right and one on his left. As evening approached, there came a rich man from Arimathea, named Joseph, who had himself become a disciple of Jesus. Going to Pilate, he asked for Jesus' body, and Pilate ordered that it be given to him. Joseph took the body, wrapped it in a clean linen cloth, and placed it in his own new tomb that he had cut out of the rock. He rolled a big stone in front of the entrance to the tomb and went away.

According to Mark 15:27, 46 (NIV) (written 50–65 AD) which says,

> They crucified two rebels with him, one on his right and one on his left. So Joseph bought some linen cloth, took down the body, wrapped it in the linen, and placed it in a tomb cut out of rock. Then he rolled a stone against the entrance of the tomb.

When Only God Knew

According to Luke 23:32–33, 50–53 (NIV) (written 60–61 AD) which says,

> Two other men, both criminals, were also led out with him to be executed. When they came to the place called the Skull, they crucified him there, along with the criminals—one on his right, the other on his left. Now there was a man named Joseph, a member of the Council, a good and upright man, who had not consented to their decision and action. He came from the Judean town of Arimathea, and he himself was waiting for the kingdom of God. Going to Pilate, he asked for Jesus' body. Then he took it down, wrapped it in linen cloth and placed it in a tomb cut in the rock, one in which no one had yet been laid.

And according to John 19:18, 38–42 (NIV) (written 80–90 AD) which says,

> There they crucified him, and with him two others—one on each side and Jesus in the middle.

> Later, Joseph of Arimathea asked Pilate for the body of Jesus. Now Joseph was a disciple of Jesus, but secretly because he feared the Jewish leaders. With Pilate's permission, he came and took the body away. He was accompanied by Nicodemus, the man who earlier had visited Jesus at night. Nicodemus brought a mixture of myrrh and aloes, about seventy-five pounds. Taking Jesus' body, the two of them wrapped it, with the spices, in strips of linen. This was in accordance with Jewish burial customs. At the place where Jesus was crucified, there was a garden, and in the garden

a new tomb, in which no one had ever been laid. Because it was the Jewish day of Preparation and since the tomb was nearby, they laid Jesus there.

g. Jesus Predicted His Death and that He Would Be Resurrected on the Third Day

Fact Stated: Matthew, Mark and Luke (written 50–61 AD)
Fact Confirmed: Immediately

John 14:6 (NIV) says, "Jesus answered, 'I am the way and the truth and the life. No one comes to the Father except through me.'"

The evidence that Jesus died after being crucified and rose on the third day and was seen has been discussed elsewhere in this book and is compelling, and it will not be repeated here. Just as Psalm 16:10 and 49:15 (NIV) (written 1440–450 BC) also said, Jesus would not "see decay" because God redeemed Him "from the realm of the dead." Because the evidence for the resurrection is so strong, however, one should take seriously what the New Testament says about Jesus and how He is the only path to eternal life.

What has not yet been discussed is the fact that, before it happened, Jesus Himself predicted (a) His own death at least three times, (b) its circumstances before it happened, i.e., that He would go to Jerusalem, be handed over to the Jewish elders, chief priests and the teachers of the law, who will condemn Him to death and then hand Him over to the Romans to suffer and be mocked, insulted, flogged, spit on and crucified, and (c) His resurrection on the third day, as the Bible reports. So, for example, see Matthew 20:17–19, which says,

> Now Jesus was going up to Jerusalem. On the way, he took the Twelve aside and said to them, "We are going up to Jerusalem, and the Son of Man will be delivered over to the chief priests and the teachers of the law. They will condemn him to death and will hand him over to the Gentiles to be mocked and

flogged and crucified. On the third day he will be raised to life!"

See also, e.g., Matthew 12:40, which reports that Jesus told the scribes and Pharisees who came to question Him, that "for as Jonah was three days and three nights in the belly of a huge fish, so the Son of Man will be three days and three nights in the heart of the earth." *See also* Matthew 16:21, 17:22–23, 26:2, Mark 8:31, 9:31, 10:33–34, Luke 9:22, 43–45, 17:25, 18:31–33.

h. Nations and Kings Will Accept Christ and Become Christian

Fact Stated: Isaiah (written 700–680 BC)
Fact First Confirmed: 272 to 337 AD (950–1040 years later ±)

Jesus was a descendant of Abraham,[1107] and Genesis 22:18 (NIV) (written 1450–1405 BC) says that through Abraham's "offspring all nations on earth will be blessed." Isaiah 49:6 (ESV) (written 740–680 BC) says that the Lord informed Isaiah that

> [i]t is too light a thing that you should be my servant to raise up the tribes of Jacob and to bring back the preserved of Israel; I will make you, [referring to Jesus,] as a light for the nations, that my salvation may reach to the end of the earth.

Not only did "the preserved of Israel" return to Israel after it was established by mandate in 1948, as discussed below, but "all nations on earth" are becoming Christian. According to one report, "as of the year 2020, Christianity had approximately 2.5 billion adherents out of a worldwide population of about 7.8 billion people," and there are now over 200 countries in the world, most of them with Christians in them.[1108] According to the Pew Research Center in 2011, a "comprehensive demographic study of more than 200 countries finds that there are 2.18 billion Christians of all ages around the world, representing nearly a third of the estimated 2010 global population of 6.9 billion."[1109] Taken as a whole, "Christians are by far the world's largest religious group."[1110]

If the Isaiah 45:6 prophecy that Jesus' salvation will "reach to the end of the earth" has not already been fulfilled, it is close to it.

Isaiah 60:1–3 (NIV) (written 740–680 BC) also prophesied that "nations shall come to Jesus' light, and kings to the brightness of Jesus' rising." We know from history that nations and kings have "come to Jesus' light." "The first openly-Christian emperor, and the first to persecute the pagan temples, was Constantine," who lived from 272 to 337 AD.[1111] "When Constantine, the emperor of Rome, became a Christian, it meant that the empire became Christian."[1112] After that, many nations and kings came to embrace Christianity.

[1113]

When Only God Knew

"Although Charlemagne was crowned Roman Emperor in the West in 800, the first use of the term 'Holy Roman Emperor' was applied when Pope John XII crowned Otto, Duke of Saxony, Emperor Otto I on February 3, 962." [1114] After that,

> Christianity expanded tremendously between the 11th and 13th centuries. It spread throughout Europe. Many European countries declared Christian [sic] as the national religion.[1115]

All as had been predicted over 1000 years before it happened to be later proven to the world.

10. Some Final Thoughts about the Prophecies about Jesus

Finally, as to Jesus, even though some of the events that fulfilled the prophecies could have been arranged and not been coincidental, too many could not have been planned by the participants in them. "Circumstances such as his birthplace, lineage, and method of execution were beyond Christ's control and could not have been accidentally or deliberately fulfilled."[1116] As Stoner says, respecting Jesus, the Messiah,

> [M]any of the prophecies concerning the Messiah could not be purposefully fulfilled—such as the town of His birth (Micah 5:2) or the nature of His betrayal (Psalm 41:9), or the manner of His death (Zechariah 13:6 and Psalm 22:16).
>
> One of the most remarkable Messianic prophecies in the Hebrew Scriptures is the one that precisely states that the Messiah will die by crucifixion. It is found in Psalm 22 where David prophesied the Messiah would die by having His hands and feet pierced

(Psalm 22:16). That prophecy was written 1,000 years before Jesus was born. When it was written, the Jewish method of execution was by stoning. The prophecy was also written many years before the Romans perfected crucifixion as a method of execution.

Even when Jesus was killed, the Jews still relied on stoning as their method of execution, but they had lost the power to implement the death penalty due to Roman occupation. That is why they were forced to take Jesus to Pilate, the Roman governor, and that's how Jesus ended up being crucified, in fulfillment of David's prophecy. The bottom line is that the fulfillment of Bible prophecy in the life of Jesus proves conclusively that He truly was God in the flesh. It also proves that the Bible is supernatural in origin.[1117]

As Stoner concluded on page 112 of his book, *Science Speaks*, "Any man who rejects Christ as the Son of God is rejecting a fact proved perhaps more absolutely than any other fact in the world."[1118]

B. Old Testament Prophecy about Edom Fulfilled after New Testament Times

Fact Stated: Isaiah and Jeremiah (written 740–570 BC)
Fact Confirmed: 12th century AD (1170–1850 years later ±)

Isaiah 34:10–13 (NIV) (written740–670 BC) prophesied the desolation that God's judgment will bring on Edom, which he would destroy, *see* Isaiah 34:5, said,

It will not be quenched night or day; its smoke will rise forever. From generation to generation, it will lie

When Only God Knew

desolate; no one will ever pass through it again. The desert owl and screech owl will possess it; the great ow and the raven will nest there. God will stretch out over Edom, the measuring line of chaos and the plumb line of desolation. Her nobles will have nothing there to be called a kingdom; all her princes will vanish away. Thorns will overrun her citadels, nettles, and brambles her strongholds. She will become a haunt for jackals, a home for owls. Jeremiah 49:17–18 (NIV) [written 627–570 BC] prophesied that "Edom will become an object of horror; all who pass by will be appalled and will scoff because of all its wounds. As Sodom and Gomorrah were overthrown, along with their neighboring towns," says the LORD, "so no one will live there; no people will dwell in it.

Edom was a land bordering ancient Israel, in what is now southwestern Jordan, between the Dead Sea and the Gulf of Aqaba, which was probably occupied about the 13th century BC.[1119] At the time that Isaiah and Jeremiah made their prophecies, "Edom prospered because of its strategic location on the trade route" and its copper industry.[1120]

But Edom was completely desolate as Isaiah and Jeremiah predicted "by the time the Muslims gained control of the area in" AD 636. As Doug Powell reported,[1121]

Edom was already in decline because of changing trade routes due to Roman occupation and a devastating earthquake in AD 363. By the time the crusaders built a castle near Petra, Edom's former capital, they found it was desolate place. From their time until Petra's rediscovery in the early nineteenth century, nothing is known of the place. The area in general is desolate and remains uninhabited to this day, fulfilling the prophecy of verse 17 and the last part of verse 18.

C. Old Testament Prophecy about Israel Fulfilled in Modern Times

1. Historical Context

Before considering evidence as to the accuracy of Old Testament prophecy about Israel that would be fulfilled in modern times, it is important to understand what happened to Israel and the Jews which led up to that fulfillment. To do that, we start with Leviticus, one of the oldest Old Testament books in the Bible.

As pointed out in Chapter 10, Leviticus 26:40–43 (NIV) (written 1450–1405 BC) talks about Jewish diaspora/exile, their being sent "into the land of their enemies," and Israel being "deserted by them" and lying "desolate without them," due to the Israelites "unfaithfulness and their hostility" toward God. It also says that God would remember His covenant with Jacob, Isaac, and Abraham that they are to live in Israel.

As also pointed out in Chapter 10, which talked particularly about the Assyrian and Babylonian diasporas/exiles, from the Christian perspective, the most significant unfaithfulness and hostility by the Israelites toward God occurred when many of them and their leaders rejected Jesus and caused Him to be crucified. This unfaithfulness and hostility by the Israelites toward God occurred thirty-five years, more or less, prior to the diaspora, which began a Jewish exile from Israel in AD 70 of more Jews from Israel than did the Assyrian or Babylonian captivity.

The Old Testament prophet Daniel also predicted that Jerusalem and the Temple would be destroyed after Jesus' crucifixion. In Daniel 9:26 (NIV) (written 536–530 BC), he prophesied that after "the Anointed One, Jesus, will be put to death," and that "the people of the ruler, meaning Rome, who will come will destroy the city and the sanctuary." And so, it happened.

In AD 70, the Roman general, "Titus, crushed the Great Revolt of AD 66, destroyed Jerusalem and the Temple," and "Israel was left in ruins, and the Jews scattered."[1122] The Jews and Christians began to leave Jerusalem in great numbers and to disperse throughout the world after the Romans destroyed their temple in AD 70 and drove them out of Jerusalem.[1123] That is one of several historical occasions called a Jewish Diaspora when the Jews were exiled from their home in the Promised Land,[1124] but it turned out to be the beginning of the longest exile and involved the most Jews. It came after the

> Roman military blockade of Jerusalem during the First Jewish Revolt. The fall of the city marked the effective conclusion of a four-year campaign against the Jewish insurgency in Judaea. The Romans destroyed much of the city, including the Second Temple.[1125]

So many Jews were exiled after Rome destroyed the Temple in Jerusalem that "the Jewish state comes to an end in 70 AD, when the Romans begin to actively drive Jews from the home they had lived in for over a millennium."[1126] "Most of the 4 million Jews living in the first century resided within travel distance of Jerusalem and the Temple."[1127] "By 70 AD, Jerusalem and Judea were left desolate, most of the people either killed or held in captivity or had become refugees fleeing to remote lands."[1128] By the time that the Jews were driven out of Israel, only a few thousand were left.

One author, referring to Deuteronomy 29 (written 1450–1404 BC), Isaiah 11:11–13 (written 740–680 BC), Jeremiah 25:11 (written 627–570 BC), Hosea 3:4–5 (written 750–710 BC), and Luke 21:23–24 (written 50–65 AD), pointed out that the

Prophet Moses foretold [with some additions by Jeremiah and Jesus] that the ancient Jewish nation would be conquered twice and that the people would be carried off as slaves each time, first by the Babylonians (for a period of seventy years), and then by a fourth world kingdom [which we know as Rome]. The second conqueror, Moses said, would take the Jews captive to Egypt in ships, selling them or giving them away as slaves to all parts of the world. Both of these predictions were fulfilled to the letter, the first in 607 BC and the second in AD 70. God's spokesmen said, further, that the Jews would remain scattered throughout the entire world for many generations, but without becoming assimilated by the peoples or of other nations, and that the Jews would one day return to the land of Palestine to re-establish for a second time their nation.[1129]

Forty or so years before it occurred, Jesus also predicted the destruction of the Temple in Jerusalem. Matthew 24:1–2 (NIV) (written 50–65 AD) says,

Jesus left the temple and was walking away when his disciples came up to him to call his attention to its buildings. "Do you see all these things?" he asked. "Truly I tell you, not one stone here will be left on another; every one will be thrown down."

As reported by Luke, the reliable historian described previously, in Luke 19:42–44 (NIV) (written 60–61 AD), Jesus wept over Jerusalem as he approached it and saw it, also prophesying about its destruction, saying

When Only God Knew

"If you, even you, had only known on this day what would bring you peace—but now it is hidden from your eyes. The days will come upon you when your enemies will build an embankment against you and encircle you and hem you in on every side. They will dash you to the ground, you and the children within your walls. They will not leave one stone on another, because you did not recognize the time of God's coming to you."

About forty years after Jesus said that, exactly as He prophesied,

[t]he magnificent "Herod's Temple" was completely destroyed, leaving not one stone upon another. It was an event that marked the beginning of the long and arduous Jewish Diaspora. Yet, it was definitely an event foreseen in Bible prophecy. Jesus not only prophesied about the destruction of Jerusalem and its Holy Temple.[1130]

As Jesus prophesied in Luke 21:24 (NIV) (written 60–61 AD, almost ten years before the Temple was destroyed) (emphasis added),

When you see Jerusalem being surrounded by armies, you will know that its desolation is near. Then let those who are in Judea flee to the mountains, let those in the city get out, and let those in the country not enter the city. For this is the time of punishment in fulfillment of all that has been written. How dreadful it will be in those days for pregnant women and nursing mothers! There will be great distress in the land and wrath against this people. They will fall by the sword and will be taken as prisoners to *all the nations. Jerusalem will be trampled on by the Gentiles* until the times of the Gentiles are fulfilled.

The Revolt of AD 66 is not, however, the only time that the Jews revolted against Roman occupation. After a third Jewish revolt in AD 135, "the Jewish people were scattered throughout the world by Emperor Hadrian;" Rome had "put up with the Jews for almost 150 years before they finally decided to wipe them out and take their homeland from them."[1131]

The Jews who were dispersed would, without being assimilated by the peoples of other nations or other nations, remained scattered throughout the world until 1948, when the modern State of Israel was founded.

2. Specific Old Testament Prophecies Made about the Jews and Israel Fulfilled in the Twentieth Century

Many other Old Testament writers, some of whom may have been contemporaries, many of whom lived hundreds and thousands of years apart and all of whom lived 2500 years before the final fulfillment of their prophecies, prophesied that (a) the Jews would be dispersed throughout the world, as did Jesus, (b) they would return to Israel from the far reaches of the earth, (c) the State of Israel would be reestablished in one day and (d) the once desolate lands of Israel would provide in abundance once the Jews returned to Israel. *See, e.g.,* the following Bible verses containing many predictions, and which will be cited below:

Deuteronomy 30:1–5 (NIV) (written 1450–1405 BC) (emphasis added) which says,

> When all these blessings and curses I have set before you come on you and you take them to heart wherever the Lord your God disperses you *among the*

When Only God Knew

nations, and when you and your children return to the Lord your God and obey him with all your heart and with all your soul according to everything I command you today, then the Lord your God will restore your fortunes and have compassion on you and gather you again *from all the nations where he scattered you.* Even if you have been banished to the *most distant land under the heavens,* from there the Lord your God will gather you and bring you back. He will bring you to the land that belonged to your ancestors, and you will take possession of it. He will make you more prosperous and numerous than your ancestors.

Psalm 107:2–3 (NIV) (written 1440–450 BC) (emphasis added) which says,

"Let the redeemed of the Lᴏʀᴅ tell their story— those he redeemed from the hand of the foe, those he gathered from the lands, from east and west, from north and south."

Isaiah 11:11–12, 27:6, 35:1–2, 41:18–19, 43:5–6, 51:3, 66:8 (NIV) (written 740–680 BC) (emphasis added) which says,

In that day the Lord will reach out his hand a second time to reclaim the surviving remnant of his people from *Assyria,* from *Lower Egypt,* from *Upper Egypt,* from *Cush,*[1132] from *Elam,*[1133] from *Babylonia,* from Hamath[1134] and from the islands of the Mediterranean.

He will raise a banner for *the nations* and gather the exiles of Israel; he will assemble the scattered people of Judah *from the four quarters of the earth.*

In days to come Jacob will take root, Israel will bud and blossom and fill all the world with fruit.

The desert and the parched land will be glad; the wilderness will rejoice and blossom. Like the crocus, it will burst into bloom; it will rejoice greatly and shout for joy...

I will make rivers flow on barren heights, and springs within the valleys. I will turn the desert into pools of water, and the parched ground into springs.

I will put in the desert the cedar and the acacia, the myrtle and the olive. I will set junipers in the wasteland, the fir and the cypress together,

Do not be afraid, for I am with you; I will bring your children *from the east and gather you from the west. I will say to the north*, "Give them up!" *and to the south*, "Do not hold them back." Bring my sons from afar and my daughters from the ends of the earth...

The Lord will surely comfort Zion and will look with compassion on all her ruins; he will make her deserts like Eden, her wastelands like the garden of the LORD. Joy and gladness will be found in her, thanksgiving and the sound of singing.

Who has ever heard of such a thing? Who has ever seen such things? *Can a country be born in a day, or a nation be brought forth in a moment?* Yet no sooner is Zion in labour than she gives birth to her children.

Jeremiah 16:14–15, 31:10 (NIV) (written 627–570 BC) (emphasis added) which says,

"However, the days are coming," declares the LORD, "when it will no longer be said, 'As surely as the LORD

When Only God Knew

lives, who brought the Israelites up out of Egypt,' [15] but it will be said, 'As surely as the LORD lives, who brought the Israelites up *out of the land of the north* and out of all the *countries* where he had banished them.' For I will restore them to the land I gave their ancestors.

Hear the word of the LORD, you *nations*; proclaim it in distant coastlands: "He who scattered Israel will gather them and will watch over his flock like a shepherd."

Ezekiel 34:13, 36:11, 34–35, 37:10–14, 21–22 (NIV) (written 590–570 BC) (emphasis added) which says,

I will bring them out *from the nations and gather them from the countries*, and I will bring them into their own land. I will pasture them on the mountains of Israel, in the ravines and in all the settlements in the land.

I will increase the number of people and animals living on you, and they will be fruitful and become numerous. I will settle people on you as in the past and will make you prosper more than before. Then you will know that I am the LORD.

The desolate land will be cultivated instead of lying desolate in the sight of all who pass through it. They will say, "This land that was laid waste has become like the garden of Eden; the cities that were lying in ruins, desolate and destroyed, are now fortified and inhabited."

So I prophesied as he commanded me, and breath entered them; they came to life and stood up on their feet—a vast army. Then he said to me: "Son of man, these bones are the people of Israel. They say, 'Our bones are dried up and our hope is gone; we are cut off.' Therefore prophesy and say to them: 'This is what the Sovereign LORD says: My people, I am going to open your graves and bring you up from them; *I will bring you back to the land of Israel.* Then you, my people, will know that I am the LORD, when I open your graves and bring you up from them. I will put my Spirit in you and you will live, and *I will settle you in your own land.* Then you will know that I the LORD have spoken, and I have done it, declares the LORD.'"

and say to them, 'This is what the Sovereign LORD says: I will take the Israelites out of the *nations* where they have gone. I will gather them from all around and bring them back into their own land. I will make them one nation in the land, on the mountains of Israel...._

Amos 9:13–15 (NIV) (written circa 760–750 BC) (emphasis added) which says,

"The days are coming," declares the LORD,
    "when the reaper will be overtaken by the plowman and the planter by the one treading grapes. New wine will drip from the mountains and flow from all the hills, and I will bring my people Israel back from exile.
    "They will rebuild the ruined cities and live in them. They will plant vineyards and drink their wine; they will make gardens and eat their fruit. *I will plant Israel in their own land,* never again to be uprooted

from the land I have given them," says the LORD your God,

and Zechariah 8:3–8, 12:2, 6 (NIV) (written 640–621 BC), which says,

This is what the LORD says: "I will return to Zion and dwell in Jerusalem. Then Jerusalem will be called the Faithful City, and the mountain of the LORD Almighty will be called the Holy Mountain."

This is what the LORD Almighty says: "Once again men and women of ripe old age will sit in the streets of Jerusalem, each of them with cane in hand because of their age. The city streets will be filled with boys and girls playing there."

This is what the LORD Almighty says: "It may seem marvelous to the remnant of this people at that time, but will it seem marvelous to me?" declares the LORD Almighty.

This is what the LORD Almighty says: "I will save my people from the *countries of the east and the west.* I will bring them back to live in Jerusalem; they will be my people, and I will be faithful and righteous to them as their God."

"I am going to make Jerusalem a cup that sends all the surrounding peoples reeling. Judah will be besieged as well as Jerusalem.

...

"On that day I will make the clans of Judah like a firepot in a woodpile, like a flaming torch among sheaves. They will consume all the surrounding peoples right and left, but Jerusalem will remain intact in her place.

About the time that Deuteronomy was written (1450–1405 BC) and well before the remainder of the books just cited were written, Leviticus 26:443–4 (NIV) (written 1450–1405 BC) prophesied that God would never allow the people of Israel to be completely destroyed. It says,

> For the land will be deserted by them and will enjoy its sabbaths while it lies desolate without them. They will pay for their sins because they rejected my laws and abhorred my decrees. Yet in spite of this, when they are in the land of their enemies, I will not reject them or abhor them so as to destroy them completely, breaking my covenant with them. I am the LORD their God.

Like the prophecies that the Jews would be dispersed, the prophecies that the Jews would not be completed destroyed as a people, the Jews would return to Israel from the far reaches of the earth, the State of Israel would be reestablished in one day, and the lands of Israel would provide in abundance would also come true, but in this century, thousands of years after they were prophesied.

These prophecies are different than the ones which apply to the Jews returning from the Babylonian exile discussed in chapter 10. These prophecies talk about a future in which there is an almost complete dispersal of the Jews throughout the world, not just to Assyria or Babylon. As is plain from emphasis above, according to these prophecies, the Jews would return from all over the earth. According to these prophecies, Israel would also be reborn in one day, and Israel would be fruitful as never before.

So did that happen? It did. Mostly in the twentieth century[1135] 2500 years, more or less, after the events were prophesied.

3. Jewish Exiles Return to Israel from All Over the Earth

Fact Stated: Genesis, Leviticus, Deuteronomy, Psalms, Isaiah, Jeremiah, Ezekiel, Amos, and Zechariah (written 1450–450 BC)

Fact Confirmed: Late 19th century AD but mostly 20th century (2300–3400 years later ±)

As the prophets predicted,[1136] Jews have returned from exile from all over the earth, and much of that is due to Adolph Hitler's "Final Solution," more commonly known as the "Holocaust." As God promised in Leviticus 26:44 (written 1450–1405 BC), the Jewish people were not completely destroyed during the Holocaust, despite Hitler's evil intent.

"In 1880, before immigration began, Palestine's Jewish population numbered about 25,000."[1137]

The first two waves of immigration took place under the Ottoman Empire. The first was between 1882 and 1903, brought 20,000 to 30,000 Russians fleeing Czarist Russia's pogroms. Between 1903 and 1914, during the second brought 35,000–40,000 more Russians.[1138]

During the 1870s and 1880s the Jewish population in Europe began to more actively discuss emigration back to Israel and the re-establishment of the Jewish Nation in its national homeland. The Zionist movement[1139] was founded officially in 1897.[1140]

The third and fourth [waves] brought 35,000 Jews from the Soviet Union, Poland, and the Baltic countries between 1919 and 1923, and 82,000 Jews from the Balkans and the Near Orient between 1924 and 1931, respectively. By the end of 1931, 174,600 Jews were living in Palestine.[1141]

In 1933, with the rise to power of Adolf Hitler and the Nazis in Germany, the Jewish situation became more severe. Economic crises, racial anti-Semitic laws, and a fear of an upcoming war led many Jews to flee from Europe to Palestine, to the United States, and to the Soviet Union.[1142]

Many Jews began to return from exile in the twentieth century as a consequence of Hitler's rise to power. "By the mid-1900s, anti-Semitism had developed into a powerful political force in Europe" and "in the early 1930s, more than 100,000 Jewish refugees came to Palestine from Nazi Germany and Poland," and "Zionism gained popularity."[1143] "Between 1939 and 1948, 118,228 Jews reached Palestine."[1144]

In 1941, following the invasion of the Soviet Union, the Final Solution began, an extensive organized operation on an unprecedented scale, aimed at the annihilation of the Jewish people, and resulting in the persecution and murder of Jews in political Europe, inclusive of European North Africa [pro-Nazi Vichy-North Africa and Italian Libya]. This genocide, in which approximately six million Jews were methodically exterminated, is known as the Holocaust or the Shoah [Hebrew term]. In Poland, three million Jews were killed in gas chambers in all concentration camps combined, with one million at the Auschwitz camp complex alone.

Palestine, which had been under a British mandate since 1920, saw large waves of Jewish migration before and during the Holocaust.[1145]

After the establishment of Israel, immigration of Holocaust survivors from Europe and a large influx of Jewish refugees from Arab countries had doubled Israel's population within one year of its independence. Overall, during the following years approximately 850,000 Sephardi and Mizrahi Jews fled or were expelled from Arab countries, Iran and Afghanistan. Of these, about 680,000 settled in Israel.

Israel's Jewish population continued to grow at a very high rate for years, fed by waves of Jewish immigration from round the world, including the massive immigration wave of Soviet Jews, who arrived in Israel in the early 1990s, according to the Law of Return. Some 380,000 Jewish immigrants from the Soviet Union arrived in 1990–91 alone.[1146]

When Only God Knew

By 2010 AD, 13,428,300 Jews were living in Israel.[1147] Over 1.5 million immigrants to Israel have come from Russia/Ukraine (Former USSR) alone, but they have also come from Afghanistan, Algeria, Argentina, Bulgaria, Czechoslovakia (Former), Egypt, Ethiopia, France, Germany, Hungary, India, Iran, Iraq, Libya, Morocco, Poland, Romania, South Africa, Sudan, Syria, Tunisia, Turkey, United Kingdom, United States Yemen and Yugoslavia (Former),[1148] 52,000 of which had been detained on Cyprus in the Mediterranean by the British government between August 1946 and May 1948[1149]—that is from all over the world, from "east and west, north and south" and from Assyria, Lower and Upper Egypt, Cush, Elam, Babylonia, Hamath in Syria and from the islands of the Mediterranean as was predicted over 2000 years before it would happen.

So, how did those Old Testament prophets know this would happen, and why did it just recently happen if not to confirm the accuracy and reliability of the Bible at a time of great secular skepticism?

4. Israel is Born in One Day

Fact Stated: Isaiah (written 740–680 BC)
Fact Confirmed: 1948 AD (2600–2680 years later ±)

In 1948,

> Israel became a state again with less than one million Jews in country… There is some debate over when the Great Diaspora began, but all agree on its official end—May 14, 1948.[1150]

"In 1947, the United Nations had split Palestine up into Arab and Jewish areas."[1151] Palestine "had been under a British mandate since 1920," but "after the mandate expired in 1948, David Ben-Gurion proclaimed on May 14 the establishment of a Jewish state"[1152]—in one day, as prophesied.

5. Israel, Despite Being Considerably Smaller, Will Defeat Its Larger Enemies

Fact Stated: Isaiah and Zechariah, e.g., (written 740–470 BC)
Fact Confirmed: 1948 AD to date (2400–2700 years later ±)

It was prophesied, thousands of years before it would occur, that Israel after the Jews returned to their homeland and though Israel was much smaller, would defeat its larger enemies. In Isaiah 41:12–14 (NIV) (written 740–680 BC), the prophet says,

> Though you search for your enemies, you will not find them. Those who wage war against you will be as nothing at all. For I am the LORD your God who takes hold of your right hand and says to you, Do not fear; I will help you.
>
> Do not be afraid, you worm Jacob,[1153] little Israel, do not fear, for I myself will help you," declares the LORD, your Redeemer, the Holy One of Israel.

Zechariah 12:2 (NIV) (written 520–470 BC) says, "I am going to make Jerusalem a cup that sends all the surrounding peoples reeling.

As soon as Israel declared itself a state, war broke out when "neighboring Arab states attacked."[1154]

The nation of Israel was created on May 14, 1948. The next day, the countries surrounding Israel declared war on the new nation. Israel has been in an almost permanent state of internal conflict ever since.[1155]

The armies of Egypt, Lebanon, Syria, Jordan and Iraq[1156] marched into the territory of what had just ceased to be the British Mandate, thus starting the 1948 Arab-Israeli War. The nascent Israel Defense Forces repulsed the Arab armies, and extended Israel's borders beyond the original Resolution 181(II) boundaries for the proposed Jewish state.[1157]

When Only God Knew

Fulfilling the prophecies in Isaiah 41:12–14 and Zechariah 12:2 that Israel would send the surrounding nations which attacked it "reeling," in 1949 that war ended, and the state of Israel started building and absorbing massive waves of hundreds of thousands of Jews from all over the world.[1158] But since that time, "Israel has been involved in a number of wars and large-scale military operations," many against much larger nations,[1159] not including more recent conflicts, which include the following:

- Reprisal operations (1950s–1960s)—Military operations carried out by the Israel Defense Forces during the 1950s and 1960s. These actions were in response to constant fedayeen (Arab guerrilla attacks "operating especially in Israel and Palestine against the Israeli government"[1160]) during which Arab guerillas infiltrated from Syria, Egypt, and Jordan into Israel to carry out attacks against Israeli civilians and soldiers.

- Suez Crisis (October 1956)—A military attack on Egypt by Britain, France, and Israel, beginning on 29 October 1956, with the intention to occupy the Sinai Peninsula and to take over the Suez Canal. The attack followed Egypt's decision of 26 July 1956 to nationalize the Suez Canal after the withdrawal of an offer by Britain and the United States to fund the building of the Aswan Dam. Although the Israeli invasion of the Sinai was successful, the US and USSR forced it to retreat. Even so, Israel managed to re-open the Straits of Tiran and pacified its southern border.

- Six-Day War (June 1967)—Fought between Israel and Arab neighbors Egypt, Jordan, and Syria. The nations of Iraq, Saudi Arabia, Kuwait, Algeria, and others[1161] also contributed troops and arms to the Arab forces. Following the war, the territory held by Israel expanded significantly ("The Purple Line"): The West Bank (including East Jerusalem) from Jordan, Golan Heights from Syria, Sinai, and Gaza from Egypt.

- War of Attrition (1967–1970)—A limited war fought between the Israeli military and forces of the Egyptian Republic, the USSR, Jordan, Syria, and the Palestine Liberation Organization[1162] from 1967 to 1970. It was initiated by the Egyptians as a way of recapturing the Sinai from the Israelis, who had been in control of the territory since the mid-1967 Six-Day War. The hostilities ended with a ceasefire signed between the countries in 1970, with frontiers remaining in the same place as when the war began.

- Yom Kippur War (October 1973)—Fought from October 6 to October 26, 1973, by a coalition of Arab states led by Egypt and Syria against Israel[1163] as a way of recapturing part of the territories which they lost to the Israelis back in the Six-Day War. The war began with a surprise joint attack by Egypt and Syria on the Jewish holiday of Yom Kippur. Egypt and Syria crossed the cease-fire lines in the Sinai and Golan Heights, respectively. Eventually, Arab forces were defeated by Israel, and there were no significant territorial changes.

- Palestinian insurgency in South Lebanon (1971–1982)—PLO, the Palestine Liberation Organization, relocate to South Lebanon from Jordan and stage attacks on the Galilee and as a base for international operations. In 1978, Israel launches Operation Litani—the first Israeli large-scale invasion of Lebanon, which was carried out by the Israel Defense Forces in order to expel PLO forces from the territory. Continuing ground and rocket attacks, and Israeli retaliations, eventually escalate into the 1982 War.

When Only God Knew

- 1982 Lebanon War (1982)—It began on 6 June 1982, when the Israel Defense Forces invaded southern Lebanon to expel the PLO from the territory. The Government of Israel ordered the invasion as a response to the assassination attempt against Israel's ambassador to the United Kingdom, Shlomo Argov, by the Abu Nidal Organization and due to the constant terror attacks on northern Israel made by the Palestinian guerilla organizations which resided in Lebanon. The war resulted in the expulsion of the PLO from Lebanon and created an Israeli Security Zone in southern Lebanon.
- South Lebanon conflict (1982–2000)—Nearly twenty years of warfare between the Israel Defense Forces and its Lebanese proxy militias with Lebanese Muslim guerrilla, led by Iranian-backed Hezbollah, within what was defined by Israelis as the "Security Zone" in South Lebanon.
- First Intifada (1987–1993)—First large-scale Palestinian uprising against Israel in the West Bank and the Gaza Strip.
- Second Intifada (2000–2005)—Second Palestinian uprising, a period of intensified violence, which began in late September 2000.
- 2006 Lebanon War (summer 2006)—Began as a military operation in response to the abduction of two Israeli reserve soldiers by the Hezbollah. The operation gradually strengthened to become a wider confrontation. The principal participants were Hezbollah paramilitary forces and the Israeli military. The conflict started on 12 July 2006 and continued until a United Nations-brokered ceasefire went into effect on 14 August 2006, though it formally ended on 8 September 2006, when Israel lifted its naval blockade of Lebanon. The war resulted in the

pacification of southern Lebanon and in the weakness of the Hezbollah (which suffered serious casualties but managed to survive the Israeli onslaught).

- Gaza War (December 2008–January 2009)—Three-week armed conflict between Israel and Hamas during the winter of 2008–2009. In an escalation of the ongoing Israeli-Palestinian conflict, Israel responded to ongoing rocket fire from the Gaza Strip with military force in an action titled "Operation Cast Lead." Israel opened the attack with a surprise airstrike on December 27, 2008. Israel's stated aim was to stop such rocket fire from and the import of arms into Gaza. Israeli forces attacked military and civilian targets, police stations, and government buildings in the opening assault. Israel declared an end to the conflict on January 18 and completed its withdrawal on January 21, 2009.

- Operation Pillar of Defense (November 2012)—Military offensive on the Gaza Strip.[1164]

6. Despite Years of Conflict, Israel Blooms Where There Was Only Desert and Desolation

Fact Stated: Deuteronomy, Isaiah, Ezekiel and Amos (written 1450–570 BC)
Fact Confirmed: 20th century AD (2500–3400 years later ±)

And yet despite all these armed conflicts and even as they were being fought, many with much larger countries, the Jews in Israel turned a desert and desolate land into a garden, just as had been prophesied in Deuteronomy 30:1–5 (written 1450–1405 BC), Isaiah 27:6, 35:1–2, 41:18–19, 51:3 (written 740–680 BC), Ezekiel 36:11, 34–35 (written 590–570 BC) and Amos 9:13–15 (written circa 760–750 BC). In 1867, well before the State of Israel was established in 1948, Mark Twain toured the land of Israel known back then as Palestine. Here's how he described it:

> A desolate country whose soil is rich enough, but is given over wholly to weeds—a silent mournful expanse…A desolation is here that not even imagination can grace with the pomp of life and action.…We never saw a human being on the whole route…There was hardly a tree or a shrub anywhere. Even the olive and the cactus, those fast friends of the worthless soil, had almost deserted the country.

Mark Twain wouldn't even recognize the land today. Out of rocky soil, swamps, and even out of deserts, Israelis have created gardens, vineyards, and farms with some of the most innovative techniques in the world.[1165]

There are many articles about how the new State of Israel made the desert and desolation that Mark Twain described into a garden with an abundance of food, fruit, vegetables, and protein from meat, as had been prophesied in the Bible thousands of years earlier. While some articles discuss that fact and at which pictures of the result can be found from the footnote below,[1166] one of the best descriptions of Israel turning a desolate land into gardens, orchards and pastures come from an article entitled *Gardening and Farming Like Israel* written in 2018 by Chris Baldelomar,[1167] a Christian author from Lubbock, Texas. It says,

> The coastal plains were swampy [when the State of Israel came into existence]. The Galilee in the Judean Hills were rocky, and the southern half of the country was mostly desert. The Jewish settlers faced a number of obstacles, from bad soil, Bedouin Raiders, to malaria carrying mosquitoes overtaking the coastal plains in the Jordan Valley.

And instead of giving up, and leaving the land, they went to work, beginning with draining the swamps, spraying the land, and changing the flow of water in irrigation canals to interrupt the mosquitoes breeding. Their first efforts were a success, and in less that [sic for than] twenty years after Isracl's statehood, the country was officially malaria free. But this was just the beginning. ... Now, the Jewish settlers were free to focus on making the desert bloom in the coastal plains. Citrus groves replaced the swamps in the Jordan Valley. What was once the center of the malaria epidemic, now became the country's breadbasket. The Negev desert blossomed with newly planted forests and vineyards. And the Arava, once the aridest part of Israel, became the site of a flourishing vegetable industry. All of this was accomplished in the first twenty years of Israel's statehood. In that time, Israel more than doubled their standard of living, and now they are using their experience to help other countries.

...

In Israel, the freshwater supply was not enough to support a growing country, so Israel started looking west to the Mediterranean. The Mediterranean Sea has become Israel's greatest natural resource because of their water technologies. Israel is producing 450 million cubic meters of drinkable water a day through a process called Sea Water Reverse Osmosis. Water can go from the ocean to the faucet in less that [sic for than] ninety minutes. And Israeli technology is now being used in more than forty countries around the world. And thanks to the Mediterranean

When Only God Knew

Sea, Israel may soon have something that was once unthinkable, a water surplus.

Many farmers are getting water for their crops literally out of thin air. Ancient Israelites used stones to collect the dew every morning. Now, and [sic for an] Israeli company is using plastic trays to do the same.

Every morning, these trays channel the dew straight into the roots of the plants. They also prevent weeds from growing between the plants and reduce water usage by up to 50 percent. Israeli farmers have always made good use of their water, but it wasn't long before they realized that in order to survive, they also needed to start reusing it. Today, Israel recycles 80 percent of its waste water.

Israelis developed a way to purify wastewater using ultraviolet light. This treated water is then used to irrigate crops. Sixty percent of the water that is irrigating fields in Israel is produced water, and not natural water.

Under the Negev desert, there is an underground ocean too salty to drink or desalinate. So Israeli settlers found a new way to use it. And instead of fighting against nature, they learned it is better to cooperate and coordinate with what you have. One Israeli company has brought the ocean to the desert by building fish farms using the warm salty water from underground. It is ideal for raising saltwater fish like tilapia, sea bass, and barramundi.

Their operation is working without chemicals, without anything, and it is very healthy, friendly for the environment, and they are making good money. Even the fish waste is put to use every week. At one fish farm, the water in the tanks are [sic] replaced, and pumped underground to irrigate a nearby olive grove. The fish waste in the water makes an ideal natural fertilizer, and the olives are growing around the fish farm, and are doing very well without any other chemicals, only by the nutrients of the fish.

Israel found new ways to use less water. Once a barren strip of desert, the Arava now has 600 farms supplying more than 60 percent of Israel's exports of fresh vegetables. In the Arava, sometimes they might get twenty millimeters of annual rain fall. A very harsh climate. The driest parts of the deserts are blooming with the help of a process called drip irrigation. Drip Irrigation was invented by an Israeli engineer named Simcha Blass. He got the idea for drip irrigation after seeing a tree that was larger than the others around it. After digging around the roots, he found it was being watered by a drip leak in an underground pipe. And it was not until plastic was introduce that he was able to experiment with drippers that would emit water in small drops. Soon after, they boosted their crop yield by 50 percent, and use 40 percent less water to do it.

Even before "organic" was a popular word, Israel was implementing organic techniques in their farms. They had the same problems every [sic] other farmers and gardeners have. How do you get rid of the pests? And their answer was to fight bugs with more bugs. Every single thing in nature has a natural enemy that eats it or attacks it. For the pests that attacked their crops, they started breeding different insects that were predators to the pests that ate their crops.

They solved an agricultural problem with how to pollinate greenhouse plants. In greenhouses which are climate controlled, you do not have winds or natural pollination. So they had to find other methods of pollination. Their solution was to breed bumble bees. The bees collect pollen for food, and they have to go and work even in cold weather conditions. Since they do not have stores of honey in the hive, they have to go to work, saving the farmers money because instead of paying people, the bees are doing the pollinating. And unlike people, they don't miss a single flower. Once farmers started using bees for pollination, the yield of the tomato crops increased by 25 percent. They also found creative ways to get rid of rodents. Instead of using poison, which is not ecologically friendly, they found that having owl barns to be an amazing solution. Two owls can capture an average of 2000–5000 mice per year.[1168]

Such abundance in such a desolate place was all part of God's plan prophesied thousands and thousands of years before it came to pass. Again, how did the writers of the Old Testament know it would happen, and why has it only very recently happened, if not as a result of God's knowledge as to the future and His intention that it would be made known now?

CONCLUSION

Well, there you have it.

It is for you, the reader, to decide if a preponderance of the evidence, clear and convincing evidence, or evidence beyond a reasonable doubt supports the conclusion that the Bible contains facts that were not generally known when they were stated, could only have come from an all-knowing and all-present being—God—so that their truth would be later verified and, for those reasons and others, the Bible is reliable and a truth on which you can rely for who Jesus was and for the faith to ask Him into your life.

I hope that you have reached or will reach the same conclusion I have.

God bless you.

—Mike

ENDNOTES

Foreword

1   John Parnell, *It's the Christian's Duty to Speak the Truth*, (no longer online), https://www.desiringgod.org/articles/its-the-christians-duty-to-speak-the-truth.

Introduction

2   Ferdinand Bada, *What Was the Age of Reason?* (First published July 23, 2019, in World Facts), World Atlas, https://www.worldatlas.com/articles/what-was-the-age-of-reason.html.

3   *Id.*

4   Phillip Power, *Intelligence & Unbelief—the Not-so Causal Relationship*, Mensa Bulletin, The Magazine of American Mensa (Aug. 2021) at 20.

5   *Id.* at 22.

6   *Id.* at 20–21

7   *Id.* at 21–22.

8   *Id.* at 22.

9   *Id.*

10   *See* Doug Powell, *Guide to Christian Apologetics*, Holman Reference (Nashville, Tennessee © 2006 by Doug Powell) at 4.

11   *See, e.g.,* Blair Parke, *How Many Books Are in the Bible?*, Christianity.com (June 25, 2020), https://www.christianity.com/wiki/bible/how-many-books-are-in-the-bible.html.

12   While archaeology itself is older, "archaeology as a scientific study is only about 150 years old."
See K. Kris Hirst, *The History of Archaeology - The First Archaeologists*, ThoughtCo (Updated Jan. 15, 2020), https://www.thoughtco.com/the-first-archaeologists-167134#.

13   Different standards for judging evidence are discussed in Chapter 1.

14   There are also philosophical and logical proofs for the accuracy of the Bible. This book will not consider those, but the reader may want to investigate them as well.

15   *See* Chapter 1 *infra* for a discussion of the various levels of courtroom proofs, which include reasonable doubt as one level.

16   *See, e.g.,* Proverbs 9:10 (written circa 971–686 BC) and Psalms 111:10 (written 1440–450 BC).

17   Revelation 20:10 (written 94–96 AD).

18   As Romans (NIV) 1:19–23 and 25 (written 56–57 AD) says,

> *[W]hat may be known about God is plain to them, because God has made it plain to them. For since the creation of the world God's invisible qualities—his eternal power and divine nature—have been clearly seen, being understood from what has been made....*
>
> *For although they knew God, they neither glorified him as God nor gave thanks to him, but their thinking became futile and their foolish hearts were darkened. Although they claimed to be wise, they became fools and exchanged the glory of the immortal God for images made to look like a mortal human being and birds and animals and reptiles.*
>
> *... They exchanged the truth about God for a lie, and worshiped and served created things rather than the Creator...*

19   John 14:6 (written 80–90 AD).

Chapter 1

20   *See, e.g., generally, United States v. Shonubi*, 895 F. Supp. 460 (E.D. N.Y. 1995).

21   *See, e.g., Reyes v. Netdeposit, LLC*, 802 F.3d 469, 495 (3d Cir. 2014) (Emphasis in original, cited cases omitted).

22   *See* Doug Powell, *Guide to Christian Apologetics* at 4 and 11, Holman Reference (Nashville, Tennessee © 2006 by Doug Powell). For ease of reference throughout this book, all quoted material has indents on each side to show it is quoted. A quotation inside previously quoted material, has further indents on each side to show it is a quotation in the previous material being quoted.

23   *See, e.g., Musacchio v. United States,* 136 S. Ct. 709, 715, 577 U.S. 237 (2015); Smith v. Equitrac Corp., 88 F. Supp. 2d 727, 731 (S.D. Tex. 2000).

24   *See, e.g., Biestek v. Berryhill,* 139 S. Ct. 1148, 1159, 203 L. Ed. 2d 504 (2019).

25   *See, e.g.,: Barnes v. Thomas,* 938 F.3d 526, 542 (4th Cir. 2019); Dependable Sales & Serv., Inc. v. TrueCar, Inc., 377 F. Supp. 3d 337, 351 (S.D.N.Y, 2019);

Hunter v. Hamilton Cty. Court of Common Pleas, 2019 U.S. Dist. LEXIS 89742, *, 2019 WL 2281542 (S.D. Ohio 2019) (citing *United States v. Solivan*, 937 F.2d 1146, 1150 (6th Cir. 1991);

Briggs v. Plichta, 2017 U.S. Dist. LEXIS 146592 *4 (W.D. Mich. Aug. 11, 2017) (Legal conclusions "do not suffice to create a genuine issue of material fact for trial");

Estakhrian v. Obenstine, 233 F. Supp. 3d 824, 837 n. 11 (C.D. Cal. 2017) (citing *Hardy v. Town of Greenwich*, 2008 U.S. Dist. LEXIS 98333, 2008 WL 5117370, *7 (D. Conn. 2008);

Garnett-Bishop v. N.Y. Cmty. Bancorp, Inc., 2017 U.S. Dist. LEXIS 29764, *109 (E.D.N.Y. 2017);

Cox v. Washington, 2015 U.S. Dist. LEXIS 167102, *6, 2015 WL 8539910 (W.D. Wash. 2015);

Williams v. City of New York, 2012 U.S. Dist. LEXIS 112, *19, 2012 WL 3245448 (N.D.N.Y. 2012) (citing *Perry v. State of N.Y. Dept. of Labor*, No. 08 CIV. 4610 (PKC), 2009 U.S. Dist. LEXIS 74006, 2009 WL 2575713, *3 (S.D.N.Y. 2009) (quoting *Bell Atl. Corp. v. Twombly*, 550 U.S. 544, 127 S. Ct. 1964 - 1965, 167 L. Ed. 2d 929 (2007);

Gonzalez v. City of Deerfield Beach, 549 F.3d 1331, 1336 (11th Cir.2008) (citing *Lawrence v. City of Philadelphia*, Pa., 527 F.3d 299, 317–318 (3d Cir. 2008);

Wynn-Howard v. USW, Local 555T, 2008 U.S. Dist. LEXIS 26728 *18; 2008 WL 768641 (W.D. Pa. Mar. 19, 2008);

Pagan v. Fruchey, 492 F.3d 766, 773 (6th Cir. 2007);

Russell v. McKinney Hosp. Venture, 235 F.3d 219, 229 (5th Cir. 2000)(citing *Hunt v. City of Markham, Ill.*, 219 F.3d 649, 652-53 (7th Cir. 2000).

26   In the United States of America, the U.S. "Constitution guarantees both criminal and civil litigants a right to an impartial jury."

See, e.g., Warger v. Shauers, 574 U. S. 40. 50 (2014).

The requirement that jurors be impartial is guaranteed by the Sixth Amendment to the Constitution.

See, e.g., generally, Holland v. Illinois, 493 U.S. 474 (1990).

27   *See, e.g.,: Mu'Min v. Virginia*, 500 U.S. 415, 420–421 (1991);

United States v. Boylan, 698 F. Supp. 376, 391 (D. Mass. 1988) (citing *United States v. Klee*, 494 F.2d 394, 396 (9th Cir.), cert. denied, 419 U.S. 835, 42 L. Ed. 2d 61, 95 S. Ct. 62 (1974).

28   *See* https://dictionary.cambridge.org/us/dictionary/english/proof.

29   Designed by katemangostar / Freepik; https://www.freepik.com/free-vector/federal-law-presentation-illustration_4332384.htm

30   *See, e.g., Fla. Standard Jury Instructions in Civil Cases*, Notes on Use for 401.1, 402.3 and 404.3.

31   *See, e.g., Cornell v. Nix*, 119 F.3d 1329, 1335 (8th Cir. 1997).

32   *See e.g., US v. Hampton*, 128 Fed. Appx. 734, 738 (11th Cir. 2005).

33   *See, e.g., Jimenez v. DaimlerChrysler Corp.*, 269 F.3d 439, 450 (4th Cir. 2001);

Fla. Standard Jury Instructions in Civil Cases, Notes on Use for 404.13 and 405.4;

Slomowitz v. Walker, 429 So.2d 797, 800 (Fla. 4th DCA 1983) (citing *In Re Boardwalk Regency Casino License Application*, 180 N.J. Super. 324, 434 A.2d 1111, 1118 (N.J.Super. App.Div.1981).

34   *See e.g., U.S. v. Lawson*, 507 F.2d 433, 440 (7th Cir. 1974).

35   *See, e.g., State v. Wilson*, 686 So.2d 569 (Fla. 1996).

36   *See* Z. Hereford, *How to Think for Yourself*, Essential Life Skills.Net, https://www. essentiallifeskills.net/think-for-yourself.html.

37   "Signed by Yale University professors, Nicholas Christakis, Paul Bloom, Carlos Eire and Noel Valis; Princeton University professors, Maria E. Garlock, Robert P. George, Joshua Katz, Thomas P. Kelly, John B. Londregan and Michael A. Reynolds; and Harvard University professors, Mary Ann Glendon, Jon Levenson, Jacqueline C. Rivers, Tyler Vander Weele and Adrian Vermeule.

See http://www.washingtontimes.com/news/2017/aug/30/ivy-league-professors-condemn-intellectual-bigotry/viewpoints (no longer online);

Some Thoughts and Advice for Our Students and All Students, James Madison Program in American Ideals and Institutions (Aug. 29, 2017), https://jmp.princeton.edu/ announcements/some-thoughts-and-advice-our-students-and-all-students.

See also Ivy League professors condemn intellectual bigotry: 'Don't be tyrannized by public opinion,' The Washington Times, https://www.washingtontimes.com/news/2017/ aug/30/ivy-league-professors-condemn-intellectual-bigotry (no longer online).

38   *See Ivy League professors condemn intellectual bigotry: 'Don't be tyrannized by public opinion,'* The Washington Times, https://www.washingtontimes.com/news/2017/aug/30/ ivy-league-professors-condemn-intellectual-bigotry (No longer available online).

See also Some Thoughts and Advice for Our Students and All Students, James Madison Program in American Ideals and Institutions (Aug. 29, 2017), https://jmp.princeton.edu/ announcements/some-thoughts-and-advice-our-students-and-all-students.

39   *See Some Thoughts and Advice for Our Students and All Students*, James Madison Program in American Ideals and Institutions (Aug. 29, 2017), https://jmp.princeton.edu/ announcements/some-thoughts-and-advice-our-students-and-all-students.

40   *Id.*

41   "John Stuart Mill (1806–73) was the most influential English language philosopher of the nineteenth century. He was a naturalist, a utilitarian, and a liberal, whose work explores the consequences of a thoroughgoing empiricist outlook."

See John Stuart Mill, Stanford Encyclopedia of Philosophy, https://plato.stanford.edu/entries/mill/ (Aug. 25, 2016).

He "profoundly influenced the shape of nineteenth century British thought and political discourse."

See Mill, John Stuart, Internet Encyclopedia of Philosophy, https://iep.utm.edu/milljs/.

42   *See* Paul L. Maier, *Biblical Archaeology: Factual Evidence to Support the Historicity of the Bible*, CRI (Mar. 30, 2009), www.equip.org/article/biblical-archaeology-factual-evidence-to-support-the-historicity-of-the-bible/.

43   *Id. See also* Chapter 3 *infra*.

Chapter 2

44   *See* Merriam Webster Dictionary, https://www.merriam-webster.com/dictionary/apologetics?src=search-dict-hed.

45   *See* Dictionary.com, https://www.dictionary.com/browse/apologetics.

46   *See, e.g.,* Doug Powell, *Holman Quick Source Guide to Christian Apologetics* (Holman Reference, Nashville, Tennessee 20060, at 356 – 357.

47   *Id.* at 358 – 359.

48   *Id.* at 360 – 361.

49   *Id.* at 363.

50   jsarber, *Examples of Scientific Accuracy in the Bible*, Bible Study Forum (Aug. 21, 2007), https://christianforumsite.com/threads/examples-of-scientific-accuracy-in-the-bible.5120/#.

51   *See Age of Reason*, All About History, http://www.allabouthistory.org/age-of-reason.htm.

Chapter 3

52   Juries are to make trustworthiness determinations during their deliberations.

See, e.g., Apple Inc. v. Samsung Elec. Co., Ltd., 839 F.3d 1034, 1045 (Fed. Cir. 2016).

The lack of trustworthiness is the reason that hearsay evidence, with some exceptions considered trustworthy, is not allowed to be considered by a fact finder in court.

See, e.g., Chambers v. Miss., 410 U.S. 284, 302 (1973);

United States v. Scheffer, 523 U.S. 303, 330 n. 17 (1997) (Stevens, J., Dissent).

53   *See, e.g.,* Paul L. Maier , *Biblical Archaeology: Factual Evidence to Support the Historicity of the Bible*, CRI (Mar. 30, 2009), www.equip.org/article/biblical-archaeology-factual-evidence-to-support-the-historicity-of-the-bible/.

54   *Id.*

55   *See, e.g., Samson Supporting Evidence Found*, Church of God News (COGwriter ©2009–2013 B. Thiel), https://www.cogwriter.com/news/old-testament-history/samson-supporting-evidence-found/.

See also Jack Wellman, *Does Archaeology Support the Bible? A Look at the Evidence*, What Christians Want to Know, https://www.whatchristianswanttoknow.com/does-archaeology-support-the-bible-a-look-at-the-evidence/ ("Every year [there is] another significant find in the Middle East, Africa, and in Europe"—"artifacts that have been unearthed [that] are specifically mentioned in the Old Testament and the New Testament").

56   *See, e.g.,* Jonathon Peterson, *When Was Each Book of the Bible Written?*, BibleGatewayBlog (Feb. 1, 2016), https://www.biblegateway.com/blog/2016/02/when-was-each-book-of-the-bible-written/;

When Were the Bible Books Written, Grace to You, https://www.gty.org/library/questions/QA176/when-were-the-bible-books-written;

When were the books of the Bible written?, Beyond Today (Posted Jan 27, 2011), https://www.ucg.org/bible-study-tools/bible-questions-and-answers/when-were-the-books-of-the-bible-written.

57   *See e.g.,* Brennan Breed, *Authorship of Job*, Ask a Scholar, Bible Odyssey n.p. (cited Feb. 7, 2021), https://www.bibleodyssey.org/en/tools/ask-a-scholar/authorship-of-job;

The Book of Job, Summary, http://www.firmfoundationri.com/images/The_Book_of_Job.pdf.

58   Also known as *Song of Solomon*.

59   *See, e.g.,* Ian Sample, Science Editor, *Scientists use 'virtual unwrapping' to read ancient biblical scroll reduced to 'lump of charcoal'*, The Guardian *Sept. 26, 2016), https://www.theguardian.com/science/2016/sep/21/jubilation-as-scientists-use-virtual-unwrapping-to-read-burnt-ancient-scroll.

60   *See* Andrew Griffin, *Scientists Finally Read the Oldest Biblical Text Ever Found*, Independent (Sept. 22, 2016) https://infostudenti.net/en/scientists-have-finally-been-able-to-read-the-oldest-biblical-text-ever-found/#.

61   For all facts, *see id.* (Emphasis added).

62   *See* Peter Surran, *The Dead Sea Scrolls; Why Are They Important*, Ministry Matters (Mar. 12, 2017), https://www.ministrymatters.com/all/entry/8052/the-dead-sea-scrolls-why-are-they-important.

63   *See* Scott Manning, *Process of Copying the Old Testament by Jewish Scribes*, Historian on the Warpath (Mar. 17, 2017), http://www.scottmanning.com/content/process-of-copying-the-old-testament-by-jewish-scribes/.

64   *See, e.g.,* Jennie Cohen, *Six Things You May Not Know About the Dead Sea Scrolls*, History Stories (Aug. 29, 2018),

https://www.history.com/news/6-things-you-may-not-know-about-the-dead-sea-scrolls.

See also Patrick Zukeran, *The Story of the Scrolls*, Probe for Answers (Apr. 17, 2006), https://probe.org/the-dead-sea-scrolls.

65   *See* Peter Surran, *The Dead Sea Scrolls; Why Are They Important*, Ministry Matters (Mar. 12, 2017), https://www.ministrymatters.com/all/entry/8052/the-dead-sea-scrolls-why-are-they-important.

66   *See* Patrick Zukeran, *The Story of the Scrolls*, Probe for Answers (Apr. 17, 2006) https://probe.org/the-dead-sea-scrolls;

Peter Surran, *The Dead Sea Scrolls; Why Are They Important*, Ministry Matters (Mar. 12, 2017), https://www.ministrymatters.com/all/entry/8052/the-dead-sea-scrolls-why-are-they-important.

67   *See* Patrick Zukeran, *The Story of the Scrolls*, Probe for Answers (Apr. 17, 2006), https://probe.org/the-dead-sea-scrolls.

68   *Id.*

69   Twelfth Dead Sea Scrolls Cave discovered west of Qumran, Behold Israel (Feb. 8, 2017), https://beholdisrael.org/twelfth-dead-sea-scrolls-cave-discovered-west-of-qumran/.

See Peter Surran, *The Dead Sea Scrolls; Why Are They Important*, Ministry Matters (Mar. 12, 2017), https://www.ministrymatters.com/all/entry/8052/the-dead-sea-scrolls-why-are-they-important;

Kevin Loria, *A New Dead Sea Scrolls Cave Has Been Discovered—and It Might Not Be the Last*, Business Insider (Feb. 9, 2017), https://www.businessinsider.com/new-dead-sea-scrolls-cave-discovered-2017-2.

70   *See, e.g.,* Jennie Cohen, *Six Things You May Not Know About the Dead Sea Scrolls*, History Stories (Aug. 29, 2018), https://www.history.com/news/6-things-you-may-not-know-about-the-dead-sea-scrolls.

71   *Id.*

72   More than 100,000 fragments were also analyzed. Archaeologists studied pottery, coins, graves, and garments at Khirbet Qumran and arrived at a date ranging from the second century BC to the first century AD. Paleographers studied the style of writing and arrived at dates raging from the third century BC to the first century AD. Scientists, using the radiocarbon dating method, dated the scrolls from the fourth century BC to the first century AD. Since all the methods came to a similar conclusion, scholars are very confident in their assigned date for the texts. The scrolls date as early as the third century BC to the first century AD.

See Patrick Zukeran, *The Story of the Scrolls*, Probe for Answers (Apr. 17, 2006) (No longer available online) https://probe.org/the-dead-sea-scrolls.

73   *See* Peter Surran, *The Dead Sea Scrolls; Why Are They Important*, Ministry Matters (Mar. 12, 2017), https://www.ministrymatters.com/all/entry/8052/the-dead-sea-scrolls-why-are-they-important.

74   *See* Patrick Zukeran, *The Story of the Scrolls*, Probe for Answers (Apr. 17, 2006) (No longer available online), https://probe.org/the-dead-sea-scrolls.

75   The "book of Samuel is "a collective name of fragments containing parts of the Books of Samuel which were found among the Dead Sea Scrolls."

    See The Samuel Scroll, Wikipedia (last edited Aug. 2, 2021), https://en.wikipedia.org/wiki/The_Samuel_Scroll.

76   *See* Patrick Zukeran, *The Story of the Scrolls*, Probe for Answers (Apr. 17, 2006) (No longer available online), https://probe.org/the-dead-sea-scrolls.

77   *Id.*

78   *Id.*

    See also Peter Surran, *The Dead Sea Scrolls; Why Are They Important*, Ministry Matters (Mar. 12, 2017), https://www.ministrymatters.com/all/entry/8052/the-dead-sea-scrolls-why-are-they-important.

79   *See* Patrick Zukeran, *The Story of the Scrolls*, Probe for Answers (Apr. 17, 2006) (No longer available online), https://probe.org/the-dead-sea-scrolls, citing James Vanderkam and Peter Flint, *The Meaning of the Dead Sea Scrolls* (San Francisco, CA.: Harper Collins Publishers, 2002) at 115;

    Peter Surran, *The Dead Sea Scrolls; Why Are They Important*, Ministry Matters (Mar. 12, 2017), https://www.ministrymatters.com/all/entry/8052/the-dead-sea-scrolls-why-are-they-important.

80   *See* Patrick Zukeran, *The Story of the Scrolls*, Probe for Answers (Apr. 17, 2006) (No longer available online), https://probe.org/the-dead-sea-scrolls.

81   *See generally* Daniel 2 (written 536–530 BC).

    See also Patrick Zukeran, *The Story of the Scrolls*, Probe for Answers (Apr. 17, 2006) (No longer available online), https://probe.org/the-dead-sea-scrolls (citing, among others, Millar Burrows, *The Dead Sea Scrolls* (New York: Viking Press, 1955), 304, quoted in Norman Geisler and William Nix, *General Introduction to the Bible* (Chicago: Moody Press, 1986) which said, "It is a matter of wonder that through something like one thousand years the text underwent so little alteration."

    See also Part IV on Prophecy *infra*.

82   *See* Peter Surran, *The Dead Sea Scrolls; Why Are They Important*, Ministry Matters (Mar. 12, 2017), https://www.ministrymatters.com/all/entry/8052/the-dead-sea-scrolls-why-are-they-important.

83   *See* JMM Team, *Did Scribes Faithfully Transmit Old Testament Manuscripts?*, Josh McDowell Ministries (Feb. 7, 2018), https://www.josh.org/faithful-transmit-old-testament/.

84   *See* Ian Werret, *How Did Scribes and the Scribal Tradition Shape the Hebrew Bible?*, Bible Odyssey, https://www.bibleodyssey.org/en/tools/bible-basics/how-did-scribes-and-the-scribal-tradition-shape-the-hebrew-bible.

85   *Id.*

86   *See, e.g., Siege of Jerusalem* (597 BC), Wikipedia (last edited Aug. 19, 2021), https://en.wikipedia.org/wiki/Siege_of_Jerusalem_(597_BC).

87   *See, e.g., Babylonian Captivity*, Encyclopedia Britannica, https://www.britannica.com/event/Babylonian-Captivity.

88   *See, e.g.,* Ezra 1:1–3 (NIV) (written 457–444 BC);

       Babylonian Captivity, Encyclopedia Britannica, https://www.britannica.com/event/Babylonian-Captivity.

89   *See* Ezra 7:6 (ESV) (written 457–444 BC).

90   *See* Nehemiah 8:1–3 (written 445–400 BC).

91   *See* Scott Manning, *Process of Copying the Old Testament by Jewish Scribes*, Historian on the Warpath (Mar. 17, 2007), http://www.scottmanning.com/content/process-of-copying-the-old-testament by jewish-scribes/;

       Meticulous Jewish Scribes, The Story of the Bible, http://www.storyofbible.com/meticulous-jewish-scribes.html.

92   *See* Walter Sullivan, *Diggers Find Imperial City of Assyrians*, The New York Times (Oct. 18, 1981), https://www.nytimes.com/1981/10/18/us/diggers-find-imperial-city-of-assyrians.html.

93   An ancient people who, by 2500 BC, lived in the northern parts of Mesopotamia, which is a region of southwest Asia in the Tigris and Euphrates river system located in the region now known as the Middle East and which includes parts of southwest Asia and lands around the eastern Mediterranean Sea.

       See, e.g., The Hurrians, Israel-a-history-of.com, https://www.israel-a-history-of.com/hurrians.html, (citing Andrew Lawler, *Who Were The Hurrians?*, Archaeology Institute of America);

       Mesopotamia, History.com, https://www.history.com/topics/ancient-middle-east/mesopotamia.

94   *Id..*

95   *Id.*

96   "These tablets include treaties, marriage arrangements, rules regarding inheritance, adoption, and the like." Paul L. Maier, *Biblical Archaeology: Factual Evidence to Support the Historicity of the Bible*, CRI (Mar. 30, 2009), https://www.equip.org/article/biblical-archaeology-factual-evidence-to-support-the-historicity-of-the-bible/.

97   *See* Cristian Violatti, *10 Archaeological Discoveries Consistent with Biblical Passages*, LstVerse/History (Nov. 4, 2016), http://listverse.com/2016/11/04/10-archaeological-discoveries-consistent-with-biblical-passages.

98   *See* Genesis16: 1–2 (written 1450–1405 BC).

99   *See* Cristian Violatti, *10 Archaeological Discoveries Consistent with Biblical Passages*, LstVerse/History (Nov. 4, 2016), http://listverse.com/2016/11/04/10-archaeological-discoveries-consistent-with-biblical-passages.

100   *Id.*

101   *See* Numbers 6:24–26 (NIV) (written 1450–1405 BC).

102   *See* Cristian Violatti, *10 Archaeological Discoveries Consistent with Biblical Passages*, LstVerse/History (Nov. 4, 2016), http://listverse.com/2016/11/04/10-archaeological-discoveries-consistent-with-biblical-passages.

103   *See How We Got the Bible*, Making Life Count Ministries, Online..

104   *See, e.g.,* Matt Slick, *Manuscript evidence for superior New Testament reliability*, Christian Apologetics & Research Ministry (Dec . 6, 2008), https://carm.org/about-the-bible/manuscript-evidence-for-superior-new-testament-reliability/;

      Top of Form Bottom of Form *Generalized Question*, Christian Chat (May 1, 2015), https://christianchat.com/bible-discussion-forum/a-generalized-question.108793/page-7.

105   *Id.*

106   *See Comparing the New Testament with Other Ancient Books,* GodWords—Theology and Other Good Stuff (with information from The Center for the Study of New Testament Manuscripts), https://godwords.org/comparing-the-new-testament-with-other-ancient-books.

107   *Id.*

108   *See, e.g., Old Testament Manuscripts,* http://kukis.org/Doctrines/OTmanuscripts.pdf;

      Case-Making 101: How does the Bible compare to other ancient documents?, Truth, Faith and Reason (Dec. 4, 2016), https://truthfaithandreason.com/case-making-101-how-does-the-bible-compare-to-other-ancient-documents/;

      E. Ray Clendenen, *Textual Criticism and Bible Translation* (May 25, 2015), https://www.challies.com/sponsored/textual-criticism-and-bible-translation/ (sponsored by Tim Challies),

109   *See Comparing the New Testament with Other Ancient Books*, GodWords—Theology and Other Good Stuff (with information from The Center for the Study of New Testament Manuscripts), https://godwords.org/comparing-the-new-testament-with-other-ancient-books.

110   *Id.*

111   *See e.g.,* Bill Pratt, *How Do Other Ancient Texts Compare to the New Testament? #10 Post of 2012* Tough Questions Answered (Dec. 11, 2012), https://www.toughquestionsanswered. org/2012/12/11/how-do-other-ancient-texts-compare-to-the-new-testament.

112   *See, e.g.,* Ronald Cram, *Top NT Archaeological Finds*, Factbridge, http://factbridge.org/sites/default/files/inline-files/Top-NT-Archaeological-Finds.pdf, at No. 10 (citing https://en.wikipedia.org/wiki/Rylands_Library_Papyrus_P52).

113   *Id.* at No. 11 (citing *Papyrus 66,* Wikipedia (last edited June 1, 2021), https://en.wikipedia.org/wiki/Papyrus_66).

114   *Id.* at No. 12 (citing *Chester Beatty Papyri,* Wikipedia (last edited Aug. 13, 2021), http://bit.ly/BeattyPapyri).

115   *Id.* at No. 13 (citing *Codex Vaticanus,* Wikipedia (last edited Aug. 7, 2021), https://en.wikipedia.org/wiki/Codex_Vaticanus).

116   *Id.* at No. 14 (citing *Codex Sinaiticus,* Wikipedia (last edited Aug. 22, 2021), https://cn.wikipedia.org/wiki/Codex_Sinaiticus).

117   *See, e.g.,* Jim Franks, *Is the Bible True? Proof 5: Consistency of the Bible's Internal Evidence,* Life Hope & Truth (Sept.—Oct. 2015), https://lifehopeandtruth.com/bible/is-the-bible-true/proof-5-consistency/.

118   *See, e.g., How Many People Wrote the Bible?,* All About Truth; https://www.allabouttruth.org/how-many-people-wrote-the-bible-faq.htm.

119   *See e.g.,* Jim Franks, *Is the Bible True? Proof 5: Consistency of the Bible's Internal Evidence,* Life Hope & Truth (Sept.—Oct. 2015), https://lifehopeandtruth.com/bible/is-the-bible-true/proof-5-consistency/.

120   *Id.*

121   *See, e.g.,* Matt Slick, *Manuscript evidence for superior New Testament reliability,* Christian Apologetics & Research Ministry (CARM) (Dec. 6, 2008), https://carm.org/manuscript-evidence.

122   *See, e.g.,* L. David McClister, *Josephus, Flavius (AD 37–c.100),* Wiley Online Library (First published Nov. 25, 2011, https://doi.org/10.1002/9780470670606.wbecc1585), https://www.academia.edu/1565034/Josephus_Flavius_AD_37_c_100;

Gary William Poole, *Flavius Josephus—Jewish priest, scholar, and historian* (alternative title: *Joseph ben Matthias*), Britannica (Anniversary information added Jan. 1, 2021, revised and updated by Melissa Petruzzello, Assistant Editor), https://www.britannica.com/biography/Flavius-Josephus.

123   *See, e.g.,* Paul L. Meier, *Josephus and Jesus,* North American Board (Published Mar. 30, 2016), https://www.namb.net/apologetics/resource/josephus-and-jesus/;

Josephus, Wikipedia, https://en.wikipedia.org/wiki/Josephus;

Josephus' Jewish Antiquities, Livius.org—Articles on ancient history (created 1997; modified Oct. 12, 2020), https://www.livius.org/sources/about/josephus-jewish-antiquities/;

Flavius Josephus - Jewish priest, scholar, and historian, Britannica (Anniversary information added Jan. 1. 2021), https://www.britannica.com/biography/Flavius-Josephus.

124   *See Josephus' Jewish Antiquities*, Livius.org—Articles on ancient history (created 1997; modified Oct. 12, 2020), https://www.livius.org/sources/about/josephus-jewish-antiquities/.

125   *Id.*

126   *Id.*

127   *See* James Tabor, *Josephus on James*, The Jewish Roman World of Jesus, https://pages.uncc.edu/james-tabor/ancient-judaism/josephus-james/.

128   *See Pliny the Younger on Jesus Christ*, Street Apologist: the blog of Vocab Malone, host of Urban Theologian Radio, https://streetapologist.wordpress.com/2013/09/28/pliny-the-younger/.

129   *See, e.g.,* William Whiston, Translator, *Letters of Pliny the Younger and the Emperor Trajan*, Frontline (From *The Works of Josephus*, Hendrickson Publishers, 1987), https://www.pbs.org/wgbh/pages/frontline/shows/religion/maps/primary/pliny.html.

130   *See e.g. Tacitus on Jesus*, Wikipedia (last edited Nov. 25, 2021), https://en.wikipedia.org/wiki/Tacitus_on_Jesus;

Tacitus (c. 55–117 CE): Nero's Persecution of the Christians, https://www.bing.com/search?q=Annals+of+Tacitus+and+nero+fastening+the +guilt+of+starting+the+fire.

131   *See* Alexander Thomson , Translator, Revised and Edited by T. Forester, Produced by Tapio Riikonen and David Widger, *Suetonius: The Lives of the Twelve Caesars by C. Suetonius Tranquillius*, an English Translation, augmented with *His Lives of the Grammarians, Rhetoricians, and Poets* (Release Date: Oct. 22, 2006; last updated: August 31, 2016),
https://www.gutenberg.org/files/6400/6400-h/6400-h.htm.

132   *See* Editors of Encyclopaedia Britannica, *Suetonius*, Roman author, Britannica (Jan. 1, 2021), https://www.britannica.com/biography/Suetonius.

133   *See* Mark Cartwright, *Suetonius*, Ancient History Encyclopedia (Jan. 21, 2016), https://www.ancient.eu/Suetonius/#:~:text=Gaius Suetonius Tranquillus.

134   If the reader is interested in reading more about Nero or the other Caesars, a translation of the *Lives of the Twelve Caesar* may also be found at Alexander Thomson and E. Forester, *The Lives of the Twelve Caesars*, OLL (George Bell & Sons, London), https://oll.libertyfund.org/title/thomson-the-lives-of-the-twelve-caesars.

135   *See* C. Suetonius Tranquillus, *Tiberius Claudius Drusus Caesar, The Lives of the Twelve Caesars* (Alexander Thomson Translation, Revised and corrected by T . Forester), https://www.gutenberg.org/files/6400/6400-h/6400-h.htm#link2 H_4_0006;

When Only God Knew

Lucrezia Nordio, *When did Suetonius write Lives of the Caesars?* (last updated Feb. 23, 2020), https://findanyanswer.com/when-did-suetonius-write-lives-of-the-caesars.

136 *See, e.g., Stories of Jesus the Nazarene from the Talmud*, Steemit, https://steemit.com/jesus/@offgridlife/stories-of-jesus-the-nazarene-from-the-talmud.

137 *Id.*

138 *Id.*

139 *Id.* (quoting from *Yeshu ha-Notzri:* ירצונה ושי — *The Historical Jesus the Nazarene in the 1st Century Jewish Tradition* (May 11, 2017), http://yeshuhanotzri.blogspot.com/2016/02/execution-of-yeshu-ha-notzri-on-eve-of.html).

140 *See* Matthew 26:2 (written 50–65 AD); Mark 14:12–25 (written 50–65 AD); Luke 22:7–14 (written 60–61 AD); John 13:1 (written 80–90 AD).

141 *See, e.g., Mara bar Serapion on Jesus*, Wikipedia (last edited June 13, 2021), https://en.wikipedia.org/wiki/Mara_bar_Serapion_on_Jesus.

142 *See, e.g., The Romans Destroy the Temple at Jerusalem*, 70 AD, Eyewitness to History. com, http://www.eyewitnesstohistory.com/jewishtemple.htm.

143 *See* Tim Stratton, *Historical References to Christ From Non-Biblical Authors*, Free Thinking Ministries (Apr. 3, 2017), https://freethinkingministries.com/historical-references-to-christ-from-non-biblical-authors/.

  See also Craig A, Evans, Editor (2004) Lives of Jesus and Jesus Outside the Bible, *The Historical Jesus—Critical Concepts in Religious Studies*, volume IV at p. 382.

144 *See e.g.,* Ben C. Smith, author and designer, *Mara bar Serapion on the wise king of the Jews* - A Syriac letter from a man to his son (File last modified Mar. 4, 2019), http://www.textexcavation.com/marabarserapiontestimonium.html.

145 *See Mara bar Serapion on Jesus*, Wikipedia (last edited June 13, 2021), https://en.wikipedia.org/wiki/Mara_bar_Serapion_on_Jesus.

146 *See, e.g., Henry Chadwick (theologian)*, Wikipedia (last edited July 14, 2021), https://en.wikipedia.org/wiki/Henry_Chadwick_(theologian).

147 *See, e.g., Can we be Confident in the New Testament? (part 2)*, My Theo-Blogy (October 16, 2012), https://mytheoblogy.wordpress.com/2012/10/16/can-we-be-confident-in-the-new-testament-part-2/.

148 *See, e.g.,* Harry Oates, *The Great Jewish Revolt of 66 CE*, Ancient History Encyclopedia (Aug. 28, 2015), https://www.ancient.eu/article/823/the-great-jewish-revolt-of-66-ce/.

149 *See, e.g., The Romans Destroy the Temple at Jerusalem, 70 AD*, Eyewitness to History.com (2005), http://www.eyewitnesstohistory.com/jewishtemple.htm.

150 *See, e.g.,* Joshua Hammer, *What is Beneath the Temple Mount?*, Smithsonian Magazine (April 2011), https://www.smithsonianmag.com/history/what-is-beneath-the-temple-mount-920764/#;

  What's beneath the Temple Mount? (Smithsonian), Elder of Ziyon (April 01, 2011) (discussing Smithsonian Article), https://elderofziyon.blogspot.com/2011/04/whats-beneath-temple-mount-smithsonian.html;

Biblical Archaeology Society Staff, *Sifting Antiquity on the Temple Mount Sifting Project*, Bible History Daily (Sept. 17, 2019), https://www.biblicalarchaeology.org/daily/biblical-sites-places/temple-at-jerusalem/temple-mount-sifting-project/.

151   *See, e.g.,* Joshua Hammer, *What is Beneath the Temple Mount?*, Smithsonian Magazine (Apr. 2011), https://www.smithsonianmag.com/history/what-is-beneath-the-temple-mount-920764/;

AnaRina Bar Tzon Kresiman, *For the FREEDOM of Zion* (Dec. 2019), https://www.alignwithzion.com/post/for-the-freedom-of-zion;

What's beneath the Temple Mount? (Smithsonian), Elder of Ziyon (Apr. 1, 2011) (discussing Smithsonian Article), https://elderofziyon.blogspot.com/2011/04/whats-beneath-temple-mount-smithsonian.html.

152   *See* Matthew 24: 1 (NIV) (written 50–65 AD) and in Luke 21: 5–7 (NIV) (written 60–61 AD).

153   *See, e.g.,* Nancy Levin, *10 Longest Books in the Bible,* Largest.org (Jan. 9, 2020), https://largest.org/culture/books-in-the-bible/.

154   *See, e.g., Gospel of Luke*, Wikipedia (last edited Aug. 9, 2021), https://en.wikipedia.org/wiki/Gospel_of_Luke.

155   *See, e.g., Acts of the Apostles*, Wikipedia (last edited Aug. 20, 2021), https://en.wikipedia.org/wiki/Acts_of_the_Apostles

156   *See, e.g., Gospel of Luke,* Wikipedia (last edited Aug. 9, 2021), https://en.wikipedia.org/wiki/Gospel_of_Luke.

157   *See Luke,* The Bible Teaching Ministry of Pastor Chuck Swindoll, https://www.insight.org/resources/bible/the-gospels/luke.

158   *See, e.g., William Mitchell Ramsay*, Wikipedia (last edited July 15, 2021), https://en.wikipedia.org/wiki/William_Mitchell_Ramsay.

159   *See, e.g., The Bible Is Unique #11 (External Evidence Test –Ramsey Tests)*, Josh McDowell Ministries, https://www.josh.org/wp-content/uploads/External-Evidence-Test-—Ramsey-Tests.pdf.

160   *See, e.g., William Mitchell Ramsay*, Wikipedia (last edited July 15, 2021), https://en.wikipedia.org/wiki/William_Mitchell_Ramsay.

161   *See, e.g.,* Ronald Cram, *Top NT Archaeological Finds,* http://factbridge.org/sites/default/files/inline-files/Top-NT-Archaeological-Finds.pdf at No. 5 (citing http://bit.ly/PhrygianAltar).

162   *See* Jason Jackson, *Luke, the Beloved Historian*, Christian Courier.com (Sept. 4, 2021), https://www.christiancourier.com/articles/1196-luke-the-beloved-historian (citing *Luke the Historian in the Light of Research*, Grand Rapids: Baker, 1977, p. 47).

         When Only God Knew

163   *See, e.g.,* Ronald Cram, *Top NT Archaeological Finds,*
       http://factbridge.org/sites/default/files/inline-files/Top-NT-Archaeological-Finds.pdf
       at No. 4 (citing http://bit.ly/Politarch-Inscription).

164   *See Definitions for politarch,* Definitions & Translations,
       https://www.definitions.net/definition/politarch.

165   *See* Leon Mauldin, *Thessalonian Politarch Inscription & its Bearing on Acts 17:6,8,*
       Leon's Message Board (Feb. 21, 2018),
       https://leonmauldin.blog/category/inscriptions/.

166   *See, e.g.,* Ernest DeWitt Burton, *Critical and Historic Notes—The Politarchs,*
       https://www.jstor.org/stable/3153438?seq=1#metadata_info_tab_contents (reprinting
       Critical and Historic Notes, The American Journal of Theology (1898), volume 2, No. 3,
       at p. 599);

       Politarchs (Acts 17:6, 8): Luke gets it right—as usual!, HolyLandPhotos' Blog (May
       3, 2016) (citing Fant, Clyde E., and Mitchell, G. Reddish, *Politarch Inscription
       at Thessalonica, Lost Treasures of the Bible—Understanding the Bible Through
       Archaeological Artifacts in World Museums* (Grand Rapids, MI: Eerdmans, 2008) pp. 366–
       70), https://holylandphotos.org/browse.asp?s=1,4,13,31,283,285&img=GNMTTHCT22;

       Politarch, Wiki2—Wikipedia Republished (last edited Feb. 1, 2021),
       https://wiki2.org/en/Politarch.

167   *See, e.g.,* Ernest DeWitt Burton, *Critical and Historic Notes—The Politarchs,*
       https://www.jstor.org/stable/3153438?seq=1#metadata_info_tab_contents (reprinting
       Critical and Historic Notes, The American Journal of Theology (1998), volume 2, No. 3,
       at p. 600.

168   *See, e.g., generally, Luke gets it right—as usual!,* HolyLandPhotos' Blog (May 3, 2016)
       (citing Fant, Clyde E., and Mitchell, G. Reddish, *Politarch Inscription at Thessalonica,
       Lost Treasures of the Bible—Understanding the Bible Through Archaeological Artifacts in
       World Museums* (Grand Rapids, MI: Eerdmans, 2008) p. 599),
       https://holylandphotos.org/browse.asp?s=1,4,13,31,283,285&img=GNMTTHCT22.

       See also Ronald Cram, *Top NT Archaeological Finds,* /
       http://factbridge.org/sites/default/files/inline-files/Top-NT-Archaeological-Finds.pdf
       at No. 4 (citing http://bit.ly/Politarch-Inscription).

169   *See* Leon Mauldin, *Thessalonian Politarch Inscription & its Bearing on Acts 17:6,8,*
       Leon's Message Board, https://leonmauldin.blog/2018/02/21/thessalonian-politarch-
       inscription-its-bearing-on-acts-1768.

170   *See, e.g.,* Stephen Chew, *Myth: Eyewitness Testimony is the Best Kind of Evidence,*
       Association for Psychological Science (APS) (Aug. 20, 2018),
       https://www.psychologicalscience.org/teaching/myth-eyewitness-testimony-is-the-best-
       kind-of-evidence.html.

171   Including by impaling, beheading, crucifixion, flaying, and being thrown to their deaths
       without denying that Jesus lived as the Bible said that he did and that he did the many

miracles which the Bible described. They all died declaring that Jesus died and that they saw him alive afterwards.

172   *See e.g., How Ancient Eyewitness Testimony Became the New Testament Gospel Record,* Cold Case Christianity with J. Warner Wallace (May 30, 2018), https://coldcasechristianity.com/writings/how-ancient-eyewitness-testimony-became-the-new-testament-gospel-record/.

173   *See, e.g., How Ancient Eyewitness Testimony Became the New Testament Gospel Record,* Cold Case Christianity with J. Warner Wallace (May 30, 2018), https://coldcasechristianity.com/writings/how-ancient-eyewitness-testimony-became-the-new-testament-gospel-record/.

174   *See* Timothy Paul Jones, *Apologetics: Were the Gospels Written While the Eyewitnesses Were Still Alive?* (May 5, 2015), https://www.timothypauljones.com/gospels-written-while-eyewitnesses/.

175   Some of the earliest transcripts do not contain Mark 16:9–20 (written 50–65 AD) which discusses Jesus' post resurrection appearances.

176   John (written 80–90 AD).

177   *See* Rob Phillips, *Can we trust the biblical manuscripts?* The Pathway (Jan. 13, 2020), https://mbcpathway.com/2020/01/13/can-we-trust-the-biblical-manuscripts/.

Part II

178   *See* Merriam Webster Dictionary, https://www.merriam-webster.com/dictionary/archaeology.

179   *See* Merriam Webster Dictionary, https://www.merriam-webster.com/dictionary/anthropology.

180   *See* Merriam Webster Dictionary, https://www.merriam-webster.com/dictionary/history.

181   *Archaeologists Are Digging up Bible Stories: 100 Stunning Discoveries that Confirm the Bible,* www.bible.ca/archeology/bible-archeology.htm.

182   *See generally* Chapter 3, *supra.*

183   *See Archaeologists are digging up bible stories: 100 stunning discoveries that confirm the Bible,* www.bible.ca/archeology/bible-archeology.htm.

184   *See* Fred Williams, *Archeological Evidence, Evidences of the Bible* (Mar. 1, 1999), https://bibleevidences.com/archaeological-evidence/.

185   *Id.* (quoting Nelson Glueck, *Rivers in the Desert,* 1960, pg. 31).

186   *Id.* (quoting William M. Ramsay, *St. Paul the Traveler and the Roman Citizen,* 1982, pg. 8, and William M. Ramsay, *The Bearing of Recent Discovery on the Trustworthiness of the New Testament,* 1915, pg. 222).

187   *Id.* (quoting A.N Sherwin-White, *Roman Society and Roman Law in the New Testament,* 1963, pg. 189).

188   While archaeology may "not prove God wrote the Bible," when considered with all of the other proofs, including the scientific and medical facts in the Bible written at a time when the truth of those facts was not readily apparent or known to the Biblical writer, apparently, the evidence supports the conclusion beyond any reasonable doubt that the Bible is god-breathed.

189   *Id.* (quoting Millar Burrows, *What Mean These Stones*, 1941, p 1).

190   *See generally* Chapter 3, *supra.*

191   *See Rivers in the Desert: A History of the Negev*, p. 31 (quoted in Ronald Cram, *Top NT Archaeological Finds*, Factbridge, factbridge.org/sites/default/files/inline-files/Top-NT-Archaeological-Finds.pdf).

192   *See Jonathan L. Reed,* Westar Institute, https://www.westarinstitute.org/membership/westar-fellows/fellows-directory/jonathan-l-reed;

      Jonathan L. Reed, HarperCollinsPublishers (Copyright © 2021 HarperCollins Publishers), https://www.harpercollins.com/author/cr-102590/jonathan-l-reed/.

193   *See The Harper Collins Visual Guide to the New Testament: What Archaeology Reveals about the First Christians*, p.100, (quoted in Ronald Cram, *Top NT Archaeological Finds*, Factbridge, factbridge.org/sites/default/files/inline-files/Top-NT-Archaeological-Finds.pdf).

194   *See John McRay*, Wikipedia (last edited Aug. 4, 2021), https://en.wikipedia.org/wiki/John_McRay.

195   *See Archaeology and the New Testament*, p.22 (quoted in Ronald Cram, *Top NT Archaeological Finds*, Factbridge, factbridge.org/sites/default/files/inline-files/Top-NT-Archaeological-Finds.pdf).

196   *See St. Paul the Traveler and Roman Citizen*, p.8 (cited and quoted in Ronald Cram, *Top NT Archaeological Finds*, Factbridge, factbridge.org/sites/default/files/inline-files/Top-NT-Archaeological-Finds.pdf).

197   *See Paul Barnett*, Wikipedia (last edited Sept. 11, 2019), https://en.wikipedia.org/wiki/Paul_Barnett.

198   *See Is the New Testament Reliable?* (quoted in Ronald Cram, *Top NT Archaeological Finds*, Factbridge, factbridge.org/sites/default/files/inline-files/Top-NT-Archaeological-Finds.pdf).

199   In this author's and in others' opinion, without fail over time archaeology does endorse particular Bible events as archaeology catches up to what the Bible reports.

200   Clifford Wilson, *Does Archaeology Support the Bible?*, Answers in Genesis (Jan. 24, 2008), Chapter 25, (Emphasis added), https://answersingenesis.org/archaeology/does-archaeology-support-the-bible/.

Chapter 4

201   *See* Genesis 37 (written 1450–1405 BC).

202   *See* Genesis 39–46, 50:18 (written 1450–1405 BC); Exodus 9:26 (ESV) (written 1450–1405 BC).

203   *See* Genesis 46:33–47:8, 27 (written 1450–1405 BC).

204   *See* Genesis 50:24–26 (written 1450–1405 BC).

205   *See* Exodus 13: (written 1450–1405 BC).

206   *See* Genesis 37:2–28; 41:37–43 (written 1450–1405 BC).

207   *See* C. R. Conder, *Ramses*, Bible Hub Encyclopedia, http://bibleatlas.org/ramses.htm;

       Simcha Jacobovici, *Statue of Biblical Joseph Found: Story Covered Up!*, Torah Archeology (Feb. 18, 2014), http://www.simchajtv.com/statue-of-biblical-joseph-found-story-covered-up/;

       Ramses 1, http://www.aldokkan.com/egypt/ramses1.htm;

       Rameses - ancient city, Egypt, Britannica, https://www.britannica.com/place/Rameses.

208   *See also Evidence for the Exodus*, Evidences of the Bible (Mar. 5, 2017), https://bibleevidences.com/evidence-for-the-exodus/.

209   *See Egyptian monuments* (detailed guide to the archaeological sites of the Nile Valley and desert areas of Egypt), Tell el-Dab'a (Avaris) (Mar. 2, 2009.), https://egyptsites.wordpress.com/2009/03/02/tell-el-daba/.

210   *See Evidence for the Exodus*, Evidences of the Bible (Mar. 5, 2017), https://bibleevidences.com/evidence-for-the-exodus/.

211   *See* Genesis 11:31 (NOV) (written 1450–1405 BC).

212   *See Evidence for the Exodus*, Evidences of the Bible (Mar. 5, 2017), https://bibleevidences.com/evidence-for-the-exodus/.

       See also Exodus 9:26 (written 1450–1405 BC).

213   *See Evidence for the Exodus*, Evidences of the Bible (Mar. 5, 2017), https://bibleevidences.com/evidence-for-the-exodus/.

214   Genesis 46:31–32 (ESV) (written 1450–1405 BC) says, "My brothers and my father's household, who were in the land of Canaan, have come to me. And the men are shepherds, for they have brought their flocks and their herds and all they have."

215   *See Evidence for the Exodus*, Evidences of the Bible (Mar. 5, 2017), https://bibleevidences.com/evidence-for-the-exodus/

216   *Id.*

217   Joseph was the second most powerful man in Egypt, next only to the pharaoh.

      See Genesis 41:39–41 (written 1450–1405 BC).

218   *See Evidence for the Exodus*, Evidences of the Bible (Mar. 5, 2017),
      https://bibleevidences.com/evidence-for-the-exodus/.

219   *See* Genesis 35:22 (written 1450–1405 BC).

220   The twelve sons of Jacob from whom the Bible says the tribes of Israel are descended are
      Reuben, Simeon, Judah, Issachar, Zebulun, Benjamin, Dan, Naphtali, Gad, Asher, Ephraim
      and Manasseh.

      See, e.g., Ancient Jewish History: The Twelve Tribes of Israel, Jewish Virtual Library
      (citing Encyclopaedia Judaica. © 2008 The Gale Group),
      https://www.jewishvirtuallibrary.org/the-twelve-tribes-of-israel;

      The Editors of Encyclopaedia Britannica, *Twelve Tribes of Israel*, Britannica (Adam
      Augustyn, corrected display issue, Jan 31, 2020),
      https://www.britannica.com/topic/Twelve-Tribes-of-Israel.

221   *See Evidence for the Exodus*, Evidences of the Bible (Mar. 5, 2017),
      https://bibleevidences.com/evidence-for-the-exodus/.

222   *Id.*

223   *Id.*

224   Genesis 50:24–25 (NIV) (written 1450–1405 BC) said, *Then Joseph said to his brothers,
      "I am about to die. But God will surely come to your aid and take you up out of this land
      to the land he promised on oath to Abraham, Isaac and Jacob." And Joseph made the
      Israelites swear an oath and said, "God will surely come to your aid, and then you must
      carry my bones up from this place."*

      Exodus 13:19 (NIV) (written 1450–1405 BC) said, *Moses took the bones of Joseph with
      him because Joseph had made the Israelites swear an oath. He had said, "God will surely
      come to your aid, and then you must carry my bones up with you from this place."*

225   *Id*;

      Simcha Jacobovici, *Statue of Biblical Joseph Found: Story Covered Up!*, Torah
      Archeology (Feb. 18, 2014),
      http://www.simchajtv.com/statue-of-biblical-joseph-found-story-covered-up/.

226   *See* Genesis 37:3, 23 (written 1450–1405 BC).

227   *See* Steven Rudd, *Introduction: Historical and Archaeological survey of the Exodus-1899
      BC: Israelites enter Egypt*, Exodus Route Restored (2005+),
      http://www.bible.ca/archeology/bible-archeology-exodus-route.htm#authorintro.

228   *Id.*

229   *See* Judges 13–16 (written circa 1043 BC).

230   According to the Old Testament, he killed 1,000 Philistine men using only the jawbone of a donkey as a weapon.

        See Judges 15:14–17 (written circa 1043 BC).

231   *See The Shiloh Excavations* (first published in the Winter 2005 issue of *Bible and Spade*), Associates for Biblical Research, https://biblearchaeology.org/research/judges-united-monarchy/3800-between-the-pillars-revisiting-samson-and-the-house-of-dagon, for two viewpoints respecting the debate.

232   *See* Judges 14:5–6 (written circa 1043 BC).

233   "The Talmudic period was from around 21 centuries ago until 15 centuries ago," during which. "the Torah-sages edited and collated the teachings of the Mishna (Oral Torah) and the Talmud (commentary) which until then had been transmitted in a form which had not yet been formally finalized."

        What is the Talmudic Period?, Answers, https://www.answers.com/Q/What_is_the_Talmudic_Period.

234   *See Samson*, Star Myths of the World, https://www.starmythworld.com/samson.

235   *Id.* (discussing *Hamlet's Mill* (1969) by Giorgio de Santillana and Hertha von Dechend).

236   *See, e.g.,* COGwriter, *Samson Supporting Evidence Found*, Church of God News (July 31, 2012), http://www.cogwriter.com/news/old-testament-history/samson-supporting-evidence-found/.

237   *See, e.g., TAU Archeologists Find Potential Evidence of Biblical Samson's Existence*, Tel Aviv University (Aug. 2, 2012), https://english.tau.ac.il/news/samson_seal.

238   *See Beit Shemesh*, Wikipedia (last edited Aug. 13, 2021) https://en.wikipedia.org/wiki/Beit_Shemesh.

239   *See* COGwriter, *Samson Supporting Evidence Found*, Church of God News (July 31, 2012), http://www.cogwriter.com/news/old-testament-history/samson-supporting-evidence-found/.

240   *See* Mark Oliver, *Were Samson's Superhuman Abilities Really That Far-fetched?*, Ancient Origins—Restructuring the Story of Humanity's Past (June 28 2018), https://www.ancient-origins.net/myths-legends-asia/samson-superhuman-abilities-really-far-fetched-0010282.

241   *See* COGwriter, *Samson Supporting Evidence Found*, Church of God News (July 31, 2012), http://www.cogwriter.com/news/old-testament-history/samson-supporting-evidence-found/.

242   *See* Mark Oliver, *Were Samson's Superhuman Abilities Really That Far-fetched?*, Ancient Origins—Restructuring the Story of Humanity's Past (June 28 2018), https://www.ancient-origins.net/myths-legends-asia/samson-superhuman-abilities-0010282.

243   *Id.*

244   *Id.*

245   *See* Judges 14:5 (written circa 1043 BC);

TAU Archeologists Find Potential Evidence of Biblical Samson's Existence, Tel Aviv University (Aug. 2, 2012), https://english.tau.ac.il/news/samson_seal.

246   *See* Mark Oliver, *Were Samson's Superhuman Abilities Really That Far-fetched?*, Ancient Origins—Restructuring the Story of Humanity's Past (June 28 2018), https://www.ancient-origins.net/myths-legends-asia/samson-superhuman-abilities-0010282.

247   *Id.*

248   Gath "was one of the five Philistine city-states, established in northeastern Philistia," whose "existence is confirmed by Egyptian inscriptions." "Philistia was a confederation of cities in the Southwest Levant." — The Levant is an approximate historical geographical term referring to a large area in the Eastern Mediterranean region of Western Asia. In its narrowest sense, it is equivalent to the historical region of Syria, which included present-day Syria, Lebanon, Jordan, Israel, Palestine and most of Turkey south-east of the middle Euphrates.

   See Gath (city), Wikipedia (last edited July10, 2021), https://en.wikipedia.org/wiki/Gath_(city);

   Philistia, Wikipedia (last edited August 1, 2021), https://en.wikipedia.org/wiki/Philistia;

   Levant, Wikipedia (last edited August 8, 2021), https://en.wikipedia.org/wiki/Levant?.

249   *Id.*

250   *See The Shiloh Excavations* (first published in the Winter 2005 issue of Bible and Spade), Nehemiah Communications, Associates for Biblical Research, https://biblearchaeology.org/research/judges-united-monarchy/3800-between-the-pillars-revisiting-samson-and-the-house-of-dagon.

251   *Id.*

252   *See, e.g.*, Genesis 10:15, 15:20, 23:3, 5, 7, 10, 16, 18, 20, 25:10, 49:32 (written 1450—1405 BC); Exodus 3:8, 17, 13:5, 23:23, 28, 33:2, 34:11 (written 1450–1405 BC); Numbers 13:29 (written 1450–1405 BC); Deuteronomy 7:1, 20:17 (written 1450–1405 BC); Joshua 3:10, 9:1, 11:3, 12:8 (written circa 1405–1385 BC); 1 Kings 10:29–11:2 (written circa 561–538 BC); 2 Chronicles 1:17 (written 450–430 BC).

253   *See* Genesis 10:15 (written 1450–2405 BC).

254   *See* Nehemiah 9:8 (written 445–400 BC).

255   *See Archaeologists are digging up bible stories: Photo Gallery of the 100 most incredible archeological objects – Introduction*, www.bible.ca/archeology/bible-archeology.htm.

256   *See* Paul L. Maier, *Biblical Archaeology: Factual Evidence to Support the Historicity of the Bible*, CRI (Mar. 30, 2009), https://www.equip.org/article/biblical-archaeology-factual-evidence-to-support-the-historicity-of-the-bible.

257   *See Archaeologists are digging up bible stories: Photo Gallery of the 100 most incredible archeological objects – Introduction*, www.bible.ca/archeology/bible-archeology.htm;

See also Paul L. Maier, *Biblical Archaeology: Factual Evidence to Support the Historicity of the Bible*, CRI (Mar. 30, 2009), https://www.equip.org/article/biblical-archaeology-factual-evidence-to-support-the-historicity-of-the-bible.

258   *Id.*

259   *See Archaeologists are digging up bible stories: Photo Gallery of the 100 most incredible archeological objects – Introduction*, www.bible.ca/archeology/bible-archeology.htm.

260   *See* Aharon Kempinski. *Hittites in the Bible: What Does Archaeology Say?*, Biblical Archaeology Review 5:5 (September/October 1979), BAS Library-Biblical Archaeology Society Online Archive, https://www.baslibrary.org/biblical-archaeology-review/5/5/3.

261   *See, e.g.,* 2 Samuel 7:4–29, 12:1–31 (written 931–722 BC); 1 Kings 1:1–53 (written circa 561–538 BC).

262   *See* Margaret Hunter, *15 Historical Proofs of the Bible*, Amazing Bible Timeline with World History (Apr. 29, 2013), https://amazingbibletimeline.com/blog/q9_historical_proof_bible/.

263   "It is thought that David ruled between 1010 and 970 BC."

    See Austin Cline, *Profile and Biography of David, Old Testament King*, Learn Religions (June 25, 2019), https://www.thoughtco.com/david-profile-and-biography-248832.

    See also 53 People in the Bible Confirmed Archaeologically, Bible History Daily (originally published 2014.), https://www.biblicalarchaeology.org/daily/people-cultures-in-the-bible/people-in-the-bible/50-people-in-the-bible-confirmed-archaeologically/#note01.

264   *See* Bible Archaeology Society Staff, *The Tel Dan Inscription: The First Historical Evidence of King David from the Bible*, Bible History Daily (Oct. 18, 2020), www.biblicalarchaeology.org/daily/biblical-artifacts/artifacts-and-the-bible/the-tel-dan-inscription-the-first-historical-evidence-of-the-king-david-bible-story.

265   *See* Margaret Hunter, *15 Historical Proofs of the Bible*, Amazing Bible Timeline with World History (Apr. 29, 2013), https://amazingbibletimeline.com/blog/q9_historical_proof_bible/.

266   *See* Cristian Violatti, *10 Archaeological Discoveries Consistent With Biblical Passages*, List Verse (Nov. 4, 2016), http://listverse.com/2016/11/04/10-archaeological-discoveries-consistent-with-biblical-passages/.

267   *See* Clifford Wilson, *Does Archaeology Support the Bible?*, Answers in Genesis, Chapter 25 (Jan. 24, 2008; last featured Aug. 27, 2014), https://answersingenesis.org/archaeology/does-archaeology-support-the-bible/.

268   *Id.*

269   *See* Joshua J. Mark, *Sargon II*, Ancient History Encyclopedia, (July 3, 2014), https://www.ancient.eu/Sargon_II/.

270   *See* Cristian Violatti, *10 Archaeological Discoveries Consistent With Biblical Passages*, List Verse (Nov. 4, 2016), http://listverse.com/2016/11/04/10-archaeological-discoveries-consistent-with-biblical-passages/.

271 *See* Paul L. Maier, *Biblical Archaeology: Factual Evidence to Support the Historicity of the Bible*, CRI (Mar. 30, 2009), https://www.equip.org/article/biblical-archaeology-factual-evidence-to-support-the-historicity-of-the-bible.

272 *See The Moabite Stone*, Bible History—Maps, Images, Archaeology, http://www.bible-history.com/resource/ff_mesha.htm.

273 *See* Paul L. Maier, *Biblical Archaeology: Factual Evidence to Support the Historicity of the Bible*, CRI (Mar. 30, 2009), https://www.equip.org/article/biblical-archaeology-factual-evidence-to-support-the-historicity-of-the-bible.

274 *Id.*

275 *See* Brian Windle, *King Uzziah: An Archaeological Biography*, Bible Archaeology Report (Aug. 7, 2020), https://biblearchaeologyreport.com/2020/08/07/king-uzziah-an-archaeological-biography/;

followed by the other citations; *53 People in the Bible Confirmed Archaeologically*, Bible History Daily (originally published in 2014.), https://www.biblicalarchaeology.org/daily/people-cultures-in-the-bible/people-in-the-bible/50-people-in-the-bible-confirmed-archaeologically/#note01;

Paul L. Maier, *Biblical Archaeology: Factual Evidence to Support the Historicity of the Bible*, CRI (Mar. 30, 2009), https://www.equip.org/article/biblical-archaeology-factual-evidence-to-support-the-historicity-of-the-bible/;

Uzziah Tablet Inscription, Bible History - Maps, Images, Archaeology, http://www.bible-history.com/archaeology/israel/uzziah-tablet.html.

276 *See, e.g.,* Joshua J. Mark, *Esarhaddon*, Ancient History Encyclopedia, (July 8, 2014), https://www.ancient.eu/Esarhaddon/;

Esarhaddon, Wikipedia (last edited Aug. 15, 2021), https://en.wikipedia.org/wiki/Esarhaddon.

277 *See, e.g.,* Shanika Gunaratna, *Ancient palace reportedly discovered under shrine destroyed by ISIS*, CBS News (Mar. 1, 2017), https://www.cbsnews.com/news/ancient-palace-reportedly-discovered-deep-under-shrine-demolished-by-isis/;

James Rogers, *Biblical king's palace uncovered beneath shrine destroyed by ISIS*, Fox News (Mar. 6, 2017), https://www.foxnews.com/science/biblical-kings-palace-uncovered-beneath-shrine-destroyed-by-isis;

Biblical king's palace uncovered beneath shrine destroyed by ISIS, End Times Headlines (Mar. 8, 2017), https://endtimeheadlines.org/2017/03/biblical-kings-palace-uncovered-beneath-shrine-destroyed-isis/.

278 *See 53 People in the Bible Confirmed Archaeologically*, Bible History Daily (originally published 2014.), https://www.biblicalarchaeology.org/daily/people-cultures-in-the-bible/people-in-the-bible/50-people-in-the-bible-confirmed-archaeologically/#note01 for a more detailed description of where they were confirmed.

279   First and Second Chronicles were written 450–430 BC

280   Jeremiah was written 627–570 BC.

281   Nehemiah was written 445–400 BC.

282   "The death of Sennacherib is recorded at Isaiah 37:38 (written 700-680 BC) and 2 Kings 19:37 (written circa 561–538 BC) and is confirmed in the records of Sennacherib's son, Esarhaddon."

      See Clifford Wilson, *Does Archaeology Support the Bible?*, Answers in Genesis (Jan. 24, 2008, last featured Aug. 27, 2014), Chapter 25, https://answersingenesis.org/archaeology/does-archaeology-support-the-bible/.

283   Daniel was written 536–530 BC.

284   Ezra was written 457–444 BC.

285   Esther was written 483–331 BC.

286   *See* Doug Powell, *Guide to Christian Apologetics* at 16, Holman Reference (Nashville, Tennessee © 2006 by Doug Powell).

287   *See* Ryan Nelson, *How Did the Apostles Die? What We Actually Know*, (Dec 17, 2019), https://overviewbible.com/how-did-the-apostles-die/.

288   *See* Matthew 10:2–4 (written 50–65 AD). See also Mark 3:14–19 (written 50–65 AD), Luke 6:13–16 (written 60–61 AD), and Acts 1:13–16 (written 62–70 AD).

289   *See* Ryan Nelson, *How Did the Apostles Die? What We Actually Know*, (Dec 17, 2019), https://overviewbible.com/how-did-the-apostles-die/.

290   Including by impaling, beheading, crucifixion, flaying, and being thrown to their deaths without denying that Jesus lived as the Bible said that he did and that he did the many miracles which the Bible described. They all died declaring that Jesus died and that they saw him alive afterwards.

291   *See* Discussion *infra.*

292   *See, e.g.,* David Snell, *How Did Each of the Original Twelve Apostles Die?*, Third Hour (Apr. 28, 2018), https://thirdhour.org/blog/faith/scripture/new-testament/original-apostles-deaths/ (citing National Geographic).

293   *See* Ryan Nelson, *How Did the Apostles Die? What We Actually Know*, (Dec 17, 2019), https://overviewbible.com/how-did-the-apostles-die/;

      Who were the 12 disciples?, Bible Info, https://www.bibleinfo.com/en/questions/who-were-twelve-disciples.

      See also Jack Wellman, *How Did The 12 Apostles Die? A Bible Study*, What Christians Want to Know (Prison Fellowship), https://www.whatchristianswanttoknow.com/how-did-the-12-apostles-die-a-bible-study.

294   *See, e.g.,* David Snell, *How Did Each of the Original Twelve Apostles Die?*, Third Hour (Apr. 28, 2018), https://thirdhour.org/blog/faith/scripture/new-testament/original-apostles-deaths/ (citing National Geographic).

295   *See Who were the 12 disciples?*, Bible Info,
https://www.bibleinfo.com/en/questions/who-were-twelve-disciples.

296   *Id.*

297   *See* David Snell, *How Did Each of the Original Twelve Apostles Die?*, Third Hour Apr. 28,
2018), https://thirdhour.org/blog/faith/scripture/new-testament/original-apostles-deaths/.

298   *See, e.g.,* David Pleacher, *Do You Know How The Apostles Died?*,
https://www.bing.com/search?q=David+Pleacher+and+Do+You+Know+How+The+
Apostles+Died.

299   *See Who were the 12 disciples?*, Bible Info,
https://www.bibleinfo.com/en/questions/who-were-twelve-disciples.

300   *See* Matthew 10: 2–4 (written 50–65 AD).

301   *See* Ryan Nelson, *How Did the Apostles Die? What We Actually Know,* (Dec 17, 2019),
https://overviewbible.com/how-did-the-apostles-die/.

302   *See* Acts 12:1–2 (written 62–70 AD).

     See also Jack Zavada, *Meet the Apostle James: First to Die for Jesus,* Learn Religions
(updated Dec. 7, 2020), https://www.learnreligions.com/profile-of-apostle-james-701062.

303   *See* Acts 12:1–2 (ESV) (written 62–70 AD).

304   *See* Acts 12:1–2 (written 62–70 AD).

     See also Phillip J. Long, *Acts 12:1-2—Why Did Herod Kill James?*, Reading Acts (Feb. 19,
2013), https://readingacts.com/2013/02/19/acts-121-2-why-did-herod-kill-james/;

     Lesser Known People of the Bible, journeyonline.org,
https://journeyonline.org/lessons/james-in-the-new-testament/?series=8751.

305   *See, e.g.,* Acts 12:1–2 (ESV) (written 62–70 AD).

     See also Phillip J. Long, *Acts 12:1-2—Why Did Herod Kill James?*, Reading Acts (Feb. 19,
2013), https://readingacts.com/2013/02/19/acts-121-2-why-did-herod-kill-james/.

306   *See, e.g., Do You Know How the 13 Apostles Died?*, http://www.bibleone.net/apostles.htm.

     See also Eusebius of Caesarea, Christian History,
https://www.christianitytoday.com/history/people/scholarsandscientists/eusebius-of-
caesarea.html;

     Eusebius, Wikipedia (last edited Aug. 27, 2021), https://en.wikipedia.org/wiki/Eusebius;

     The Editors of Encyclopaedia Britannica, *Caesarea* (Alternative Titles: *Ḥorbat Qesari,
Caesarea Maritima, Caesarea Palestinae, Strato's Tower, Straton's Tower*), Britannica
(article added to new online database July 20, 1998),
https://www.britannica.com/place/Caesarea.

307   *See, e.g.,* Ryan Nelson, *How Did the Apostles Die? What We Actually Know,* (Dec 17, 2019), https://overviewbible.com/how-did-the-apostles-die/.

308   *See e.g.,* The Editors of Encyclopaedia Britannica, *Saint James - apostle, the Lord's brother* (alternative title: *the Lord's Brother James*), Britannica (last updated: Jan 1, 2021), https://www.britannica.com/biography/Saint-James-the-Lords-brother;

Ryan Nelson, *How Did the Apostles Die? What We Actually Know,* (Dec 17, 2019), https://overviewbible.com/how-did-the-apostles-die/.

309   *See, e.g.,* Paul Pavao, *The Death of James the Just, Brother of Jesus Christ,* Christian for Everyman, Greatest Stories Ever Told. 2014 (accessed Feb. 20, 2021) https://www.christian-history.org/death-of-james.html.

310   *Id.*

311   *See* Matthew 4:5 (written 50–65 AD); Luke 4:9 (written 60–61 AD).

See also Margaret Hunter, *When and how did the Twelve Apostles die?,* Amazing Bible Timeline with World History (Apr. 29, 2013), https://amazingbibletimeline.com/blog/q6_apostles_die.

312   *See e.g.,* Margaret Hunter, *15 Historical Proofs of the Bible,* Amazing Bible Timeline with World History (Apr. 29, 2013), https://amazingbibletimeline.com/blog/q9_historical_proof_bible/;

Paul Pavao, *The Death of James the Just, Brother of Jesus Christ,* Christian for Everyman, Greatest Stories Ever Told. 2014 (accessed Feb. 20, 2021) https://www.christian-history.org/death-of-james.html.

313   *See* Matthew 10:3 (written 50–65 AD).

314   *See, e.g.,* Ryan Nelson, *How Did the Apostles Die? What We Actually Know,* (Dec 17, 2019), https://overviewbible.com/how-did-the-apostles-die/.

315   *See* Ryan Nelson, *Who Was James Son of Alphaeus? The Beginner's Guide,* (Sept 11, 2019), https://overviewbible.com/james-son-of-alphaeus/.

316   *See, e.g., The Bible Is Unique #11 (External Evidence Test –RamseyTests),* https://www.josh.org/wp-content/uploads/External-Evidence-Test—-Ramsey-Tests.pdf.

317   *See, e.g., William Mitchell Ramsay,* Wikipedia (last edited Oct. 25, 2020), https://en.wikipedia.org/wiki/William_Mitchell_Ramsay.

318   *See, e.g.,* Ronald Cram, *Top NT Archaeological Finds,* http://factbridge.org/sites/default/files/inline-files/Top-NT-Archaeological-Finds.pdf at No. 5 (citing http://bit.ly/PhrygianAltar).

319   *See* Ryan Nelson, *How Did the Apostles Die? What We Actually Know,* (Dec 17, 2019), https://overviewbible.com/how-did-the-apostles-die/.

320   *See* Jack Wellman, *How Did The 12 Apostles Die? A Bible Study,* What Christians Want to Know (Prison Fellowship), https://www.whatchristianswanttoknow.com/how-did-the-12-apostles-die-a-bible-study.

321   *Id.*

     See also David Pleacher, *Do You Know How The Apostles Died?*,
https://www.pleacher.com/forwards/religion/apostle.html.

322   *See* Acts 7:58, 8:1–3, 9:1–29, 22:3–5, 26:9–11 (written 62–70 AD).

323   *See* Acts 9:3–9 (written 62–70 AD).

324   *See, e.g. Who Wrote Most of the New Testament?* (May 3, 2014),
https://apologika.blogspot.com/2014/05/who-wrote-most-of-new-testament.html.

325   *See, e.g.,* Melissa Petruzzello, *St. Paul's Contributions to the New Testament*, Britannica,
https://www.britannica.com/list/st-pauls-contributions-to-the-new-testament.

326   *See e.g.,* David Pleacher, *Do You Know How The Apostles Died?*,
https://www.pleacher.com/forwards/religion/apostle.html.

327   *See* Bethany Pyle, *How Did the Apostle Paul Die?*, Christianity.com (originally published Aug. 05, 2019),
https://www.christianity.com/wiki/people/how-did-the-apostle-paul-die.html.

     See also How did the apostle Paul die?, Got Questions,
https://www.gotquestions.org/how-did-Paul-die.html.

328   *See* Ryan Nelson, *How Did the Apostles Die? What We Actually Know,* (Dec 17, 2019),
https://overviewbible.com/how-did-the-apostles-die/.

329   *See, e.g.,* Margaret Hunter, *15 Historical Proofs of the Bible*, Amazing Bible Timeline with World History (Apr. 2019, 2013),
https://amazingbibletimeline.com/blog/q9_historical_proof_bible/;

     Ryan Nelson, *How Did the Apostles Die? What We Actually Know*, (Dec 17, 2019),
https://overviewbible.com/how-did-the-apostles-die/.

330   *See* Margaret Hunter, *15 Historical Proofs of the Bible*, Amazing Bible Timeline with World History (Apr. 29, 2013),
https://amazingbibletimeline.com/blog/q9_historical_proof_bible/.

331   *See* Ryan Nelson, *How Did the Apostles Die? What We Actually Know*, (Dec 17, 2019),
https://overviewbible.com/how-did-the-apostles-die/.

332   *See* David Snell, *How Did Each of the Original Twelve Apostles Die?*, Third Hour (Apr. 28, 2018),
https://thirdhour.org/blog/faith/scripture/new-testament/original-apostles-deaths/.

333   *Id.*

334   *See, e.g., Philip the Apostle*, Wikipedia (last edited June 12, 2021),
https://en.wikipedia.org/wiki/Philip_the_Apostle;

     Mary Jane Chaignot, *Bible Study-Bible Characters and Themes—Philip*, Bible Wise,
https://www.biblewise.com/bible_study/characters/philip.php;

Mark Cartwright, *Phrygia*, Ancient History Encyclopedia (published Sept. 5, 2019), https://www.ancient.eu/phrygia/.

335   *See, e.g., Philip the Apostle*, Wikipedia (last edited June 12, 2021), https://en.wikipedia.org/wiki/Philip_the_Apostle;

Mary Jane Chaignot, *Bible Study–Bible Characters and Themes-Philip*, Bible Wise, https://www.biblewise.com/bible_study/characters/philip.php.

336   *See, e.g.,* Thomas J. Craughwell, *Archaeologists discover the tomb of St. Philip the Apostle*, Our Sunday Visitor (Aug. 17, 2011), https://www.osvnews.com/2011/08/17/archaeologists-discover-the-tomb-of-st-philip-the-apostle/.

337   *See* Jack Wellman, *How Did the 12 Apostles Die? A Bible Study*, What Christians Want to Know (Prison Fellowship), https://www.whatchristianswanttoknow.com/how-did-the-12-apostles-die-a-bible-study/.

338   *See* Mary Jane Chaignot, *Bible Study-Bible Characters and Themes-Philip*, Bible Wise, https://www.biblewise.com/bible_study/characters/philip.php.

339   *See* Ryan Nelson, *How Did the Apostles Die? What We Actually Know*, (Dec 17, 2019), https://overviewbible.com/how-did-the-apostles-die/.

340   (Dec 17, 2019), https://overviewbible.com/how-did-the-apostles-die/#:~:text.

341   *See also, e.g.,* Nina Garsoïan, *Moses of Chorene* (cross reference *"Movsēs XorenacʻI"*), Encyclopaedia Iranica (originally published: Jan. 1, 2000), https://iranicaonline.org/articles/moses-chorene-crossref;

Moses of Chorene, Livius.org-Articles on ancient history (modified on 12 October 2020), https://www.livius.org/articles/person/moses-of-chorene/;

Kevin Knight, Editor, *Moses of Chorene*, New Advent, https://www.newadvent.org/cathen/10598a.htm.

The History of Armenia is also known as History of Armenia Major.

Compare Moses of Chorene (created 2019; last modified Oct. 12, 2020), Livius.org, https://www.livius.org/articles/person/moses-of-chorene/;

Moses of Chorene (Alternate title: *Moses Chorenensis*), Catholic Online (Copyright 2021 Catholic Online), https://www.catholic.org/encyclopedia/view.php?id=8221.

342   *See also, e.g.,* Alexander Mikaberidze and George Nikoladze, *Caucasian Iberia*, Colchis and the Eastern Kingdom of Iberia, http://realhistoryww.com/world_history/ancient/Misc/Colchis_East_Iberia/Colchis_and_East_Iberia.htm.

343   *See also, e.g.,* Jacobus de Voragine, *The Golden Legend: Readings on the Saints* (Princeton University Press—2012), https://b-ok.cc/book/2642016/156cf3.

344   *See also, e.g.,* The Editors of Encyclopaedia Britannica, *Justus Lipsius*, Belgian scholar (alternative title: *Joest Lips*), Britannica (anniversary information added Oct. 14, 2020), https://www.britannica.com/biography/Justus-Lipsius.

345   All six points mentioned in Ryan Nelson, *How Did the Apostles Die? What We Actually Know, Who Was Simon the Zealot?* (Aug. 7–Dec 17, 2019), https://overviewbible.com/how-did-the-apostles-die/.

346   *See* David Snell, *How Did Each of the Original Twelve Apostles Die?*, Third Hour (Apr. 28, 2018), https://thirdhour.org/blog/faith/scripture/new-testament/original-apostles-deaths/.

347   *See* Ryan Nelson, *How Did the Apostles Die? What We Actually Know*, (Dec 17, 2019), https://overviewbible.com/how-did-the-apostles-die/.

348   *See* Jack Wellman, *How Did The 12 Apostles Die? A Bible Study*, What Christians Want to Know (Prison Fellowship), https://www.whatchristianswanttoknow.com/how-did-the-12-apostles-die-a-bible-study.

349   *See* David Snell, *How Did Each of the Original Twelve Apostles Die?*, Third Hour (Apr. 28, 2018), https://thirdhour.org/blog/faith/scripture/new-testament/original-apostles-deaths/;

    Jack Wellman, *How Did The 12 Apostles Die? A Bible Study*, What Christians Want to Know (Prison Fellowship), https://www.whatchristianswanttoknow.com/how-did-the-12-apostles-die-a-bible-study.

350   *See* John 20:25 (written 80–90 AD).

351   *See* John 20: 26—28 (written 80–90 AD).

352   *See* Margaret Hunter, *15 Historical Proofs of the Bible*, Amazing Bible Timeline with World History (Apr. 29, 2013), https://amazingbibletimeline.com/blog/q9_historical_proof_bible/.

353   *Id.*

354   *See* Ryan Nelson, *How Did the Apostles Die? What We Actually Know* (Dec 17, 2019), https://overviewbible.com/how-did-the-apostles-die/.

355   *See, e.g., John the Apostle,* Wikipedia (last edited Feb. 17, 2021), https://en.wikipedia.org/wiki/John_the_Apostle.

356   *See, e.g.,* See Margaret Hunter, *15 Historical Proofs of the Bible*, Amazing Bible Timeline with World History (Apr. 29, 2013), https://amazingbibletimeline.com/blog/q9_historical_proof_bible/;

    Genelle Austin-Lett and Mary Jane Chaignot, *Boiled in Oil*, Bible Wise, https://www.biblewise.com/bible_study/questions/boiled-in-oil.php.

357   *See, e.g., Ephesus,* Wikipedia (last edited on Feb. 20, 2021), https://en.wikipedia.org/wiki/Ephesus.

358   *See, e.g.,* Gary William Poole, Assoc. Ed., *Flavius Josephus-Jewish priest, scholar, and historian* (alternative title: *Joseph ben Matthias*), Britannica (last updated: Jan 1, 2021), https://www.britannica.com/biography/Flavius-Josephus.

359   *Id.*

360   *See* William Whiston, Translator, *Josephus' Description of Jesus*, Frontline (The Antiquities of the Jews, Book 18, Chapter 3, from The Works of Josephus, Hendrickson Publishers, 1987), https://www.pbs.org/wgbh/pages/frontline/shows/religion/maps/primary/josephusjesus.html.

361   *See* William Whiston, Translator, *The Antiquities of the Jews* by Flavius Josephus (last updated: Aug. 9, 2017), https://www.gutenberg.org/files/2848/2848-h/2848-h.htm.

      See also James Tabor, *Josephus on James*, The Jewish Roman World of Jesus (Josephus, *Antiquities* Book 20: chapter 9), https://pages.uncc.edu/james-tabor/ancient-judaism/josephus-james/.

362   *See, e.g., Lucian*, Wikipedia (last edited Feb. 20, 2021), https://en.wikipedia.org/wiki/Lucian.

363   *See Suetonius*, All About the Journey (© 2002–2021, AllAboutTheJourney.org), https://www.allaboutthejourney.org/suetonius.htm.

364   *See, e.g.,* Roberts-Donaldson, Translator, *Mara Bar-Serapion*, Early Christian Writings, http://www.earlychristianwritings.com/mara.html.

      See also Don Stewart, *What Do Early Non-Christian Writings Say about Jesus?*, Blue Letter Bible, https://www.blueletterbible.org/faq/don_stewart/don_stewart_185.cfm.

365   *See* Don Stewart, *What Do Early Non-Christian Writings Say about Jesus?*, Blue Letter Bible, https://www.blueletterbible.org/faq/don_stewart/don_stewart_185.cfm.

366   *See, e.g.,* William Whiston, Translator, *Letters of Pliny the Younger and the Emperor Trajan*, Frontline (from the Works of Josephus, Hendrickson Publishers, 1987), https://www.pbs.org/wgbh/pages/frontline/shows/religion/maps/primary/pliny.html;

      #102: Pliny's Letter to Trajan, Christian History Institute (introduction by Stephen Tomkins. Edited and prepared for the web by Dan Graves), https://christianhistoryinstitute.org/study/module/pliny.

367   *See, e.g.*, The Editors of Encyclopaedia Britannica, *Pliny the Younger - Roman author* (alternative title: *Gaius Plinius Caecilius Secundus*), Britannica (modified July 03, 2019), https://www.britannica.com/biography/Pliny-the-Younger.

368   William Whiston, Translator, *Letters of Pliny the Younger and the Emperor Trajan*, Frontline (from the Works of Josephus, Hendrickson Publishers, 1987), https://www.pbs.org/wgbh/pages/frontline/shows/religion/maps/primary/pliny.html.

      See also Don Stewart, *What Do Early Non-Christian Writings Say about Jesus?*, Blue Letter Bible, https://www.blueletterbible.org/faq/don_stewart/don_stewart_185.cfm.

369   *See* William Whiston, Translator, *Letters of Pliny the Younger and the Emperor Trajan*, Frontline (from the Works of Josephus, Hendrickson Publishers, 1987), https://www.pbs.org/wgbh/pages/frontline/shows/religion/maps/primary/pliny.html.

370   *See, e.g., Book Ten, Letter 96 to the Emperor Trajan*, http://www.vroma.org/~hwalker/Pliny/Pliny10-096-E.html.

371   *See, e.g.,* Vocab Malone, *Suetonius on "Chrestus"-#4 in a Series on Non-Biblical References to Jesus,* Street Apologist: the blog of Vocab Malone, host of Urban Theologian Radio, https://streetapologist.wordpress.com/2013/09/22/suetonius-on-chrestus/.

372   *See* Alfred John Church and William Jackson Brodribb, Translators, *The Annals by Tacitus* (written 109 AD), Book XV, http://classics.mit.edu/Tacitus/annals.11.xv.html.

       See also Don Stewart, *What Do Early Non-Christian Writings Say about Jesus?-Cornelius Tacitus (Early Second Century),* Blue Letter Bible, https://www.blueletterbible.org/faq/don_stewart/don_stewart_185.cfm.

373   *See* Luke 3:1 (written 60–61).

374   *See* Matthew 27:2 (written 60–61).

375   *See* Luke 23:2 (written 60–61).

376   *See, e.g.,* https://www.reasonablefaith.org/question-answer/P70/thallus-on-the-darkness-at-noon;

       See also Don Stewart, *What Do Early Non-Christian Writings Say about Jesus?,* Blue Letter Bible, https://www.blueletterbible.org/faq/don_stewart/don_stewart_185.cfm.

377   *See Thallus (historian),* Wikipedia (last edited Feb. 21, 2021), https://en.wikipedia.org/wiki/Thallus_(historian).

378   *See, e.g.,* Don Stewart, *What Do Early Non-Christian Writings Say about Jesus?,* Blue Letter Bible, https://www.blueletterbible.org/faq/don_stewart/don_stewart_185.cfm.

379   *See, e.g.,,* Sextus Julius Africanus, Wikipedia (last edited Dec. 30, 2020), https://en.wikipedia.org/wiki/Sextus_Julius_Africanus;

       Jason Colavito, *Sextus Julius Africanus,* The Chronography (translation in the *Ante-Nicene Christian Library—1869*), http://www.jasoncolavito.com/julius-africanus-chronography.html.

380   *See* The Editors of Encyclopaedia Britannica, *Sextus Julius Africanus, Christian historian,* Britannica (added to new online data base July 20, 1998), https://www.britannica.com/biography/Sextus-Julius-Africanus.

381   *See* George Syncellus 9th Century AD translation of Julius Africanus quote of Thallus, *Thallus,* Religions Wiki (last edited Oct. 17 2016), https://religions.wiki/index.php/Thallus.

       See also Jason Colavito, *Sextus Julius Africanus,* The Chronography (translation in the *Ante-Nicene Christian Library—1869*), http://www.jasoncolavito.com/julius-africanus-chronography.html;

       Nonbiblical Accounts of New Testament Events and/or People, Truediscipleship (guest article—Sept. 5, 2021), https://truediscipleship.com/nonbiblical-accounts-of-new-testament-events-andor-people/.

382   *See, e.g.,* William Lane Craig, *#160 Thallus on the Darkness at Noon,* Reasonable Faith (May 20, 2010), https://www.reasonablefaith.org/writings/question-answer/thallus-on-the-darkness-at-noon.

383   *See* Matthew 26:2 (written 50–65 AD); Mark 14:1–2,12 (written 50–65 AD); Luke 22:1–2, 7 (written 60–61 AD); John 13:1 (written 80–90 AD).

384   *See* Danny R. Faulkner, *Did the Moon Appear as Blood on the Night of the Crucifixion?,* Answers in Genesis (Feb. 12, 2014), https://answersingenesis.org/jesus/crucifixion/did-the-moon-appear-as-blood-on-the-night-of-the-crucifixion/.

       See also Aron Moss, *Why Is Passover on a Full Moon?,* Chabad.org, https://www.chabad.org/holidays/passover/pesach_cdo/aid/4250850/jewish/Why-Is-Passover-on-a-Full-Moon.htm;

       When is Passover 2022? Learn What Time it Starts and Ends, 18 Doors, https://18doors.org/When_is_Passover_Anyway_A_Guide_to_Jewish_Time/? ("Passover… is tied to the phases of the sun and the moon {and] "will always begin on a full moon in the spring").

385   *See* Don Stewart, *What Do Early Non-Christian Writings Say about Jesus?,* Blue Letter Bible, https://www.blueletterbible.org/faq/don_stewart/don_stewart_185.cfm (citing Joseph Klausner, *Jesus of Nazareth,* London: Collier-Macmillan, 1929, at p. 34)

386   *See About Don Stewart,* Educating Our World https://educatingourworld.com/.

387   *See* Don Stewart, *What Do Early Non-Christian Writings Say about Jesus?,* Blue Letter Bible, https://www.blueletterbible.org/faq/don_stewart/don_stewart_185.cfm.

388   *See Execution of Yeshu ha Notzri on the Eve of Passover - Talmud, Sanhedrin 43a,* Yeshu ha-Notzri : ירצונה ושי, The Historical Jesus the Nazarene in the 1st Century Jewish Tradition, י- (May 11, 2017) (quoting *Talmud Sanhedrin 43a*), https://yeshuhanotzri.blogspot.com/2016/02/execution-of-yeshu-ha-notzri-on-eve-of.html.

389   *See* Don Stewart, *What Do Early Non-Christian Writings Say about Jesus?,* Blue Letter Bible, https://www.blueletterbible.org/faq/don_stewart/don_stewart_185.cfm.

390   *See* Matthew 3:1 (written 50–65 AD); Mark 1: 1–4 (written 50–65 AD); Luke 3:1–4 (written 60–61 AD); John 1:6—7, 19–34 (written 80-90 AD).

391   *See* Matthew 3:1–17, 11:1–18, 17:11–13, 21:32 (written 50–65 AD); Mark 1:1–11, 14–15, 2:18, 6:14, 17–29, 8:27–28 (written 50–65 AD); Luke 1:5–25, 36, 39—42, 57–66, 76–80, 3:1–22, 7:20, 24 –33 (written 60–61 AD); John 1:6–8, 19–34, 3:22–36, 10:40–41 (written 80–90 AD); Acts 19:3–4 (written 62–70 AD).

392   *See* Deuteronomy 18:15 (written 1450–1405 BC); Isaiah 40:3 (ESV) (written 740–680 BC); Malachi 3:1 4:5–6 (written 433–424 BC).

393   *See, e.g.,* Gary William Poole, Assoc. Ed., *Flavius Josephus-Jewish priest, scholar, and historian* (alternative title: *Joseph ben Matthias*), Britannica (last updated: Jan 1, 2021), https://www.britannica.com/biography/Flavius-Josephus.

394   *See, e.g.,* Matthew 14:1–1 (written 50–65 AD).

395   *See, e.g.*, Gary William Poole, Assoc. Ed., *Flavius Josephus-Jewish priest, scholar, and historian* (alternative title: *Joseph ben Matthias*), Britannica (last updated: Jan 1, 2021), https://www.britannica.com/biography/Flavius-Josephus.

396   *See* Matthew 26:3–4, 57–65 (written 50–65 AD); Luke 3:2 (written 60–61 AD); John 11:45–57, 18:13–14, 19–24, 28 (written 80–90 AD).

397   *See* Paul L. Maier, *Biblical Archaeology: Factual Evidence to Support the Historicity of the Bible*, CRI (Mar. 30, 2009), www.equip.org/article/biblical-archaeology-factual-evidence-to-support-the-historicity-of-the-bible/.

      See also Ronald Cram, *Top NT Archaeological Finds*, Factbridge, http://factbridge.org/sites/default/files/inline-files/Top-NT-Archaeological-Finds.pdf at No. 9 (citing http://bit.ly/CaiaphasOssuary).

398   *See, e.g.,* Matthew 27:2 (written 50–65 AD); Mark 15:1 (written 50–65 AD); Luke 3:1 (written 60–61 AD); John 18:38 (written 80–90 AD); Acts 4:27 (written 62–70 AD); 1 Timothy 1:16 (written 62–64 AD).

399   *See, e.g.,* Rusty Russel, *Fallen Empires-The Pilate Inscription*, Bible History Online, https://www.bible-history.com/empires/pilate.html;

      Doug Powell, *Guide to Christian Apologetics at 19*, Holman Reference (Nashville, Tennessee © 2006 by Doug Powell).

400   *See, e.g.,* The Editors of Encyclopaedia Britannica, *Pontius Pilate, governor of Judea* (alternative title: *Marcus Pontius Pilatus*), Britannica (top questions updated—May 16, 2019), https://www.britannica.com/biography/Pontius-Pilate.

401   *See Mount Gerizim*, Wikipedia (last edited Jan. 13, 2021), https://en.wikipedia.org/wiki/Mount_Gerizim;

      The Editors of Encyclopaedia Britannica , *Nāblus, city—West Bank* (alternative titles: *Flavia Neapolis, Julia Neapolis, Nabulus, Neapolis*), Britannica (article revised and updated, May 18, 2008, Laura Etheredge) https://www.britannica.com/place/Nablus.

402   *See, e.g., Nablus*, Wikipedia (last edited Feb. 18, 2021), https://en.wikipedia.org/wiki/Nablus.

403   *See, e.g.,* Matt Slick, *The writings of Josephus mention many biblical people and places*, Christian Apologetics and Research Ministry (CARM) (Dec 7, 2008), https://carm.org/questions/about-doctrine/writings-josephus-mention-many-biblical-people-and-places.

      See also Pontius Pilate (4), Livius.org—Articles on ancient history (last modified April 21, 2020), http://www.livius.org/articles/person/pontius-pilate/pontius-pilate-4/.

404   Tacitus reported in his Annals of Christ having suffered the extreme penalty during the reign of Tiberius at the hands of Pilate.

      See Margaret Hunter, *15 Historical Proofs of the Bible*, Amazing Bible Timeline with World History (Apr. 29, 2013), https://amazingbibletimeline.com/blog/q9_historical_proof_bible/.

See also Jewish Rabbinical writings from what is known as the Tannaitic period, between 70 AD and 200 AD; for example, Sanhedrin 43a which described Jesus' hanging on Passover eve.

See Margaret Hunter, *15 Historical Proofs of the Bible*, Amazing Bible Timeline with World History (Apr. 29, 2013), https://amazingbibletimeline.com/blog/q9_historical_proof_bible/.

405   *See* Rusty Russel, *Fallen Empires - The Pilate Inscription*, Bible History Online, https://www.bible-history.com/empires/pilate.html;

Daniel Peterson, *The 'Pilate Stone' in Israel's Caesarea-by-the-Sea*, Deseret News (May 3, 2018), https://www.deseret.com/2018/5/3/20644446/the-pilate-stone-in-israel-s-caesarea-by-the-sea?;

Ronald Cram, *Top NT Archaeological Finds* at No. 17, Factbridge, http://factbridge.org/sites/default/files/inline-files/Top-NT-Archaeological-Finds.pdf (citing http://bit.ly/PilotStoneInscription).

406   *See, e.g., Caesarea Maritima*, Wikipedia (last edited Feb. 9, 2021), https://en.wikipedia.org/wiki/Caesarea_Maritima.

407   *See, e.g.,* Raj Richard, *Exciting Archeological Discoveries Validating the Bible*, Reasoned Musings (June 1, 2015), http://rajkumarrichard.blogspot.com/2015/06/exciting-archeological-discoveries.html.

408   *Id.*;

Ronald Cram, *Top NT Archaeological Finds* at No. 17, Factbridge, http://factbridge.org/sites/default/files/inline-files/Top-NT-Archaeological-Finds.pdf.

409   *Id.*

410   *Id.*

411   *See* Ronald Cram, *Top NT Archaeological Finds* at No. 27, Factbridge, http://factbridge.org/sites/default/files/inline-files/Top-NT-Archaeological-Finds.pdf.

412   *See, e.g., Gallio Inscription-Delphi Inscription*, Vici.org (added and last updated by Elżbieta on Sept. 19, 2017), https://vici.org/vici/44673/.

413   *See, e.g.,* Ronald Cram, *Top NT Archaeological Finds* at No. 5, Factbridge, http://factbridge.org/sites/de-fault/files/inline-files/Top-NT-Archaeological-Finds.pdf (citing http://bit.ly/PhrygianAltar).

See also Titus Kennedy, *The Gallio Inscription*, Drive Thru History (July 14, 2020), https://drivethruhistory.com/the-gallio-inscription/;

Delphi Inscription, Wikipedia (last edited Jan. 7, 2021), https://en.wikipedia.org/wiki/Delphi_Inscription.

414   *See, e.g., Historical Evidence for Quirinius & the Census*, Bible Believer's Archaeology (Copyright © 2021), vol. 3 excerpt, http://www.biblehistory.net/newsletter/quirinius.htm.

415   *See, e.g., When was Publius Quirinius governor of Syria?—Census in Luke 2:2*, NeverThirsty (Copyright © Like The Master Ministries), https://www.neverthirsty.org/bible-qa/qa-archives/question/when-was-publius-quirinius-governor;

Bryan Windle, *Quirinius: An Archaeological Biography*, Bible Archaeology Report (Dec. 19, 2019), https://biblearchaeologyreport.com/2019/12/19/quirinius-an-archaeological-biography/.

416   *See, e.g., Historical Evidence for Quirinius*, Bible Believers Archaeology (Copyright © 2021), vol. 3, http://www.biblehistory.net/newsletter/cyrenius.htm;

See also Ronald Cram, *Top NT Archaeological Finds* at No. 26, http://fact-bridge.org/sites/default/files/inline-files/Top-NT-Archaeological-Finds.pdf (citing http://bit.ly/-1LF4PE6).

417   *See* Bryan Windle, *Quirinius: An Archaeological Biography*, Bible Archaeology Report (Dec. 19, 2019), https://biblearchaeologyreport.com/2019/12/19/quirinius-an-archaeological-biography/.

418   *See, e.g.*, Miguel Angel, *Lysanias, Ruler of Abilene*, Bible 7 Evidence, http://bible7evidence.blogspot.com/2014/10/lysanias-ruler-of-abilene.html.

419   *See e.g., Project History—History of the Dig Site—Abila*, John Brown University, https://www.jbu.edu/abila/history/.

420   *See e.g.*, Miguel Angel, *Lysanias, Ruler of Abilene*, Bible 7 Evidence, http://bible7evidence.blogspot.com/2014/10/lysanias-ruler-of-abilene.html.

421   *See, e.g., Lysanias*, BiblicalTraining, https://www.biblicaltraining.org/library/lysanias;

Bill Wilson, Compiler, *The Best of Josh McDowell, A Ready Defense* (Nashville, Tenn., Thomas Nelson Publishers, copyright 1993) at 109–110;

Ronald Cram, *Top NT Archaeological Finds*, http://factbridge.org/sites/default/files/inline-files/Top-NT-Archaeological-Finds.pdf.

422   *See* Acts 28:1 (written 62–70 AD).

423   *See, e.g., Malta and the Apostle Paul*, Bible Study, https://www.biblestudy.org/apostlepaul/malta.html.

424   *Id.*

425   *See, e.g., History of Malta—Roman Rule*, Wikipedia (last edited Jan. 26, 2021), https://en.wikipedia.org/wiki/History_of_Malta#Roman_rule.

According to David Pafford, who attended Fuller Theological Seminary in Pasadena, California and holds a Masters in Theology and a M.B.A. from William Woods University, is in ministry for and was elected a National General Presbyter for the Assemblies of God (*see* David Pafford, *About David Pafford*, David Pafford Online, http://davidpafford.com/about-david-pafford/).

The theory is sometimes expressed that they had come, not to Malta (Sicula Melita) but to Melita Illyrica (Mljet) in the Adriatic Gulf. Nonetheless, according to Williams, the theory rests on too narrow a definition of the Sea of Adria, "which by the tenth century AD, when the theory was first supposed, was limited, as now, to the sea between Italy and the Balkans."[7] In any case, Williams believes J.S. Smith, he postulates that Mljet is too far from the probable route of the ship. Smith calculated that it is about 475 nautical miles from Fair Havens. He assumed that if the wind direction was east by north east and the average rate of drift of a large ship on the starboard tack, which is approximately one and a half miles per hour, that the ship would be less than three miles from the entrance of Saint Paul's Bay. This according to his calculation would be on the midnight of the 14th day. [8] Lastly, Marshall adds that at the entry of the bay is a shoal, now sunk below its level in ancient times, which could well be where the vessel ran aground.[9] From studying both theories, I believe in the overwhelming conclusion that the shipwreck happened on Malta (Sicula Melita).

David Pafford, *Acts 28, Paul on Malta*, http://davidpafford.com/acts-28-paul-on-malta/.

426 *See, e.g., Malta and the Apostle Paul*, Bible Study, https://www.biblestudy.org/apostlepaul/malta.html;

Acts 27 (written 62–70 AD).

427 *See* Acts 28:7 (written 62–70 AD).

428 *See, e.g., Verse-by-Verse Bible Commentary, Acts 28:7*, StudyLight.Org, https://www.studylight.org/commentary/acts/28-7.html (citing Coffman's Commentaries on the Bible, in turn citing G. H. C. MacGregor, *The Interpreter's Bible* (New York: Abingdon Press, 1954), Vol. IX, p. 343.

George Hogarth Carnaby MacGregor a/k/a G. H. C. MacGregor lived from 1892–1963 AD, was the Professor of Divinity and Biblical Criticism from 1933 to 1963 at Glasgow University in Scotland and was responsible for 53 works in 270 publications in 3 languages and 3,048 library holdings.

See, e.g., George MacGregor, The University of Glasgow Story (University of Glasgow), https://www.universitystory.gla.ac.uk/biography/?id=WH2235&type=P;

George Hogarth Carnaby MacGregor, BibleTruth, https://bibletruthpublishers.com/george-hogarth-carnaby-macgregor-collections/lucl155;

Online Books by G. H. C. Macgregor, The Online Books Page, http://onlinebooks.library.upenn.edu/webbin/book/lookupname?key=Macgregor%2C%20 G.%20H.%20C.%20%28George%20Hogarth%20Carnaby%29%2C%201864-1900.

429 *See, e.g., James Strong and John McClintock*, Publius, McClintock and Strong Biblical Cyclopedia, *The Cyclopedia of Biblical, Theological, and Ecclesiastical Literature* (Haper and Brothers Publishers, N.Y., 1880), https://www.biblicalcyclopedia.com/P/publius.html (citing Lewin's St. Paul, ii, 209).

430 *See* Acts 13:4–7 (written 62–70 AD).

431   *See* Archae27, *Sergius Paulus the Proconsul and the Apostle Paul*, APXAIOC Institute of
       Biblical Archaeology (copyright © 2021), https://apxaioc.com/?p=20#:~:text.

432   *See, e.g., Sergius Paulus*, Bible Believer's Archaeology (Copyright © 2021), vol. 3 excerpt
       http://www.biblehistory.net/newsletter/paulus.htm.

433   *Id.*

       See also Ronald Cram, *Top NT Archaeological Finds* at No. 3, Factbridge,
       http://factbridge.org/sites/default/files/inline-files/Top-NT-Archaeological-Finds.pdf
       (citing http://www.hwhouse.com/images/4.SERGIUS_PAULUS_INSCRIPTION.pdf).

434   *See, e.g., Sergius Paulus*, Bible Believer's Archaeology (Copyright © 2021), vol. 3 excerpt
       http://www.biblehistory.net/newsletter/paulus.htm.

       See also Sergius Paulus (Copyright © 2021 www.BibleHistory.net),
       https://www.biblehistory.net/newsletter/paulus.htm.

435   *See, e.g., Sergius Paulus*, Wikipedia (last edited Dec. 7, 2020),
       https://en.wikipedia.org/wiki/Sergius_Paulus.

436   *See, e.g., Sergius Paulus*, Bible Believer's Archaeology (Copyright © 2021), vol. 3
       excerpt, http://www.biblehistory.net/newsletter/paulus.htm.

Chapter 5

437   *See* Jack Zavada, *Biblical History of Ancient Babylon*, Learn Religions (updated Dec. 4,
       2019), https://www.learnreligions.com/history-of-babylon-3867031.

438   Jack Zavada is a Christianity writer who "began his 45-year career as a police and
       government newspaper reporter and Associated Press wire editor;" he is "a freelance writer
       who concentrates on Christian topics. During his 45-year career, he has written thousands
       of newspaper and magazine articles covering areas from sports and business to the Bible
       and theology." *See* Mary Faorchild, *Jack Zavada*, Learn Religions (Aug. 12, 2018),
       https://www.learnreligions.com/jack-zavada-701410,

439   *See* Jack Zavada, *Biblical History of Ancient Babylon*, Learn Religions (updated Dec. 4,
       2019), https://www.learnreligions.com/history-of-babylon-3867031.

440   *Id.*

441   "[A]lso spelled Nebuchadrezzar II, (born c. 630–died c. 561 [BC]), second and greatest
       king of the Chaldean dynasty of Babylonia (reigned c. 605–c. 561 [BC]). He was known
       for his military might, the splendour of his capital, Babylon, and his important part in
       Jewish history."

       See Henry W.F. Saggs, *Nebuchadnezzar II—king of Babylon* (alternative titles: *Nabu-
       Kudurri-usur II, Nebuchadrezzar II*), Britannica (top questions updated, The Editors of
       Encyclopaedia Britannica, Sept. 18, 2019),

       https://www.britannica.com/biography/Nebuchadnezzar-II.

Henry W.F. Saggs is Emeritus Professor of Semitic Languages, University College, Cardiff, University of Wales and the author of *The Greatness That Was Babylon* and others.

Id.

442   "Robert Koldewey, (born Sept. 10, 1855, Blankenburg am Harz, duchy of Brunswick [Germany]—died Feb. 4, 1925, Berlin, Ger.), German architect and archaeologist who revealed the semilegendary Babylon of the Bible as a geographic and historical reality."

See, e.g., The Editors of Encyclopaedia Britannica (last updated: Jan 31, 2021), *Robert Koldewey, German architect and archaeologist*, Britannica (anniversary information added Jan 31, 2021), https://www.britannica.com/biography/Robert-Koldewey.

443   *See* Clifford Wilson, *Does Archaeology Support the Bible?*, Answers in Genesis, Chapter 25 (Jan. 24, 2008; last featured Aug. 27, 2014), https://answersingenesis.org/archaeology/does-archaeology-support-the-bible/.

444   *See* Jack Zavada, *Biblical History of Ancient Babylon*, Learn Religions (updated Dec. 4, 2019), https://www.learnreligions.com/history-of-babylon-3867031.

445   "The name 'Abraham' appears in Mesopotamian records, and the various nationalities the patriarch encountered, as recorded in Genesis, are entirely consistent with the peoples known at that time and place. Other details in the biblical account regarding Abraham, such as the treaties he made with neighboring rulers and even the price of slaves, mesh well with what is known elsewhere in the history of the ancient Near East."

Paul L. Maier, *Biblical History: The Faulty Criticism of Biblical Historicity*, CRI (Mar. 30, 2019) http://www.equip.org/article/biblical-history-the-faulty-criticism-of-biblical-historicity/.

446   "Sir Leonard Woolley, (born April 17, 1880, London—died Feb. 20, 1960, London), British archaeologist whose excavation of the ancient Sumerian city of Ur (in modern Iraq) greatly advanced knowledge of ancient Mesopotamian civilization."

See The Editors of Encyclopaedia Britannica, *Sir Leonard Woolley-British archaeologist* (alternative title: *Sir Charles Leonard Woolley*), Britannica (last updated: Feb 16, 2021), https://www.britannica.com/biography/Leonard-Woolley.

447   *See, e.g.,* Paul L. Maier, *Biblical History: The Faulty Criticism of Biblical Historicity*, CRI (Mar. 30, 2019), http://www.equip.org/article/biblical-history-the-faulty-criticism-of-biblical-historicity/.

448   *See* Joyce Chepkemoi, *Where Was Mesopotamia Located*, World Atlas (June 6 2017), https://www.worldatlas.com/articles/where-was-mesopotamia-located.html.

449   *See* A.T. Clay, *Ur*, Bible Hub (© 2004–2021 by Bible Hub), https://biblehub.com/topical/u/ur.htm (citing Easton's Bible Dictionary).

450   *See* Cristian Violatti, *10 Archaeological Discoveries Consistent With Biblical Passages*, List Verse (Nov. 4, 2016), http://listverse.com/2016/11/04/10-archaeological-discoveries-consistent-with-biblical-passages/.

451 *See* Marshall Beeber, *Ruins of Sodom and Gomorrah Found!*, Messianic Literary Corner, http://www.messianic-literary.com/sodom.htm.

452 *See, e.g.,* Paul L. Maier, *Biblical Archaeology: Factual Evidence to Support the Historicity of the Bible*, CRI (Mar. 30, 2009), https://www.equip.org/article/biblical-archaeology-factual-evidence-to-support-the-historicity-of-the-bible.

453 *See* Numbers 21:1 (written 1450–1405 BC).

454 *See* Genesis 26:31–33 (written 1450–1405 BC).

455 *See* Amos 7:12–13 (written 760–750 BC).

456 *See* Joshua 15:10 (written 1405–1385 BC).

457 *See* Joshua 17:11 (written 1405–1385 BC); 1 Samuel 31:10, 12 (written 931–722 BC); 2 Samuel 21:12 (written 930–722 BC); 1 Chronicles 7:29 (written 450–430 BC).

458 *See* Judges 18:29 (written circa 1043 BC).

459 *See* Joshua 16:10 (written 1405–1385 BC); 1 Kings 9:15–19 (written 561–583 BC).

460 *See* 1 Samuel 11:4, 13:15 (written 931–722 BC); Isaiah 10:29 (written 700–680 BC).

461 *See* Genesis 11:31–32 (written 1450–1405 BC).

462 *See* Joshua 11:1 (written 1405–1385 BC); 1 Kings 9:15 (written circa 561–538 BC); Jeremiah 49:28 (written 627–570 BC).

463 *See* Joshua 12:2 (written 1405–1385 BC).

464 *See* Numbers 22:1(written 1450–1405 BC).

465 *See* Joshua 10:3–5; 12:11 (written 1405–1385 BC).

In 701 BC, the Assyrian king Sennacherib invaded Judah. Many cities fell to the invading army, including the southern city of Lachish mentioned in 2 Kings 18:13–17 (written circa 561–538 BC). Several archaeological finds are consistent with this event. At the site of Lachish, archaeologists have uncovered arrowheads, a siege ramp, a counter-ramp, the crest of a helmet, and a chain used by the defenders against the siege ram. At the site of the ancient Assyrian city of Nineveh in northern Iraq, a relief sculpture depicting the capture of Lachish was retrieved from the palace of Sennacherib and is currently displayed in the British Museum.

See Cristian Violatti, *10 Archaeological Discoveries Consistent With Biblical Passages*, List Verse (Nov. 4, 2016), http://listverse.com/2016/11/04/10-archaeological-discoveries-consistent-with-biblical-passages/.

466 *See* 1 Kings 9:15 (written circa 561–538 BC).

467 *See* 2 Kings 19:36 (written circa 561–538 BC); Jonah 1:1–2, 3:3, 4:11 (written 785–760 BC).

468 *See* Genesis 12:6, 33:18 (written 1450–1405 BC).

469 *See* Joshua 18:1–10 (written 1405–1385 BC); Judges 21:19 (written circa 1043 BC).

470 *See* Nehemiah 1:1 (written 445–400 BC); Esther 1:1–2 (written 483–331 BC).

471   *See* Paul L. Maier, *Biblical Archaeology: Factual Evidence to Support the Historicity of the Bible*, CRI (Mar. 30, 2009), https://www.equip.org/article/biblical-archaeology-factual-evidence-to-support-the-historicity-of-the-bible;

   Matt Slick, *Archaeological evidence verifying biblical cities*, Christian Apologetics and Research Ministry (CARM) (Dec 7, 2008), https://carm.org/evidence-and-answers/archaeological-evidence-verifying-biblical-cities/.

472   *See* Paul L. Maier, *Biblical Archaeology: Factual Evidence to Support the Historicity of the Bible*, CRI (Mar. 30, 2009), https://www.equip.org/article/biblical-archaeology-factual-evidence-to-support-the-historicity-of-the-bible.

473   *See* Anugrah Kumar, *Evidence for Bible's Tower of Babel Discovered*, The Christian Post (May 8, 2017), https://www.christianpost.com/news/evidence-bible-tower-of-babel-discovered.html.

474   Martin Schøyen, born on January 31, 1940, is a Norwegian businessman, traveler, historian, paleographer and collector of books. "He started collecting books in 1955. Currently his private collection[,] the Schøyen Collection[,] contains [over] 13,000 manuscript items[;] the oldest book is about 5000 years old."

   See, e.g., Martin Schøyen, Howold, https://www.howold.co/person/martin-schoyen.

475   His name is "also spelled Nebuchadrezzar II, (born c. 630—died c. 561 [BC]), second and greatest king of the Chaldean dynasty of Babylonia (reigned c. 605–c. 561" BC

   See Henry W.F. Saggs, *Nebuchadnezzar II—king of Babylon* (alternative titles: *Nabu-Kudurri-usur II, Nebuchadrezzar II*), Britannica (top questions updated, The Editors of Encyclopaedia Britannica, Sept. 18, 2019), https://www.britannica.com/biography/Nebuchadnezzar-II.

476   *See, e.g.,* N.S. Gill, *Nabopolassar, King of Babylon*, ThoughtCo (updated Mar. 8, 2017), https://www.thoughtco.com/babylonian-king-nabopolassar-120004.

477   *See* Anugrah Kumar, *Evidence for Bible's Tower of Babel Discovered*, The Christian Post, (May 9, 2017), https://www.christianpost.com/news/evidence-bible-tower-of-babel-discovered.html.

   See also Ancient Code Team, *Ancient Babylonian Tablet Shows the Tower of Babel and Describes Construction*, Ancient Code, https://www.ancient-code.com/ancient-babylonian-tablet-proves-the-tower-of-babel-was-real/.

478   *See* RE, *Ancient Babylonian tablet PROVES the Tower of Babel was REAL*, Rise Earth (May 12, 2017, Source: Smithsonian), https://riseearth.org/ancient-babylonian-tablet-proves-tower.html.

479   "Herodotus was a Greek writer and geographer credited with being the first historian" who was "born in about 485 BC" and died around 425 BC.

   See, e.g., History.com Editors *Herodotus*, History.com (updated: Oct 24, 2019) https://www.history.com/topics/ancient-history/herodotus.

480   The Seleucid Empire, which existed from 312-63 BC, "was the vast political entity established by Seleucus I Nicator" (meaning "Victor" or "Unconquered"). He had been one of the generals of Alexander the Great, lived from about 358–281 BC and ruled the Seleucid Empire from 305–281 BC, after Alexander's death in 323 BC

   See, e.g., Joshua J. Mark, *Seleucid Empire,* Ancient History Encyclopedia (Oct. 2, 2019), https://www.ancient.eu/Seleucid_Empire/.

481   *See Tower of Babel Stele,* The Schøyen Collection (Published: Andrew George, ed.: Cuneiform Royal Inscriptions and Related Texts in the Schøyen Collection, Cornell University Studies in Assyriology and Sumerology, vol. 17, Manuscripts in the Schøyen Collection, Cuneiform texts VI. CDL Press, Bethesda, MD, 2011, text 76, pp. 153-169, pls. LVIII-LXVII), https://www.schoyencollection.com/history-collection-introduction/babylonian-history-collection/tower-babel-stele-ms-2063.

482   *See, e.g., Bethsaida,* seetheholyland.net (administered by Bethsaida Excavations Project (et-Tell) (© 2021, See the Holy Land), https://www.seetheholyland.net/bethsaida/.

483   *See, e.g.,* Jim Gerrish, *The Evangelical Triangle,* The Word of God Today (Nov. 2002), http://www.wordofgodtoday.com/evangelical-triangle/.

484   *See also* Luke 10:13–14 (written 60–61 AD).

485   "Tyre and Sidon are port cities located in modern Lebanon on the Mediterranean coast. Sidon is believed to have existed prior to 2000 BC, with Tyre being just a little younger."

   See Why did Jesus mention Tyre and Sidon in Luke 10:14?, Got Questions (© 2002–2021 Got Questions Ministries, last updated: Aug. 30, 2021), https://www.gotquestions.org/Tyre-and-Sidon.html.

   The Old Testament mentions Israel's dealings with these cities, including the Israelites' failure to conquer Sidon in the conquest of the Promised Land (Judges 1:31), their worship of Sidonian gods on several occasions (Judges 10:6–16; 1 Kings 11), and their obtaining materials from Sidon and Tyre for the building of the temple [in Jerusalem at the direction of David by Solomon, his son,] (1 Chronicles 22:[1–16]). King Hiram of Tyre provided many of the temple furnishings for Solomon (1 Kings 7:13–51). Tyrians and Sidonians are also mentioned in helping rebuild the temple in Ezra's time (Ezra 3:7). Queen Jezebel was a Sidonian (1 Kings 16:31). The Sidonian city of Zarephath was where a widow took care of Elijah and the Lord provided oil and flour for her through the famine; later, the widow's son became ill, and Elijah raised him from the dead (1 Kings 17:8–24).

   The Old Testament also has several prophecies against Tyre and Sidon that predicted a complete overthrow (Isaiah 23; Jeremiah 25; 27; 47; Ezekiel 26–28; Joel 3; Amos 1:9–10; Zechariah 9:1–4). Nebuchadnezzar besieged Tyre from 585–572 BC. Alexander the Great conquered Tyre in 322 BC, completely destroying the city. The Persian king Artaxerxes conquered Sidon.

   Id.

"Jesus used the pagan cities of Tyre and Sidon to highlight the way God's chosen people refused Him."

Id.

"The people of Tyre and Sidon did not have the same opportunities of those in Chorazin, Bethsaida and Capernaum—to hear and respond to the ministry of Jesus."

See, e.g., Lowell Grisham, *Chorazin, Bethsaida, and Capernaum*, Episcopal Café (Oct. 17, 2011), https://www.episcopalcafe.com/chorazin_bethsaida_and_capernaum/.

486   *See* Jim Gerrish, *The Cursed City of Chorazin*, Word of God Today (2004), http://www.wordofgodtoday.com/cursed-city-chorazin/.

487   *See, e.g.*, The Editors of Encyclopaedia Britannica, *Medusa—Greek mythology*, Britannica (corrected display issue-Jan 31, 2020), https://www.britannica.com/topic/Medusa-Greek-mythology;

     Gorgons, Greek Mythology, https://www.greekmythology.com/Myths/Creatures/Gorgons/gorgons.html.

488   *See, e.g.,* Jim Gerrish, *The Cursed City of Chorazin*, Word of God Today (2004), http://www.wordofgodtoday.com/cursed-city-chorazin/.

489   *See* Matthew 11:21 (written 50–65 AD); Mark 6:45, 8:22 (written 50–65 AD); Luke 9:10, 10:13 (written 60–61 AD); John 1:44, 12:21 (written 80–90 AD).

490   "Gaius Plinius Secundus (AD 23/24–79), called Pliny the Elder, was a Roman author, a naturalist and natural philosopher, a naval and army commander of the early Roman Empire, and a friend of emperor Vespasian." *Plini the Elder*, Wikipedia (last edited on Feb. 21, 2021), https://en.wikipedia.org/wiki/Pliny_the_Elder.

491   *See Bethsaida*, Wikipedia (last edited Feb. 20, 2021), https://en.wikipedia.org/wiki/Bethsaida.

     See also Chapter 3, *supra.*

492   *Id.*

493   *See also* John 12:21 (written 80–90 AD) again stating that the apostle Philip was from Bethsaida.

494   *See* John 1:43–51 (written 80–90 AD).

495   "Herod, by name Herod the Great, Latin Herodes Magnus, (born 73 [BC]—died March/ April, 4 [BC in], Jericho, Judaea), Roman-appointed king of Judaea (37–4 [BC]), who built many fortresses, aqueducts, theatres, and other public buildings and generally raised the prosperity of his land but who was the center of political and family intrigues in his later years. The New Testament portrays him as a tyrant, into whose kingdom Jesus of Nazareth was born." The Magi visited Herod on their way to Bethlehem, and Herod ordered all the children two years old and under to be killed, because the Magi and the Jewish priests and scribes told him that the King of the Jews was to be born in Bethlehem.

See, e.g., Stewart Henry Perowne, *Herod—king of Judea* (alternative titles: *Herod the Great, Herodes Magnus*), Britannica (last updated: Feb 9, 2021), https://www.britannica.com/biography/Herod-king-of-Judaea;

Matthew 2:1–16 (written 50–65 AD).

496   *See, e.g., Bethsaida*, Seetheholyland (© 2021, See the Holy Land), https://www.seetheholyland.net/tag/bethsaida-julias/;

       Bethsaida, Wikipedia (last edited Feb, 20, 2021), https://en.wikipedia.org/wiki/Bethsaida.

497   *See Bethsaida*, Seetheholyland (© 2021, See the Holy Land) https://www.seetheholyland.net/tag/bethsaida-julias/#.

498   "The Kingdom of Geshur is first mentioned in Deuteronomy 3:14 [(written 1450–1405 BC)], noting it as a border nation of the tribes of Manasseh. It lay on the north-east of the Sea of Galilee and east of the River Jordan."

       See, e.g., Heidi Kinner, *The Kingdom of Geshur*, HeidiKinner.org (posted May 20, 2016), http://heidikinner.org/2016/05/20/the-kingdom-of-geshur/.

       It coexisted with the Old Testament "kingdoms of Israel and Judah to its south, and with the kingdom of Aram to the north (in present-day Syria;" scholars are confident Bethsaida was its capital.

       See Philippe Bohstrom, *Fortifications Found Show Biblical Kingdom of Geshur More Powerful Than Thought*, Haaretz (updated: Apr. 10, 2018), https://www.haaretz.com/archaeology/biblical-geshur-a-3000-year-old-superpower-1.5413366/.

499   *See Bethsaida*, Wikipedia (last edited Feb, 20, 2021), https://en.wikipedia.org/wiki/Bethsaida.

500   *Id.*

501   *See* James Rogers, *Lost Roman City That Was Home to Jesus' Apostles Found, Say Archaeologists*, Fox News (last update Sept. 26, 2017), https://www.foxnews.com/science/lost-roman-city-that-was-home-to-jesus-apostles-found-say-archaeologists.

502   *See Bethsaida*, Wikipedia (last edited Feb. 20, 2021), https://en.wikipedia.org/wiki/Bethsaida.

503   *See* Matthew 4:12–13, 8:5, 11:23, 17:24 (written 50–65 AD); Mark 1:21, 2:1, 9:33 (written 50–65 AD); Luke 4:23, 31,7:1, 10:15 (written 60–61 AD); John 2:12, 4:46, 6:17, 24, 59 (written 80–90 AD).

504   *See* Matthew 4:13, 8:5, 17:24 (written 50–65 AD); Mark 1:21, 2:1, 9:33 (written 50–65 AD); Luke 4:23, 31,7:1, 10:15 (written 60–61 AD); John 2:12, 4:46, 6: 17, 24, 59 (written 80–90 AD)

505   *See* Matthew 4:13, 8:5 (written 50–65 AD); Mark 1:21, 2:1, 9:33 (written 50–65 AD); Luke 4:23, 31,7:1 (written 60–61 AD); John 2:12, 4:46, 6: 59 (written 80–90 AD).

506   *See* Matthew 4:13 (written 50–65 AD).

      See also Capernaum—The town of Jesus, Traveling Israel (all rights reserved Cahanovitc Oren 2021), https://www.travelingisrael.com/capernaum/.

507   *See, e.g.* Kat Cendana, *Matthew, Apostle*, Amazing Bible Timeline with World History (Aug. 8, 2016), https://amazingbibletimeline.com/blog/apostle-matthew/.

508   *See* Mark 1:16–18 (written 50–65 AD).

      See also, e.g., David Padfield, *Capernaum* (copyright 2017 David Padfield), https://www.padfield.com/acrobat/history/Capernaum.pdf#.

509   *See* Mark 1:19–20 (written 50–65 AD).

      See also, e.g., David Padfield, *Capernaum* (copyright 2017 David Padfield), https://www.padfield.com/acrobat/history/Capernaum.pdf#.

510   *See* Mark 2:13–14 (written 50–65 AD).

      See also, e.g., David Padfield, *Capernaum* (copyright 2017 David Padfield), https://www.padfield.com/acrobat/history/Capernaum.pdf#.

511   *Id.*

512   *See* Mark 1:21– 26 (written 50–65 AD);

513   *See* Mark 1:29–31 (written 50–65 AD);

514   *See* Chapter 3 *supra.*

515   *See* Luke 4:39–41 (written 50–65 AD);

516   *See, e.g., Capernaum—The town of Jesus*, Traveling Israel (all rights reserved Cahanovitc Oren 2021), https://www.travelingisrael.com/capernaum/.

517   *See Capernaum*, https://www.israeljerusalem.com/capernaum-israel.htm#:~:text=After-lying-buried-for-centuries-the-ruins-Capernaum.

518   Sir Charles William Wilson, who lived from 1836–1905, was an English army officer and topographer who also directed the survey of Jerusalem in 1864–66 and the survey of Sinai in1868–69 and later served as consul in Turkey.

      See, e.g., Wilson, Sir Charles William, Jewish Virtual Library (Sources: Encyclopaedia Judaica. © 2008 The Gale Group. All Rights Reserved), www.jewishvirtuallibrary.org/wilson-sir-charles-william-x00b0.

519   *See, e.g., Capernaum,* Wikipedia (last edited Feb, 20, 2021), https://en.wikipedia.org/wiki/Capernaum.

520   *See e.g., Capernaum—The town of Jesus*, Traveling Israel (all rights reserved Cahanovitc Oren 2021), https://www.travelingisrael.com/capernaum/.

521   The Hasmonean dynasty was a ruling dynasty of Judea and surrounding regions which ruled Judea beginning about 140 BC In 63 BC, the kingdom was invaded by the Roman Republic, broken up and set up as a Roman client state. The dynasty survived for 103 years

before yielding to the Herodian dynasty in 37 BC With the installation of Herod the Great as king in 37 BC, the Hasmonean dynasty ended.

See, e.g., Hasmonean dynasty, Wikipedia (last edited Feb. 20, 2021), https://en.wikipedia.org/wiki/Hasmonean_dynasty.

522 *See, e.g., Capernaum*, Wikipedia (last edited Feb, 20, 2021), https://en.wikipedia.org/wiki/Capernaum.

523 *See Chorazin*, Seetheholyland (© 2021, See the Holy Land), https://www.seetheholyland.net/chorazin/;

Jim Gerrish, *The Cursed City Of Chorazin*, Word of God Today (2004), http://www.wordofgodtoday.com/cursed-city-chorazin/.

524 *See Chorazin*, Seetheholyland (© 2021, See the Holy Land) https://www.seetheholyland.net/chorazin/;

Jim Gerrish, *The Cursed City Of Chorazin*, Word of God Today (2004), http://www.wordofgodtoday.com/cursed-city-chorazin/.

525 *Id.*

526 *See* Matthew 11:20–24 (written 50–65 AD).

See also Chorazin, Seetheholyland (© 2021, See the Holy Land), https://www.seetheholyland.net/chorazin/;

Jim Gerrish, *The Cursed City Of Chorazin*, Word of God Today (2004), http://www.wordofgodtoday.com/cursed-city-chorazin/.

527 *See* Matthew 11:21 (written 50–65 AD); Luke. 10:13 (written 60–61 AD),

528 *See Chorazin* Seetheholyland (© 2021, See the Holy Land), https://www.seetheholyland.net/chorazin/.

529 *See, e.g.* The Editors of Encyclopaedia Britannica, *Eusebius of Caesarea, Christian bishop and historian* (alternative title: *Eusebius Pamphili*), Britannica (Michael Ray revised details of his imprisonment, Oct. 26, 2017), https://www.britannica.com/biography/Eusebius-of-Caesarea.

530 *See Chorazin*, Seetheholyland (© 2021, See the Holy Land), https://www.seetheholyland.net/chorazin/.

531 *See* John Black, *The 'Cursed' city of Chorazin*, Ancient Origins (updated Nov. 1, 2013), https://www.ancient-origins.net/ancient-places-asia/cursed-city-chorazin-00988.

532 *See* Nikola Petrovski, *Chorazin: Jesus Christ Put a Curse on This Place*, Abandoned Spaces (Aug. 6, 2019) https://www.abandonedspaces.com/towns/bible.html

533 The Palestine Exploration Fund was "founded under the royal patronage of Queen Victoria in 1865 by a group of distinguished academics and clergymen" with the original mission of promoting "research into the archaeology and history, manners and customs and culture, topography, geology and natural sciences of biblical Palestine and the Levant," " a vast

geographical region situated in the Eastern Mediterranean" without fixed boundaries and it changes over time, but containing countries "characterized by similar linguistic, cultural, and religious traits, including "Iraq, Syria, Lebanon, Cyprus, Turkey (Hatay Province), Israel, Jordan, and Palestine," but has also been considered to be 'the territory from Greece to Egypt."

See, e.g., History, The Palestine Exploration Fund, https://www.pef.org.uk/about/history/;

Joyce Chepkemoi, *Where is the Levant?*, World Atlas (July 24, 2018), https://www.worldatlas.com/articles/where-is-the-levant.html.

534   *See, e.g.,* Jim Gerrish, *The Cursed City of Chorazin,* Word of God Today (2004), http://www.wordofgodtoday.com/cursed-city-chorazin/.

See also Nikola Petrovski, *Chorazin: Jesus Christ Put a Curse on This Place,* Abandoned Spaces (Aug. 6, 2019), https://www.abandoned-spaces.com/towns/bible.html.

535   *Id.*

536   *See* The Editors of Encyclopaedia Britannica, *Ephesus, ancient city, Turkey* (alternative title: *Ephesos*), Britannica, https://www.britannica.com/place/Ephesus.

537   *See Ephesus,* Wikipedia (last edited on 20 February 2021), https://en.wikipedia.org/wiki/Ephesus;

The Editors of Encyclopaedia Britannica, *Ionia—ancient region, Turkey*, Britannica, https://www.britannica.com/place/Ionia;

"Anatolia, Turkish Anadolu, also called Asia Minor, [is] the peninsula of land that today constitutes the Asian portion of Turkey."

See also, e.g., John E. Woods, *Anatolia—historical region, Asia* (alternative title: *Anadolu, Asia Minor*), Britannica (corrected styling issues and added cross-references., Apr. 30, 2015), https://www.britannica.com/place/Anatolia (no longer online);

The Ancient City of Ephesus, Ephesus Tours @Tripadvisor (©2021), https://ancientephesus.com/ephesus (no longer online).

538   *See Ephesus,* Wikipedia (last edited on 20 February 2021), https://en.wikipedia.org/wiki/Ephesus.

539   "Ionia is the name given during ancient times to the central region of Anatolia's Aegean shore in Asia Minor, present-day Turkey, one of the most important centres of the Greek world;" "colonized by Greeks from the Athens region around 1000" BC

See, e.g., Cristian Violatti, *Ionia,* Ancient History Encyclopedia (May 27, 2014), https://www.ancient.eu/ionia/.

'The Ionian League was a confederation of twelve Ionian cities that existed from the mid-7th century BC to the 4th century BC."

See, e.g., *Ionian League*, Historica,
https://historica.fandom.com/wiki/Ionian_League.

540   *See Ephesus*, Wikipedia (last edited on 20 February 2021),
https://en.wikipedia.org/wiki/Ephesus.

See also Ancient Rome—Republic to Empire, Ducksters,
https://www.ducksters.com/history/ancient_rome/republic_to_empire.php;

Ancient Rome, Wikipedia (last edited Feb. 19, 2021),
https://en.wikipedia.org/wiki/Ancient_Rome#:~:text=In historiography%2C.

The term "classical Greece" refers to the period between the Persian Wars at the beginning
of the fifth century BC and the death of Alexander the Great in 323 BC The classical period
was an era of war and conflict—first between the Greeks and the Persians, then between
the Athenians and the Spartans—but it was also an era of unprecedented political and
cultural achievement. Besides the Parthenon and Greek tragedy, classical Greece brought
us the historian Herodotus, the physician Hippokrates and the philosopher Socrates. It also
brought us the political reforms that are ancient Greece's most enduring contribution to the
modern world: the system known as demokratia, or "rule by the people."

See History.com Editors, *Classical Greece*, History (last updated Aug. 3, 2020),
https://www.history.com/topics/ancient-history/classical-greece.

The Ionian League was "a democratic confederation based upon" constitutional principles
made up of twelve Ionian cities including Ephesus.

See Government of the Ionian League (©-2021),
https://unchartedsuns.com/inventories/government-of-the-ionian-league/;

Hasan Gülday, *Introduction into The Ionian League*, Licensed Tour Guide in Turkey,
https://toursaroundturkey.com/introduction-ionian-league/.

541   *See Ephesus*, Wikipedia (last edited Feb. 20, 2021), https://en.wikipedia.org/wiki/Ephesus.

One of the reasons that the Temple of Artemis at Ephesus is considered one of the Seven
Wonders of the Ancient World is because it was huge, double the dimensions of other
Greek temples including the Parthenon.

See, also e.g., Mark Cartwright, *Temple of Artemis at Ephesus*, Ancient History
Encyclopedia (July 26, 2018), https://www.ancient.eu/Temple_of_Artemis_at_Ephesus.

542   *See, e.g.,* The Editors of Encyclopaedia Britannica, *Artemis- Greek goddess*, Britannica
(corrected display issue, July 5, 2018),
https://www.britannica.com/topic/Artemis-Greek-goddess.

543   The Roman politician and general who lived from 83–30 BC, was an ally of Julius Caesar
and the main rival of his successor Octavian (later Augustus), both of whom were "integral
to Rome's transition from republic to empire," but whose "romantic and political alliance

with the Egyptian queen Cleopatra was his ultimate undoing."

History.com Editors, *Mark Antony*, History (updated Oct. 24, 2019), https://www.history.com/topics/ancient-history/mark-antony.

544   *See, e.g.,* History.com Editors, *Augustus*, History (updated Aug. 21, 2018), https://www.history.com/topics/ancient-history/emperor-augustus;

The Editors of Encyclopaedia Britannica, *Battle of Actium—ancient Roman history*, Britannica, https://www.britannica.com/event/Battle-of-Actium-ancient-Roman-history.

545   *See* The Editors of Encyclopaedia Britannica, *Ephesus, ancient city, Turkey* (alt. title: *Ephesos*), Britannica, https://www.britannica.com/place/Ephesus.

546   *See* Acts 18:19, 21 and 24, 19:1, 17, 23, 26 and 35, 20:16 and 17 (written 62–70 AD); 1 Corinthians 15:32 and 16:82 (written 55 AD); Ephesians 1:1 (written 60–62 AD); 1 Timothy 1:3 and 18 written 62–64 AD); 2 Timothy 4:12 (written 66–67 AD). and Revelation 1:11 and 2:1 (written 94–96 AD).

547   *See Ephesus*, Wikipedia (last edited Feb. 20, 2021), https://en.wikipedia.org/wiki/Ephesus.

548   *See* The Editors of Encyclopaedia Britannica, *Ephesus, ancient city, Turkey* (alternative title: *Ephesos*), Britannica, https://www.britannica.com/place/Ephesus.

549   *See Ephesus,* Wikipedia (last edited Feb. 20, 2021), https://en.wikipedia.org/wiki/Ephesus.

550   *Id.*

See also The Editors of Encyclopaedia Britannica, *Ephesus, ancient city, Turkey* (alternative title: *Ephesos*), Britannica, https://www.britannica.com/place/Ephesus.

551   The Seljuks were originally Turkic nomads who inhabited the steppes of Central Asia and Southeast Russia. The name of this people is taken from their traditional ancestor, Seljuk, who was a chief of the Qinik, a branch of the Oghuz Turks. Around 950 AD, Seljuk migrated to Khwarezm[,also spelled Khorezm, also called Chorasmia, an historic region in the territories of present-day Turkmenistan and Uzbekistan, while serving in the Khazar army[, the army of "an interesting and largely overlooked Turkic tribal Empire which was established in the late 6th Century."

The Seljuk Empire was a medieval empire that existed between the 11th and 12th centuries. They are most famous for their invasions and battles against the Byzantine Empire and later their role in the First Crusade. Although the Seljuks were originally a Turkic people, they intermarried with the Persians and adopted much of their culture and language. At its most extent, the Seljuk (Seljuq) Empire stretched from Central Asia in the east all the way to Anatolia [in Turkey] in the west.

See Wu Mingren, *The Seljuks: Nomads Who Built an Empire and Took on Byzantine Power*, Ancient Origins (updated Apr. 22, 2019), https://www.ancient-origins.net/history-important-events/seljuks-0011773;

The Editors of Encyclopaedia Britannica, *Khwārezm, historical region, Central Asia* (alternative titles: *Chorasmia, Khorezm*), Britannica; (Modified link of Web site Apr. 3,

2020), https://www.britannica.com/place/Khwarezm;

Dugdale-Pointon, T. (14 June 2011), *Khazar Khaganate*, http://www.historyofwar.org/articles/wars_khazar.html.

552 *See, e.g.,* The Editors of Encyclopaedia Britannica, *Ephesus, ancient city, Turkey* (alternative title: *Ephesos*), Britannica, https://www.britannica.com/place/Ephesus.

553 *See Ephesus City in Ruins*, Biblical Ephesus, http://biblicalephesus.com/ephesus.

554 *See John Turtle Wood*, Wikipedia (last edited June 8, 2020), https://en.wikipedia.org/wiki/John_Turtle_Wood.

555 *Id.*

556 *See, e.g.,* The Editors of Encyclopaedia Britannica, *Ephesus, ancient city, Turkey* (alternative title: *Ephesos*), Britannica, https://www.britannica.com/place/Ephesuss.

557 *See Ephesus*, Wikipedia (last edited Feb. 20, 2021), https://en.wikipedia.org/wiki/Ephesus.

558 Karl Mautner Ritter von Markhof was a wealthy Austrian businessman who lived from 1834—1896.

See, e.g., Carl Ferdinand Ritter Mautner von Markhof, Mautner Markhof, https://www.dynastiemautnermarkhof.com/en/adolf-ignaz-ritter-mautner-von-markhof/carl-ferdinand/.

559 *See Ephesus*, Wikipedia (last edited Feb. 20, 2021), https://en.wikipedia.org/wiki/Ephesus.

560 *Id.*

561 *See* Joshua 19:46 (written circa 1405–1385 BC) ; 2 Chronicles 2:16 (written 450–430 BC); Ezra 3:7 (written BC457–444); Jonah 1:3; (written 785–760 BC); Acts 3:7, 9:36, 38, 42 and 43, 10:5,8,23 and 32, 11:5 and 13 (written 62–70 AD).

562 *See Jaffa*, seetheholyland.net (© 2021, See the Holy Land), https://www.seetheholyland.net/tag/joppa/;

Jacqueline Schaalje, *Archaeology in Jaffa*, The Jewish Magazine (May Shavuot 2001 Edition), http://www.jewish-mag.com/43mag/jaffa/jaffa.htm.

563 *See, e.g., Joppa*, All About Archaeology (copyright © 2002-2020 AllAboutArchaeology.org), https://www.allaboutarchaeology.org/joppa-faq.htm.

564 *See Jaffa*, seetheholyland.net (© 2021, See the Holy Land), https://www.seetheholyland.net/tag/joppa/.

565 *See, e.g., Joppa*, Experience the Land of the Bible (© 2016 Land of the Bible), https://www.land-of-the-bible.com/Joppa# (no longer online);

Jacqueline Schaalje, *Archaeology in Jaffa*, The Jewish Magazine (May Shavuot 2001 Edition), http://www.jewishmag.com/43mag/jaffa/jaffa.htm.

566 *See Jaffa*, seetheholyland.net (© 2021, See the Holy Land), https://www.seetheholyland.net/tag/joppa/.

567   *See, e.g., Joppa*, Experience the Land of the Bible (© 2016 Land of the Bible),
       https://www.land-of-the-bible.com/Joppa# (no longer online).

568   *See* Joshua 19:40–46 (written circa 1405–1385 BC).

569   *See, e.g., Joppa*, All About Archaeology (copyright © 2002-2020, AllAboutArchaeology.
       org), https://www.allaboutarchaeology.org/joppa-faq.htm.

570   *See* Acts 9:36–41 (written circa 62–70 AD).

571   *See* Acts 9:42–43 (written circa 62–70 AD)

572   *See* Acts 10 (written circa 62–70 AD)

573   *See, e.g., Joppa*, Experience the Land of the Bible (© 2016 Land of the Bible),
       https://www.land-of-the-bible.com/Joppa# (no longer online).

574   *See Jaffa*, seetheholyland.net (© 2021, See the Holy Land),
       https://www.seetheholyland.net/tag/joppa/

575   *See, e.g., Joppa*, Experience the Land of the Bible (© 2016 Land of the Bible),
       https://www.land-of-the-bible.com/Joppa# (no longer online);

       Jaffa, seetheholyland.net (© 2021, See the Holy Land),
       https://www.seetheholyland.net/tag/joppa.

576   *See, e.g., Joppa*, Experience the Land of the Bible (© 2016 Land of the Bible),
       https://www.land-of-the-bible.com/Joppa# (no longer online);

       Joppa, seetheholyland.net (© 2021, See the Holy Land),
       https://www.seetheholyland.net/tag/joppa/.

577   *See, e.g., Great Commanders—Edmund Allenby: The bull*, National Army Museum,
       https://www.nam.ac.uk/explore/edmund-allenby#.

578   *See, e.g., Joppa*, Experience the Land of the Bible (© 2016 Land of the Bible),
       https://www.land-of-the-bible.com/Joppa# (no longer online).

579   Pompey was a military leader and politician during the fall of the Roman Republic. He
       lived from 106 BC to 48 BC.

       See, e.g., James Lloyd, *Pompey*, World History Encyclopedia (Jan. 27. 2013),
       https://www.ancient.eu/pompey/#.

580   *See, e.g., Joppa*, Experience the Land of the Bible (© 2016 Land of the Bible),
       https://www.land-of-the-bible.com/Joppa# (no longer online).

581   The Roman emperor from 69–79 AD.

       See, e.g., Guy Edward Farquhar Chilver, *Vespasian—Roman emperor* (alternative
       titles: *Caesar Vespasianus Augustus, Titus Flavius Vespasianus*), Britannic (anniversary
       information added–June 20, 2020), https://www.britannica.com/biography/Vespasian.

582   *See, Joppa* (© Copyright 2016 Land of the Bible),
       https://www.land-of-the-bible.com/Joppa (no longer online).

See also, Jacqueline Schaalje, *Archaeology in Jaffa*, The Jewish Magazine (May Shavuot 2001 Edition), http://www.jewishmag.com/43mag/jaffa/jaffa.htm.

583   *See Jaffa*, Wikipedia (last edited Feb. 20, 2021),
https://en.wikipedia.org/wiki/Jaffa#Archaeology.

584   *See* Jacqueline Schaalje, *Archaeology in Jaffa*, The Jewish Magazine (May Shavuot 2001 Edition), http://www.jewishmag.com/43mag/jaffa/jaffa.htm.

585   *Id.*

586   *Id.*

587   *See* Martin Peilstöcker, *The History and Archaeology of Jaffa 1*, Chapter 2 The History of Archaeological Research in Jaffa, 1948–2009 (Cotsen Institute of Archaeology Press at UCLA, pp. 17-32- copyright date: 2011),
https://www.jstor.org/stable/j.ctvdjrrkm#:~:text=Directed.

588   "A tell (alternately spelled tel, til, or tal) is a special form of archaeological mound, a human-built construction of earth and stone."

       See K. Kris Hirst, *What Is a Tell? the Remnants of Ancient Mesopotamian Cities*, ThoughtCo (updated Mar. 22, 2019),
https://www.thoughtco.com/what-is-a-tell-169849#:~:text.

589   *See* Jacqueline Schaalje, *Archaeology in Jaffa*, The Jewish Magazine (May Shavuot 2001 Edition), http://www.jewishmag.com/43mag/jaffa/jaffa.htm.

590   *Id.*

591   *See Jaffa*, Wikipedia (last edited Feb. 20, 2021,),
https://en.wikipedia.org/wiki/Jaffa#Archaeology.

592   *See, e.g.,* Ronald Cram, *Top NT Archaeological Finds*, Factbridge,
http://factbridge.org/sites/default/files/inline-files/Top-NT-Archaeological-Finds.pdf
at No. 21 (citing. http://bit.ly/SkepticalOfNazareth, http://bit.ly/NazarethHouse).

593   *Id*

594   *See Can We Trust the New Testament as an Historical Document?*, Airrington Ministries (copyright 1989—2020, Airrington Ministries),
http://airrington.com/?page_id=879#:~:text.

595   *See* Ronald Cram, *Top NT Archaeological Finds*, Factbridge,
http://factbridge.org/sites/default/files/inline-files/Top-NT-Archaeological-Finds.pdf
at No. 18 (citing http://bit.ly/PoolOf-Bethesda).

596   *Id.*

597   *Id.* at No. 19 (citing http://articles.latimes.com/2005/-aug/09/science/sci-siloam9).

598   *Id.* at No. 22 (citing http://bit.ly/CapernaumSyna-gogue).

Chapter 6

599   *See* Paul L. Maier, *Biblical Archaeology: Factual Evidence to Support the Historicity of the Bible*, CRI (Mar. 30, 2009), www.equip.org/article/biblical-archaeology-factual-evidence-to-support-the-historicity-of-the-bible.

600   "Sir Leonard Woolley, (born April 17, 1880, London—died Feb. 20, 1960, London), British archaeologist whose excavation of the ancient Sumerian city of Ur (in modern Iraq) [also] greatly advanced knowledge of ancient Mesopotamian civilization."

        See The Editors of Encyclopaedia Britannica, *Sir Leonard Wooley, British archaeologist* (alternative title: *Sir Charles Leonard Woolley*), Britannica (updated Feb. 16, 2021), https://www.britannica.com/biography/Leonard-Woolley.

601   According to Genesis 11:31 (written 1450–1405 BC), Terah took his son Abram, later to be named Abraham who was to become the patriarch of the Jewish people, Abram's wife Sarai, later to be named Sarah, and his grandson, Lot, from Ur of the Chaldeans into the land of Canaan.

602   *See* Cristian Violatti, *10 Archaeological Discoveries Consistent With Biblical Passages*, List Verse (Nov. 4, 2016), https://listverse.com/2016/11/04/10-archaeological-discoveries-consistent-with-biblical-passages.

603   *See* Clifford Wilson, *Does Archaeology Support the Bible?*, Answers in Genesis (Jan. 24, 200814), Chapter 25, https://answersingenesis.org/archaeology/does-archaeology-support-the-bible/
        (citing N. Osanai, A comparative study of the flood accounts in the Gilgamesh Epic and Genesis, www.answersingenesis.org/go/gil-gamesh);

        Paul L. Maier, Biblical Archaeology: *Factual Evidence to Support the Historicity of the Bible*, CRI (Mar. 30, 2009), www.equip.org/article/biblical-archaeology-factual-evidence-to-support-the-historicity-of-the-bible/.

        As pointed out above, for example, the Babylonian Gilgamesh Flood legend described an ark that was shaped like a cube, not at all stable.

        See, e.g., Gilgamesh (Epic): Which Came First–Noah's Flood or the Gilgamesh Epic?, Genesis apologetics, https://genesisapologetics.com/faqs/gilgamesh-epic-which-came-first-noahs-flood-or-the-gilgamesh-epic/#:~:text.

604   *See* Genesis 11:31, 15:7 (written 1450–1405 BC).

        See also Acts 7:2–4 (written AD, 62–70).

605   *See* Genesis 12:1–3 17:8 (written 1450–1405 BC).

        See also Canaan (The Promised Land), Places, http://www.bibletutor.com/level1/program/start/places/canaan.htm.

When Only God Knew

606 *See* Genesis 12:1–4, 6–10, 20; 13:1–18; 15:7; 16:3; 17:8; 20:1; 22:1–2; 23:1–20 (written 1450–1405 BC).

See also Acts 7:2–4 (written AD, 62–70).

607 *See, e.g.,* Paul L. Maier, *Biblical History: The Faulty Criticism of Biblical Historicity*, CRI (Mar. 30, 2009), http://www.equip.org/article/biblical-history-the-faulty-criticism-of-biblical-historicity.

608 *Id.*

609 *Id.*

610 *Id.*

611 *Id.*

612 *Id.*

613 *Id.*

614 *Id.*

615 *See* Exodus (written 1450–1405 BC).

616 *See Evidence for the Exodus*, Evidences of the Bible (Mar. 5, 2017), https://bibleevidences.com/evidence-for-the-exodus/.

617 *See, e.g.,* Mark McWhorter, *Wisdom's Corner, Pithom and Raamse* (Published by The Old Paths Bible School-copyright 2002), http://www.oldpaths.org/Classes/Children/WC/Stories/wc06_24.html.

See also Pithom, Bible Hub (© 2004-2021 by Bible Hub), https://biblehub.com/topical/p/pithom.htm (citing Eaton's Bible Dictionary which said that in Pithom there has "recently (1883) been discovered the ruins of supposed grain-chambers, and other evidences to show that this was a great "store city." Its immense ruin-heaps show that it was built of bricks, and partly also of bricks without straw").

618 *See Evidence for the Exodus*, Evidences of the Bible (Mar. 5, 2017), https://bibleevidences.com/evidence-for-the-exodus (citing *Israel's Exodus in Transdisciplinary Perspective*).

See also The Ipuwer Papyrus—Were The 10 Biblical Plagues Real?, Early Church History, https://earlychurchhistory.org/communication/the-ipuwer-papyrus-were-the-10-biblical-plagues-real/.

619 *See, e.g.,* Roger Waite and Todd Dragger, Compilers, *The Plagues of Egypt* (2008), http://www.cbcg.org/franklin/The_Plagues_Of_Egypt.pdf.

620 *See Evidence for the Exodus*, Evidences of the Bible (Mar. 5, 2017), https://bibleevidences.com/evidence-for-the-exodus/.

621 *See Egyptian Evidence for the Exodus*, http://www.angelfire.com/ill/hebrewisrael/ipuwer.html.

See also *Biblical Archeology of the Exodus-The Ipuwer Papyrus*, Biblical Archeology,
http://www.truthnet.org/Biblicalarcheology/5/Exodus-archeology.htm.

622   *See, e.g.*, Roger Waite and Todd Dragger, Compilers, *The Plagues of Egypt* (2008),
http://www.cbcg.org/franklin/The_Plagues_Of_Egypt.pdf.

623   *Compare* Marina Sohma, *Does the Ipuwer Papyrus Provide Evidence for the Events of the
Exodus*, Ancient Origins (updated Nov. 6, 2016), https://www.ancient-origins.net/artifacts-
ancient-writings/does-ipuwer-papyrus-provide-evidence-events-exodus-006951,

The Ipuwer Papyrus—Were The 10 Biblical Plagues Real?, Early Church History,
https://earlychurchhistory.org/communication/the-ipuwer-papyrus-were-the-10-biblical-
plagues-real/,

and *Is there extra-biblical evidence of the ten plagues in Egypt?*, Got Questions (©
Copyright 2002-2021 Got Questions Ministries - last updated: April 26, 2021),
https://www.gotquestions.org/evidence-ten-plagues.html.

624   Pharoah Ramses II is generally considered by many scholars to have been the pharaoh who
initially refused to let the Hebrew slaves go.

See, e.g., Jean-Pierre Isbouts, *Who was the Egyptian pharaoh challenged Moses?*, National
Geographic (Mar. 20, 2018),
https://www.nationalgeographic.com/culture/article/pharaoh-king-punished-god.

625   *See also Exodus Evidence: An Egyptologist Looks at Biblical History*, Biblical
Archaeology Review 42:3 (May/June 2016),
https://www.baslibrary.org/biblical-archaeology-review/42/3/2.

See also, Biblical Archaeology Society Staff, *The Exodus: Fact or Fiction? - Evidence of
Israel's Exodus from Egypt*, Biblical History Daily (Oct. 23, 2020),
https://www.biblicalarchaeology.org/daily/biblical-topics/exodus/exodus-fact-or-fiction/.

626   *See* Joe Kovacs, *Chariots in Red Sea: 'Irrefutable Evidence'*, WND (June 7, 2012),
http://www.wnd.com/2012/06/chariots-in-red-sea-irrefutable-evidence/.

See also, e.g., Chariots Found In The Bottom Of The Red Sea, National Geographic (Aug.
5, 2021), https://nationalgeographyc.blogspot.com/2021/08/chariots-found-in-bottom-of-
red-sea.html.

627   *See* Joe Kovacs, *Chariots in Red Sea: 'Irrefutable Evidence'*, WND (June 7, 2012),
http://www.wnd.com/2012/06/chariots-in-red-sea-irrefutable-evidence/.

628   *Id.*

629   *Id.*

630   *See, e.g., Chris Mooney, No, really: There is a scientific explanation for the parting of the
Red Sea in Exodus*, The Washington Post (Dec. 8, 2014),
https://www.washingtonpost.com/news/wonk/wp/2014/12/08/no-really-there-is-a-
scientific-explanation-for-the-parting-of-the-red-sea-in-exodus/.

631   *Id.*

632   *Id.*

633   *See, e.g.,* Yam Suph, Wikipedia (last edited Apr.3, 2021), https://en.wikipedia.org/wiki/Yam_Suph.

634   *Id.*

       See also Chris Mooney, *Scientific explanation behind the parting of Red Sea*, News Leader (Dec. 13, 2014), https://www.newsleader.com/story/life/2014/12/13/scientific-explanation-behind-parting-red-sea/20288229/.

635   *Id.*

636   *See* Navah, *Yam Suph—Red Sea or Sea of Reeds*, Time of Reckoning (Aug 21, 2020), https://timeofreckoning.org/category/yam-suph-red-sea-or-sea-of-reeds#:~:text.

637   *See, e.g., Who Were the Philistines?*, Conversation Starters (House Church Network Association), http://www.hcna.us/columns/phili.html#.

638   *See, e.g., Sinai Peninsula*, Wikipedia (last updated Aug. 9, 2021), https://en.wikipedia.org/wiki/Sinai_Peninsula.

639   Copied from Nations Online Project, nationsonline.org, © 1998-2021, https://www.nationsonline.org/oneworld/map/Sinai_map.htm.

640   *See, e.g., Sinai Peninsula map*, https://www.nationsonline.org/oneworld/map/Sinai_map.htm.

641   *See, e.g., Goshen*, All About Archaeology (© 2002-2021 AllAboutArchaeology.org), https://www.allaboutarchaeology.org/goshen.htm.

642   *See* Steve Rudd, *The Exodus Route: Red Sea Camp at the Straits of Tiran*, https://www.bible.ca/archeology/bible-archeology-exodus-route-straits-of-tiran.htm.

643   *See, e.g., Gulf of Aqaba*, Wikipedia (last edited July 18, 2021), https://en.wikipedia.org/wiki/Gulf_of_Aqaba.

644   *See, e.g.,* Steve Rudd, *The Exodus Route: Goshen to the Red Sea*, https://www.bible.ca/archeology/bible-archeology-exodus-route-goshen-red-sea.htm.

645   *See, e.g.,* Amanda Briney, *Suez Canal History and Overview*, ThoughtCo (updated September 09, 2019), https://www.thoughtco.com/suez-canal-red-sea-mediterranean-sea-1435568.

646   *See, e.g.,* Reuters Staff, *Pharaonic-era sacred lake unearthed in Egypt*, Reuters (Oct. 15, 2009), (Online).

647   *See* Joshua 6:8–20 (written 1405–1385 BC).

648   *See* Joshua 6:21, 24 (written 1405–1385 BC).

649   *See* Paul L. Maier, *Biblical History: The Faulty Criticism of Biblical Historicity*, CRI (Mar. 30, 2009), http://www.equip.org/article/biblical-history-the-faulty-criticism-of-biblical-historicity/. (Emphasis added).

650   *Id.*

651   *Id.*

652   *Id.*

653   *See* Bryant Wood and Gary Byer of Associates for Biblical Research, *Is the Bible accurate concerning the existence and destruction of the walls of Jericho?*, Christian Answers.net, http://www.christiananswers.net/q-abr/abr-a011.html.

654   *Id.*

655   *Id.*

656   *See* Paul L. Maier, *Biblical History: The Faulty Criticism of Biblical Historicity*, CRI (Mar. 30, 2009), http://www.equip.org/article/biblical-history-the-faulty-criticism-of-biblical-historicity/.

One author said, "there is evidence now that [Kathleen Kenyon] messed up her dating of the fall of Jericho quite badly."

Gary Hastert, *Did The Fall of Jericho Happen The Way It Was Described In Jericho 5 & 6?* (Sept. 28, 2014), https://garyhastert.wordpress.com/2014/09/28/did-the-fall-of-jericho-happen-the-way-it-was-described-in-jericho-5-6/.

See also Meranda Devan, *Archaeological Proof Of Jericho*, Why God, http://whygodreallyexists.com/archives/archaeological-proof-of-jericho.

But see John Noble Wilford, *Believers Score in Battle Over the Battle of Jericho*, The New York Times (Feb. 22, 1990), www.nytimes.com/1990/02/22/world/believers-score-in-battle-over-the-battle-of-jericho.html discussing other viewpoints.

657   "Stratigraphic studies deal primarily with sedimentary rocks but may also encompass layered igneous rocks (e.g., those resulting from successive lava flows) or metamorphic rocks formed either from such extrusive igneous material or from sedimentary rocks."

The Editors of Encyclopaedia Britannica, *Stratigraphy-geology*, Britannica (added to new online database, July 20, 1998), https://www.britannica.com/science/stratigraphy-geology.

Dr. Wood may have had advantages that Dame Kenyon did not have. Following failed attempts during the last half of the 19th century by the International Geological Congress (founded 1878) to standardize a stratigraphic scale, it was not until after the International Union of Geological Sciences was founded in 1961 that a Commission on Stratigraphy to standardize a stratigraphic scale was established.

See The Editors of Encyclopaedia Britannica, Britannica, https://www.britannica.com/science/stratigraphy-geology.

658   Dr. Wood may have also had the advantage over Dame Kenyon in that area as well; carbon-14 dating had been around forty to forty-five years longer when he did his work at Jericho.

See The Editors of Encyclopaedia Britannica, *Carbon-14 dating—scientific technology* (alternative title: *radiocarbon dating*), Britannica (corrected display issue, Feb, 7, 2020), https://www.britannica.com/science/carbon-14-dating.

659   *See* Paul L. Maier, *Biblical History: The Faulty Criticism of Biblical Historicity*, CRI (Mar. 30, 2009),
      http://www.equip.org/article/biblical-history-the-faulty-criticism-of-biblical-historicity/.

660   *See* Paul L. Maier, *Biblical Archaeology: Factual Evidence to Support the Historicity of the Bible*, CRI (Mar. 30, 2009), http://www.equip.org/article/biblical-archaeology-factual-evidence-to-support-the-historicity-of-the-bible/.

661   *Id.*

      See also Biblical Archaeology Society Staff, *Hezekiah's Tunnel Reexamined*, Bible History Daily (Nov. 28, 2020), https://www.biblicalarchaeology.org/daily/biblical-sites-places/jerusalem/hezekiahs-tunnel-reexamined/

      and *Siloam tunnel*, Wikipedia (last edited on Jan. 25, 2021), https://en.wikipedia.org/wiki/Siloam_tunnel.

662   *Id.*

663   *See* Paul L. Maier, *Biblical Archaeology: Factual Evidence to Support the Historicity of the Bible*, CRI (Mar. 30, 2009), www.equip.org/article/biblical-archaeology-factual-evidence-to-support-the-historicity-of-the-bible/.

664   The southern kingdom of the Israelites which, after King Solomon died, was controlled by two of the twelve Jewish tribes.

      See, e.g., Who Are the Tribes of Judah?, Jewish Vice (published Aug. 30, 2018 - © 2021, Jewish Voice Ministries International),
      https://www.jewishvoice.org/read/blog/who-are-tribes-judah#:~:text.

665   *See, e.g., The Fourth Expedition To Lachish*, Southern Adventist University,
      https://www.southern.edu/administration/archaeology/lachish/index.html#!#:~:text;

      Cristian Violatti, *10 Archaeological Discoveries Consistent With Biblical Passages*, List Verse (Nov. 4, 2016), https://listverse.com/2016/11/04/10-archaeological-discoveries-consistent-with-biblical-passages;

      Noah Wiener, *Lachish: Open Access to BAR Articles on Lachish Archaeology*, Bible History Daily (Aug. 14, 2016), https://www.biblicalarchaeology.org/daily/biblical-sites-places/biblical-archaeology-sites/lachish/.

666   *See* Cristian Violatti, *10 Archaeological Discoveries Consistent With Biblical Passages*, List Verse (Nov. 4, 2016), https://listverse.com/2016/11/04/10-archaeological-discoveries-consistent-with-biblical-passages.

667   *See* 1 Corinthians 15:5–8 (written 55 AD).

668   *See and compare, e.g.,* Ken Curtis, *Whatever Happened to the Twelve Apostles?*, Christianity.com (originally published Apr. 28, 2010), https://www.christianity.com/church/church-history/timeline/1-300/whatever-happened-to-the-twelve-apostles-11629558.html;

Steven Gertz, *How do we know 10 of the disciples were martyred?*, CT, https://www.christianitytoday.com/history/2008/august/how-do-we-know-10-of-disciples-were-martyred.html;

Ray Konig, *What happened to the Apostles?*, About-Jesus.org (© About-Jesus.org), http://www.about-jesus.org/martyrs.htm;

Jack Wellman, *Which Of The Apostles Were Martyred?*, What Christians Want to Know (Copyright © 2010-2021 Telling Ministries LLC), https://www.whatchristianswanttoknow.com/which-of-the-apostles-were-martyred/.

669   *See* Chapter 3, *supra*, for a general discussion about Luke.

670   *See* Chapter 5, *supra*, for discussion about Capernaum.

671   Gerasenes was a city on the eastern shore of the Sea of Galilee.

See, e.g., Gerasenes, Bible Hub (© 2004-2021 by Bible Hub), https://biblehub.com/topical/g/gerasenes.htm.

672   Tyre and Sidon "are on the Mediterranean coast in what was Phoenicia in the first century AD and what is Lebanon today, just north of Israel. Tyre is located about 20 kilometers (14 miles) north of the current Israeli-Lebanese border, and Sidon is located about 20 miles (32 kilometers) north of Tyre."

See Tyre and Sidon, BibleVerseStudy.com, https://www.bibleversestudy.com/acts/acts12-tyre-and-sidon.htm.

Decapolis, league of 10 ancient Greek cities in eastern Palestine that was formed after the Roman conquest of Palestine in 63 BC, when Pompey the Great reorganized the Middle East to Rome's advantage and to his own. The name Decapolis also denotes the roughly contiguous territory formed by these cities, all but one of which lay east of the Jordan River.

The Editors of Encyclopaedia Britannica, *Decapolis, ancient Greek league, Palestine*, Britannica (article revised, Apr. 12, 2002), https://www.britannica.com/place/Decapolis-ancient-cities-Palestine/additional-info#history.

673   *See* Chapter 5, *supra*, for discussion about Bethsaida.

674   Lake of Gennesaret is in "northern Israel and is the largest body of fresh water in Israel;" it "supplies fresh water not only to Israel but also to the neighboring country of Jordan."

See, e.g., Lake of Gennesaret (© ISRAELJERUSALEM.COM), https://www.israeljerusalem.com/lake-of-gennesaret.htm

675   *See also* Zechariah 12:10 (written 520–470 BC)

676   *See, e.g.,* Ronald Cram, *Top NT Archaeological Finds*, Factbridge, http://factbridge.org/sites/default/files/inline-files/Top-NT-Archaeological-Finds.pdf at No. 8 (citing http://bit.ly/Yehohanan).

When Only God Knew

677   *Id.*

678   *Id.*

679   *Id.*

680   *See generally*, Chapter 3, *supra*.

681   *See* Peter Hawkins, *Jesus' Resurrection: Eyewitness Accounts*, Life Hope & Truth, https://lifehopeandtruth.com/god/who-is-jesus/jesus-resurrection/.

     See also Stephen Nielsen, *13 Post-Resurrection Appearances of Jesus* (Published Apr. 11, 2020). https://stephennielsen.com/2020/04/11/13-post-resurrection-appearances-of-jesus/.

682   *See* Jack Zavada, *7 Proofs of the Resurrection*, Learn religions (updated Apr. 26, 2019), https://www.learnreligions.com/proofs-of-the-resurrection-700603.

     See also, e.g., Ed Jarrett, *What Is the Importance of the Empty Tomb?*, Christianity.com (originally published Feb. 14, 2020), https://www.christianity.com/wiki/jesus-christ/the-importance-of-the-empty-tomb.html;

     How Do Women Eyewitnesses Lend Credibility To The Resurrection Accounts?, The John Ankerberg Show (Mar. 6, 2018), https://jashow.org/articles/how-do-women-eyewitnesses-lend-credibility-to-the-resurrection-accounts/ (no longer online);

     The Courage and Conviction of the First Believers, the WORD Among Us (© 2021 The Word Among Us), https://wau.org/resources/article/the_courage_and_conviction_of_the_first_believers/;

     Bill Pratt, *How Does James' Belief in Jesus Corroborate the Resurrection?*, Tough Questions Answered (Aug. 11, 2017), https://www.toughquestionsanswered.org/2017/08/11/how-does-james-belief-in-jesus-corroborate-the-resurrection/.

683   *See, e.g., Jewish Time Divisions In The 1st Century AD*, Agape Bible Study (Copyright © 1991, revised 2012 Agape Bible Study), https://www.agapebiblestudy.com/charts/jewishtimedivision.htm;

     #5a Hours of the Day, Days of the Month, Months of the Year in Scripture - #5a1 Calculating Hours of the Day in Scripture, Bibletime Studies, (Online).

684   "In the apostolic period, Iconium was one of the chief cities in the southern part of the Roman province Galatia, and it probably belonged to the "Phrygian region" mentioned in Acts 16:6."

     Iconium, BibleHub Atlas, https://bibleatlas.org/iconium.htm.

     "Phrygia was the name of an ancient Anatolian kingdom (12th-7th century BCE) and, following its demise, the term was then applied to the general geographical area it once covered in the western plateau of Asia Minor."

Mark Caldwell, *Phrygia—Definition*, World History Encyclopedia (published Sept. 5, 2019), https://www.ancient.eu/phrygia/.

685   Lycaonia "[w]as a country in the central and southern part of Asia Minor whose boundaries and extent varied at different periods." In the time of Paul, it was bounded on the West by Pisidia and Phrygia.

       See, e.g., Lycaonia, BibleHub, https://bibleatlas.org/lycaonia.htm.

686   *See, e.g., Ronald Cram, *Top NT Archaeological Finds*, Factbridge, http://factbridge.org/sites/default/files/inline-files/Top-NT-Archaeological-Finds.pdf at No. 6 (citing http://bit.ly/PhrygianAltar).

687   *Id.*

688   *Id.*

689   *Id.*

690   *See Biblical Archaeology 44: Iconium was not in Lycaonia*, Theo-sophical Ruminations (posted by Theosophical Ruminator under Archaeology, Sept. 26, 2011), https://theosophical.wordpress.com/2011/09/26/biblical-archaeology-44-iconium-was-not-in-lycaonia/.

Part III

691   *See, e.g.* Dictionary.com, https://www.dictionary.com/browse/science.

692   *See, e.g.* Merriam Webster, https://www.merriam-webster.com/dictionary/science.

693   *See* Jeremy Gyorke, *Is the Bible Scientifically Accurate?*, Patch (posted Jan 15, 2014), https://patch.com/michigan/wyandotte/is-the-bible-scientifically-accurate.

694   Phillip Power, *Intelligence & Unbelief—the Not-so causal Relationship*, Mensa Bulletin, The Magazine of American Mensa (Aug. 2021) at 22.

695   Johannes Kepler, who lived from 1571 to 1639, "discovered three major laws of planetary motion, conventionally designated as follows: (1) the planets move in elliptical orbits with the Sun at one focus; (2) the time necessary to traverse any arc of a planetary orbit is proportional to the area of the sector between the central body and that arc (the "area law"); and (3) there is an exact relationship between the squares of the planets' periodic times and the cubes of the radii of their orbits (the "harmonic law"). Kepler himself did not call these discoveries "laws," as would become customary after Isaac Newton derived them from a new and quite different set of general physical principles."

       See Robert H. Westman, *Johannes Kepler-German Astronomer*, Britannica (anniversary information added Dec 23, 2020) https://www.britannica.com/biography/Johannes-Kepler.

696   *See* Jeremy Gyorke, *Is the Bible Scientifically Accurate?*, Patch (posted Jan 15, 2014), https://patch.com/michigan/wyandotte/is-the-bible-scientifically-accurate.

697   *Id.*

698 *See* Phillip Power, *Intelligence & Unbelief—the Not-so causal Relationship*, Mensa Bulletin, The Magazine of American Mensa (Aug. 2021) at 21.

699 *Id.* at 21.

700 *See, e.g., René Descartes*, Stanford Encyclopedia of Philosophy (first published Dec 3, 2008; substantive revision Jan 16, 2014), https://plato.stanford.edu/entries/descartes/.

701 *See* Phillip Power, *Intelligence & Unbelief—the Not-so causal Relationship*, Mensa Bulletin, The Magazine of American Mensa (Aug. 2021) at 20-21.

702 *Id.* at 21–22.

703 *Id.* at 22.

704 Systematically postulated by Charles Darwin when he published his famous book *On the Origin of Species* in 1859.

705 *See, e.g.,* Doug Powell, *Guide to Christian Apologetics at 69*, Holman Reference (Nashville, Tennessee © 2006 by Doug Powell) (citing Allan Sandage, *A Scientist Reflects on Religious Belief*, available online at Leadership U., http://www.leaderu.com/truth/1truth15.html).

706 *See* James Bishop, *How Science Led A World Leading Astronomer, Allan Sandage, To God*, Rason for Jesus (Oct. 10, 2017), https://reasonsforjesus.com/how-science-led-a-world-leading-astronomer-allan-sandage-to-god/.

707 *See, e.g.,* Jeremy Gyorke, *Is the Bible Scientifically Accurate?*, Patch (posted Jan 15, 2014), https://patch.com/michigan/wyandotte/is-the-bible-scientifically-accurate.

     See also Martin Vika, *Science As Proof Of The Bible*, Course Hero, https://www.coursehero.com/file/55628896/77807466-Science-as-Proof-of-the-Bible.pdf/.

708 *See, e.g.,* Jeremy Gyorke, *Is the Bible Scientifically Accurate?*, Patch (posted Jan 15, 2014), https://patch.com/michigan/wyandotte/is-the-bible-scientifically-accurate.

709 *Id.*

710 *See* David R. Reagan, *Applying the Science of Probability to the Scriptures—Do statistics prove the Bible's supernatural origin?*, Lamb and Lion Ministries, https://christinprophecy.org/articles/applying-the-science-of-probability-to-the-scriptures.

711 *Id.*

Chapter 7

712 Portions quoted directly from Jason Lisle, *How Do You Know the Bible Is True?*, Answers in Genesis (Mar. 22, 2011), https://answersingenesis.org/is-the-bible-true/how-do-we-know-that-the-bible-is-true/.

713 *See History of biology*, Wikipedia (last edited Aug. 8, 2021, https://en.wikipedia.org/wiki/History_of_biology.

714 *Compare* Michael Brown, *Mitochondrial Eve*, Molecular History Research Center (posted January 1, 1998), http://www.mhrc.net/mitochondrialEve.htm;

Wynne Perry, *Age Confirmed for 'Eve,' Mother of All Humans*, Live Science (Aug. 18, 2010), https://www.livescience.com/10015-age-confirmed-eve-mother-humans.html;

Rice University (source), *'Mitochondrial Eve:' Mother of all humans lived 200,000 years ago*, ScienceDaily (Aug. 17, 2010), https://www.sciencedaily.com/releases/2010/08/100817122405.htm.

715   Short for Mitochondrial DNA. "Mitochondrial DNA is the small circular chromosome found inside mitochondria. The mitochondria are organelles[, the 'tiny cellular structure that performs specific functions within a cell,'] found in cells that are the sites of energy production. The mitochondria, and thus mitochondrial DNA, are passed from mother to offspring."

See William Gahl, *Mitochondrial DNA*, National Human Genome Research Institute, https://www.genome.gov/genetics-glossary/Mitochondrial-DNA (no longer online);

See also Regina Bailey, *What Is an Organelle?*, ThoughtCo (updated June 17, 2019), https://www.thoughtco.com/organelles-meaning-373368.

716   *See, e.g.,* Alasdair Wilkins, *How Mitochondrial Eve connected all humanity and rewrote human evolution*, Gizmodo (Jan. 24, 2012), https://io9.gizmodo.com/5878996/how-mitochondrial-eve-connected-all-humanity-and-rewrote-human-evolution;

Brian Thomas, *Mother of All Humans Lived 6,000 Years Ago*, Institution of Creation Research (Sept. 7, 2010), https://www.icr.org/article/mother-all-humans-lived-6000-years, and others.

717   *Compare* Michael Brown, *Mitochondrial Eve*, Molecular History Research Center (posted January 1, 1998), http://www.mhrc.net/mitochondrialEve.htm;

Wynne Perry, *Age Confirmed for 'Eve,' Mother of All Humans*, Live Science (Aug. 18, 2010), https://www.livescience.com/10015-age-confirmed-eve-mother-humans.html;

Rice University (source), *'Mitochondrial Eve:' Mother of all humans lived 200,000 years ago*, ScienceDaily (Aug. 17, 2010), https://www.sciencedaily.com/releases/2010/08/100817122405.htm;

Brian Thomas, *Mother of All Humans Lived 6,000 Years Ago*, Institute of Creation Research (Sept. 7, 2010), https://www.icr.org/article/mother-all-humans-lived-6000-years.

718   *See* Unknown Author, *(False) Scientific Facts in the Bible by Carol Brooks: A Critique* (Oct. 19, 2012), https://biblevsfacts.blogspot.com/2012/10/scientific-facts-in-bible-by-carol.html.

As of March 20, 2021, no comments have been received to this article in the almost ten years since it was published.

719   *See* Chapter 1 at note 6.

720   *See, e.g., The Elements of Life: The elements that compose 99.9% of your body*, TKSST, https://thekidshouldseethis.com/post/elements-human-body.

721   *See, e.g.,* Anne Marie Helmenstine, *Element Discovery Timeline - When Were the Elements Discovered?*, ThoughtCo (updated Oct, 03, 2018), https://www.thoughtco.com/element-discovery-timeline-606607.

722   *See* Carol Brooks, *Scientific Facts in the Bible*, https://www.inplainsite.org/html/scientific_facts_in_the_bible.html (citing Fred Williams, Advanced Scientific Knowledge).

      See also Scientific Evidence, Evidences of the Bible (Mar. 1, 1999), https://bibleevidences.com/science/;

      Soil Nutrient Management for Maui County, College of Tropical Agricultural and Human Resources (CTAHR), University of Hawaii at Manoa (copyright ©2007-2021 University of Hawaii), www.ctahr.hawaii.edu/mauisoil/c_nutrients.aspx.

723   *See* Anne Marie Helmenstine, *What Are the Elements in the Human Body?-Elemental Composition of a Human Being*, ThoughCo (Feb. 24, 2020), https://www.thoughtco.com/elements-in-the-human-body-p2-602188

724   *Id.*

725   *See, e.g., Chemical elements listed by elements in earthcrust*, Lenntech (copyright © 1998-2021 Lenntech B.V.), https://www.lenntech.com/periodic chart elements/earthcrust.htm.

726   *See, e.g.,* Anne Marie Helmenstine, *Element Discovery Timeline - When Were the Elements Discovered?*, ThoughtCo (Oct. 3, 2018). https://www.thoughtco.com/element-discovery-timeline-606607.

727   *Id.*

728   *See* T.L. Winslow, *TLW's Chemical Elementscope™ (Chemical Element Historyscope)* (original pub. date: Mar. 31, 2016. last updated: Jan. 12, 2021), historyscoper.com/chemicalelementscope.html;

      Chemical elements listed by the discovery year, Lenntech (copyright © 1998-2021 Lenntech B.V.), http://www.lenntech.com/periodic-chart-elements/discovery-year.htm.

729   *Id.*

730   While sulfur was known during ancient times, it was not until 1777 that Antoine Lavoisier, the prominent French chemist who lived from 1743 to 1794, convinced the rest of the scientific community that sulfur was an element.

      See, e.g., The Element Sulfur, JLab Science Education, https://education.jlab.org/itselemental/ele016.html;

      Arthur L. Donovan, *Antoine Lavoisier - French chemist* (alternative title: *Antoine-Laurent Lavoisier*), Britannica (last updated: Jan 25, 2021), https://www.britannica.com/biography/Antoine-Lavoisier.

731   *See Molecular Genetics - The Theory of Biogenesis*, Toppr,
      https://www.toppr.com/guides/biology/molecular-genetics/the-theory-of-biogenesis.

732   *See Biogenesis*, Wikipedia (last edited Feb. 25, 2021),
      https://en.wikipedia.org/wiki/Biogenesis.

733   *See The Bible and Biogenesis*, The Last Dialogue (The Last Dialogue|© 2021),
      https://www.thelastdialogue.org/article/bible-and-biogenesis/.

734   The Greek philosopher who lived 384-322 BC and was introduced to West in the 13th
      Century AD , whose philosophy was eventually subsumed by the Catholic Church.

      See, e.g., History.com Editors, *Aristotle*, History (updated Aug 22, 2019, original: Nov 9,
      2009), https://www.history.com/topics/ancient-history/aristotle.

735   *See, e.g., Molecular Genetics - The Theory of Biogenesis*, Toppr,
      https://www.toppr.com/guides/biology/molecular-genetics/the-theory-of-biogenesis/;

      Biogenesis, Wikipedia (last edited Feb. 25, 2021),
      https://en.wikipedia.org/wiki/Biogenesis.

736   *See Molecular Genetics - The Theory of Biogenesis*, Toppr,
      https://www.toppr.com/guides/biology/molecular-genetics/the-theory-of-biogenesis/;

737   *Id.*

738   *See* President of the B.A.A.S., *Biogenesis and Abiogenesis, Critiques and Addresses*
      (1870), Collected Essays VIII, https://mathcs.clarku.edu/huxley/CE8/B-Ab.html.

739   Francesco Redi's was an innovative scientist, physician, and poet who lived from 1626 to
      1697.

      See Francesco Redi, Famous Scientists, famousscientists.org. (Nov. 12, 2016),
      https://www.famousscientists.org/francesco-redi/,

740   *See Molecular Genetics - The Theory of Biogenesis*, Toppr,
      https://www.toppr.com/guides/biology/molecular-genetics/the-theory-of-biogenesis/.

741   Rudolf Carl Virchow (born October 13, 1821, and died September 5, 1902), was a German
      pathologist and statesman and one of the most prominent physicians of the 19th century.

      See E. Ashworth Underwood, *Rudolf Virchow—German Scientist* (alternative title: *Rudolf
      Carl Virchow*), Britannica (last updated Sept. 1, 2021),
      https://www.britannica.com/biography/Rudolf-Virchow.

742   *See, e.g.,* Lauren Posey, *What is Biogenesis?-Definition & Theory*, Study.com (© copyright
      2003-2021 Study.com),
      https://study.com/academy/lesson/what-is-biogenesis-definition-theory.html.

743   Louis Pasteur (born 1822 and died 1895), was the "French chemist and microbiologist who
      was one of the most important founders of medical microbiology. Pasteur's contributions
      to science, technology, and medicine are nearly without precedent. He pioneered the study
      of molecular asymmetry; discovered that microorganisms cause fermentation and disease;
      originated the process of pasteurization; saved the beer, wine, and silk industries in France;

and developed vaccines against anthrax and rabies."

See, e.g., Agnes Ullmann, *Louis Pasteur—French chemist and microbiologist*, Britannica (last updated: Feb 12, 2021), https://www.britannica.com/biography/Louis-Pasteur.

744   *See Molecular Genetics—The Theory of Biogenesis*, Toppr, https://www.toppr.com/guides/biology/molecular-genetics/the-theory-of-biogenesis/.

745   *See Biogenesis*, Wikipedia (last edited Feb. 25, 2021), https://en.wikipedia.org/wiki/Biogenesis.

746   *See, e.g.,* The Editors of Encyclopaedia Britannica, *Prothrombin—biochemistry*, Britannica (article revised and updated., Jan. 4, 2007), https://www.britannica.com/science/prothrombin;

Richard Bowen, *Vitamin K*, VIVO Pathophysiology, http://www.vivo.colostate.edu/hbooks/pathphys/topics/vitamink.html.

747   *See, e.g.,* Carol Brooks, *Scientific Facts in the Bible*, https://www.inplainsite.org/html/scientific_facts_in_the_bible.html (citing *Vitamins and Hormones* by Harris, Kenneth Vivian Thimann. Page 115);

Blood Clotting in Infants, The Last Dialogue (The Last Dialogue|© 2021), https://www.thelastdialogue.org/article/bible-miracle-blood-clotting-in-infants/.

748   *See, e.g.,* BibleAsk Team, *Why did God command circumcision on the eighth day?*, https://bibleask.org/why-did-god-command-circumcision-on-the-eighth-day/.

749   *See, e.g.,* John D. Stewart, M.D., and G. Margaret Rourke, B.A., *Prothrombin and Vitamin K Therapy*, The New England Journal of Medicine (Sept. 14, 1939), vol. 221, no. 11, http://www.nejm.org/doi/pdf/10.1056/NEJM193909142211101.

750   *See* Ferland G., *The Discovery of Vitamin K and Its Clinical Applications*, Annals of Nutrition and Metabolism (copyright © 2012 S. Karger AG, Basel), https://www.karger.com/Article/Abstract/343108.

751   *See, e.g., The Circulatory System - Part II: The Heart and Circulation of Blood,* http://lsa.colorado.edu/essence/texts/heart.html;

Kim Ann Zimmermann, *The Circulatory System: An Amazing Circuit That Keeps Our Bodies Going*, Live Science (Aug. 08, 2019), https://www.livescience.com/22486-circulatory-system.html.

752   *Id.*

753   William Harvey (1578 to 1657 AD) "was an English physician who was the first to describe accurately how blood was pumped around the body by the heart."

See BBC, *William Harvey (1578–1657)*, History (BBC © 2014), http://www.bbc.co.uk/history/historic_figures/harvey_william.shtml.

754   *See, e.g.,* Institute of Creation Research, *life of the flesh*, Discover and Defend (Content ©2021 Institute for Creation Research), http://www.icr.org/books/defenders/858;

C N Trueman, "William Harvey," History Learning Site (Mar. 17, 2015; Mar. 24, 2021), http://www.historylearningsite.co.uk/a-history-of-medicine/william-harvey/.

755   *See, e.g.,* Carol Brooks, *Scientific Facts in the Bible*, https://www.inplainsite.org/html/scientific_facts_in_the_bible.html.

756   *See* Oliver Stewart, *Bloodletting: A Brief Historical Perspective and Modern Medical Applications*, Clinical Correlations (Oct. 31, 2019), https://www.clinicalcorrelations.org/2019/10/31/bloodletting-a-brief-historical-perspective-and-modern-medical-applications//.

757   *Id.*

758   *See, e.g.,* Gerry Greenstone, *The history of bloodletting*, BCMJ (January, February 2010), Vol. 52, No. 1, http://www.bcmj.org/premise/history-bloodletting.

759   *Id.*

760   *Id.*

761   *Id.*

762   *See, e.g.,* D.P. Thomas, *The demise of bloodletting* (copyright © 2014 Royal College of Physicians of Edinburgh), http://www.rcpe.ac.uk/sites/default/files/thomas_0.pdf.

763   *Id.*

764   *See, e.g.,* Gerry Greenstone, *The history of bloodletting*, BCMJ (January, February 2010), Vol. 52, No. 1, http://www.bcmj.org/premise/history-bloodletting.

765   The Talmud "is the generic term for the documents that comment and expand upon the Mishnah ("repeating"), the first work of rabbinic law, published around the year 200 CE by Rabbi Judah the Patriarch in the land of Israel."

       See, e.g., MJL, *What Is the Talmud?*, Jewish Learning (Copyright © 2002-2021. My Jewish Learning), https://www.myjewishlearning.com/article/talmud-101/.

       The Mishnah is "a document in six primary sections, or orders, dealing with agriculture, sacred times, women and personal status, damages, holy things, and purity laws;" it lays "out different opinions concerning Jewish law."

       Id.

766   Moses Maimonides was a "Jewish philosopher, jurist, and physician [and] the foremost intellectual figure of medieval Judaism."

       See, e.g., Ben Zion Bokser, *Moses Maimonides-Jewish philosopher, scholar, and physician* (alternative titles: *Abū 'Imran Mūsā ibn Maymūn ibn 'Ubayd Allāh, Moses ben Maimon, Rambam*), Britannica (anniversary information added December 9, 2020), https://www.britannica.com/biography/Moses-Maimonides.

       He lived from March 30, 1135, to December 13, 1204, His original name was Moses ben Maimon, but he was also called Rambam and had the "Arabic name Abū 'Imran Mūsā ibn Maymūn ibn 'Ubayd Allāh."

Id.

767 *See Bloodletting, Encyclopaedia Judaica*, Jewish Virtual Library (copyright © 2008 The Gale Group), https://www.jewishvirtuallibrary.org/bloodletting (Emphasis added).

768 The Areopagus was the earliest aristocratic council of ancient Athens whose "name was taken from the Areopagus ("Ares' Hill"), a low hill northwest of the Acropolis, which was its meeting place" in Athens.

See, e.g., The Editors of Encyclopaedia Britannica, Britannica (Article added to new online July 20, 1998). https://www.britannica.com/topic/Areopagus-Greek-council.

769 *See Doing Away With "Race"*, Kingdom Come (Jan. 29, 2021), https://www.kingdom-come.net/?p=1543.

See also Chris Noland, *Gospel Life: Race Relations* (July 11, 2019), https://chrisnoland.org/2019/07/11/gospel-life-race-relations/

Both contain excerpts from Ken Ham, *One Blood* (originally published under the name, *Darwin's Plantation* in 2007).

770 *See Blood Transfusion*, encyclopedia.com (Oxford University Press—updated May 14, 2018), http://www.encyclopedia.com/medicine/divisions-diagnostics-and-procedures/medicine/blood-transfusion.

771 *See* Dariush D. Farhud and Marjan Zarit Yeganeh, *A Brief History of Human Blood Groups*, Iranian Journal of Public Health (Jan. 1, 2013), https://www.ncbi.nlm.nih.gov/pmc/articles/PMC3595629/.

772 *See Facts About Blood and Blood Types*, American Red Cross, http://www.redcrossblood.org/learn-about-blood/blood-types.html.

See also Dennis O'Neil, *Distribution of Blood Types* (Copyright © 1998-2012 Dennis O'Neil), https://www2.palomar.edu/anthro/vary/vary_3.htm.

773 Larry Adelman, *Race and Gene Studies: What Differences Make a Difference?*, http://www.pbs.org/race/000_About/002_04-background-01-02.htm

774 "An allele is one of two or more versions of a gene."

See, e.g., Leslie G. Biesecker, *Allele*, National Human Genome Research Institute, https://www.genome.gov/genetics-glossary/Allele.

775 *See A History of the Male and Female Genitalia*, https://web.stanford.edu/class/history13/earlysciencelab/body/femalebodypages/genitalia.html.

776 *See, e.g.,* Marc V., "Aristotle's Ideas," *10 Monumental Historical Misconceptions About the Female Body*, List Verse (Jan. 19, 2014), http://listverse.com/2014/01/19/10-historical-misconceptions-about-the-female-body/.

777 *See, e.g.,* Carol Brooks, *Scientific Facts in the Bible* (Part II), www.inplainsite.org, https://www.inplainsite.org/html/scientific_facts_in_the_bible.html.

778   *See, e.g.,* M. Cobb, *An Amazing 10 Years: The Discovery of Egg and Sperm in the 17th Century,* Reproduction in Domestic Animals (copyright 2012 Blackwell Verlag GmbH), Suppl. 4, 2–6, https://onlinelibrary.wiley.com/doi/pdf/10.1111/j.1439-0531.2012.02105.x;

M. Cobb, *An Amazing 10 Years: The Discovery of Egg and Sperm in the 17th Century,* PubMed.gov (Reprod Domest Anim. 2012 Aug;4), https://pubmed.ncbi.nlm.nih.gov/22827343/.

779   Georg Moritz Ebers (1837–1898), a "prolific German novelist and Egyptologist[, is] best known for his discovery and publication of the Ebers Egyptian Medical Papyrus."

See C.D. Merriman for Jalic Inc., *Georg Ebers,* The Literature Network (copyright © Jalic Inc 2005), http://www.online-literature.com/georg-ebers/.

780   *See, e.g.,* Evan Andrews, *7 Unusual Ancient Medical Techniques,* History (© 2021 A&E Television Networks, LLC), https://www.history.com/news/7-unusual-ancient-medical-techniques.

781   *See, e.g.,* B. B. Wagner, *The Ebers Papyrus: Medico-Magical Beliefs and Treatments Revealed in Ancient Egyptian Medical Text,* Ancient Origins, Ancient Origins (updated July 22, 2019), https://www.ancient-origins.net/artifacts-ancient-writings/ebers-papyrus-0012333.

782   *See* Carol Brooks, *Scientific Facts in the Bible—Part II,* https://www.inplainsite.org/html/scientific_facts_in_the_bible.html;

S.E. Massengill, *A sketch of medicine and pharmacy and a view of its progress by the Massengill family from the fifteenth to the twentieth century,* Internet Archive (Bristol, Tenn.-Va. The S. E. Massengill Company), www.archive.org/stream/ sketchofmedicine00massuoft/sketchofmedicine00massuoft_djvu.txt.

783   *See, e.g.,* Joshua J. Mark, *Egyptian Medical Treatments,* World History Encyclopedia (published Feb, 20, 2017), https://www.worldhistory.org/article/51/egyptian-medical-treatments/;

Carol Brooks, *Scientific Facts in the Bible—part II,* https://www.inplainsite.org/html/scientific_facts_in_the_bible.html;

S.E. Massengill, *A sketch of medicine and pharmacy and a view of its progress by the Massengill family from the fifteenth to the twentieth century,* Internet Archive (Bristol, Tenn.-Va. The S. E. Massengill Company), www.archive.org/stream/ sketchofmedicine00massuoft/sketchofmedicine00massuoft_djvu.txt.

784   *See* Carol Brooks, *Scientific Facts in the Bible—Part II,* https://www.inplainsite.org/html/scientific_facts_in_the_bible.html citing Robert (Bob) M. Brier and Hoyt Hobbs. *Daily life of the ancient Egyptians Revised Edition* (Publisher: Greenwood; Revised edition (September 30, 2008) Pg. 280).

785   *See, e.g.,* Douglas J. Brewer and Emily Teeter, *Ancient Egyptian Society and Family Life,* Fathom Archive (This seminar is extracted from Chapter 7 of *Egypt and Egyptians,*

Cambridge University Press, 2001. Copyright Douglas J. Brewer and Emily Teeter 1999), http://fathom.lib.uchicago.edu/2/21701778/.

786 *See*, Carol Brooks, *Scientific Facts in the Bible—Part II*, https://www.inplainsite.org/html/scientific_facts_in_the_bible.html.

787 *See, e.g.*, Tzvi Freeman , *What Is Torah?—A Comprehensive Overview*, Chabad.org (© Copyright), https://www.chabad.org/library/article_cdo/aid/1426382/jewish/Torah.htm.

788 *See, e.g.,* Carol Brooks, *Scientific Facts in the Bible*, https://www.inplainsite.org/html/scientific_facts_in_the_bible.html.

789 *See, e.g.,* Joe Leech, *11 Evidence-Based Health Benefits of Eating Fish*, healthline (June 11, 2019), https://www.healthline.com/nutrition/11-health-benefits-of-fish.

790 *See, e.g.,* Is Shrimp Healthy or Harmful to Your Health, Smarternutrition (© 2021, Smarter Nutrition.), (no longer online).

791 *See* Leviticus 11:7–8 (NIV) (written 1450–1405 BC) which says, "⁷ And the pig, though it has a divided hoof, does not chew the cud; it is unclean for you. ⁸ You must not eat their meat or touch their carcasses; they are unclean for you."

792 *See e.g., Trichinosis*, Source: Medical Parasitology, Stanford University, https://web.stanford.edu/group/parasites/ParaSites2001/trichinosis/index.html.

793 "Cirrhosis is scarring of the liver" which can lead to many health complications, including death if untreated.

     See, e.g., Cirrhosis—Also called: Hepatic fibrosis, Medline Plus (some copyrighted content), https://medlineplus.gov/cirrhosis.html.

794 *See* Carol Brooks, *Scientific Facts in the Bible—Part II*, https://www.inplainsite.org/html/scientific_facts_in_the_bible.html (citing NCBI. *Relationship between pork consumption and cirrhosis*. https://www.ncbi.nlm.nih.gov/pubmed/2858627).

795 *See* European Food Safety Authority, *Hepatitis E: raw pork is main cause of infection in EU* (published July 11, 2017), https://www.efsa.europa.eu/en/press/news/170711.

796 "Germ theory, in medicine, [is] the theory that certain diseases are caused by the invasion of the body by microorganisms, organisms too small to be seen except through a microscope."

     The Editors of Encyclopaedia Britannica, *Germ theory-Medicine*, Britannica (article added to new online database July 20, 1998), https://www.britannica.com/science/germ-theory/.

797 *See, e.g.,* Carol Brooks, *Scientific Facts in the Bible—Part II*, https://www.inplainsite.org/html/scientific_facts_in_the_bible.html.

798 *See, e.g.,* Kat Eschner, *The Idea of Surgeons Washing Their Hands is Only 154 Years Old*, Smithsonian Magazine (Mar. 16, 2017), https://www.smithsonianmag.com/smart-news/idea-sterilizing-surgical-instruments-only-150-years-old-180962498/.

799   *See* Carol Brooks, *Scientific Facts in the Bible—Part II*,
      https://www.inplainsite.org/html/scientific_facts_in_the_bible.html.

800   Now called Eötvös Loránd University, it was founded in 1635 as a Catholic university for
      teaching theology and philosophy. In 1770, it was named Royal University of Pest until
      1873, then University of Budapest until 1921, when it was renamed Royal Hungarian
      Pázmány Péter University after its founder.

      See, Eötvös Loránd University, Wikipedia (last edited Sept. 4, 2021),
      https://en.wikipedia.org/wiki/Eötvös_Loránd_University.

801   *See, e.g.,* Carol Brooks, *Scientific Facts in the Bible—Part II*,
      https://www.inplainsite.org/html/scientific_facts_in_the_bible.html.

802   *Id.*

803   *See, e.g., Bible Verses about Quarantine—What does the Bible say about quarantine?*,
      Christianity.com (© 2021 Christianity.com),
      https://www.christianity.com/bible/bible-verses-about-quarantine-59.

804   *See also* Leviticus 13:1–4 (written 1450–1405 BC).

805   *See* American Standard Version, the Common English Bible, the Contemporary Version,
      the Easy-to-Read Version, the Modern English Version, New American Standard Bible,
      New International Version all at Leviticus 13:31–33.

806   Translated "leprosy" in the King James Version,

807   *See, e.g.,* Carol Brooks, *Scientific Facts in the Bible—Part II*,
      https://www.inplainsite.org/html/scientific_facts_in_the_bible.html.

808   *See Microbiology of M.leprae*, World Health Organization,
      https://www.who.int/lep/microbiology/en/,.

      See also Merriam Webster, https://www.merriam-webster.com/dictionary/leprosy.

809   *See* Carol Brooks, *Scientific Facts in the Bible—Part II*,
      https://www.inplainsite.org/html/scientific_facts_in_the_bible.html.

810   "The Black Death was a devastating global epidemic of bubonic plague that struck Europe
      and Asia in the mid-1300s."

      History.com Editors, *Black Death*, History (updated: July 6, 2020, original: Sept. 17,
      2010), https://www.history.com/topics/middle-ages/black-death.

811   *See, e.g.,* Beyond Today Editor, *Bible Commentary—Leviticus 13–15—Laws Regulating
      Disease and Bodily Discharges*, Beyond Today (posted May 22, 2002),
      https://www.ucg.org/bible-study-tools/bible-commentary/bible-commentary-
      leviticus-13-15.

812   *See, e.g.,* Jeremy Gyorke, *Is the Bible Scientifically Accurate?*, Patch (Jan 15, 2014),
      https://patch.com/michigan/wyandotte/is-the-bible-scientifically-accurate.

813   *See, e.g., History of Quarantine*, Centers for Disease Control and Prevention,
      https://www.cdc.gov/quarantine/historyquarantine.html.

814   *See, e.g., A Brief Summary of Louis Pasteur's Germ Theory of Disease*, BiologyWise (Copyright © Biology Wise & Buzzle.com, Inc.), https://biologywise.com/louis-pasteurs-germ-theory-of-disease;

       Germ Theory Of Disease, Vedantu, https://www.vedantu.com/biology/germ-theory-of-disease.

815   *See, e.g.,* John F. Walvoord, *4. Nebuchadnezzar's Pride And Punishment (contributed by www.walvoord.com)*, From the series: Daniel The Key To Prophetic Revelation, Bible.org, https://bible.org/seriespage/4-nebuchadnezzar-s-pride-and-punishment.

816   *See, e.g.,* Prospector, *Nebuchadnezzar and boanthropy*, The Pharmaceutical Journal (July 10, 2013—last updated Mar. 17, 2021), https://www.pharmaceutical-journal.com/opinion/blogs/nebuchadnezzar-and-boanthropy.

817   Barend Joseph Stokvis, who lived from 1834 to 1902, was a physician and professor of physiology and pharmacology at the University of Amsterdam.

       See, e.g., Barend Joseph Stokvis, Wikipedia (last edited Dec. 22, 2019), https://en.wikipedia.org/wiki/Barend_Joseph_Stokvis.

818   *See History of Porphyria*, American Porphyria Foundation (2010-2021 American Porphyria Foundation), https://porphyriafoundation.org/for-patients/about-porphyria/history-of-porphyria/;

       Nick Lane, *Born to the Purple: The Story of Porphyria,* Scientific American (Dec. 16, 2002), https://www.scientificamerican.com/article/born-to-the-purple-the-st/.

819   *See, e.g.,* http://theinfoscience.blogspot.com/2015/12/boanthropy.html (no longer online).

820   *See, e.g.,* Chuck Swindoll, *Proverbs*, The Bible Teaching Ministry of Pastor Chuck Swindoll (© 2021 Insight for Living Ministries), https://insight.org/resources/bible/the-wisdom-books/proverbs.

821   *See* https://www.psychologytoday.com/us/blog/evidence-based-living/201902/exploring-the-link-between-health-and-happiness.

822   *Id.*

823   *See* Mayo Clinic Staff, *Stress relief from laughter? It's no joke*, Mayo Clinic (Apr. 05, 2019), https://www.mayoclinic.org/healthy-lifestyle/stress-management/in-depth/stress-relief/art-20044456.

824   *See Probable Occasions on Which Each Psalm Was Composed*, https://www.blueletterbible.org/study/parallel/paral18.cfm.

825   *Id.*

826   *See* David, *Christians are Happier,* Welcome To: Ways To Faith, (Feb. 14, 2020), https://waystofaith.net/better/christians-are-happier/

827   *See* Michelle Darrisaw, *It Turns out, Regular Church-Goers Are Happier, a New Pew Study Finds*, The Oprah Magazine (Feb. 8, 2019), https://www.oprahmag.com/life/health/a26251703/religion-happiness-pew-study/;

Stoyan Zaimov, *Christians Happiest Among All Faith Groups, Survey Reveals*, The Christian Post (Feb. 3, 2016), https://www.christianpost.com/news/christians-among-happiest-faith-groups-non-religious-least-uk-national-statistics-survey.html.

Chapter 8

828   Portions from "How Do You Know The Bible Is True?," Online, Copyright © 1998, 1999, 2005 by Clarifying Christianity (SM).

829   *See Paleontology*, National Geographic Resource Library | Encyclopedic Entry, https://www.nationalgeographic.org/encyclopedia/paleontology/.

830   *See, e.g., Best Evidences—Science and the Bible Refute Millions of Years* (copyright © Answers in Genesis), Answers in Genesis, P.O. Box 510, Hebron, Ky 41048.

831   *See, Pyramids Were Built with Help From Dinosaurs, Claims Top Egyptologist*, World News Daily Report (Feb. 12, 2021), https://worldnewsdailyreport.com/pyramids-were-built-with-help-from-dinosaurs-claims-top-egyptologist/.

832   *Id.*

833   *Id.*

834   *See, e.g., Great Pyramid of Giza*, https://sites.google.com/site/greatpyramidofgizakhufu/.

835   An apatosaurus was "one of the largest land animals of all time," weighing as much as 45 tons and measuring about 75 feet long, including its long neck and tail; it had "four massive and pillarlike legs, and its tail was extremely long" and "was first described by American paleontologist O.C. Marsh in 1877;" its "fossil remains are found in North America and Europe." A brachiosaurus was also a massive animal with a long giraffe-like neck that was about 23 feet high, 85 feet long and weighed between 30 and 80 tons; the "first remains of this dinosaur were discovered in 1903 by Elmer S. Riggs in Western Colorado." An average-sized Brontosaurus weighed 33.6 tons, less on average than either an apatosaurus or a brachiosaurus; a fossil of a brontosaurus "was first discovered in western North America in 1874 and first described in 1879 by American paleontologist Othniel Charles Marsh."

    See, e.g., The Editors of Encyclopaedia Britannica, *Apatosaurus - dinosaur genus*, Britannica (article updated Aug. 27, 2020), https://www.britannica.com/animal/Apatosaurus/;

    About Brachiosaurus, https://www.newdinosaurs.com/brachiosaurus/;

    John Rafferty, *Brontosaurus-dinosaur genus* (alternative title: *Brontosaurus*), Britannica (last changed Sept. 15, 2020), https://www.britannica.com/animal/Brontosaurus.

836   *See Probable Occasions on Which Each Psalm Was Composed*, https://www.blueletterbible.org/study/parallel/paral18.cfm.

837   Henry Morris lived from October 6, 1918, to February 25, 2006, and is considered the father of the modern creation science movement.

See, e.g., Christine Dao, *Man of Science, Man of God: Henry M. Morris*, Institute of Creation Research (Feb. 1, 2009),
https://www.icr.org/article/science-man-god-henry-m-morris/.

838   *See Leviathan—Behemoths—Mythical Animals in the Bible*, Bible Study,
https://www.biblestudy.org/bible-study-by-topic/mythical-animals-in-the-bible/leviathan-behemoth.html.

839   *Id.*

840   Petroglyphs, artifacts, and even little clay figurines found in North America resemble modern depictions of dinosaurs. Rock carvings in South America depict men riding diplodocus-like creatures and, amazingly, bear the familiar images of triceratops-like, pterodactyl-like, and tyrannosaurus rex-like creatures. Roman mosaics, Mayan pottery, and Babylonian city walls all testify to man's trans-cultural, geographically unbounded fascination with these creatures. …In addition to the substantial amount of anthropic and historical evidences for the coexistence of dinosaurs and man, there are physical evidences, like the fossilized footprints of humans and dinosaurs found together at places in North America and West-Central Asia.

        See, e.g., What Does the Bible Say About Dinosaurs?, Got Questions (© Copyright 2002-2021 Got Questions Ministries—last updated April 26, 2021),
https://www.gotquestions.org/dinosaurs-Bible.html.

841   The first dinosaur bone was discovered in in 1676 in England, but it was thought to be the leg bone of a giant; it "wasn't given a scientific name until 1824 by William Buckland."

        See, e.g., Jeffrey Rank, *What was the First Dinosaur Discovered?*, Dinosaurs Report (© 2021 Dinosaur Report), https://www.dinosaurreport.com/first-dinosaur-discovered/;

        First Dinosaur Fossil Discoveries, ZoomDinosaur.com (Copyright ©1998-2018 EnchantedLearning.com),
https://www.enchantedlearning.com/subjects/dinosaurs/dinofossils/First.shtml.

842   Mary Ann Woodhouse Mantell, who was born in 1795 in London, England and who made this find, was married to Dr. Gideon Mantell. a physician who is wrongly "remembered as the sole 'discoverer'" of the reptile named *Iguanodon;* Mary Ann eventually left Gideon and died of an opium overdose in 1869.

        See, e.g., Mary Ann Mantell-Biography, IMDb (© 1990-2021 by IMDb.com, Inc.),
https://www.imdb.com/name/nm9057905/bio;

        Mary Ann Woodhouse Mantell, Trowel Blazers (© 2021 TrowelBlazers),
https://trowelblazers.com/mary-ann-woodhouse-mantell/;

        jschuethbfr, *Micro Musings. The woman who discovered dinosaurs*, Bias in the Fossil Record (Mar. 15, 2021), https://fossilbiasblog.com/2021/03/15/micro-musings-the-woman-who-discovered-dinosaurs/.

843   *See, e.g., Apologetics: Bible and Dinosaur*, savedbygrace2009 (Aug. 31, 2016), https://savedbygrace2009.wordpress.com/2016/08/31/apologetics-bible-and-dinosaurs/.

844   *See, e.g., First Dinosaur Fossil Discoveries*, ZoomDinosaurs.com https://www.enchantedlearning.com/subjects/dinosaurs/dinofossils/First.shtml.

845   *See* Bonnie Sachatello-Sawyer and Liza Charlesworth, *When Was the First Dinosaur Discovered?*, Scholastic (© 2021 Scholastic Inc.) (adapted from *Dinosaurs: The Very Latest Information and Hands-On Activities From the Museum of the Rockies*, by Liza Charlesworth and Bonnie Sachatello-Sawyer), https://www.scholastic.com/teachers/articles/teaching-content/when-was-first-dinosaur-discovered/ (no longer online).

See also, Howard Markel and Johanna Mayer, *The Origin Of The Word 'Dinosaur,'* Science Friday (July 6, 2015), https://www.sciencefriday.com/articles/the-origin-of-the-word-dinosaur.

846   *See, e.g., Dinosaurs Mentioned in the Bible*, Scientists for Jesus (Oct. 22, 2013), https://scientistsforjesus.blogspot.com/2013/10/dinosaurs-in-bible.html

847   *See, e.g.,* Ken Ham and Tim Chaffey, *Tannin: Sea Serpent, Dinosaur, Snake, Dragon, or Jackal?*, Answers in Genesis (Aug. 8, 2012), https://answersingenesis.org/dinosaurs/tannin-sea-serpent-dinosaur-snake-dragon-or-jackal/.

848   *See, e.g.,* Howard Markel and Johanna Mayer, *The Origin Of The Word 'Dinosaur,'* Science Friday (July 6, 2015), https://www.sciencefriday.com/articles/the-origin-of-the-word-dinosaur/.

849   *See, e.g.,* William T. Pelletier, *The Bible and Science*, The Woodside News (May 2012), https://biblescienceguy.files.wordpress.com/2012/05/2012-05-dragons.pdf.

Sir Richard Owen lived from 1804 to 1892, was a "British anatomist and paleontologist who is remembered for his contributions to the study of fossil animals, especially dinosaurs." "He was the first to recognize them as different from today's reptiles; in 1842 he classified them in a group he called Dinosauria."

See, e.g., The Editors of Encyclopaedia Britannica, *Richard Owen-British anatomist and paleontologist* (alternative title: *Sir Richard Owen*), Britannica (anniversary information added Dec. 14, 2020), https://www.britannica.com/biography/Richard-Owen.

850   *See, e.g., Whale* (Copyright © 2021, Bible Study Tools), https://www.biblestudytools.com/dictionary/whale.

851   *See, e.g., Dinosaurs and the Bible-Clarifying Christianity* (Copyright © 1998, 2005 Clarifying Christianity), http://clarifyingchristianity.com/dinos.shtml,

852   *See, e.g.,* loswl1, *Scientific Accuracy in the Bible Revealed*, Inspiksmarket (June 13, 2011), https://www.inspiks.com/scientific-accuracy-in-the-bible-revealed/;

Dinosaurs and the Bible—Clarifying Christianity (Copyright © 1998, 2005 Clarifying Christianity), http://clarifyingchristianity.com/dinos.shtml;

Mark Stephens, *Dinosaurs: What is the Real Story?* (Mar. 1, 2008-Copyright © TASC, Inc), https://tasc-creationscience.org/article/dinosaurs-what-real-story;

Behemoth, Fiery Flying Serpents, and Sea Monsters, Creation, Dinosaurs, and the Bible, https://creationbuff.wordpress.com/category/dragons/.

853 *See, e.g.,* Ken Ham and Tim Chaffey, *Tannin: Sea Serpent, Dinosaur, Snake, Dragon, or Jackal?*, Answers in Genesis (Aug. 8, 2012), https://answersingenesis.org/dinosaurs/tannin-sea-serpent-dinosaur-snake-dragon-or-jackal/

854 *See, e.g.,* James Burch, *Dragons Don't Exist. So Why Are They Everywhere?* (published Sept. 6, 2019), https://allthatsinteresting.com/dragon-legends.

855 *See* A. Sutherland, *Dragons And Dragon Kings In Ancient Mythology*, Ancient Pages (Nov. 2, 2016), https://www.ancientpages.com/2016/11/02/dragons-dragon-kings-ancient-mythology/.

856 *Id.*

857 *See, e.g.,* Vigdis Hocken and Aparna Kher, *2021: Year of the Ox—Chinese Animal Signs*, timeanddate.com (© Time and Date AS 1995–2021), https://www.timeanddate.com/calendar/chinese-zodiac-signs.html.

858 *See, e.g.,* Carolyne Larrington, *Dragons and their Origins*, English Heritage (posted Mar. 15, 2019), http://blog.english-heritage.org.uk/origin-of-dragons/;

Dragons of Fame - Dragons of North America (© Kylie 'drago' McCormick-last updated Oct. 9, 2017), http://www.blackdrago.com/fame_northamer.htm;

List of dragons in mythology and folklore, Wikipedia (last edited Aug. 5, 2021), https://en.wikipedia.org/wiki/List_of_dragons_in_mythology_and_folklore.

859 *Id.*

860 *Id.*

861 *Id.*

862 *Id.*

863 *See, e.g.,* Fen Montaigne, *The Fertile Shore*, Smithsonian Magazine (January/February 2020), https://www.smithsonianmag.com/science-nature/how-humans-came-to-americas-180973739.

864 *See, e.g.,* Michele Debczak, *Humans First Arrived in North America 30,000 Years Ago, New Studies Suggest*, Mental Floss (July 22, 2020), https://https://www.mentalfloss.com/article/626734/humans-first-arrived-north-america-30000-years-ago.

865 *See and compare* Amanda Briney, *A Geographic Overview of the Bering Strait - the Land Bridge Between Eastern Asia and North America*, ThoughtCo (updated Feb. 15, 2019), https://www.thoughtco.com/geographic-overview-bering-land-bridge-1435184;

Amanda Briney. *An Overview of the Last Global Glaciation*, ThoughtCo (updated July 27, 2019), https://www.thoughtco.com/the-last-glaciation-1434433.

See also History.com Editors, *Ice Age*, History (last updated June 7, 2019, original publication date Mar. 11, 2015), https://www.history.com/topics/pre-history/ice-age;

Staff Writer, *When Did the Ice Age Start and End?* (Last updated Mar. 27, 2020), https://www.reference.com/science/did-ice-age-start-end-c16afd2754205865.

866   *See* James Burch, *Dragons Don't Exist. So Why Are They Everywhere?*, ATI (Published Sept. 6, 2019), https://allthatsinteresting.com/dragon-legends.

867   *See, e.g. The History of Dragons*, Draconika Dragons (Copyright 2004-2019, Kevin Owen), http://www.draconika.com/history.php.

868   *See, e.g., Dragons in History*, sheperdmoonlight (Jan. 10, 2011), https://sheperdmoonlight.wordpress.com/2011/01/10/dragons-in-history/;

Do you believe in the Existence of this two amazing creatures??, https://theexistanceofmermaidsanddragons.weebly.com/background-info.html;

Do You Believe In Dragons? ~ Palaeontologists discover a dragon's skull in South Dakota, United Lighthouse (Mar 14, 2019), https://www.universallighthouseblog.com/post/do-you-believe-in-dragons---palaeontologists-discover-a-dragon-s-skull-in-south-dakota.

869   *See, e.g., Dragons in History*, sheperdmoonlight (Jan. 10, 2011), https://sheperdmoon-light.wordpress.com/2011/01/10/dragons-in-history/.

See Do you believe in the Existence of this two amazing creatures??, https://theexistanceofmermaidsanddragons.weebly.com/background-info.html;

Do You Believe In Dragons? ~ Palaeontologists discover a dragon's skull in South Dakota, United Lighthouse (Mar 14, 2019), https://www.universallighthouseblog.com/post/do-you-believe-in-dragons---palaeontologists-discover-a-dragon-s-skull-in-south-dakota.

870   *See Dragons in History*, Genesis Park, https://www.genesispark.com/exhibits/evidence/historical/dragons/#.

871   *Various dinosaurs and pterosaurs from the Hell Creek Formation. From back to front: Ankylosaurus, Tyrannosaurus, Quetzalcoatlus, Triceratops, Struthiomimus, Pachycephalosaurus, Acheroraptor and Anzu respectively.* Durbed. 31 December 2012. Image converted to grayscale.https://commons.wikimedia.org/wiki/File:Hell_Creek_dinosaurs_and_pterosaurs_by_durbed.jpg.

872   *Statue of a dragon guarding one of the beautiful bridges in downtown Ljubljana, Slovenia.* June 2008. Photo by Ville Miettinen. Image converted to grayscale. https://commons.wikimedia.org/wiki/File:Dragon_Ljubljana.jpg.

873   *See, e.g.,* Anne Marie Helmenstine, *Incompatible Chemical Mixture*, ThoughtCo (updated Oct. 1, 2018), (no longer online), https://www.thoughtco.com/dangerous-chemical-incompatibilities-602404;

Which material, when mixed with water, will cause a fire?, Quora, https://www.quora.com/Which-material-when-mixed-with-water-will-cause-a-fire;

What two chemicals, when mixed, makes an explosion?, Quora, https://www.quora.com/What-two-chemicals-when-mixed-makes-an-explosion;

Water-Reactive Chemicals, Montana Office of Risk Management, https://www.umt.edu/risk-management/safety-compliance/safety-fact-sheets/water-reactive-chemicals.php;

Potassium Chlorate and Sugar: Instant Fire, https://www.angelo.edu/faculty/kboudrea/demos/instant_fire/instant_fire.htm;

Robbie Gonzalez, *Ten amazing (and occasionally explosive) chemical reactions, caught on video*, Gizmodo (Feb, 20, 2012), https://gizmodo.com/ten-amazing-and-occasionally-explosive-chemical-react-5886602.

874 *See, e.g.,* Melissa—TodayIFoundOut.com, *Chlorine Trifluoride: The Chemical That Sets Fire to Asbestos on Contact*, Gizmodo (July 56, 2015), https://gizmodo.com/chlorine-trifluoride-the-chemical-that-sets-fire-to-as-1715935811.

875 *See Bombardier beetles*, National Geographic, https://www.nationalgeographic.com/animals/invertebrates/facts/bombardier-beetle.

876 *See Bombardier beetle*, Wikipedia (last edited Aug. 22, 2021), https://en.wikipedia.org/wiki/Bombardier_beetle.

See also, e.g., Bombardier Beetles, The National Wildlife Federation, https://www.nwf.org/Educational-Resources/Wildlife-Guide/Invertebrates/Bombardier-Beetles.

877 *See* Evan Lubofsky, *The Discovery of Hydrothermal Vents—Scientists celebrate 40th anniversary and chart future research*, Oceanus (June 11, 2018), https://www.whoi.edu/oceanus/feature/the-discovery-of-hydrothermal-vents/.

See also, e.g., Deep Sea Hydrothermal Vents, National Geographic, https://www.nationalgeographic.org/media/deep-sea-hydrothermal-vents/.

878 *See, e.g.,* Gordon Churchyard , *A Song of *Praise to God—Psalm 135* (© 1999-2002, Wycliffe Associates (UK), https://www.easyenglish.bible/psalms/psalm135-taw.htm.

879 *See A Multi-Phased Journey*, NASA Earth Observatory (published Oct 1, 2010), https://earthobservatory.nasa.gov/features/Water/page2.php.

880 *See, e.g., Is there any river that doesn't meet a sea?*, Quora, https://www.quora.com/Is-there-any-river-that-doesn-t-meet-a-sea.

881 *See, How many gallons of water flow into the Atlantic Ocean from the Amazon River each second?*, Answers (Copyright ©2021 Answers, LLC), https://www.answers.com/Q/How_many_gallons_of_water_flow_into_the_Atlantic_Ocean_from_the_Amazon_River_each_second.

882 *See, e.g.,* Carol Brooks, *Scientific Facts in the Bible—Part I*, https://www.inplainsite.org/html/scientific_facts_in_the_bible.html.

883   *See Oceans and Seas and the Water Cycle*, USGS– U.S. Department of the Interior, https://www.usgs.gov/special-topic/water-science-school/science/oceans-and-seas-and-water-cycle?

884   *See A Multi-Phased Journey*, NASA Earth Observatory (published Oct 1, 2010), https://earthobservatory.nasa.gov/features/Water/page2.php.

885   *See, e.g.,* Tiffany Means, *The Chemistry of Weather: Condensation and Evaporation*, ThoughtCo (updated Nov. 5, 2019), https://www.thoughtco.com/condensation-and-evaporation-3444344.

886   *Id.*

887   *See* Numerous writers, *Condensation*, National Geographic Resource Library | Encyclopedic Entry (last updated Jan. 21, 2011), https://www.nationalgeographic.org/encyclopedia/condensation/.

888   *See* The Editors of Encyclopaedia Britannica, *Atmospheric circulation—meteorology*, Britannica (article revised and updated June 27, 2007), https://www.britannica.com/science/atmospheric-circulation.

889   *See, e.g.,* Brian Williams, *Global Circulation* (last updated Jan. 6, 2020), https://www.briangwilliams.us/weather-climate/c-global-circulation.html;

Olin Jeuck Eggen, *Edmond Halley—British scientist* (alternative title: *Edmund Halley*), Britannica (anniversary information added Jan. 10, 2021), https://www.britannica.com/biography/Edmond-Halley.

890   *See, e.g.,* Anselm H. Amadio, *Aristotle—Greek philosopher* (alternative title: *Aristoteles*), Britannica (last updated: Mar 2, 2021), https://www.britannica.com/biography/Aristotle.

891   *See, e.g., Scientific Evidence*, Evidences of the Bible (Mar. 1, 1999), https://bibleevidences.com/science/

892   *See* A. Sutherland, *Ancient Greeks Had Great Understanding of Weather And Climate*, Ancient Pages (Sept. 7, 2015), https://www.ancientpages.com/2015/09/07/ancient-greeks-had-great-understanding-of-weather-and-climate/.

893   *See, e.g., Weather Forecasting Through the Ages*, Earth Observatory (published Feb 25, 2002), https://earthobservatory.nasa.gov/features/WxForecasting/wx2.php.

894   *See* A. Sutherland, *Ancient Greeks Had Great Understanding of Weather And Climate*, Ancient Pages (Sept. 7, 2015), https://www.ancientpages.com/2015/09/07/ancient-greeks-had-great-understanding-of-weather-and-climate/.

895   *See* Carol Brooks, *Scientific Facts in the Bible -Part I*, https://www.inplainsite.org/html/scientific_facts_in_the_bible.html.

896   *See* loswl1, *Scientific Accuracy in the Bible Revealed*, Inspiksmarket (June 13, 2011), https://www.inspiks.com/scientific-accuracy-in-the-bible-revealed/.

897   *See, e.g.,* Anne E. Egger, *The Hydrologic Cycle: Water's journey through time*, Vision Learning, https://www.visionlearning.com/en/library/Earth-Science/6/The-Hydrologic-Cycle/99;

Christopher J. Duffy, *The terrestrial hydrologic cycle: an historical sense of balance*, Wiley Online Learning (Mar. 31, 2017), https://onlinelibrary.wiley.com/doi/full/10.1002/wat2.1216#.

898   *See Ernest Rutherford*, The Nobel Prize 9sept. 8, 2021), https://www.nobelprize.org/prizes/chemistry/1908/rutherford/facts/;

Rutherford: splitting the atom, Manchester (last updated Sept. 30, 2009), http://news.bbc.co.uk/local/manchester/hi/people_and_places/history/ newsid_8282000/8282223.stm.

The idea of atoms stretches back to ancient Greece when the philosopher Democritus declared that all matter is made of tiny particles. The philosopher Plato even decided— wrongly—that different substances had different shaped atoms, like pyramids or cubes. The first modern evidence for atoms appears in the early 1800s when British chemist John Dalton discovered that chemicals always contain whole number ratios of atoms.

See Know how scientists discovered atoms and the instruments that help them view these small particles Britannica (© *American Chemical Society,* A Britannica Publishing Partner), https://www.britannica.com/video/187021/discovery-atoms-instruments-scientists-particles#:~:text.

899   *See, e.g.,* Michael Madsen, *Pioneering Nuclear Science: The Discovery of Nuclear Fission*, IAEA (Dec. 20, 2013), https://www.iaea.org/newscenter/news/pioneering-nuclear-science-discovery-nuclear-fission.

900   *Id.*

901   *See, e.g.,* Francie Diep, *Computer Models Show What Exactly Would Happen to Earth After A Nuclear War*, Popular Science (July 18, 2014), https://www.popsci.com/article/science/computer-models-show-what-exactly-would-happen-earth-after-nuclear-war/.

902   *See, e.g.,* Lester Stone II, *What Would Happen in an All-Out Nuclear War?*, History News Network (Copyright 2021), https://historynewsnetwork.org/article/129966.

903   *See, e.g.,* David Bressan, *Even A Small Nuclear War Would Still Have Effects on Global Scale*, Forbes (Aug 12, 2017), https://www.forbes.com/sites/davidbressan/2017/08/12/even-a-small-nuclear-war-would-still-have-effects-on-global-scale/.

904   *See, e.g.,* Carol Brooks, *Scientific Facts in the Bible—Part I*, https://www.inplainsite.org/html/scientific_facts_in_the_bible.html.

905   *See, e.g., How Long Is a Cubit?*, Ark Encounter (copyright 2021 Answers in Genesis), https://arkencounter.com/noahs-ark/cubit/.

906   *See* Carol Brooks, *Scientific Facts in the Bible—Part II*, https://www.inplainsite.org/html/scientific_facts_in_the_bible.html (citing Hong, S.W. et al., *Safety investigation of Noah's Ark in a seaway*, TJ 8(1):26–36, 1994—all the co-authors are on the staff of the Korea Research Institute of Ships and Ocean Engineering).

See also Helen Thompson, *Could Noah's Ark Float? In Theory, Yes!*, Smithsonian Magazine (Apr. 4, 2014), https://www.smithsonianmag.com/science-nature/could-noahs-ark-float-theory-yes-180950385/.

907   *See* Tim Lovett, *Thinking Outside the Box*, Answers in Genesis (March 19, 2007; last featured January 12, 2016), https://answersingenesis.org/noahs-ark/thinking-outside-the-box/#study.

908   *Id.*

909   *See* Carol Brooks, *Scientific Facts in the Bible - Part II*, https://www.inplainsite.org/html/scientific_facts_in_the_bible.html.

      See also Tim Lovett, *Thinking Outside the Box*, Answers in Genesis (March 19, 2007; last featured January 12, 2016), https://answersingenesis.org/noahs-ark/thinking-outside-the-box/#study.

910   *See About Tsunamis*, US Dept of Commerce - National Oceanic and Atmospheric Administration - National Weather Service, https://www.weather.gov/safety/tsunami-about.

911   *See, e.g.,* Helen Thompson, *Could Noah's Ark Float? In Theory, Yes!*, Smithsonian Magazine (Apr. 4, 2014), https://www.smithsonianmag.com/science-nature/could-noahs-ark-float-yes-180950385/

912   *Id.*

913   *See* John Fincham, *A History of Naval Architecture* (London, Whittaker and Co. 1851), "Introduction to the History of Ship Building" at ix, Internet Archive, https://archive.org/details/bub_gb_0adWAAAAcAAJ/page/n27/mode/2up.

914   *See History of Naval Architecture Through the Ages*, Bright Hub Engineering (Jan. 25, 2009), http://www.brighthubengineering.com/naval-architecture/23596-ship-building-and-design-an-overview/.

915   *See* Jeff Miller, *God and the Laws of Thermodynamics: A Mechanical Engineer's Perspective*, Apologetics Press (Copyright © 2007 Apologetics Press, Inc.), https://www.apologeticspress.org/apcontent.aspx?category=9&article=2106.

916   *Id.*

917   *See* Jeff Miller, *God and the Laws of Thermodynamics: A Mechanical Engineer's Perspective*, Apologetics Press (Copyright © 2007 Apologetics Press, Inc.), https://www.apologeticspress.org/apcontent.aspx?category=9&article=2106; (quoting Tracy Walters, *A Reply to John Patterson's Arguments*, Origins Research, (Fall/Winter, 1986) quoted therein at 9[2]:8-0).

918   *See* Jeff Miller, *God and the Laws of Thermodynamics: A Mechanical Engineer's Perspective*, Apologetics Press (Copyright © 2007 Apologetics Press, Inc.), https://www.apologeticspress.org/apcontent.aspx?category=9&article=2106.

919   *Id.*

      See also Nick Connor, *What is First Law of Thermodynamics—Definition*, Thermal Engineering (May 22, 2019), https://www.thermal-engineering.org/what-is-first-law-of-thermodynamics-definition/.

920   *See* loswl1, *Scientific Accuracy in the Bible Revealed*, Inspiksmarket (June 13, 2011), https://www.inspiks.com/scientific-accuracy-in-the-bible-revealed/.

921   *See* Jeff Miller, *God and the Laws of Thermodynamics: A Mechanical Engineer's Perspective*, Apologetics Press (Copyright © 2007 Apologetics Press, Inc.), https://www.apologeticspress.org/apcontent.aspx?category=9&article=2106.

> Endless studies and experiments have confirmed its validity over and over again under a multitude of different conditions.

Id.

922   *See* Jeff Miller, *God and the Laws of Thermodynamics: A Mechanical Engineer's Perspective*, Apologetics Press (Copyright © 2007 Apologetics Press, Inc.), https://www.apologeticspress.org/apcontent.aspx?category=9&article=2106.

See also Jee Main, *Second Law Of Thermodynamics*, https://byjus.com/jee/second-law-of-thermodynamics/#:~:text.

923   *See* Jeff Miller, *God and the Laws of Thermodynamics: A Mechanical Engineer's Perspective*, Apologetics Press (Copyright © 2007 Apologetics Press, Inc.), https://www.apologeticspress.org/apcontent.aspx?category=9&article=2106.

See also Harold I. Sharlin, *William Thomson, Baron Kelvin-Scottish engineer, mathematician, and physicist* (alternative titles: *Lord Kelvin, Sir William Thomson, William Thomson, Baron Kelvin of Largs*), Britannica (anniversary information added Dec. 13, 2020), https://www.britannica.com/biography/William-Thomson-Baron-Kelvin.

924   *See* Jeff Miller, *God and the Laws of Thermodynamics: A Mechanical Engineer's Perspective*, Apologetics Press (Copyright © 2007 Apologetics Press, Inc.), https://www.apologeticspress.org/apcontent.aspx?category=9&article=2106 (citing Curt Suplee, *Milestones of Science* (Washington, D.C.: National Geographic Society, 2000) at page 156).

925   *See, e.g., Nicolas Léonard Sadi Carnot, the Considered Father of Thermodynamics*, Solar Energy (published: June 4, 2020), https://solar-energy.technology/thermodynamics/laws-of-thermodynamics/first-law-thermodynamics/history#:~:text.

926   *Id;*

Ben G. Bareja, *Contribution to the History of Photosynthesis: Julius Robert Mayer*, Crops Review (August 25, 2021), https://www.cropsreview.com/robert-mayer.html#:~:text.

927   *See* Jeff Miller, *God and the Laws of Thermodynamics: A Mechanical Engineer's Perspective*, Apologetics Press (Copyright © 2007 Apologetics Press, Inc.), https://www.apologeticspress.org/apcontent.aspx?category=9&article=2106.

928   *Id.* (quoting from page 2 of the Fourth Edition of a prominent textbook used in schools of engineering across America, *Thermodynamics: An Engineering Approach* written by Yunus A. Cengel and Michael A. Boles, (New York: McGraw-Hill, 2002).

929 *See* Jeff Miller, *God and the Laws of Thermodynamics: A Mechanical Engineer's Perspective*, Apologetics Press (Copyright © 2007 Apologetics Press, Inc.), https://www.apologeticspress.org/apcontent.aspx?category=9&article=2106.

930 *Id.* (citing Yunus A. Cengel and Michael A. Boles, *Thermodynamics: An Engineering Approach* (New York: McGraw-Hill, 2002) at page 2).

931 *See Justus von Liebig*, Famous Scientists—The Art of Genius (Famous Scientists-© 2021), https://www.famousscientists.org/justus-von-liebig/.

932 *See* Jeff Miller, *God and the Laws of Thermodynamics: A Mechanical Engineer's Perspective*, Apologetics Press (Copyright © 2007 Apologetics Press, Inc.), https://www.apologeticspress.org/apcontent.aspx?category=9&article=2106 (citing Wilbur M. Smith, *Therefore Stand* (New Canaan, CT: Keats Publishing, 1981) at pages 307-308).

933 *See When was it first discovered (or comprehended) that air has weight?*, History of Science and Mathematics—Beta, https://hsm.stackexchange.com/questions/5767/when-was-it-first-discovered-or-comprehended-that-air-has-weight#.

934 *Id.*

935 *Id.*

   Robert Kiser, *Scientific details declared long before being discovered by scientist*, People Get Ready (Apr. 1. 2021), http://peoplegetready.org/christian-apologetics/scientific-details-declared-long-discovered-scientist/;

   The Editors of Encyclopaedia Britannica, *Evangelista Torricelli-Italian physicist and mathematician*, Britannica (anniversary information added Oct. 21, 2020), https://www.britannica.com/biography/Evangelista-Torricelli.

936 *See, e.g.,* Mary Bellis, *When Was the First TV Invented?*, ThoughtCo (updated Dec. 31, 2020), https://www.thoughtco.com/the-invention-of-television-1992531.

937 *See, e.g.,* Mary Bellis, *The Inventors Behind the Creation of Television*, ThoughtCo (updated Jan. 13, 2020), https://www.thoughtco.com/television-history-1992530.

938 *See, e.g.,* Mary Bellis, *When Was the First TV Invented?*, ThoughtCo (updated Dec. 31, 2020), https://www.thoughtco.com/the-invention-of-television-1992531.

939 *Id.*

940 *Id.*

941 *See* Erik Gregersen, *Philo Farnsworth-American inventor* (alternative title: *Philo Taylor Farnsworth II*), Britannica (last updated Mar. 7, 2021), https://www.britannica.com/biography/Philo-Farnsworth

942 *See, e.g.,* Mary Bellis, *When Was the First TV Invented?*, ThoughtCo (updated Dec. 31, 2020), https://www.thoughtco.com/the-invention-of-television-1992531.

Chapter 9

943   *See generally* Doug Powell, *Guide to Christian Apologetics* at 21, Holman Reference (Nashville, Tennessee © 2006 by Doug Powell).

944   *Id.* at 50.

945   *See* James Bishop, *How Science Led A World Leading Astronomer, Allan Sandage, To God*, Reason for Jesus (Oct. 10, 2017), https://reasonsforjesus.com/how-science-led-a-world-leading-astronomer-allan-sandage-to-god/.

946   *See* Doug Powell, *Guide to Christian Apologetics* at 52, Holman Reference (Nashville, Tennessee © 2006 by Doug Powell) (citing Hugh Ross, *The Creator and the Cosmos* (Colorado Springs: NavPress, 1993, 2001) at 154–157).

947   *See* Doug Powell, *Guide to Christian Apologetics* at 52–56, Holman Reference (Nashville, Tennessee © 2006 by Doug Powell).

948   *See* Carol Brooks, *Scientific Facts in the Bible—Part I*, https://www.inplainsite.org/html/scientific_facts_in_the_bible.html.

     See also The Big Bang, The Last Dialogue (The Last Dialogue|© 2021), https://www.thelastdialogue.org/article/bible-confirms-big-bang-theory/.

949   *See* Carol Brooks, *Scientific Facts in the Bible—Part I*, https://www.inplainsite.org/html/scientific_facts_in_the_bible.html.

950   *See, e.g.,* Anselm H. Amadio, *Aristotle-Greek philosopher* (alternative title: *Aristoteles*), Britannica (Bibliography revised and updated Mar. 30, 2020) https://www.britannica.com/biography/Aristotle.

951   *See, e.g.,* Geoff Haselhurst, *Cosmology-Uniting Space, Time, Matter, Motion & Universe*, On Truth & Reality (copyright © 1997–2018), https://www.spaceandmotion.com/cosmos-space-time-matter-motion.htm;

     Marcelo Gleiser, *The Universe According To Albert Einstein: Relativity*, 13.7 Cosmos & Culture-Commentary On Science And Societ (NPR USF Media—Mar. 14, 2018), https://www.npr.org/sections/13.7/2018/03/14/593156411/the-universe-according-to-albert-einstein-relativity.

952   *See Newton's Views on Space, Time, and Motion*, Stanford Encyclopedia of Philosophy (first published Aug 12, 2004; substantive revision Aug 22, 2011), https://plato.stanford.edu/entries/newton-stm/.

953   *See, e.g.,* Anselm H. Amadio, *Aristotle-Greek philosopher* (alternative title: *Aristoteles*), Britannica (last updated: Mar 2, 2021), https://www.britannica.com/biography/Aristotle.

954   *See, e.g., Ancient Philosophy*, Exactly What Is Time? (Copyright © 2021 - Exactly What Is Time?), http://www.exactlywhatistime.com/philosophy-of-time/ancient-philosophy/.

955   *See, e.g., Big Bang Theory & Relevant Creation Philosophies*, BrainMass (copyright 2004-2021 BrainMass, Inc.), https://brainmass.com/physics/big-bang-theory/big-bang-theory-relevant-creation-philosophies-147948#:~:text.

956   *See, e.g.,* Geoff Haselhurst, *Albert Einstein Cosmology*, On Truth & Reality (Copyright 1997–2018), https://www.spaceandmotion.com/Physics-Albert-Einstein-Cosmology.htm.

957   *Id.* at 52–56.

958   *See* Andrew Zimmerman Jones, *Understanding the Big-Bang Theory*, ThoughtCo (updated June 11, 2019), https://www.thoughtco.com/what-is-the-big-bang-theory-2698849.

959   *See, e.g.,* Akash Peshin, *What Caused the Big Bang?*, Science ABC (updated Dec: 2, 2019), https://www.scienceabc.com/nature/universe/caused-big-bang.html.

960   *See, e.g.,* Charlie Wood, *The Big Bang Theory: How the Universe Began*, Live Science (June 12, 2019), https://www.livescience.com/65700-big-bang-theory.html.

961   *See* Andrew Zimmerman Jones, *Understanding the Big-Bang Theory,* ThoughtCo (updated June 11, 2019), https://www.thoughtco.com/what-is-the-big-bang-theory-2698849.

962   *See* John C. Mather and Gary F Hinshaw (2008), *Cosmic background explorer*, Scholarpedia (accepted Mar. 18, 2008), http://www.scholarpedia.org/article/Cosmic_background_explorer#:~:text.

963   *See, e.g., Big Bang*, Wikipedia (last edited Aug. 21, 2021), https://en.wikipedia.org/wiki/Big_Bang.

       See also Jersey Pangilinan, *The Big Bang theory.docx-The Big Bang theory is the ...*, Course Hero (Copyright © 2021. Course Hero, Inc.), https://www.coursehero.com/file/88575484/The-Big-Bang-theory-docx/.

964   *See* Andy Briggs, *What is the Big Bang?*, EarthSky (posted by Andy Briggs in Astronomy Essentials | Space | June 11, 2020), https://earthsky.org/space/definition-what-is-the-big-bang.

965   *See, e.g., The Big Bang*, Origins | Cern—The Heart of the Matter (copyright 2000 The Exploration), https://www.exploratorium.edu/origins/cern/ideas/bang.html.

966   *See* Paul Sutter, *Will we ever know exactly how the universe ballooned into existence?*, Live Science (Apr. 15, 2021), https://www.livescience.com/why-physicists-cant-see-inflation-big-bang.html.

967   *See, e.g.,* University of Central Florida, *What caused the Big Bang?*, Science Daily (Oct. 31, 2019), https://www.sciencedaily.com/releases/2019/10/191031154921.htm.

968   *See, e.g.,* Akash Peshin, *What Caused the Big Bang?*, Science ABC (updated Dec: 2, 2019), https://www.scienceabc.com/nature/universe/caused-big-bang.html.

969   *See What Is the Big Bang?*, NASA Science (last updated March 17, 2021), https://spaceplace.nasa.gov/big-bang/en/.

970   *See* Matt Strassler, *Big Bang: Expansion, NOT Explosion, Of Particular Significance* (Mar. 16, 2014), https://profmattstrassler.com/articles-and-posts/relativity-space-astronomy-and-cosmology/history-of-the-universe/big-bang-expansion-not-explosion/.

971   *See, e.g.,* The European Space Agency, *How many stars are there in the Universe?*, (ESA / Science & Exploration / Space Science / Herschel),

https://www.esa.int/Science_Exploration/Space_Science/Herschel/How_many_stars_are_there_in_the_Universe.

972   *See, e.g.,* Fraser Cain, *How Many Stars are There in the Universe?,* Universe Today (posted June 3, 2013), https://www.universetoday.com/102630/how-many-stars-are-there-in-the-universe/.

973   *See* Michael Lam, *How could an explosive Big Bang be the birth of our universe?,* Phys Org (May 1, 2020), https://phys.org/news/2020-05-explosive-big-birth-universe.html.

974   *See* Steven Ball, *A Christian Physicist Examines the Big Bang Theory* (Sept. 2003), https://www.letu.edu/academics/arts-and-sciences/files/big-bang.pdf.

975   *Id.*

976   *Id.*

977   *See, e.g.,* Tutai Pere, *Science and the book of Genesis,* Cook Island News (Aug. 26, 2016, citing Austin American Statesman, Oct. 19, 1997), https://www.cookislandsnews.com/church-talk/science-and-the-book-of-genesis/.

978   *See, e.g.,* Akash Peshin, *Why Is The Universe Expanding?,* Science ABC (updated Apr. 10, 2019), https://www.scienceabc.com/nature/universe/why-is-the-universe-expanding.html;

      Carol Brooks, *Scientific Facts in the Bible—Part I,* https://www.inplainsite.org/html/scientific_facts_in_the_bible.html.

979   *See, e.g., The Expanding Universe,* Sloan Digital Sky Survey/SkyServer, https://skyserver.sdss.org/dr1/en/astro/universe/universe.asp#:~:text.

980   *See, e.g.,* Synonyms & Antonyms, https://www.synonyms.com/synonym/stretching.

981   *See* The European Space Agency, *How many stars are there in the Universe?,* (ESA/ Science & Exploration/Space Science/Herschel, https://www.esa.int/Science_Exploration/Space_Science/Herschel/How_many_stars_are_there_in_the_Universe.

982   © ESA, NASA and Peter Anders (Göttingen University Galaxy Evolution Group, Germany), Converted to greyscale. https://www.esa.int/Science_Exploration/Space_Science/Herschel/How_many_stars_are_there_in_the_Universe.

983   *See How many stars can you see?,* Posted by EarthSky in Astronomy Essentials | Human World (Feb. 26, 2018), https://earthsky.org/astronomy-essentials/how-many-stars-could-you-see-on-a-clear-moonless-night.

984   *See* e.g., Jeremy Gyorke, *Is the Bible Scientifically Accurate?,* Patch (posted Jan 15, 2014), https://patch.com/michigan/wyandotte/is-the-bible-scientifically-accurate.

985   *See, e.g.,* loswl1, *Scientific Accuracy in the Bible Revealed-The Innumerable Stars in the Universe,* Inspiksmarket (June 13, 2011), https://www.inspiks.com/scientific-accuracy-in-the-bible-revealed/.

986   *See, e.g.,* Eduardo Vila-Echagüe, Editor, *Almagest Star Catalogue for Guide Users* (Aug. 2000), https://www.projectpluto.com/almagest.htm.

987   *See* D. Juste, B. van Dalen, D. N. Hasse and C. Burnett (eds.), *Ptolemy's Science of the Stars in the Middle Ages*, Brepols (© 2021 Brepols Publishers), http://www.brepols.net/Pages/ShowProduct.aspx?prod_id=IS-9782503586397-1;

Review of Gerd Graßhoff's *The History of Ptolemy's Star Catalogue*, https://www.springer.com/gp/book/9780387971810.

988   *See, e.g., The Birth of Modern Astronomy*, lumen, https://courses.lumenlearning.com/astronomy/chapter/the-birth-of-modern-astronomy/.

989   *See, e.g.,* Robert S. Westman, *Nicolaus Copernicus-Polish astronomer* (alternative titles: *Mikołaj Kopernik, Nikolaus Kopernikus*), Britannica (last updated: Mar 2, 2021), https://www.britannica.com/biography/Nicolaus-Copernicus.

990   *See, e.g., History of astronomy*, Wikipedia (last edited Aug. 3, 2021), https://en.wikipedia.org/wiki/History_of_astronomy.

991   *See, e.g.,* Robert S. Westman, *Nicolaus Copernicus-Polish astronomer* (alternative titles: *Mikołaj Kopernik, Nikolaus Kopernikus*), Britannica (last updated: Mar. 2, 2021), https://www.britannica.com/biography/Nicolaus-Copernicus.

992   *See, e.g.,* Albert Van Helden, *Galileo-Italian philosopher, astronomer and mathematician* (alternative title: *Galileo Galilei*), Britannica (anniversary information added Feb. 12, 2021), https://www.britannica.com/biography/Galileo-Galilei.

993   *See* Frank Verbunt and Robert H. van Gent, *Three editions of the Star Catalogue of Tycho Brahe*, Astrophysics -> Instrumentation and Methods for Astrophysics (Cornell University Mar. 19. 2010), https://arxiv.org/abs/1003.3836.

Tycho Brahe, who lived from 1546 to 1601, was a "Danish astronomer whose work in developing astronomical instruments and in measuring and fixing the positions of stars paved the way for future discoveries."

See Olin Jeuck Eggen, *Tycho Brahe - Danish astronomer*, Britannica (material added Jan. 28, 2021, https://www.britannica.com/biography/Tycho-Brahe-Danish-astronomer.

994   *See, e.g., Johannes Hevelius (1611–1687)*, NCAR/UCAR HAO (© 2021 UCAR), https://www2.hao.ucar.edu/Education/FamousSolarPhysicists/johannes-hevelius;

Johann and Elisabeth Hevelius, Catalogus stellarum fixarum (Gdansk, 1687), bound with the Uranographia, http://lynx-open-ed.org/node/384.

995   Fraser Cain, *How Many Stars are There in the Universe?*, Universe Today (posted June 3, 2013), https://www.universetoday.com/102630/how-many-stars-are-there-in-the-universe/.

Andrea Kissack, Senior Science and Environment Editor and narrator of the QUEST television program at KQED television station in Los Angeles, California estimated the number of stars in the universe. She said, "Astronomers have estimated that there are about 200 billion stars in the Milky Way Galaxy. Galaxies come in many sizes, both much larger and considerably smaller than our home galaxy. I don't know what the average number of stars in each galaxy is, but for the sake of this calculation I chose a conservative 10 billion stars per galaxy. Astronomers have also estimated that there are between 50 billion and

100 billion galaxies in the Universe, based on observations made by the Hubble Space Telescope. Again being conservative, I chose the lower figure of 50 billion. So, with those numbers, I calculate a number of stars in the Universe at 10 billion times 50 billion, or 500 billion billion—or in exponential notation, 5 X 1020."

See Andrea Kissack, *Stars and Sand Grains*, KQED (Nov 21, 2008), https://www.kqed.org/quest/957/stars-and-sand-grains.

996   *See, e.g.,* The European Space Agency, *How many stars are there in the Universe?*, (ESA / Science & Exploration / Space Science / Herschel), https://www.esa.int/Science_Exploration/Space_Science/Herschel/How_many_stars_are_there_in_the_Universe.

997   *See Number of Grains of Sand in the World*, Infomory.com (Apr. 20, 2010), http://infomory.com/numbers/number-of-grains-of-sand-in-the-world/#:~:text.

998   *See* Robert Krulwich, *Which Is Greater, The Number Of Sand Grains On Earth Or Stars In The Sky?*, Krulwich Wonders—Robert Krulwich On Science (NPR) (Sept. 17, 2012), https://www.npr.org/sections/krulwich/2012/09/17/161096233/which-is-greater-the-number-of-sand-grains-on-earth-or-stars-in-the-sky.

999   *See, e.g.,* Merriam Webster, https://www.merriam-webster.com/dictionary/continuum and https://www.merriam-webster.com/dictionary/spectra.

1000   *See, e.g., Spectroscopy in Astronomy*, lumen, https://courses.lumenlearning.com/astronomy/chapter/spectroscopy-in-astronomy/.

1001   Sir Isaac Newton, who lived from 1642 to [1727, was the "English physicist and mathematician, who was the culminating figure of the Scientific Revolution of the 17th century."

       See Richard S. Westfall, *Isaac Newton-English physicist and mathematician* (alternative title: *Sir Isaac Newton*), Britannica (last updated: Mar 27, 2021), https://www.britannica.com/biography/Isaac-Newton.

1002   *Id.*

1003   *See, e.g., Spectroscopy and the Birth of Astrophysics*, Tools of Cosmology (Copyright ©2021), https://history.aip.org/exhibits/cosmology/tools/tools-spectroscopy.htm.

1004   *See* Neil deGrasse Tyson, *Being an Astronomer: Neil deGrasse Tyson*, Ology Home (American Museum of Natural History), https://www.amnh.org/explore/ology/astronomy/being-an-astronomer-neil-degrasse-tyson.

1005   *See, e.g.,* Elizabeth Landau, *Symphony of stars: The science of stellar sound waves*, NASA's Exoplanet Exploration (July 30, 2018), https://exoplanets.nasa.gov/news/1516/symphony-of-stars-the-science-of-stellar-sound-waves/.

1006   *See, e.g., Karl Jansky*, Magnet Academy - from the National High Magnetic Field Laboratory (Copyright © 2012-2021), https://nationalmaglab.org/education/magnet-academy/history-of-electricity-magnetism/pioneers/karl-jansky;

The Editors of the Encyclopaedia Britannica, *Karl Jansky-American engineer* (alternative title: *Karl Guthe Jansky0*, Britannica (anniversary information added—Feb. 10, 2021), https://www.britannica.com/biography/Karl-Jansky;

Karl Guthe Jansky, National Radio Astronomy Observatory (© 2021 The National Radio Astronomy Observatory), https://public.nrao.edu/gallery/karl-guthe-jansky/.

1007   *See, e.g.,* Ancient Code Team, *NASA has discovered that Stars, Moons and Planets give off music: This is what is sounds like*, Ancient Code (© 2021 Ancient Code), https://www.ancient-code.com/nasa-has-discovered-that-stars-moons-and-planets-give-off-music-this-is-what-is-sounds-like/.

1008   *Id.*

See also, e.g., Deborah Byrd, *Do stars make sounds?*, Science Wire | Space (Mar. 24, 2015), https://earthsky.org/space/do-stars-make-sounds;

NASA Shares 'sounds From Around The Milky Way,' Netizens Say 'heavens Singing Praises,' RepublicWorld.com (last updated: Sept. 23, 2020), https://www.republicworld.com/technology-news/science/nasa-shares-sounds-from-around-the-milky-way-netizens-amazed.html.

1009   From 1679 to 1680, Jasper Danckaerts, who lived from 1639 to 1702/1704 and resided "in what is now the US state of Maryland," traveled "through the territory which had previously been part of the New Netherland" on the North American continent and kept a journal in which he "documented the version of this story as it is told by the Iroquois."

See, e.g., Comparitive Religion: the World Turtle, Universal Life Church (Sept. 27, 2013), https://www.ulc.org/ulc-blog/comparative-religion-the-world-turtle;

Jasper Danckaerts, Wikipedia (last edited Apr. 2, 2021,), https://en.wikipedia.org/wiki/Jasper_Danckaerts.

1010   *See, e.g.,* Jeff Kelly, *10 Bizarre Theories About the Earth That People Believe—#9: Geoterrapinism Theory*, ListVerse (May 29, 2013), https://listverse.com/2013/05/29/10-bizarre-theories-about-the-earth-that-people-believe/.

1011   *See, e.g.,* Eric Grundhauser, *Why Is the World Always on the Back of a Turtle?*, Atlas Obscura (Oct. 20, 2017), https://www.atlasobscura.com/articles/world-turtle-cosmic-discworld.

1012   The Titans were the twelve "deities in Greek mythology that preceded the Olympians" and were, according to Greek mythology, "the children of the primordial deities Uranus (heaven) and Gaea (earth)."

See, e.g., Titans, Greek Mythology (GreekMythology.com © Copyright 1997-2021), https://www.greekmythology.com/Titans/titans.html.

1013   *See, e.g.,* Madeleine, *Atlas Holding the World Story*, Theoi Greek Mythology (posted Nov. 26, 2019), https://www.theoi.com/articles/atlas-holding-the-world-story/.

When Only God Knew

1014 *See, e.g., What did the ancient Mayas believe?*, Bitesize (*Copyright © 2021* BBC), https://www.bbc.co.uk/bitesize/topics/zq6svcw/articles/z2gkk2p.

1015 *See, e.g., Maya Civilization-Cosmology and Religion*, (© Canadian Museum of History), https://www.historymuseum.ca/cmc/exhibitions/civil/maya/mmc03eng.html.

1016 *See, e.g., Folklore-Quake Myths*, In the Line of Danger (Copyright ©2005 The Jackson Sun.), http://orig.jacksonsun.com/earthquake/folklore.html (no longer online)

1017 *See, e.g., What is the Aether?*, Energy Wave Theory (2020), https://energywavetheory.com/explanations/aether/.

1018 *See, e.g., Ether*, WolframResearch (© 1996–2007 Eric W. Weisstein), https://scienceworld.wolfram.com/physics/Ether.html.

1019 *See, e.g.,* Anne Marie Helmenstine, *Aether Definition in Alchemy and Science*, ThoughtCo (updated Nov. 2, 2019), https://www.thoughtco.com/aether-in-alchemy-and-science-604750.

1020 *See, e.g., What is the Aether?*, Energy Wave Theory (2020), https://energywavetheory.com/explanations/aether/.

1021 *See, e.g.,* The Editors of Encyclopaedia Britannica, *Michelson-Morley experiment—physics*, Britannica (changed by Erik Gregersen, July 27, 2020), https://www.britannica.com/science/Michelson-Morley-experiment/additional-info#history.

1022 *See, e.g., Ether*, WolframResearch (© 1996–2007 Eric W. Weisstein), https://scienceworld.wolfram.com/physics/Ether.html.

1023 *See, e.g., What is the Aether?*, Energy Wave Theory (2020), https://energywavetheory.com/explanations/aether/.

1024 *See* James Miller, *Who Discovered The Earth Moves Around The Sun?*, Astronomy Trek (Nov. 29, 2012), https://www.astronomytrek.com/who-discovered-the-earth-moves-around-the-sun/;

James Evans, *Aristarchus of Samos-Greek astronomer*, Britannica (bibliography revised. Dec. 11, 2014), https://www.britannica.com/biography/Aristarchus-of-Samos.

1025 *See, e.g., Earth Facts*, Space Facts, https://space-facts.com/earth/.

1026 *See e.g.,* M. Baumgarten, *Moses' Education in Egypt*, Bible Hub (Copyright © 2002, 2003, 2006, 2011 by Biblesoft, Inc.), https://biblehub.com/sermons/auth/baumgarten/moses'_education_in_egypt.htm;

The Editors of Encyclopaedia Britannica, *Manetho-Egyptian priest and historian*, Britannica (Article revised and updated—Oct. 23, 2008), https://www.britannica.com/biography/Manetho.

1027 *See* John W. Ritenbaugh, *What the Bible says about Education of Moses (From Forerunner Commentary)*, Bible Tools (© Copyright 1992-2021 Church of the Great God) https://www.bibletools.org/index.cfm/fuseaction/Topical.show/RTD/cgg/ID/13931/Education-Moses.htm.

1028 *See e.g.,* The Editors of Encyclopaedia Britannica, *Geb-Egyptian god* (alternative title: *Seb*), Britannica (revised and updated—July 10, 2008), https://www.britannica.com/topic/Geb.

1029 *See* James Miller, *Star Constellation Facts: Boötes,* Astronomy Trek (Feb. 23, 2016), https://www.astronomytrek.com/star-constellation-facts-bootes/.

1030 *See, e.g.,* Jacob Silverman, *Is there a hole in the universe?*, howstuffworks, https://science.howstuffworks.com/dictionary/astronomy-terms/hole-in-universe.htm.

 See also, Reuters Staff, *Gaping hole found in universe,* Reuters (Aug. 23, 2007), https://www.reuters.com/article/us-space-hole-idUSN2329057520070823.

1031 *See* Dominic Ford, *The Constellation Boötes*, In-The-Sky.org (© Dominic Ford 2011– 2021), https://in-the-sky.org/data/constellation.php?id=10.

1032 *See, e.g.,* Michael Anissimov, *What is the Boötes Void?*, WiseGeek (last modified Feb. 1, 2021), https://www.wise-geek.com/what-is-the-bootes-void.htm;

 Boötes void, Wikipedia (last edited July 10, 2021), https://en.wikipedia.org/wiki/Boötes_void;

 "Robert P. Kirshner (born August 15, 1949) is an American astronomer, Chief Program Officer for Science for the Gordon and Betty Moore Foundation, and the Clowes Research Professor of Science at Harvard University."

 See, e.g., Robert Kirshner, Wikipedia, https://en.wikipedia.org/wiki/Robert_Kirshner.

1033 *See, e.g.,* Michael Anissimov, *What is the Boötes Void?*, WiseGeek (last modified Feb. 1, 2021), https://www.wise-geek.com/what-is-the-bootes-void.htm.

Part IV

1034 *See How Much Of The Bible Is Prophecy?*, Grace thru faith (Copyright © 2021), https://gracethrufaith.com/ask-a-bible-teacher/much-bible-prophecy/.

1035 *See, e.g., Odds of Christ Fulfilling Prophecy*, Good News Dispatch, https://www.goodnewsdispatch.org/math.html#:~:text=Probability%2C, also known as "odds."

1036 Peter Stoner is the author of author of Science Speaks and was chairman of the mathematics and astronomy departments at Pasadena City College until 1953 when he moved to Westmont College in Santa Barbara, California. There he served as chairman of the science division and eventually professor emeritus of science.

 See Peter Stoner, Wikipedia (last edited May 9, 2021), https://en.wikipedia.org/wiki/Peter_Stoner.

1037 *See Odds of Christ Fulfilling Prophecy*, Good News Dispatch (© Copyright 2008-2016 Good News Dispatch), https://www.goodnewsdispatch.org/math.html;

David R. Reagan, *Applying the Science of Probability to the Scriptures-Do statistics prove the Bible's supernatural origin?*, Lamb and Lion Ministries (© 2021 Lamb and Lion Ministries),
https://christinprophecy.org/articles/applying-the-science-of-probability-to-the-scriptures/

1038 *Id.*

1039 *See* Doug Powell, *Guide to Christian Apologetics* at 254–255, Holman Reference (Nashville, Tennessee © 2006 by Doug Powell).

1040 *See, e.g.,* Don Stoner, *Chapter 3-The Christ of Prophecy*, www.unapologetic.co.uk, https://oldschoolcontemporary.wordpress.com/2015/12/22/dr-peter-stoners-the-prophecy-of-christ/.

1041 *See* Author Unknown, *The Odds of Eight Messianic Prophecies Coming True* (Berean Publishers June 9, 2020),
https://www.bereanpublishers.com/the-odds-of-eight-messianic-prophecies-coming-true/.

Chapter 10

1042 *See, e.g., What is the significance of the Eastern Gate of Jerusalem?*, Got Questions (© Copyright 2002-2021 Got Questions Ministries),
https://www.gotquestions.org/eastern-gate-Jerusalem.html.

1043 *See* Chapter 11 *infra.*

1044 *See* Hershel Shanks, *Ancient Jerusalem: The Village, the Town, the City*, Biblical History Daily (as published in Biblical Archaeology Review, May/June 2016),
https://www.biblicalarchaeology.org/daily/biblical-sites-places/jerusalem/ancient-jerusalem/.

1045 *See Jerusalem*, Wikipedia (last edited Sept. 6, 2021),
https://en.wikipedia.org/wiki/Jerusalem,

1046 *See, e.g., Age of Abraham, Isaac and Jacob*, Desiring to Know the Lord more… (Jan. 7, 2010), https://simplydesiringtoknowthelordmore.blogspot.com/2010;

Margaret Hunter, *How Long Was Joseph In Potiphar's House? How Long In Prison?*, Amazing Bible Timeline with World History (June 29, 2013),
https://amazingbibletimeline.com/blog/q27_joseph_how_long_in_prison/.

1047 *See, e.g., Joseph*, The Biblical Timeline, http://www.thebiblicaltimeline.org/joseph/.

1048 *See, e.g., The Hebrews and Slavery in Egypt How long? How many escaped?*, QuotesCosmos (© 2017 QuotesCosmos), https://www.quotescosmos.com/bible/bible-stories/The-Hebrews-and-Slavery-in-Egypt.html;

How long were the Children of Israel enslaved in Egypt, according to the Bible?, Biblical Hermeneutics (© 2021 Stack Exchange Inc),
https://hermeneutics.stackexchange.com/questions/6041/how-long-were-the-children-of-israel-enslaved-in-egypt-according-to-the-bible.

1049   *See, e.g.,* Joshua 5:6 (NIV) which says, "The Israelites had moved about in the wilderness forty years until all the men who were of military age when they left Egypt had died, since they had not obeyed the Lord. For the Lord had sworn to them that they would not see the land he had solemnly promised their ancestors to give us, a land flowing with milk and honey."

1050   *See What Happened To Tyre?*, Bible Reading Archaeology (Sept.13, 2017), https://biblereadingarcheology.com/2017/09/13/what-happened-to-tyre/.

1051   *See, e.g.,* Yehuda Altein and Alex Heppenheimer, *The Prophet Ezekiel,* Chabad.org (© 1993-2021 Chabad-Lubavitch Media Center), https://www.chabad.org/library/article_cdo/aid/112374/jewish/The-Prophet-Ezekiel.htm.

1052   *See* David R. Reagan, *Applying the Science of Probability to the Scriptures-Do statistics prove the Bible's supernatural origin?*, Lamb and Lion Ministries (© 2021 Lamb and Lion Ministries), https://christinprophecy.org/articles/applying-the-science-of-probability-to-the-scriptures/.

1053   *Id.*

1054   The Ezekiel 26:12 "prophecy accurately describes how Alexander the Great built a land bridge from the mainland to the island of Tyre, when… Alexander's forces took rubble from Tyre's mainland and tossed it—stones, timber and soil—into the sea, to build the land bridge" that would permit them to take the island where the city had been moved.

       See Biblical prophecy fulfilled by the Phoenician city-state of Tyre, 100prophecies.org (©100prophecies.org), https://www.100prophecies.org/page8.htm.

1055   *See e.g.,* Ken DeMyer, *Tyre Prophecy Probability* (November 2006), http://users.adam.com.au/bstett/BTyreDeMyer111.htm.

1056   Tiglath-pileser III, lived from 745–727 BC and "inaugurated the last and greatest phase of Assyrian expansion" in the 8th century BC

       See, e.g., Donald John Wiseman, *Tiglath-pileser III-king of Assyria* (Alternative title: *Tukulti-apil-esharra III*), Britannica (Article revised—Dec 1, 2000), https://www.britannica.com/biography/Tiglath-pileser-III#.

1057   Sargon II who lived from 722–705 BC "was one of the most important kings of the Neo-Assyrian Empire as founder of the Sargonid Dynasty which would rule the empire for the next century until its fall."

       See, e.g., Joshua J. Mark, *Sargon II*, World History Encyclopedia (published July 2014), https://www.worldhistory.org/Sargon_II/.

1058   Shalmaneser V reigned as the king of from726–721 BC "who subjugated ancient Israel and undertook a punitive campaign to quell the rebellion of Israel's king Hoshea."

       See, e.g., The Editors of Encyclopaedia Britannica, *Shalmaneser V - king of Assyria and Babylon* (Alternative titles: *Shulmanu-Asharidu V, Ululai*), Britannica (Article added to new online database-July 20, 1998), https://www.britannica.com/biography/Shalmaneser-V.

1059   *See, e.g., Jewish diaspora*, Wikipedia (last edited Aug. 28, 2021), https://en.wikipedia.org/wiki/Jewish_diaspora.

1060   *See, e.g., The Babylonian Captivity with Map*, Bible History (Copyright © 2020 Bible History), https://www.bible-history.com/map_babylonian_captivity/map_of_the_deportation_of_judah_the_destruction_of_jerusalem.html#:~:text.

1061   *Id.*

1062   *Id.*

1063   *See* Charles Feigelstock, *Persian ruler Cyrus the Great of Persia conquers Babylon* (Copyright © Famous Daily), http://www.famousdaily.com/history/cyrus-the-great-of-persia-conquers-babylon.html.

       See also Herodotus on Cyrus' capture of Babylon, Articles on ancient history, Livius.org (copyright © 1995–2021 Livius.org), https://www.livius.org/sources/content/herodotus/cyrus-takes-babylon/;

       How Cyrus Conquered Babylon, Foundation for Intercession (Issue #323—June 2015); God's Kingdom Ministries, https://godskingdom.org/studies/ffi-newsletter/2015/how-cyrus-conquered-babylon.

       "Herodotus was a Greek writer and geographer credited with being the first historian."

       See History.com Editors, *Herodotus*, History (Updated Oct 24, 2019-Original: Feb 4, 2010), https://www.history.com/topics/ancient-history/herodotus.

1064   *See Biblical prophecies fulfilled by Babylon and the neo-Babylonian Empire*, 100prophecies.org (©100prophecies.org), https://www.100prophecies.org/page2.htm.

1065   *See Herodotus on Cyrus' capture of Babylon*, Articles on ancient history, Livius.org, (copyright © 1995–2021 Livius.or), https://www.livius.org/sources/content/herodotus/cyrus-takes-babylon/.

1066   *See How Cyrus Conquered Babylon*, Foundation for Intercession (Issue #323—June 2015), God's Kingdom Ministries, https://godskingdom.org/studies/ffi-newsletter/2015/how-cyrus-conquered-babylon.

1067   *See* Antoine Simonin, *The Cyrus Cylinder*, World History Encyclopedia (Published Jan. 18, 2012), https://www.worldhistory.org/article/166/the-cyrus-cylinder/.

1068   *See, e.g., Bible prophecies fulfilled by Israel during ancient times*, 100Prophecies.org (©100prophecies.org), https://www.100prophecies.org/page5.htm.

1069   Talking about Cyrus the Great and Cyrus II, who lived from 590 or 580 BC to 529 BC and was the "conqueror who founded the Achaemenian empire, [centered] on Persia and comprising the Near East from the Aegean Sea eastward to the Indus River" in India.

       See, e.g., Richard N. Frye, *Cyrus the Great-king of Persia* (alternative title: *Cyrus II*), Britannica (top questions updated Jun. 21, 2019), https://www.britannica.com/biography/Cyrus-the-Great.

Cyrus ruled Persia from about 559 to 529 BC.

See also, Cyrus the Great - Charter of human rights, Persepolis (May 11, 2021), https://www.persepolis.nu/persepolis-cyrus.htm

1070 *See, e.g., The later years of exile & the return to Judah,* The Bible Journey(Chris & Jenifer Taylor © 2021), https://www.thebiblejourney.org/biblejourney2/35-the-exiles-return-to-judah/the-later-years-of-exile-amp-the-return-to-judah-538428bc/;

Kat Cendana, *Jews Return from Captivity in Babylon and Begin to Rebuild the Temple,* Amazing Bible Timeline with World History (posted May 6, 2016), https://amazingbibletimeline.com/blog/jews-return-from-captivity-in-babylon-and-begin-to-rebuild-the-temple/;

The Editors of Encyclopaedia Britannica, *Temple of Jerusalem—Judaism,* Britannica (article revised to make clear that the Western Wall was part of the retaining wall surrounding the Temple Mount. -Sept. 17, 2020), https://www.britannica.com/topic/Temple-of-Jerusalem.

1071 *See, e.g.,* Shapour Suren-Pahlav, *Cyrus the Greats' Cylinder-The World's First Charter of the Human Rights* (June 1998), https://www.cais-soas.com/CAIS/History/hakhamaneshian/Cyrus-the-great/cyrus_cylinder.htm#:~:text..

1072 *Id.*

See also Paul L. Maier, *Biblical Archaeology: Factual Evidence to Support the Historicity of the Bible,* CRI (Mar. 30, 2009), www.equip.org/article/biblical-archaeology-factual-evidence-to-support-the-historicity-of-the-bible/;

Cristian Violatti, *10 Archaeological Disco-veries Consistent With Biblical Passages,* ListVerse (Nov. 3, 2016), http://listverse.com/2016/11/04/10-archaeological-discoveries-consistent-with-biblical-passages/.

Chapter 11

1073 Matthew 2 reports that when the wise men from the east told King Herod about Jesus' birth, Herod tried to murder Him by having all the male children in Bethlehem under the age of two killed. While some commentators on the event believe that the story of the killing of the infants under two is not accurate, and there does not appear to be any secular evidence supporting that particular fact, commentators generally agree that such was in Herod's nature. Herod was ruthless and evil and willing to kill anyone, including his wife and two sons, in order to protect his position. Herod became increasing cruel toward the end of his reign. Thinking that his own family was about to overthrow him he murdered one of his wives (Mariamne), her mother, two of her sons, and his own eldest son. This led the Roman Emperor Augustus to comment that it would be safer to be Herod's pig (hus in

Greek) than his son (huios).

See, e.g., Don Stewart, *Who Were the Herods?,* Blue Letter Bible, https://www.blueletterbible.org/faq/don_stewart/don_stewart_1312.cfm.

The fact that the infanticide at Jesus' birth was not recorded is not proof that it did not happen. Some commentators believe that the number of children killed at Jesus' birth may have been too few—estimates of two-year-olds in Bethlehem at the time are as low as six or seven - to grab secular writers' attention to note in their writings.

See Is there secular evidence Herod killed babies under the age of two?, Never Thirsty (Copyright © Like The Master Ministries), https://www.neverthirsty.org/bible-qa/qa-archives/question/is-there-secular-evidence-herod-killed-babies-under-the-age-of-two/;

How many Holy Innocents were killed by King Herod?, Aleteia, https://aleteia.org/2017/12/28/how-many-holy-innocents-were-killed-by-king-herod/.

See also Slaughter of the Innocents-Herod's Slaughter of the Innocents, https://www.bibleversestudy.com/matthew/matthew2-slaughter-of-the-innocents.htm;

Wayne Jackson, *Did Matthew Fabricate the Account of Herod's Slaughter of the Bethlehem Infants?,* Christian Courier (Access date: July 5, 2021), https://www.christiancourier.com/articles/638-did-matthew-fabricate-the-account-of-herods-slaughter-of-the-bethlehem-infants.

There is other evidence, however, that Herod killed children under the age of two on another occasion. The non-Christian writer, Ambrosius Theodosius Macrobius (395–423 AD) wrote, *"On hearing that the son of Herod, king of the Jews, had been slain when Herod ordered that all boys in Syria under the age of two to be killed, Augustus said, 'It's better to be Herod's pig, than his son.'"*

See Is there secular evidence Herod killed babies under the age of two?, Never Thirsty, https://www.neverthirsty.org/bible-qa/qa-archives/question/is-there-secular-evidence-herod-killed-babies-under-the-age-of-two/ (citing Macrobius, *Saturnalia,* Book 2, section 4:11. p. 349).

1074 *See* David Teitelbaum, *Old Testament Prophecies about the Birth of Jesus,* Christian Chapel Bible Church (© 2021 Christ Chapel Bible Church), https://ccbcfamily.org/old-testament-prophecies-birth-jesus/.

1075 *See, e.g., Micah (prophet),* Wikipedia (last edited Sept. 5, 2021) https://en.wikipedia.org/wiki/Micah_(prophet).

1076 *See, e.g.,* Ron Jones, *Is There Any Evidence That Jesus Was Born in Bethlehem of Judea as the Gospels Record?* (© The Titus Institute, 2006), https://titusinstitute.com/defendingfaith/jesusbornbethlehem.php;

The Evidence Clearly Establishes That Jesus Was Born in Bethlehem, Catholic Strength, https://catholicstrength.com/2018/07/18/the-evidence-clearly-establishes-that-jesus-was-born-in-bethlehem.

1077 *See* David R. Reagan, *Applying the Science of Probability to the Scriptures-Do statistics prove the Bible's supernatural origin?*, Lamb and Lion Ministries (© 2021 Lamb and Lion Ministries), https://christinprophecy.org/articles/applying-the-science-of-probability-to-the-scriptures/.

1078 *See* Margaret Hunter Malachi, *Bible Prophet*, Amazing Bible Timeline with World History (Nov. 29, 2012), https://amazingbibletimeline.com/blog/bible-prophet-malachi/.

1079 *See, e.g., Who Was Isaiah?*, Zondervan Academic (Dec. 11, 2018), https://zondervanacademic.com/blog/isaiah#.

1080 *See, e.g.,* John Strugnell, *St. John the Baptist, Jewish prophet and Christian saint*, Britannica (Alternative Title: *Yaḥyā*) (Bibliography Revised, Melissa Petruzzello, January 19, 2017), https://www.britannica.com/biography/Saint-John-the-Baptist;

John the Baptist (citing Flavius Josephus, *Antiquities of the Jews* 18.5.2), Wikipedia (last edited Sept. 8, 2021), https://en.wikipedia.org/wiki/John_the_Baptist#cite_note-23.

1081 *See* David R. Reagan, *Applying the Science of Probability to the Scriptures-Do statistics prove the Bible's supernatural origin?*, Lamb and Lion Ministries (© 2021 Lamb and Lion Ministries), https://christinprophecy.org/articles/applying-the-science-of-probability-to-the-scriptures/.

1082 This particular "Zechariah was a prophet who lived in the sixth century before the birth of Christ. He was one of those captives in Babylon but" "together with some 50,000 of his Hebrew kinsmen, returned to their native Palestine [from the Babylonian captivity] (cir. 536 BC)."

See Wayne Jackson, *Zechariah's Amazing Prophecy of the Betrayal of Christ* (Access date: June 26, 2021), https://www.christiancourier.com/articles/913-zechariahs-amazing-prophecy-of-the-betrayal-of-christ.

See also the book of Ezra in the Bible.

1083 *See, e.g.,* Christianity.com Editorial Staff, *Why Did Jesus Ride a Donkey into Jerusalem? The Triumphal Entry*, Christianity.com (Feb. 5, 2021), https://www.christianity.com/wiki/jesus-christ/why-did-jesus-ride-a-donkey-into-jerusalem.html.

1084 *See* David R. Reagan, *Applying the Science of Probability to the Scriptures-Do statistics prove the Bible's supernatural origin?*, Lamb and Lion Ministries (© 2021 Lamb and Lion Ministries), https://christinprophecy.org/articles/applying-the-science-of-probability-to-the-scriptures/.

1085 *See, e.g., Jesus Was Betrayed By a Friend Called Judas*, Never Thirsty (Copyright © Like The Master Ministries), https://www.neverthirsty.org/about-christ/prophecies-about-christ/death-of-jesus/jesus-was-betrayed-by-a-friend-called-judas/.

1086 *See, e.g., 10 Things You Didn't Know About Judas Iscariot*, beliefnet (Copyright 2021 Beliefnet, Inc.), https://www.beliefnet.com/faiths/christianity/galleries/10-things-you-didnt-know-about-judas-iscariot.aspx.

1087 *See, e.g., Was Jesus nailed to the cross by the hands or by the wrists?*, http://www.bibleserralta.com/JesusNailedByHisHands.html.

1088 *See* David R. Reagan, *Applying the Science of Probability to the Scriptures-Do statistics prove the Bible's supernatural origin?*, Lamb and Lion Ministries (© 2021 Lamb and Lion Ministries), https://christinprophecy.org/articles/applying-the-science-of-probability-to-the-scriptures/.

1089 *Id.*

1090 *See, e.g., Merriam Webster*, https://www.merriam-webster.com/dictionary/potter%27s%20field.

1091 *See, e.g.,* Ellen Goosey, *Why Are Common Graves Called Potter's Fields?*, Mental Floss (May 30, 2020), https://www.mentalfloss.com/article/624933/potters-field-name-origin.

1092 *See* David R. Reagan, *Applying the Science of Probability to the Scriptures - Do statistics prove the Bible's supernatural origin?*, Lamb and Lion Ministries (© 2021 Lamb and Lion Ministries), https://christinprophecy.org/articles/applying-the-science-of-probability-to-the-scriptures/.

1093 *See What Did Pontius Pilate Write About Jesus?* (© 2021 Copyright Theosis Christian) (citing and quoting from *The Report of Pilate the Procurator Concerning Our Lord Jesus Christ. Sent to the August Caesar in Rome*), https://www.theosischristian.com/what-did-pontius-pilate-write-about-jesus/.

1094 *See The meaning of Affliction in the Bible (From International Standard Bible Encyclopedia)*, Bible Tools (©Copyright 1992-2021 Church of the Great God), https://www.bibletools.org/index.cfm//fuseaction/Def.show/RTD/ISBE/ID/254/Affliction.htm.

1095 *Id.;*

      Affliction, King James Bible Dictionary, http://www.kingjamesbibledictionary.com/Dictionary/affliction.

1096 *See Affliction*, Dictionary.com, https://www.dictionary.com/browse/affliction.

1097 *See* David R. Reagan, *Applying the Science of Probability to the Scriptures - Do statistics prove the Bible's supernatural origin?*, Lamb and Lion Ministries (© 2021 Lamb and Lion Ministries), https://christinprophecy.org/articles/applying-the-science-of-probability-to-the-scriptures/.

1098 *See What Did Pontius Pilate Write About Jesus?* (© 2021 Copyright Theosis Christian) (citing and quoting from *The Report of Pilate the Procurator Concerning Our Lord Jesus Christ. Sent to the August Caesar in Rome*), https://www.theosischristian.com/what-did-pontius-pilate-write-about-jesus/.

1099 John C. Robinson, *Crucifixion in the Roman World: The Use of Nails at the Time of Christ.* Studia Antiqua 2, no. 1 (2002), BYU ScholarsArchive (June 2002), https://scholarsarchive.byu.edu/studiaantiqua/vol2/iss1/6.

See also Ancient Crucifixion, https://www.bible-history.com/biblestudy/crucifixion.html.

1100 *See also Did the crucifixion nails go through Jesus' hands or wrists?*, Compelling Truth (copyright 2011-2021 Got Questions Mnistries), https://www.compellingtruth.org/nails-hands-wrists.html.

1101 *See* David R. Reagan, *Applying the Science of Probability to the Scriptures-Do statistics prove the Bible's supernatural origin?*, Lamb and Lion Ministries (© 2021 Lamb and Lion Ministries), https://christinprophecy.org/articles/applying-the-science-of-probability-to-the-scriptures/.

1102 *Id.*

1103 *See, e.g.,* Luke Wayne, *Is there historical evidence of Jesus' miracles?*, CARM (Aug. 17, 2016), https://carm.org/about-jesus/is-there-historical-evidence-of-jesus-miracles/.

1104 *See The Miracles of Jesus* (Copyright © 2021 BibleHistory.net). https://www.biblehistory.net/newsletter/jesus_miracles.htm.

1105 *See, e.g., Gall*, Easton's Bible Dictionary, https://www.biblestudytools.com/dictionary/gall/.

1106 *See, e.g., Casting lots—What was that?*, Compelling Truth (copyright 2011–2021 Got Questions Mnistries), https://www.compellingtruth.org/casting-lots.html.

1107 *See, e.g., The Messiah would be the descendant of Abraham through whom all nations would be blessed*, Jews for Jesus, https://jewsforjesus.org/jewish-resources/messianic-prophecy/the-messiah-would-be-the-descendant-of-abraham-through-whom-all-nations-would-be-blessed/.

See also Abraham's Family Tree Chart, https://www.biblestudy.org/maps/map-of-lineage-from-abraham-to-jesus.html.

1108 *See, Christianity by country*, Wikipedia (last edited Sept. 3, 2021), / https://en.wikipedia.org/wiki/Christianity_by_country.

1109 *See Global Christianity—A Report on the Size and Distribution of the World's Christian Population*, Pew Research Center (Dec. 19, 2011), https://www.pewforum.org/2011/12/19/global-christianity-exec/.

1110 *Id.*

1111 *See, e.g., Constantine the Great*, Wikipedia (last edited on 9 September 2021), https://en.wikipedia.org/wiki/Constantine_the_Great.

1112 *See, e.g.,* Berel Wein, *The Roman Empire Adopts Christianity* (adapted by Yaakov Astor), Free Crash Course in Jewish History (Copyright © JewishHistory.com & The Destiny Foundation), https://www.jewishhistory.org/the-roman-empire-adopts-christianity/.

1113 Louis-Félix Amiel — *Charlemagne empereur d'Occident*. Converted to greyscale. https://commons.wikimedia.org/wiki/File:Louis-Félix_Amiel_-_Charlemagne_ empereur_d'Occident_(742-814).jpg.

See also https://www.bing.com/images/search?q=free+pictures+of+charlemagne.

1114   *See* Mandy Kinne, *Who was the first ruler of the Holy Roman Empire?*, HistoryNet,
https://www.historynet.com/who-was-the-first-ruler-of-the-holy-roman-empire.htm.

1115   *See Power Struggle between Popes and Kings*,
https://www.essaycrackers.com/blog/power-struggle-popes-kings/.

1116   *See, e.g.*, Mary Fairchild, *Old Testament Prophecies of Jesus-47 Predictions of the Messiah
Fulfilled in Jesus Christ*, Learn Religion (updated Oct. 19, 2020),
https://www.learnreligions.com/prophecies-of-jesus-fulfilled-700159.

1117   *See* David R. Reagan, *Applying the Science of Probability to the Scriptures - Do statistics
prove the Bible's supernatural origin?*, Lamb and Lion Ministries (© 2021 Lamb and Lion
Ministries),
https://christinprophecy.org/articles/applying-the-science-of-probability-to-the-scriptures/

1118   *See* Author Unknown, *The Odds of Eight Messianic Prophecies Coming True*, Berean
Publishers (June 9, 2020),
https://www.bereanpublishers.com/the-odds-of-eight-messianic-prophecies-coming-true/.

1119   *See* The Editors of Encyclopaedia Britannica, *Edom-ancient country, Middle East*
(Alternative Title: *Iduma*), Encyclopaedia Britannica (Article added to new online
database—July 20, 1998), https://www.britannica.com/place/Edom.

1120   *Id.*

1121   *See* Doug Powell, *Guide to Christian Apologetics* at 244–246, Holman Reference
(Nashville, Tennessee © 2006 by Doug Powell) (citing John Urquhart, *The Wonders of
Prophecy* (Harrisburg, PA: Christian Alliance, 1925), 163).

1122   *Id.*

1123   *See, e.g., Ancient Jewish History: The Diaspora*, Jewish Virtual Library,
https://www.jewishvirtuallibrary.org/the-diaspora.

1124   *See, e.g., Jewish Diaspora-Summary*, JewishWikipedia.com,
http://www.jewishwikipedia.info/diaspora.html.

The first exile was the Assyrian exile, the expulsion from the Kingdom of Israel (Samaria)
begun by Tiglath-Pileser III of Assyria in 733 BCE. This process was completed by
Sargon II with the destruction of the kingdom in 722 BCE, concluding a three-year siege
of Samaria begun by Shalmaneser V. The next experience of exile was the Babylonian
captivity, in which portions of the population of the Kingdom of Judah were deported
in 597 BCE and again in 586 BCE by the Neo-Babylonian Empire under the rule of
Nebuchadnezzar II.

See, e.g., Jewish diaspora, Wikipedia, https://en.wikipedia.org/wiki/Jewish_diaspora.

1125   *See, e.g.*, Kathleen Lohnes, *Siege of Jerusalem-Jewish-Roman war*, Britannica (article
thoroughly revised Aug. 29, 2018),
https://www.britannica.com/event/Siege-of-Jerusalem-70.

1126   *See, e.g., Ancient Jewish History: The Diaspora*, Jewish Virtual Library,
https://www.jewishvirtuallibrary.org/the-diaspora.

1127   *See* Phil Hopersberger, Land of the Bible (© Copyright 2016) http://www.land-of-the-bible.com/The_Great_Diaspora (no longer online).

1128   *Id.*

1129   *See* Hugh Ross, *Fulfilled Prophecy: Evidence for the Reliability of the Bible, Reasons to Believe* (Aug. 22, 2003), https://reasons.org/explore/publications/articles/fulfilled-prophecy-evidence-for-the-reliability-of-the-bible

1130   *See, e.g.,* Darrell G. Young, *The Fall of Jerusalem in 70 AD-Oh Jerusalem, Thou that Killeth the Prophets,* Focus on Jerusalem Prophecy Ministry (February 2004), https://focusonjerusalem.com/thefallofjerusalem.html.

1131   *See* Margaret Hunter, *Diaspora of the Jews,* Amazing Bible Timeline with World History (Mar. 2, 2013), https://amazingbibletimeline.com/blog/diaspora-of-the-jews/.

1132   "No modern nation corresponds exactly to ancient Cush. Located along the middle course of the Nile—between the junction of the Blue and White Nile and the First Cataract—the territory of Cush lies partly in Egypt and partly in the Republic of Sudan."

      See Jennifer Drummond, *The Kingdom of Cush - The Hebrew Bible's Forgotten Civilization,* Bible History Daily (Jan. 28, 2021), Biblical Archaeological Society, https://www.biblicalarchaeology.org/daily/cush/.

      Cush is also believed to be modern day Ethiopia.

      See, e.g., La Vista Church of Christ, http://lavistachurchofchrist.org/LVanswers/2004/2004-08-11.htm.

1133   Elam "was an ancient civilization centered in the far west and southwest of modern-day Iran."

      See Elam, Wikipedia. https://en.wikipedia.org/wiki/Elam.

      See also Linda Watson, *The Ancient People in the Middle East—Where are they today?,* http://12tribehistory.com/the-ancient-people-in-the-middle-east-where-are-they-today/.

1134   Hamath is a city located in the northwestern part of what is known today as Syria.

      See, e.g., Craig C. White, *Hamath and Arpad (Tell Rifaat),* High Time to Awake, https://hightimetoawake.com/hamah-and-aleppo-and-arpad/.

1135   "In 1917, British Foreign Secretary Arthur James Balfour wrote a letter to Baron Rothschild, a wealthy and prominent leader in the British Jewish community."

      In the brief correspondence, Balfour expressed the British government's support for the establishment of a Jewish home in Palestine. This letter was published in the press one week later and eventually became known as the "Balfour Declaration."

      The text was included in the Mandate for Palestine—a document issued by the League of Nations in 1923 that gave Great Britain the responsibility of establishing a Jewish national homeland in British-controlled Palestine.

See History.com Editors, *Zionism*, https://www.history.com/topics/middle-east/zionism.

1136 *See* Genesis 15:18 (written 1450–1405 BC), Deuteronomy 30:1–5 (written 1450–1405 BC), Psalm 107:2–3 (written 1440–450 BC), Isaiah 11:11–12, 43:5–6 (written 740–680 BC), Jeremiah 16:14–15, 31:10 (written 627–570 BC, Ezekiel 34:13, 37:11–14, 21–22 (written 590–570 BC), Amos 9:13–15 (written circa 760–750 BC) and Zechariah 8:3–8, 12:2 (written 640–621 BC).

1137 *See Jewish Immigration to Historical Palestine*, Factsheet Series No. 181 (created: November 2013), Canadians for Justice and Peace in the Middle East, https://www.cjpme.org/fs_181.

1138 *Id.*

1139 "Zionism is a religious and political effort that brought thousands of Jews from around the world back to their ancient homeland in the Middle East and reestablished Israel as the central location for Jewish identity. ... Zionism is a movement to recreate a Jewish presence in Israel. The name comes from the word "Zion," which is a Hebrew term that refers to Jerusalem."

  See History.com Editors, *Zionism*, https://www.history.com/topics/middle-east/zionism.

1140 *See, e.g., Jewish history*, Wikipedia, https://en.wikipedia.org/wiki/Jewish_history.

1141 *See Jewish Immigration to Historical Palestine*, Factsheet Series No. 181 (created: November 2013), Canadians for Justice and Peace in the Middle East, https://www.cjpme.org/fs_181.

1142 *See, e.g., Jewish history*, Wikipedia, https://en.wikipedia.org/wiki/Jewish_history.

1143 *See, e.g., Migration of Jews to Palestine in the 20th Century*, (Sources: Bard, Mitchell, and Schwartz, Moshe. *1001 Facts Everyone Should Know About Israel*. Lanham, Maryland: Rowman and Littlefield Publishers, Inc., 2005, and *World Book Encyclopedia*. 2009), https://media.nationalgeographic.org/assets/file/jews_MIG.pdf.

1144 *Id.*

1145 *See, e.g., Jewish history*, Wikipedia, https://en.wikipedia.org/wiki/Jewish_history.

1146 *See, e.g., History of the Jews and Judaism in the Land of Israel*, Wikipedia, https://en.wikipedia.org/wiki/History_of_the_Jews_and_Judaism_in_the_Land_of_Israel#State_of_Israel_(1948–present).

1147 *See, e.g., Historical Jewish population comparisons*, Wikipedia, https://en.wikipedia.org/wiki/Historical_Jewish_population_comparisons.

1148 *See, e.g., Immigration to Israel: Total Immigration, by Country of Origin - (1948 - Present)*, Jewish Virtual Library (Source: Israel Central Bureau of Statistics.), https://www.jewishvirtuallibrary.org/total-immigration-to-israel-by-country-of-origin;

  History of the Jews and Judaism in the Land of Israel, Wikipedia, https://en.wikipedia.org/wiki/History_of_the_Jews_and_Judaism_in_the_Land_of_Israel#State_of_Israel_(1948–present).

1149 *See* following notes.

1150   *See, e.g.,* Phil Hopersberger, Land of the Bible (© Copyright 2016) http://www.land-of-the-bible.com/The_Great_Diaspora (no longer online).

1151   *See, e.g., Migration of Jews to Palestine in the 20th Century,* (Sources: Bard, Mitchell, and Schwartz, Moshe. *1001 Facts Everyone Should Know About Israel.* Lanham, Maryland: Rowman and Littlefield Publishers, Inc., 2005, and *World Book Encyclopedia.* 2009), https://media.nationalgeographic.org/assets/file/jews_MIG.pdf.

1152   *See, e.g., Jewish history,* Wikipedia, https://en.wikipedia.org/wiki/Jewish_history.

1153   Israel was likely so named, according to one author, because "[w]orms are small, and worms are lowly," which Israel was and still is compared to its much larger enemies.

See, e.g., Why does God call Jacob a worm in Isaiah 41:14?, https://www.gotquestions.org/worm-Jacob.html.

According to another author, the "'worm Jacob' denotes here smallness, weakness, and helplessness" or "despicable and trampled upon," "weak and despised," "trodden under foot," a "creature of the dust, prostrate and helpless" "abject, weak, and wretched," all an ample description of Israel at its founding.

See Isaiah 41:14 (quoting F. Jarratt, "Thou worm Jacob,"), https://biblehub.com/sermons/isaiah/41-14.htm.

1154   *See, e.g., Jewish history,* Wikipedia, https://en.wikipedia.org/wiki/Jewish_history.

1155   *See, e.g., Migration of Jews to Palestine in the 20th Century,* (Sources: Bard, Mitchell, and Schwartz, Moshe. *1001 Facts Everyone Should Know About Israel.* Lanham, Maryland: Rowman and Littlefield Publishers, Inc., 2005, and *World Book Encyclopedia.* 2009), https://media.nationalgeographic.org/assets/file/jews_MIG.pdf.

1156   As late as 1950, Israel had a population of less than 1,300,000 while Egypt, Lebanon, Syria, Jordan and Iraq had a population of over 31,000,000.

See List of countries by past and projected future population, Wikipedia, https://en.wikipedia.org/wiki/List_of_countries_by_past_and_projected_future_population#Estimates_between_the_years_1950_and_1980_(in_thousands).

1157   *See, e.g., History of the Jews and Judaism in the Land of Israel,* Wikipedia, https://en.wikipedia.org/wiki/History_of_the_Jews_and_Judaism_in_the_Land_of_Israel#State_of_Israel_(1948–present).

1158   *See, e.g., Jewish history,* Wikipedia, https://en.wikipedia.org/wiki/Jewish_history.

1159   *See* notes 1152–1154 *infra.*

1160   *See, e.g.,* "fedayeen," Oxford Languages, Oxford University Press, https://languages.oup.com/.

"The fedayeen made efforts to infiltrate territory in Israel in order to strike military[8] as well as civilian targets in the aftermath of the 1948 Arab–Israeli War."

See Adnan Abu-Amer, *'Jihadi Salafis'— A New Component in the Palestinian Political Context,* Palestine-Israel Journal, https://www.pij.org/articles/1631/jihadi-salafis-a-new-componentin-the-palestinian-political-context..

1161 In 1967, Israel won that war despite the fact that it had a population of only 2,619,102 while Egypt, Jordan, Syria., Iraq, Saudi Arabia, Kuwait, Algeria, and others had populations totaling over 59,000,000.

See List of countries ordered by their population size—1967, PopulationPyramid.net (© December 2019), https://www.populationpyramid.net/population-size-per-country/1967/.

1162 In 1965, Israel had a population of less than 2,600,000 which increased by 1970 to 2,895,000. During that same period of time Egypt, Russia, Jordan and Syria saw their populations increase from over 162,000,000 to over 167,000,000.

See List of countries by past and projected future population, Wikipedia, https://en.wikipedia.org/wiki/List_of_countries_by_past_and_projected_future_population#Estimates_between_the_years_1950_and_1980_(in_thousands).

1163 From 1970 to 1975, Israel saw its population increase from to 2,895,000 to 3,342,000 while total populations of Egypt and Syria ranged from almost 40,000,000 to over 44,000,000.

See List of countries by past and projected future population, Wikipedia, https://en.wikipedia.org/wiki/List_of_countries_by_past_and_projected_future_population#Estimates_between_the_years_1950_and_1980_(in_thousands).

1164 *See, e.g., List of wars involving Israel,* https://military.wikia.org/wiki/List_of_wars_involving_Israel.

1165 *See* Chris Baldelomar, *Gardening and Farming Like Israel,* Flat City Farms (Feb. 22, 2018), https://flatcityfarms.com/2018/02/gardening-and-farming-like-israel/.

1166 *See, e.g.,* LFTBH Administrator, *Prophecy Being Fulfilled: Israeli Desert Blooms!,* Looking for the Blessed Hope (Feb. 22, 2020), https://looking4theblessedhope.com/2020/02/22/prophecy-being-fulfilled-israeli-desert-blooms/;

The Desert Bursts into Bloom & 3 Other Unusual Events, One for Israel (Mar. 4, 2020), https://www.oneforisrael.org/bible-based-teaching-from-israel/the-desert-bursts-into-bloom-3-other-unusual-events/;

A true farming miracle in Israel's Arava desert,-YouTube, https://www.youtube.com/watch?v=n6xMjJr-oqg;

How Israel Made the Desert Bloom, Solve Israel's Problems (Dec. 23, 2011), https://solveisraelsproblems.com/how-israel-made-the-desert-bloom/.

1167 *See* Chris Baldelomar, *Gardening and Farming Like Israel,* Flat City Farms (Feb. 22, 2018), https://flatcityfarms.com/2018/02/gardening-and-farming-like-israel/.

1168 *Id.*

CPSIA information can be obtained
at www.ICGtesting.com
Printed in the USA
BVHW031939011022
648402BV00028B/508

9 781685 560805